Managing With People in Mind

MANAGING WITH PEOPLE IN MIND

A Harvard Business Review Paperback

Harvard Business Review paperback No. 90085

The *Harvard Business Review* articles in this collection
are available individually. Discounts apply to quantity
purchases. For information and ordering, contact Operations Department, Harvard Business School Publishing
Division, Boston, MA 02163. Telephone: (617) 495-6192.
Fax: (617) 495-6985.

Contents

The Manager's Role

**The Manager's Job: Folklore and Fact
(An HBR Classic)**
Henry Mintzberg
3

The textbook definition of the manager's job is tidy, rational, and wrong. Mintzberg debunks the myths and offers a more accurate picture of real managerial roles and skills. *(March - April 1990)*

Wagon Masters and Lesser Managers
J.S. Ninomiya
18

Like wagon train masters, good managers are concerned about their fellow travelers as well as themselves. *(March - April 1988)*

Supervision: Substance and Style
Saul W. Gellerman
25

The style of an effective supervisor is intertwined with the substance of the job to be accomplished. *(March - April 1976)*

The Manager: Master and Servant of Power
Fernando Bartolomé and André Laurent
37

How managers can understand the effects of power on both their superiors and their subordinates. *(November - December 1986)*

Effective Daily Management

How to Make People Decisions
Peter F. Drucker
45

A magic wand won't help make good people decisions, but hard work and disciplined thought will. *(July - August 1985)*

Management Time: Who's Got the Monkey?
William Oncken, Jr. and Donald L. Wass
49

The classic analogy that underscores the value of assigning, delegating, and controlling. *(November - December 1974)*

Making Time to Manage
Robert C. Dorney
55

Time management is more about management than about time. *(January - February 1988)*

How to Run a Meeting
Antony Jay
59

How to right things that go wrong in meetings. *(March - April 1976)*

How to Make a Team Work
Maurice Hardaker and Bryan K. Ward
75

At IBM, managers set goals, accept responsibilities, and become a real team—using the technique of Process Quality Management. *(November - December 1987)*

Overcoming Group Warfare
Robert R. Blake and Jane S. Mouton
81

Two proven approaches to resolving conflicts between groups that need to cooperate but are already in the heat of battle. *(November - December 1984)*

How to Deal with Resistance to Change
Paul R. Lawrence
93

Change is primarily thwarted by human, not technical, factors and is not helped by shallow notions of participative management. *(January - February 1969)*

Managing Your Boss
John J. Gabarro and John P. Kotter
101

It is as important, and as challenging, to manage your supervisor as it is to manage your subordinates. *(May - June 1993)*

The Subordinate's Predicaments
Eric H. Neilsen and Jan Gypen
111

How subordinates can overcome their tendency to react defensively to their superiors. *(September - October 1979)*

Management Communication and the Grapevine
Keith Davis
123

Don't try to abolish the management grapevine—analyze, influence, and *use* it.

ABCs of Job Interviewing
James M. Jenks and Brian L.P. Zevnik
131

A hasty glance at a resume is not a wise way to prepare for interviewing a job candidate. A written outline and questions that focus on a candidate's past performance are keys to a revealing interview. *(July - August 1989)*

People and Organizations

In Praise of Hierarchy
Elliot Jaques
137

Despite the heralded arrival of the flat organization, hierarchy has not had its day. The reason: Hierarchy is organic, arising from the nature of work. *(January - February 1990)*

Managing Without Managers
Ricardo Semler
144

A company in Brazil lets workers make corporate decisions, come to work when they want, and look over the company books at any time. Managers set their own salaries. The result isn't chaos and bankruptcy, but an annual growth rate of 40 percent. *(September - October 1989)*

The Case of the Omniscient Organization
Gary T. Marx
153

To improve its performance, a floundering company institutes a stringent screening process for job applicants and close monitoring of employees that includes audio and video surveillance and drug testing. Experts debate the merits of technology-assisted control of employees. *(March - April 1990)*

Solving Managerial Dilemmas

Skilled Incompetence
Chris Argyris
165

Are some skilled communicators creating organizational chaos by adeptly avoiding conflict with coworkers? *(September - October 1986)*

The Abrasive Personality
Harry Levinson
171

When abrasive people attain high positions in the organization, top management has a real problem to solve. *(May - June 1978)*

The Case of the Mismanaged Ms.
Sally Seymour
181

A female executive battles sexual discrimination and the "old-boy" network. *(November - December 1987)*

Discipline Without Punishment—At Last
David N. Campbell, R.L. Fleming, and Richard C. Grote
193

How to implement a nonpunitive approach to employee discipline. *(July - August 1985)*

How to Deal with Bizarre Employee Behavior
Terry L. Leap and Michael D. Crino
201

How serious is it when an employee throws a pie in a consultant's face? Would you know what to do? *(May - June 1986)*

Beyond Testing: Coping with Drugs at Work
James T. Wrich
205

A program for combating the devastating effects of drug abuse and creating an addiction-free workplace. *(January - February 1988)*

How Technology Brings Blind People into the Workplace
Julia Anderson
213

How technology has provided the visually impaired greater access to more jobs. *(March - April 1989)*

The Manager's Role

HBR CLASSIC

The Manager's Job: Folklore and Fact

by Henry Mintzberg

The classical view says that the manager organizes, coordinates, plans, and controls; the facts suggest otherwise.

If you ask managers what they do, they will most likely tell you that they plan, organize, coordinate, and control. Then watch what they do. Don't be surprised if you can't relate what you see to these words.

When a manager is told that a factory has just burned down and then advises the caller to see whether temporary arrangements can be made to supply customers through a foreign subsidiary, is that manager planning, organizing, coordinating, or controlling? How about when he or she presents a gold watch to a retiring employee? Or attends a conference to meet people in the trade and returns with an interesting new product idea for employees to consider?

These four words, which have dominated management vocabulary since the French industrialist Henri Fayol first introduced them in 1916, tell us little about what managers actually do. At best, they indicate some vague objectives managers have when they work.

The field of management, so devoted to progress and change, has for more than half a century not seriously addressed *the* basic question: What do managers do? Without a proper answer, how can we teach management? How can we design planning or information systems for managers? How can we improve the practice of management at all?

What do managers do? Even managers themselves don't always know.

Our ignorance of the nature of managerial work shows up in various ways in the modern organization—in boasts by successful managers who never spent a single day in a management training pro-

Henry Mintzberg is the Bronfman Professor of Management at McGill University. His latest book is Mintzberg on Management: Inside Our Strange World of Organizations *(Free Press, 1989). This article appeared originally in HBR July-August 1975. It won the McKinsey Award for excellence.*

gram; in the turnover of corporate planners who never quite understood what it was the manager wanted; in the computer consoles gathering dust in the back room because the managers never used the fancy on-line MIS some analyst thought they needed. Perhaps most important, our ignorance shows up in the inability of our large public organizations to come to grips with some of their most serious policy problems.

Somehow, in the rush to automate production, to use management science in the functional areas of marketing and finance, and to apply the skills of the behavioral scientist to the problem of worker motivation, the manager – the person in charge of the organization or one of its subunits – has been forgotten.

I intend to break the reader away from Fayol's words and introduce a more supportable and useful description of managerial work. This description derives from my review and synthesis of research on how various managers have spent their time.

In some studies, managers were observed intensively; in a number of others, they kept detailed diaries; in a few studies, their records were analyzed. All kinds of managers were studied – foremen, factory supervisors, staff managers, field sales managers, hospital administrators, presidents of companies and nations, and even street gang leaders. These "managers" worked in the United States, Canada, Sweden, and Great Britain.

A synthesis of these findings paints an interesting picture, one as different from Fayol's classical view as a cubist abstract is from a Renaissance painting. In a sense, this picture will be obvious to anyone who has ever spent a day in a manager's office, either in front of the desk or behind it. Yet, at the same time, this picture throws into doubt much of the folklore that we have accepted about the manager's work.

Folklore and Facts About Managerial Work

There are four myths about the manager's job that do not bear up under careful scrutiny of the facts.

Folklore: The manager is a reflective, systematic planner. The evidence on this issue is overwhelming, but not a shred of it supports this statement.

Fact: Study after study has shown that managers work at an unrelenting pace, that their activities are characterized by brevity, variety, and discontinuity, and that they are strongly oriented to action and dislike reflective activities. Consider this evidence:

Half the activities engaged in by the five chief executives of my study lasted less than nine minutes, and only 10% exceeded one hour.[1] A study of 56 U.S. foremen found that they averaged 583 activities per eight-hour shift, an average of 1 every 48 seconds.[2] The work pace for both chief executives and foremen was unrelenting. The chief executives met a steady stream of callers and mail from the moment they ar-

How often can you work for a half an hour without interruption?

rived in the morning until they left in the evening. Coffee breaks and lunches were inevitably work related, and ever-present subordinates seemed to usurp any free moment.

A diary study of 160 British middle and top managers found that they worked without interruption for a half hour or more only about once every two days.[3]

Of the verbal contacts the chief executives in my study engaged in, 93% were arranged on an ad hoc basis. Only 1% of the executives' time was spent in open-ended observational tours. Only 1 out of 368 verbal contacts was unrelated to a specific issue and could therefore be called general planning. Another researcher found that "in *not one single case* did a manager report obtaining important external information from a general conversation or other undirected personal communication."[4]

Is this the planner that the classical view describes? Hardly. The manager is simply responding to the pressures of the job. I found that my chief executives terminated many of their own activities, often leaving meetings before the end, and interrupted their desk work to call in subordinates. One president not only placed his desk so that he could look down a long hallway but also left his door open when he was alone – an invitation for subordinates to come in and interrupt him.

Clearly, these managers wanted to encourage the flow of current information. But more significantly, they seemed to be conditioned by their own work loads. They appreciated the opportunity cost of their own time, and they were continually aware of their ever-present obligations – mail to be answered, callers to attend to, and so on. It seems that a manager is always plagued by the possibilities of what might be done and what must be done.

When managers must plan, they seem to do so implicitly in the context of daily actions, not in some abstract process reserved for two weeks in the organization's mountain retreat. The plans of the chief executives I studied seemed to exist only in their heads – as flexible, but often specific, intentions. The traditional literature notwithstanding, the job of managing does not breed reflective planners; managers respond to stimuli, they are conditioned by their jobs to prefer live to delayed action.

Folklore: The effective manager has no regular duties to perform. Managers are constantly being told to spend more time planning and delegating and less time seeing customers and engaging in negotiations. These are not, after all, the true tasks of the manager. To use the popular analogy, the good manager, like the good conductor, carefully orchestrates everything in advance, then sits back, responding occasionally to an unforeseeable exception. But here again the pleasant abstraction just does not seem to hold up.

Fact: Managerial work involves performing a number of regular duties, including ritual and ceremony, negotiations, and processing of soft information that links the organization with its environment. Consider some evidence from the research:

A study of the work of the presidents of small companies found that they engaged in routine activities because their companies could not afford staff specialists and were so thin on operating personnel that a single absence often required the president to substitute.[5]

One study of field sales managers and another of chief executives suggest that it is a natural part of both jobs to see important customers, assuming the managers wish to keep those customers.[6]

Someone, only half in jest, once described the manager as the person who sees visitors so that other people can get their work done. In my study, I found that certain ceremonial duties – meeting visiting dignitaries, giving out gold watches, presiding at Christmas dinners – were an intrinsic part of the chief executive's job.

Studies of managers' information flow suggest that managers play a key role in securing "soft" external information (much of it available only to them because of their status) and in passing it along to their subordinates.

Folklore: The senior manager needs aggregated information, which a formal management information system best provides. Not too long ago, the words *total information system* were everywhere in the management literature. In keeping with the clas-

Being a manager often involves a little pomp and ceremony.

DRAWINGS BY MICHAEL CRAWFORD

sical view of the manager as that individual perched on the apex of a regulated, hierarchical system, the literature's manager was to receive all important information from a giant, comprehensive MIS.

But lately, these giant MIS systems are not working—managers are simply not using them. The enthusiasm has waned. A look at how managers actually process information makes it clear why.

Fact: Managers strongly favor verbal media, telephone calls and meetings, over documents. Consider the following:

In two British studies, managers spent an average of 66% and 80% of their time in verbal (oral) communication.[7] In my study of five American chief executives, the figure was 78%.

> ## Today's gossip may be tomorrow's fact— that's why managers cherish hearsay.

These five chief executives treated mail processing as a burden to be dispensed with. One came in Saturday morning to process 142 pieces of mail in just over three hours, to "get rid of all the stuff." This same manager looked at the first piece of "hard" mail he had received all week, a standard cost report, and put it aside with the comment, "I never look at this."

These same five chief executives responded immediately to 2 of the 40 routine reports they received during the five weeks of my study and to 4 items in the 104 periodicals. They skimmed most of these periodicals in seconds, almost ritualistically. In all, these chief executives of good-sized organizations initiated on their own—that is, not in response to something else—a grand total of 25 pieces of mail during the 25 days I observed them.

An analysis of the mail the executives received reveals an interesting picture—only 13% was of specific and immediate use. So now we have another piece in the puzzle: not much of the mail provides live, current information—the action of a competitor, the mood of a government legislator, or the rating of last night's television show. Yet this is the information that drove the managers, interrupting their meetings and rescheduling their workdays.

Consider another interesting finding. Managers seem to cherish "soft" information, especially gossip, hearsay, and speculation. Why? The reason is its timeliness; today's gossip may be tomorrow's fact. The manager who misses the telephone call revealing that the company's biggest customer was seen golfing with a main competitor may read about a dramatic drop in sales in the next quarterly report. But then it's too late.

To assess the value of historical, aggregated, "hard" MIS information, consider two of the manager's prime uses for information—to identify problems and opportunities[8] and to build mental models (e.g., how the organization's budget system works, how customers buy products, how changes in the economy affect the organization). The evidence suggests that the manager identifies decision situations and builds models not with the aggregated abstractions an MIS provides but with specific tidbits of data.

Consider the words of Richard Neustadt, who studied the information-collecting habits of Presidents Roosevelt, Truman, and Eisenhower: "It is not information of a general sort that helps a President see personal stakes; not summaries, not surveys, not the *bland amalgams*. Rather...it is the odds and ends of *tangible detail* that pieced together in his mind illuminate the underside of issues put before him. To help himself he must reach out as widely as he can for every scrap of fact, opinion, gossip, bearing on his interests and relationships as President. He must become his own director of his own central intelligence."[9]

The manager's emphasis on this verbal media raises two important points. First, verbal information is stored in the brains of people. Only when people write this information down can it be stored in the files of the organization—whether in metal cabinets or on magnetic tape—and managers apparently do not write down much of what they hear. Thus the strategic data bank of the organization is not in the memory of its computers but in the minds of its managers.

Second, managers' extensive use of verbal media helps to explain why they are reluctant to delegate tasks. It is not as if they can hand a dossier over to subordinates; they must take the time to "dump memory"—to tell subordinates all about the subject. But this could take so long that managers may find it easier to do the task themselves. Thus they are damned by their own information system to a "dilemma of delegation"—to do too much or to delegate to subordinates with inadequate briefing.

Folklore: Management is, or at least is quickly becoming, a science and a profession. By almost any definition of *science* and *profession*, this statement is false. Brief observation of any manager will quickly lay to rest the notion that managers practice a science. A science involves the enaction of systematic, analytically determined procedures or programs. If we do not even know what procedures managers use, how can we prescribe them by scientific analysis?

Research on Managerial Work

In seeking to describe managerial work, I conducted my own research and also scanned the literature to integrate the findings of studies from many diverse sources with my own. These studies focused on two different aspects of managerial work. Some were concerned with the characteristics of work —how long managers work, where, at what pace, with what interruptions, with whom they work, and through what media they communicate. Other studies were concerned with the content of work —what activities the managers actually carry out, and why. Thus, after a meeting, one researcher might note that the manager spent 45 minutes with three government officials in their Washington office, while another might record that the manager presented the company's stand on some proposed legislation in order to change a regulation.

A few of the studies of managerial work are widely known, but most have remained buried as single journal articles or isolated books. Among the more important ones I cite are:

□ Sune Carlson developed the diary method to study the work characteristics of nine Swedish managing directors. Each kept a detailed log of his activities. Carlson's results are reported in his book *Executive Behaviour*. A number of British researchers, notably Rosemary Stewart, have subsequently used Carlson's method. In *Managers and Their Jobs*, she describes the study of 160 top and middle managers of British companies.

□ Leonard Sayles's book *Managerial Behavior* is another important reference. Using a method he refers to as "anthropological," Sayles studied the work content of middle and lower level managers in a large U.S. corporation. Sayles moved freely in the company, collecting whatever information struck him as important.

□ Perhaps the best-known source is *Presidential Power*, in which Richard Neustadt analyzes the power and managerial behavior of Presidents Roosevelt, Truman, and Eisenhower. Neustadt used secondary sources—documents and interviews with other parties.

□ Robert H. Guest, in *Personnel*, reports on a study of the foreman's working day. Fifty-six U.S. foremen were observed and each of their activities recorded during one eight-hour shift.

□ Richard C. Hodgson, Daniel J. Levinson, and Abraham Zaleznik studied a team of three top executives of a U.S. hospital. From that study they wrote *The Executive Role Constellation*. They addressed the way in which work and socioemotional roles were divided among the three managers.

□ William F. Whyte, from his study of a street gang during the Depression, wrote *Street Corner Society*. His findings about the gang's workings and leadership, which George C. Homans analyzed in *The Human Group*, suggest interesting similarities of job content between street gang leaders and corporate managers.

My own study involved five American CEOs of middle- to large-sized organizations—a consulting firm, a technology company, a hospital, a consumer goods company, and a school system. Using a method called "structural observation," during one intensive week of observation for each executive, I recorded various aspects of every piece of mail and every verbal contact. In all, I analyzed 890 pieces of incoming and outgoing mail and 368 verbal contacts.

And how can we call management a profession if we cannot specify what managers are to learn? For after all, a profession involves "knowledge of some department of learning or science" *(Random House Dictionary)*.[10]

Fact: The managers' programs—to schedule time, process information, make decisions, and so on— remain locked deep inside their brains. Thus, to describe these programs, we rely on words like *judgment* and *intuition*, seldom stopping to realize that they are merely labels for our ignorance.

I was struck during my study by the fact that the executives I was observing—all very competent—are fundamentally indistinguishable from their counterparts of a hundred years ago (or a thousand years ago). The information they need differs, but they seek it in the same way—by word of mouth. Their decisions concern modern technology, but the procedures they use to make those decisions are the same as the procedures used by nineteenth century managers. Even the computer, so important for the specialized work of the organization, has apparently had no influence on the work procedures of general managers. In fact, the manager is in a kind of loop, with increasingly heavy work pressures but no aid forthcoming from management science.

Considering the facts about managerial work, we can see that the manager's job is enormously complicated and difficult. Managers are overburdened with obligations yet cannot easily delegate their tasks. As a result, they are driven to overwork and forced to do many tasks superficially. Brevity, fragmentation, and

The Manager's Roles

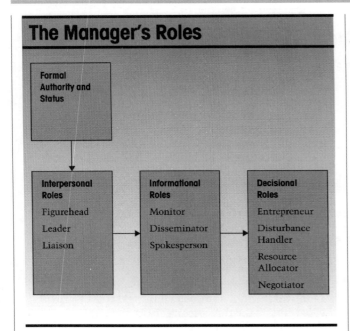

Formal Authority and Status

Interpersonal Roles

Figurehead

Leader

Liaison

Informational Roles

Monitor

Disseminator

Spokesperson

Decisional Roles

Entrepreneur

Disturbance Handler

Resource Allocator

Negotiator

verbal communication characterize their work. Yet these are the very characteristics of managerial work that have impeded scientific attempts to improve it. As a result, management scientists have concentrated on the specialized functions of the organization, where it is easier to analyze the procedures and quantify the relevant information.[11]

But the pressures of a manager's job are becoming worse. Where before managers needed to respond only to owners and directors, now they find that subordinates with democratic norms continually reduce their freedom to issue unexplained orders, and a growing number of outside influences (consumer groups, government agencies, and so on) demand attention. Managers have had nowhere to turn for help. The first step in providing such help is to find out what the manager's job really is.

Back to a Basic Description of Managerial Work

Earlier, I defined the manager as that person in charge of an organization or subunit. Besides CEOs, this definition would include vice presidents, bishops, foremen, hockey coaches, and prime ministers. All these "managers" are vested with formal authority over an organizational unit. From formal authority comes status, which leads to various interpersonal relations, and from these comes access to information. Information, in turn, enables the manager to make decisions and strategies for the unit.

The manager's job can be described in terms of various "roles," or organized sets of behaviors identified with a position. My description, shown in "The Manager's Roles," comprises ten roles. As we shall see, formal authority gives rise to the three interpersonal roles, which in turn give rise to the three informational roles; these two sets of roles enable the manager to play the four decisional roles.

Interpersonal Roles

Three of the manager's roles arise directly from formal authority and involve basic interpersonal relationships. First is the *figurehead* role. As the head of an organizational unit, every manager must perform some ceremonial duties. The president greets the touring dignitaries. The foreman attends the wedding of a lathe operator. The sales manager takes an important customer to lunch.

The chief executives of my study spent 12% of their contact time on ceremonial duties; 17% of their incoming mail dealt with acknowledgments and requests related to their status. For example, a letter to a company president requested free merchandise for a crippled schoolchild; diplomas that needed to be signed were put on the desk of the school superintendent.

Duties that involve interpersonal roles may sometimes be routine, involving little serious communication and no important decision making. Nevertheless, they are important to the smooth functioning of an organization and cannot be ignored.

Managers are responsible for the work of the people of their unit. Their actions in this regard constitute the *leader* role. Some of these actions involve leadership directly—for example, in most organizations the managers are normally responsible for hiring and training their own staff.

In addition, there is the indirect exercise of the leader role. For example, every manager must motivate and encourage employees, somehow reconciling their individual needs with the goals of the organization. In virtually every contact with the manager, subordinates seeking leadership clues ask: "Does she approve?" "How would she like the report to turn out?" "Is she more interested in market share than high profits?"

The influence of managers is most clearly seen in the leader role. Formal authority vests them with great potential power; leadership determines in large part how much of it they will realize.

The literature of management has always recognized the leader role, particularly those aspects of it related to motivation. In comparison, until recently it has hardly mentioned the *liaison* role, in which the manager makes contacts outside the vertical chain of command. This is remarkable in light of the finding of virtually every study of managerial work that managers spend as much time with peers and other people outside their units as they do with their own subordinates—and, surprisingly, very little time with their own superiors.

In Rosemary Stewart's diary study, the 160 British middle and top managers spent 47% of their time with peers, 41% of their time with people inside their unit, and only 12% of their time with their superiors. For Robert H. Guest's study of U.S. foremen, the figures were 44%, 46%, and 10%. The chief executives of my study averaged 44% of their contact time with people outside their organizations, 48% with subordinates, and 7% with directors and trustees.

The contacts the five CEOs made were with an incredibly wide range of people: subordinates; clients, business associates, and suppliers; and peers—managers of similar organizations, government and trade organization officials, fellow directors on outside boards, and independents with no relevant organizational affiliations. The chief executives' time with and mail from these groups is shown in "The Chief Executive's Contacts." Guest's study of foremen shows, likewise, that their contacts were numerous and wide-ranging, seldom involving fewer than 25 individuals, and often more than 50.

Informational Roles

By virtue of interpersonal contacts, both with subordinates and with a network of contacts, the manager emerges as the nerve center of the organizational unit. The manager may not know everything but typically knows more than subordinates do.

Studies have shown this relationship to hold for all managers, from street gang leaders to U.S. presidents. In *The Human Group*, George C. Homans explains how, because they were at the center of the information flow in their own gangs and were also in close touch with other gang leaders, street gang leaders were better informed than any of their followers.[12] As for presidents, Richard Neustadt observes: "The essence of [Franklin] Roosevelt's technique for information-gathering was competition. 'He would call you in,' one of his aides once told me, 'and he'd ask you to get the story on some complicated business, and you'd come back after a couple of days of hard labor and present the juicy morsel you'd uncovered under a stone somewhere, and *then* you'd

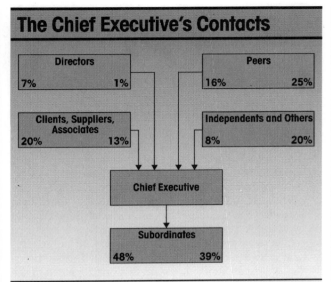

The Chief Executive's Contacts

Directors		Peers	
7%	1%	16%	25%

Clients, Suppliers, Associates		Independents and Others	
20%	13%	8%	20%

Chief Executive

Subordinates	
48%	39%

Note: The first figure indicates the proportion of total contact time spent with each group and the second figure, the proportion of mail from each group.

find out he knew all about it, along with something else you *didn't* know. Where he got this information from he wouldn't mention, usually, but after he had done this to you once or twice you got damn careful about *your* information.'"[13]

We can see where Roosevelt "got this information" when we consider the relationship between the interpersonal and informational roles. As leader, the manager has formal and easy access to every staff member. In addition, liaison contacts expose the manager to external information to which subordinates often lack access. Many of these contacts are with other managers of equal status, who are themselves nerve centers in their own organization. In this way, the manager develops a powerful database of information.

Processing information is a key part of the manager's job. In my study, the CEOs spent 40% of their contact time on activities devoted exclusively to the transmission of information; 70% of their incoming mail was purely informational (as opposed to requests for action). Managers don't leave meetings or hang up the telephone to get back to work. In large part, communication *is* their work. Three roles describe these informational aspects of managerial work.

As *monitor*, the manager is perpetually scanning the environment for information, interrogating liaison contacts and subordinates, and receiving unsolicited information, much of it as a result of the network of personal contacts. Remember that a good part of the information the manager collects in the monitor role arrives in verbal form, often as gossip, hearsay, and speculation.

Retrospective Commentary

Henry Mintzberg

Over the years, one reaction has dominated the comments I have received from managers who read "The Manager's Job: Folklore and Fact": "You make me feel so good. I thought all those other managers were planning, organizing, coordinating, and controlling, while I was busy being interrupted, jumping from one issue to another, and trying to keep the lid on the chaos." Yet everything in this article must have been patently obvious to these people. Why such a reaction to reading what they already knew?

Conversely, how to explain the very different reaction of two media people who called to line up interviews after an article based on this one appeared in the *New York Times.* "Are we glad someone finally let managers have it," both said in passing, a comment that still takes me aback. True, they had read only the account in the *Times,* but that no more let managers have it than did this article. Why that reaction?

One explanation grows out of the way I now see this article – as proposing not so much another view of management as another face of it. I like to call it the insightful face, in contrast to the long-dominant professional or cerebral face. One stresses commitment, the other calculation; one sees the world with integrated perspective, the other figures it as the components of a portfolio. The cerebral face operates with the words and numbers of rationality; the insightful face is rooted in the images and feel of a manager's integrity.

Each of these faces implies a different kind of "knowing," and that, I believe, explains many managers' reaction to this article. Rationally, they "knew" what managers did – planned, organized, coordinated, and controlled. But deep down that did not feel quite right. The description in this article may have come closer to what they really "knew." As for those media people, they weren't railing against management as such but against the cerebral form of management, so pervasive, that they saw impersonalizing the world around them.

In practice, management has to be two-faced – there has to be a balance between the cerebral and the insightful. So, for example, I realized originally that managerial communication was largely oral and that the advent of the computer had not changed anything fundamental in the executive suite – a conclusion I continue to hold. (The greatest threat the personal computer poses is that managers will take it seriously and come to believe that they can manage by remaining in their offices and looking at displays of digital characters.) But I also thought that the dilemma of delegating could be dealt with by periodic debriefings –

disseminating words. Now, however, I believe that managers need more ways to convey the images and impressions they carry inside of them. This explains the renewed interest in strategic vision, in culture, and in the roles of intuition and insight in management.

The ten roles I used to describe the manager's job also reflect management's cerebral face, in that they decompose the job more than capture the integration. Indeed, my effort to show a sequence among these roles now seems more consistent with the traditional face of management work than an insightful one. Might we not just as well say that people throughout the organization take actions that inform managers who, by making sense of those actions, develop images and visions that inspire people to subsequent efforts?

Perhaps my greatest disappointment about the research reported here is that it did not stimulate new efforts. In a world so concerned with management, much of the popular literature is superficial and the academic research pedestrian. Certainly, many studies have been carried out over the last 15 years, but the vast majority sought to replicate earlier research. In particular, we remain grossly ignorant about the fundamental content of the manager's job and have barely addressed the major issues and dilemmas in its practice.

But superficiality is not only a problem of the literature. It is also an occupational hazard of the manager's job. Originally, I believed this problem could be dealt with; now I see it as inherent in the job. This is because managing insightfully depends on the direct experience and personal knowledge that come from intimate contact. But in organizations grown larger and more diversified, that becomes difficult to achieve. And so managers turn increasingly to the cerebral face, and the delicate balance between the two faces is lost.

Certainly, some organizations manage to sustain their humanity despite their large size – as Tom Peters and Robert Waterman show in their book *In Search of Excellence.* But that book attained its outstanding success precisely because it is about the exceptions, about the organizations so many of us long to be a part of – not the organizations in which we actually work.

Fifteen years ago, I stated that "No job is more vital to our society than that of the manager. It is the manager who determines whether our social institutions serve us well or whether they squander our talents and resources." Now, more than ever, we must strip away the folklore of the manager's job and begin to face its difficult facts.

In the *disseminator* role, the manager passes some privileged information directly to subordinates, who would otherwise have no access to it. When subordinates lack easy contact with one another, the manager may pass information from one to another.

In the *spokesperson* role, the manager sends some information to people outside the unit—a president makes a speech to lobby for an organization cause, or a foreman suggests a product modification to a supplier. In addition, as a spokesperson, every manager must inform and satisfy the influential people who control the organizational unit. For the foreman, this may simply involve keeping the plant manager informed about the flow of work through the shop.

The president of a large corporation, however, may spend a great amount of time dealing with a host of influences. Directors and shareholders must be advised about finances; consumer groups must be assured that the organization is fulfilling its social responsibilities; and government officials must be satisfied that the organization is abiding by the law.

Decisional Roles

Information is not, of course, an end in itself; it is the basic input to decision making. One thing is clear in the study of managerial work: the manager plays the major role in the unit's decision-making system. As its formal authority, only the manager can commit the unit to important new courses of action; and as its nerve center, only the manager has full and current information to make the set of decisions that determines the unit's strategy. Four roles describe the manager as decision maker.

As *entrepreneur*, the manager seeks to improve the unit, to adapt it to changing conditions in the environment. In the monitor role, a president is constantly on the lookout for new ideas. When a good one appears, he initiates a development project that he may supervise himself or delegate to an employee (perhaps with the stipulation that he must approve the final proposal).

There are two interesting features about these development projects at the CEO level. First, these projects do not involve sin-

gle decisions or even unified clusters of decisions. Rather, they emerge as a series of small decisions and actions sequenced over time. Apparently, chief executives prolong each project both to fit it into a busy, disjointed schedule, and so that they can comprehend complex issues gradually.

Second, the chief executives I studied supervised as many as 50 of these projects at the same time. Some projects entailed new products or processes; others involved public relations campaigns, improvement of the cash position, reorganization of a weak department, resolution of a morale problem in a foreign division, integration of computer operations, various acquisitions at different stages of development, and so on.

Chief executives appear to maintain a kind of inventory of the development projects in various stages of development. Like jugglers, they keep a number of projects in the air; periodically, one comes down, is given a new burst of energy, and sent back into orbit. At various intervals, they put new projects on-stream and discard old ones.

While the entrepreneur role describes the manager as the voluntary initiator of change, the *disturbance handler* role depicts the manager involuntarily responding to pressures. Here change is beyond the manager's control. The pressures of a situation are too severe to be ignored—a strike looms, a major customer has gone bankrupt, or a supplier reneges on a contract—so the manager must act.

Few CEOs approve a proposal—they approve the person.

Leonard R. Sayles, who has carried out appropriate research on the manager's job, likens the manager to a symphony orchestra conductor who must "maintain a melodious performance,"[14] while handling musicians' problems and other external disturbances.

> ## The scarcest resource managers have to allocate is their own time.

Indeed, every manager must spend a considerable amount of time responding to high-pressure disturbances. No organization can be so well run, so standardized, that it has considered every contingency in the uncertain environment in advance. Disturbances arise not only because poor managers ignore situations until they reach crisis proportions but also because good managers cannot possibly anticipate all the consequences of the actions they take.

The third decisional role is that of *resource allocator*. The manager is responsible for deciding who will get what. Perhaps the most important resource the manager allocates is his or her own time. Access to the manager constitutes exposure to the unit's nerve center and decision maker. The manager is also charged with designing the unit's structure, that pattern of formal relationships that determines how work is to be divided and coordinated.

Also, as resource allocator, the manager authorizes the important decisions of the unit before they are implemented. By retaining this power, the manager can ensure that decisions are interrelated. To fragment this power encourages discontinuous decision making and a disjointed strategy.

There are a number of interesting features about the manager's authorization of others' decisions. First, despite the widespread use of capital budgeting procedures—a means of authorizing various capital expenditures at one time—executives in my study made a great many authorization decisions on an ad hoc basis. Apparently, many projects cannot wait or simply do not have the quantifiable costs and benefits that capital budgeting requires.

Second, I found that the chief executives faced incredibly complex choices. They had to consider the impact of each decision on other decisions and on the organization's strategy. They had to ensure that the decision would be acceptable to those who influence the organization, as well as ensure that resources would not be overextended. They had to understand the various costs and benefits as well as the feasibility of the proposal. They also had to consider questions of timing. All this was necessary for the simple

approval of someone else's proposal. At the same time, however, the delay could lose time, while quick approval could be ill-considered and quick rejection might discourage the subordinate who had spent months developing a pet project.

One common solution to approving projects is to pick the person instead of the proposal. That is, the manager authorizes those projects presented by people whose judgment he or she trusts. But the manager cannot always use this simple dodge.

The final decisional role is that of *negotiator*. Managers spend considerable time in negotiations: the president of the football team works out a contract with the holdout superstar; the corporation president leads the company's contingent to negotiate a new strike issue; the foreman argues a grievance problem to its conclusion with the shop steward.

These negotiations are an integral part of the manager's job, for only he or she has the authority to commit organizational resources in "real time" and the nerve-center information that important negotiations require.

The Integrated Job

It should be clear by now that these ten roles are not easily separable. In the terminology of the psychologist, they form a gestalt, an integrated whole. No role can be pulled out of the framework and the job be left intact. For example, a manager without liaison contacts lacks external information. As a result, that manager can neither disseminate the information that employees need nor make decisions that adequately reflect external conditions. (This is a problem for the new person in a managerial position, since he or she has to build up a network of contacts before making effective decisions.)

Here lies a clue to the problems of team management.[15] Two or three people cannot share a single managerial position unless they can act as one entity. This means that they cannot divide up the ten roles unless they can very carefully reintegrate them. The real difficulty lies with the informational roles. Unless there can be full sharing of managerial information—and, as I pointed out earlier, it is primarily verbal—team management breaks down. A single managerial job cannot be arbitrarily split, for example, into internal and external roles, for information from both sources must be brought to bear on the same decisions.

To say that the ten roles form a gestalt is not to say that all managers give equal attention to each role. In fact, I found in my review of the various research studies that sales managers seem to spend relatively more of their time in the interpersonal roles, presumably a reflection of the extrovert nature of the marketing activity. Production managers, on the other hand, give relatively more attention to the decisional roles, presumably a reflection of their concern with efficient work flow. And staff managers spend the most time in the informational roles, since they are experts who manage departments that advise other parts of the organization. Nevertheless, in all cases, the interpersonal, informational, and decisional roles remain inseparable.

Toward More Effective Management

This description of managerial work should prove more important to managers than any prescription they might derive from it. That is to say, *the managers' effectiveness is significantly influenced by their insight into their own work.* Performance depends on how well a manager understands and responds to the pressures and dilemmas of the job. Thus managers who can be introspective about their work are likely to be effective at their jobs. The questions in "Self-Study Questions for Managers" may sound rhetorical; none is meant to be. Even though the questions cannot be answered simply, the manager should address them.

Let us take a look at three specific areas of concern. For the most part, the managerial logjams—the dilemma of delegation, the database centralized in one brain, the problems of working with the management scientist—revolve around the verbal nature of the manager's information. There are great dangers in centralizing the organization's data bank in the minds of its managers. When they leave, they take their memory with them. And when subordinates are out of convenient verbal reach of the manager, they are at an informational disadvantage.

The manager is challenged to find systematic ways to share privileged information. A regular debriefing session with key subordinates, a weekly memory dump on the dictating machine, maintaining a diary for limited circulation, or other similar methods may ease the logjam of work considerably. The time spent disseminating this information will be more than regained when decisions must be made. Of course, some will undoubtedly raise the question of confidentiality. But managers would be well advised to weigh the risks of exposing privileged information against having subordinates who can make effective decisions.

What managers often learn on the job is how to be superficial.

Self-Study Questions for Managers

1. Where do I get my information, and how? Can I make greater use of my contacts? Can other people do some of my scanning? In what areas is my knowledge weakest, and how can I get others to provide me with the information I need? Do I have sufficiently powerful mental models of those things I must understand within the organization and in its environment?

2. What information do I disseminate? How important is that information to my subordinates? Do I keep too much information to myself because disseminating it is time consuming or inconvenient? How can I get more information to others so they can make better decisions?

3. Do I tend to act before information is in? Or do I wait so long for all the information that opportunities pass me by?

4. What pace of change am I asking my organization to tolerate? Is this change balanced so that our operations are neither excessively static nor overly disrupted? Have we sufficiently analyzed the impact of this change on the future of our organization?

5. Am I sufficiently well-informed to pass judgment on subordinates' proposals? Can I leave final authorization for more of the proposals with subordinates? Do we have problems of coordination because subordinates already make too many decisions independently?

6. What is my vision for this organization? Are these plans primarily in my own mind in loose form? Should I make them explicit to guide the decisions of others better? Or do I need flexibility to change them at will?

7. How do my subordinates react to my managerial style? Am I sufficiently sensitive to the powerful influence of my actions? Do I fully understand their reactions to my actions? Do I find an appropriate balance between encouragement and pressure? Do I stifle their initiative?

8. What kind of external relationships do I maintain, and how? Do I spend too much of my time maintaining them? Are there certain people whom I should get to know better?

9. Is there any system to my time scheduling, or am I just reacting to the pressures of the moment? Do I find the appropriate mix of activities or concentrate on one particular function or problem just because I find it interesting? Am I more efficient with particular kinds of work, at special times of the day or week? Does my schedule reflect this? Can someone else schedule my time (besides my secretary)?

10. Do I overwork? What effect does my work load have on my efficiency? Should I force myself to take breaks or to reduce the pace of my activity?

11. Am I too superficial in what I do? Can I really shift moods as quickly and frequently as my work requires? Should I decrease the amount of fragmentation and interruption in my work?

12. Do I spend too much time on current, tangible activities? Am I a slave to the action and excitement of my work, so that I am no longer able to concentrate on issues? Do key problems receive the attention they deserve? Should I spend more time reading and probing deeply into certain issues? Could I be more reflective? Should I be?

13. Do I use the different media appropriately? Do I know how to make the most of written communication? Do I rely excessively on face-to-face communication, thereby putting all but a few of my subordinates at an informational disadvantage? Do I schedule enough of my meetings on a regular basis? Do I spend enough time observing activities firsthand, or am I detached from the heart of my organization's activities?

14. How do I blend my personal rights and duties? Do my obligations consume all my time? How can I free myself from obligations to ensure that I am taking this organization where I want it to go? How can I turn my obligations to my advantage?

If there is a single theme that runs through this article, it is that the pressures of the job drive the manager to take on too much work, encourage interruption, respond quickly to every stimulus, seek the tangible and avoid the abstract, make decisions in small increments, and do everything abruptly.

Here again, the manager is challenged to deal consciously with the presures of superficiality by giving serious attention to the issues that require it, by stepping back in order to see a broad picture, and by making use of analytical inputs. Although effective managers have to be adept at responding quickly to numerous and varying problems, the danger in managerial work is that they will respond to every issue equally (and that means abruptly) and that they will never work the tangible bits and pieces of information into a comprehensive picture of their world.

To create this comprehensive picture, managers can supplement their own models with those of specialists. Economists describe the functioning of markets, operations researchers simulate financial flow processes, and behavioral scientists explain the needs and goals of people. The best of these models can be searched out and learned.

In dealing with complex issues, the senior manager has much to gain from a close relationship with the organization's own management scientists. They have something important that the manager lacks—time to probe complex issues. An effective working relationship hinges on the resolution of what a colleague and I have called "the planning dilemma."[16] Managers have the information and the authority; analysts have the time and the technology. A successful working relationship between the two will be effected when the manager learns to share information and the analyst learns to adapt to the manager's needs. For the analyst, adaptation means worrying less about the elegance of the method and more about its speed and flexibility.

Analysts can help the top manager schedule time, feed in analytical information, monitor projects, develop models to aid in making choices, design contingency plans for disturbances that can be anticipated, and conduct "quick and dirty" analyses for those that cannot. But there can be no cooperation if the analysts are out of the mainstream of the manager's information flow.

You can't teach swimming or management in a lecture hall.

The manager is challenged to gain control of his or her own time by turning obligations into advantages and by turning those things he or she wishes to do into obligations. The chief executives of my study initiated only 32% of their own contacts (and another 5% by mutual agreement). And yet to a considerable extent they seemed to control their time. There were two key factors that enabled them to do so.

First, managers have to spend so much time discharging obligations that if they were to view them as just that, they would leave no mark on the organization. Unsuccessful managers blame failure on the obligations. Effective managers turn obligations to advantages. A speech is a chance to lobby for a cause; a meeting is a chance to reorganize a weak department; a visit to an important customer is a chance to extract trade information.

Second, the manager frees some time to do the things that he or she—perhaps no one else—thinks important by turning them into obligations. Free time is made, not found. Hoping to leave some time open for contemplation or general planning is tantamount to hoping that the pressures of the job will go away. Managers who want to innovate initiate projects and obligate others to report back to them. Managers who need certain environmental information establish channels that will automatically keep them informed. Managers who have to tour facilities commit themselves publicly.

The Educator's Job

Finally, a word about the training of managers. Our management schools have done an admirable job of training the organization's specialists—management scientists, marketing researchers, accountants, and organizational development specialists. But for the most part, they have not trained managers.[17]

Management schools will begin the serious training of managers when skill training takes a serious place next to cognitive learning. Cognitive learning is detached and informational, like reading a book or listening to a lecture. No doubt much important cognitive material must be assimilated by the manager-to-be. But cognitive learning no more makes a manager than it does a swimmer. The latter will drown the first time she jumps into the water if her coach never takes her out of the lecture hall, gets her wet, and gives her feedback on her performance.

In other words, we are taught a skill through practice plus feedback, whether in a real or a simulated situation. Our management schools need to identify the skills managers use, select students who show potential in these skills, put the students into situations where these skills can be practiced and developed, and then give them systematic feedback on their performance.

My description of managerial work suggests a number of important managerial skills—developing peer relationships, carrying out negotiations, motivating subordinates, resolving conflicts, establishing information networks and subsequently disseminating information, making decisions in conditions of extreme ambiguity, and allocating resources. Above all, the manager needs to be introspective in order to continue to learn on the job.

No job is more vital to our society than that of the manager. The manager determines whether our social institutions will serve us well or whether they will squander our talents and resources. It is time to strip away the folklore about managerial work and study it realistically so that we can begin the difficult task of making significant improvements in its performance.

See references on following page

References

1. All the data from my study can be found in Henry Mintzberg, *The Nature of Managerial Work* (New York: Harper & Row, 1973).

2. Robert H. Guest, "Of Time and the Foreman," *Personnel*, May 1956, p. 478.

3. Rosemary Stewart, *Managers and Their Jobs* (London: Macmillan, 1967); see also Sune Carlson, *Executive Behaviour* (Stockholm: Strombergs, 1951).

4. Francis J. Aguilar, *Scanning the Business Environment* (New York: Macmillan, 1967), p. 102.

5. Unpublished study by Irving Choran, reported in Mintzberg, *The Nature of Managerial Work*.

6. Robert T. Davis, *Performance and Development of Field Sales Managers* (Boston: Division of Research, Harvard Business School, 1957); George H. Copeman, *The Role of the Managing Director* (London: Business Publications, 1963).

7. Stewart, *Managers and Their Jobs*; Tom Burns, "The Directions of Activity and Communication in a Departmental Executive Group," *Human Relations* 7, no. 1 (1954): 73.

8. H. Edward Wrapp, "Good Managers Don't Make Policy Decisions," HBR September-October 1967, p. 91. Wrapp refers to this as spotting opportunities and relationships in the stream of operating problems and decisions; in his article, Wrapp raises a number of excellent points related to this analysis.

9. Richard E. Neustadt, *Presidential Power* (New York: John Wiley, 1960), pp. 153-154; italics added.

10. For a more thorough, though rather different, discussion of this issue, see Kenneth R. Andrews, "Toward Professionalism in Business Management," HBR March-April 1969, p. 49.

11. C. Jackson Grayson, Jr., in "Management Science and Business Practice," HBR July-August 1973, p. 41, explains in similar terms why, as chairman of the Price Commission, he did not use those very techniques that he himself promoted in his earlier career as a management scientist.

12. George C. Homans, *The Human Group* (New York: Harcourt, Brace & World, 1950), based on the study by William F. Whyte entitled *Street Corner Society*, rev. ed. (Chicago: University of Chicago Press, 1955).

13. Neustadt, *Presidential Power*, p. 157.

14. Leonard R. Sayles, *Managerial Behavior* (New York: McGraw-Hill, 1964), p. 162.

15. See Richard C. Hodgson, Daniel J. Levinson, and Abraham Zaleznik, *The Executive Role Constellation* (Boston: Division of Research, Harvard Business School, 1965), for a discussion of the sharing of roles.

16. James S. Hekimian and Henry Mintzberg, "The Planning Dilemma," *The Management Review*, May 1968, p. 4.

17. See J. Sterling Livingston, "Myth of the Well-Educated Manager," HBR January-February 1971, p. 79.

Reprint 90210

The wagon trains demanded leadership. Ward Bond was a great manager.

Wagon Masters and Lesser Managers

by J.S. NINOMIYA

Over the past several years, I've seen more and more books and articles about managerial effectiveness and how it can increase productivity. I've also seen more and more companies try to improve executive skills through education programs, sensitivity training, and participatory management. Yet at the same time I see businesses continuing to promote people into administrative ranks with apparently little consideration for their ability to manage others, their willingness to include subordinates in decision making, or their suitability as teachers and role models for a coming generation of supervisors. Many of these newly promoted managers perform in the managerial styles of a past era, characterized by self-serving attitudes, empire building, and autocratic methods. Eventually they too need sensitivity training and remedial seminars to try to correct their ineffective behavior.

In short, too many companies are making the same mistake with managers that the auto industry used to make with quality: build it now, fix it later. We've finally started building automobiles right in the first place. Now we need to do the same with managers: hire and promote the right men and women to begin with instead of trying to "fix" them years later after they've done their damage.

I am neither a social scientist nor a management consultant. For the last 20 years, I've worked at middle management jobs in the auto industry, where I have supervised many people and worked for many supervisors. In addition, I worked on a research team in the 1970s that took me into the offices of colleagues in the oil and auto industries, and there, for weeks at a time, I was able to watch managerial behavior in other companies from a fly-on-the-wall perspective. In my experience, it is rare that managers are selected for their supervisory ability. Indeed, most of those I've known lacked what I consider the most basic requirements for effective management—an understanding of the human condition and an appreciation of people. Most managers today are still selected solely on the basis of business expertise or success in nonsupervisory positions, and the styles they develop are inadequate, to say the least.

It may help to describe some of these styles. Here are seven I meet regularly:

The Godfather. Despite the current emphasis on teamwork and participatory management, the Godfather style still prevails. Godfathers typically demand complete control of their organizations and total loyalty from their employees. Subordinates are given freedom in their routine duties, but their goals

In his 27 years at Ford, J.S. Ninomiya has held a variety of line, research, and management positions. He is currently safety planning manager for the company's environmental and safety engineering staff.

are dictated from above. A Godfather's image and ego require frequent nurturing, usually in the form of successful confrontations with outsiders. To be recognized as good employees, subordinates need only stand at ringside and root for the boss.

People who have been subjected to this style for many years rarely become good managers themselves. Most often they become new Godfathers. At the opposite extreme, they become submissive and ineffectual.

Groups led by Godfathers are normally goal oriented and known for getting things done. Outsiders see them as well-oiled machines. Superiors depend on them. Because they rely on one person for nearly all decisions, however, the goals of Godfather groups are often self-serving and not always in the best interests of the organization as a whole.

The Ostrich. Ostriches love the status quo and fear discord. They always hope problems will simply go away and would rather stick their heads in the sand than face unpleasantness of any kind.

Ostriches believe firmly in nonconfrontational approaches to problem solving, and they avoid issues and debate. They are often capable and knowledgeable in their own areas of expertise, but they are usually better suited to serve as assistants than as managers. The fact is, progress cannot be achieved without conflict, and a preference for the status quo stifles growth and can weaken morale. Ostriches are more concerned with a superior's opinion of their job performance than with the morale of their subordinates, who often lack initiative, imagination, and productivity, especially if they've had their Ostrich managers for a long time.

The Do-It-Yourselfer. Do-It-Yourselfers want to handle everything themselves, especially the more challenging assignments. The only tasks they ordinarily delegate are the ones that they find trivial or that require special skills. They are often capable individuals; many are workaholics. All live by the motto: "If you want a job done well, do it yourself!" They spend long hours at their jobs and are seen by upper management as candidates for promotion.

Unfortunately, they often make themselves indispensable. In several cases I know, a Do-It-Yourselfer's sudden illness has brought an entire department to a standstill. In addition, people who work for them often react like the people who work for Ostriches. Unable to get recognition and challenging assignments, they turn into mere hired hands. If the goals of an organization include productivity improvement and personnel development, then Godfathers, Ostriches, and Do-It-Yourselfers make poor managers.

The Detailer. Detailers want to know everything their subordinates do "in detail." In larger organizations, Detailers are so busy trying to keep up with their employees that they are virtually incapable of managing groups of any size. As they see it, their task is to be wiser and know more than their subordinates, so that they can make correct decisions by themselves. Detailers don't like group decisions and find delegating difficult. When they do delegate, they stay constantly in touch to make sure that subordinates do not arrive at independent decisions. Detailers generally lack confidence in others and make subordinates redo assignments again and again.

The decisions made by Detailers are often good ones, but they are rarely prompt. Since the usefulness of a decision is seldom a function of the time it takes to make it, a good but leisurely decision is often too late to be useful. Detailers are best suited for supervising small groups that can afford to work slowly.

The Politician. Many of us like to work for Politicians because they tell us what we want to hear. Their superiors like having them around for the same reason. One of the drawbacks to this style is that Politicians tend to overdo it. A colleague of mine received 37 notes of commendation in one year, though the boss who sent them rated his overall performance average. Praise of this kind produces nothing but frustration and resentment. No one looks forward to the 38th insincere note from the boss.

Another drawback is that Politicians tend to stratify employees and management. On hearing objections from his or her own boss, for example, the Politician may abruptly overturn a decision previously approved by subordinates. What passes for managerial skill is nothing more than a talent for dodging bullets. Politicians with fast reflexes may succeed for a while, but few manage to dodge forever.

The Arbitrator. Arbitrators are often very successful at dealing with large groups because they possess a deep understanding of people and human conflict. They believe in teamwork and team decisions. If an organization's goal is to promote harmony and increase productivity, then this style is effective, especially in mid-management ranks. On the other hand, if what the organization needs is a vocal spokesperson and a competitive leader, then the Arbitrator may not meet the need. Arbitrators are usually personable and well liked, but they do have a weakness for compromise at the wrong moment, and they tend to be so friendly with subordinates that they find it hard to crack down when the going gets tough.

The Eager Beaver. In the same way that beavers build ever larger dams to interrupt the flow of water, so Eager Beavers create ever greater workloads and eventually interrupt the smooth functioning of their organizations. These managers measure their worth by the number of letters and reports they generate and by how hard their subordinates work. They are seldom content unless their subordinates put in overtime and work weekends at least occasionally. In many cases, even those who don't need to put in overtime are pressured into it. In my experience, unnecessary work

The Godfather's heavyweight ego puts him in the center of the ring.

The Ostrich's fear of discord leaves conflict unresolved.

demoralizes employees, and constant work pressure wears them down.

Many managers of the past were Eager Beavers and Godfathers who rationalized hiring more and more employees on the grounds of minimizing overtime expenditures. But the fact is, these empire builders don't change their habits even when their departments double in size. Eager Beavers and Godfathers did so much empire building at Ford between 1979 and 1982 that new management was able to cut back the number of employees by more than one-third without affecting productivity.

On the positive side, Eager Beavers are thorough. On the negative side, they produce a mass of useless information that often gets filed in wastebaskets.

A catalog of management styles could go on and on, but these seven styles, singly or in combination, describe more than three-quarters of all the managers I've known and many I have worked for. Every one of them meets some of the needs of an organization some of the time, but not one of them is what I would call an effective manager. Six of the seven types have more weaknesses than strengths, and they all train subordinates in their own inadequate image.

The effective manager is more difficult to describe, for the very reason that he or she refuses to be typecast. The trouble with most of us is not that we sometimes act like, say, Godfathers, but that we act like Godfathers all the time. An effective manager is sometimes a Godfather and sometimes a Do-It-Yourselfer, often an Arbitrator and occasionally even an Ostrich. After 27 years, I think I know good managers when I see them, and I think I know what it is they do. I even think I know how to find them. Let me illustrate with one of my favorite examples.

Some of the most effective managers this country has ever seen were the wagon masters of the west-

ward movement in the last century. A wagon master had two jobs. He had to keep the wagons moving toward their destination day after day despite all obstacles. He also had to maintain harmony and a spirit of teamwork among the members of his party and to resolve daily problems before they became divisive. A wagon master's worth was measured by his ability to reach the destination safely and to keep spirits high along the way. He had to do both in order to do either. I see the skills of effective managers as essentially the same, and I can sum them up in the roles they play:

Decision Maker. To begin with, effective managers are decisive. Despite all our newfound emphasis on teamwork and consensus, decision-making ability is by far the most important tool a manager needs on a daily basis. Teamwork is right for many decisions. Managers alone must make many others, including most of those involving job assignments, people, and interorganizational disputes. But here as elsewhere, an executive's responsibility is twofold – to make the right decision but also to encourage subordinate participation. In my experience the best policy is to involve as many employees as practical, to present them with the whole issue to be resolved (not just pieces of it), to sincerely seek and appreciate their suggestions, and throughout the process, to display the kind of decisiveness it would take to act alone.

Listener and Communicator. Many managers hear their subordinates but do not "listen." It takes enormous effort to get to know employees individually and to learn how to sense the group dynamics in an organization. A supervisor, like the leader of a wagon train, must be sensitive to moods and attitudes. By listening and communicating well, managers can fulfill the basic human need employees have to be recognized and appreciated. Good listening is also part of an effective style in meetings. The successful managers I've known never dominate the table but let everyone express his or her views.

Teacher. One of the responsibilities of a good manager is to train subordinates to become managers. This does not mean having one or two favorites who are seen as anointed successors. It means training everyone who has potential. There are many ways to help people learn to make decisions: delegate responsibility, even to the lowest ranks; include subordinates where feasible in every project; hold regular discussion sessions; let employees represent the company with outside contacts. The effective managers I've known use all these ways of building positive self-images in their employees.

Indeed, good managers all seem to have one thing in common: they delegate well, and trusting people to do the right thing, give minimal direction. They don't reprimand subordinates who fail but encourage them to try again and to seek the help of coworkers and their own subordinates whenever possible. Good supervisors rarely find themselves burdened with unimaginative staff work because they constantly challenge the limits of their subordinates' creativity.

Peacemaker. Effective managers know how to minimize conflict. Some supervisors simply ignore its existence or become abusive and threaten to dismiss everyone involved. But managers who want their organizations to function productively face day-to-day problems directly. One way is to confront employees in order to determine the causes of conflict. Another is to encourage work groups like quality circles; a third is to rotate jobs and reassign people. Every workplace has conflicts. Effective managers sense them early and deal with them head-on.

Visionary. Wagon masters pushed their wagons toward specific destinations—Oregon, the California gold fields. Effective managers set goals that are just as firm and meaningful. Identifying goals is no less important than creating the means to achieve them. We have all looked for a car in a crowded parking lot. We trudge up one aisle and down the next, growing increasingly frustrated and embarrassed. Any clear sense of where we had left the car would have saved us enormous time and energy. In an effective organization, collective as well as individual goals are well defined and understood. Good managers never let themselves or their subordinates lose sight of them.

Self-Critic. How many times have you heard the expression "The boss is always right" or "The boss is the boss"? Not many managers are self-confident enough to admit their mistakes. Most believe that making mistakes is the worst corporate offense, and they don't allow the notion of human error to enter their philosophies. In fact, some insist on having their way even when they know they're wrong. Worse yet, subordinates who recognize the boss's mistakes can't correct them for fear of reprisal. Employees lose respect for their supervisors, and blunders achieve the status of doctrine. Effective manag-

The Politician's relentless insincerity wears subordinates down.

ers are quick to admit their own mistakes and don't dwell on the mistakes of others. They want to learn from mistakes so as not to repeat them. They know that while assessing damage and causes is often important, assigning blame is not.

Team Captain. Consensus decision making is one of the most powerful tools at a manager's disposal. Working alone, executives may find it difficult to make decisions affecting the whole organization – retooling a plant, reorganizing departments, even remodeling office space – because they are so often limited by the self-serving and conflicting information arriving from different departments. Teamwork decisions can minimize mistakes in such situations and ward off much dissatisfaction among employees whose voices would not otherwise be heard.

Leader. An executive's attitude toward subordinates is perhaps the most important trait of all. Effective managers have drive and determination, but they also have qualities like trust, modesty, politeness, patience, and sensitivity. Good managers genuinely like and appreciate people. They don't just manipulate or command; they lead. And they understand their dual function. Getting the wagons to Oregon without the passengers is no achievement. Keeping everyone in high spirits right up to the moment they perish in the desert is not success.

The need for good managers is growing. Many companies are downsizing in an effort to operate more efficiently. They are combining departments and cutting the work force but creating larger groups to be supervised. If we have fewer managers, we need them to be even more effective, which means that the ability to manage people is becoming more and more important. Yet the way we select managers hasn't changed much, and the managers we find are not much better than they ever were.

One short-term approach to the problem is to retrain today's executives. I've seen numerous efforts to introduce participatory management, promote teamwork, alter managerial attitudes, even change the so-called corporate culture. These are all moves in the right direction, but the results are often disappointing. Many people simply cannot see their own shortcomings. Others pay only lip service to such programs. Most disappointing of all, many seem to overestimate how much they've learned and changed in the course of retraining. After some recent participatory management workshops at Ford, for example, managers and their employees were asked to rate the benefits: nearly two-thirds of the executives felt they had become better supervisors, but

only a quarter of the subordinates shared that view. We must be careful not to fool ourselves with rosy self-assessments, or to believe we have solved a problem when we have really only talked about it.

For the long term, we need to make changes in the way we hire, reward, and evaluate managers. We need to improve the methods we already use – better personality profiles, better interviewing techniques, a better environment for people to work in once they've been hired. In addition, I have three unconventional suggestions:

First, abandon excessive perks. I believe effective managers always treat subordinates as people first and employees second. I know one such manager who left thank-you notes on his desk for the evening cleaning crew (who, as you might guess, kept his office immaculate). I know executives who take turns with their subordinates cleaning the office coffee maker and others who automatically pick up trash on their plants' floors instead of stepping over it. The people who work for such managers can be vehement in their unwillingness to work for anyone else.

On the other hand, I've met managers who think they are cast in a different mold from their employees – even when they all come from similar backgrounds. These executives consider themselves members of an elite and take pride in the symbols of their status, which they believe will increase their authority and make them more effective.

In fact, perks and status symbols often act as obstacles to good management. After many years of enjoying these rewards, some managers develop such a sense of privilege that they begin to look on employee concerns and complaints as encroachments on their prerogatives.

Demonstrations of rank have nothing to do with good management; yet in the United States the practice of granting special privileges is almost universal.

I recently discussed this subject with a vice president of one of the country's largest companies. He maintained that management perks were needed to inspire people to achieve corporate goals. Without them, he felt, people would have no incentive to work harder. I agreed that perks can be useful in some cases to reward achievements. But what about the rewards of approval and self-satisfaction? He was puzzled. Who would work harder for nothing but self-satisfaction? I asked then how he justified rewarding his executives but not his workers since, in his own view, people will not perform without the prospect of rewards. He said he could not reward everyone or his company would face bankruptcy.

I suspect that this man's view – the carrot for executives, the stick, presumably, for others – is shared by many in top management. There are other industrial countries, however, where such privilege is rare, yet productivity remains high.

Several years ago, a friend of mine—an American executive at a large U.S. corporation—went to work for a Japanese company in the United States. Previously, he had been a profit-oriented manager with short-term goals and had enjoyed a wide range of perks and privileges. The last time I saw him I was astonished at the change in his outlook. He had become a respected manager of people, with long-term goals and a vision for his company's future. He no longer had all the accustomed perks. He was no longer isolated in his executive suite but spent much of his time on the factory floor.

I am not suggesting that all managers adopt the Japanese style and abandon traditional American values. I cannot say that all perks are bad business practice. Many successful companies use them, some as a means of projecting company images to outsiders.

The Eager Beaver's gnawing ambition dams up the company works.

Still, the thought of doing without them is attractive. Managers need to mix with subordinates to promote a spirit of teamwork, to nurture commitment to the job, to monitor the heartbeat of the company, and to remind themselves how well and how quickly many of their subordinates could fill their shoes.

Second, ignore narrow expertise. Common sense tells us to hire supervisors with expertise in the field they're expected to manage, but there are several drawbacks to this practice. To begin with, one of the most frequent complaints of managers themselves is that they become typecast in their particular expertise and have little opportunity to grow into other areas of business. Their promotional paths are

similarly limited. But the man or woman who feels stifled by typecasting is not likely to be a truly effective manager, stimulated by new challenges, open to new ideas, creative, enthusiastic, optimistic. Moreover, expertise tends to become outdated, and in my experience this phenomenon presents two very real dangers. One is that entrenched managers will suppress innovation. Another, more dangerous possibility is that a manager with fossilized expertise may give subordinates too little room to grow.

Managers whose technical expertise is in another area will take a broader view of organizational goals, will depend more on subordinates, and will insist on teamwork, thus freeing themselves to manage people—the task for which they were hired.

In my view, the same considerations ought to apply to the old question of whether to promote from within or hire from without. Most people dislike the idea of bringing in outsiders from other companies or even transferring them from other departments. This is probably because most people fear for their own chances of promotion. But what matters is to broaden the perspectives of the organization and to find executives who can manage people. Inside or outside is irrelevant.

Third, get references from a candidate's old subordinates. This may sound radical. It is certainly unorthodox. I know of only one organization that contacted the candidate's former subordinates. Why should the references of past subordinates be less important than the references of past employers? When we hire someone to manage people, we need to know what previous employees thought. Unlike old bosses, who often write complimentary letters in behalf of people they were happy to see go, old subordinates are likely to say what they mean. There is no better judge of a supervisor's character than the people who depend on him or her to hear their complaints, arbitrate their differences, sharpen their skills, and lead them to the fulfillment of their goals.

I am convinced that the key to all our business goals—better quality, bigger sales, increased profits—is this emphasis on people. Like wagon masters, effective managers understand that their own success is inseparable from the success of their fellow travelers. Good managers get things done by caring about the people who do them.   ▽

Reprint 88209

Supervision: substance and style

To be effective, a manager needs to pay attention to what he does as well as how he does it

Saul W. Gellerman

Managers readily admit that their style has a bearing on their overall effectiveness. Many, however, are frankly mystified by the ballyhoo that has surrounded the topic for several years, and for good reason. The subject is a difficult one, since in reality the style a manager brings to his or her job is inextricably intertwined with the substance of that job—what it is to which the manager directs his attention. The manager should therefore look at substance and style together, and that is what the author did in analyzing the jobs of several first-line supervisors in the packaging plant of a major food processing company. As a result, the supervisors themselves were able to understand and improve the structure of their jobs, and the author was able to identify some general principles on how substance and style interact.

Saul W. Gellerman is president of his own consulting firm, which specializes in motivation and productivity in organizations. The author of a diverse number of books, articles, films, and audio tape cassettes, he has adapted this article from his book, *Managers and Subordinates*, published in 1976 by The Dryden Press, Hinsdale, Illinois, a division of the Holt, Rinehart & Winston CBS publishing group.

Reprint 76203

What determines how effective a first line supervisor will be in motivating his or her subordinates?

Without question, the supervisor's effectiveness is determined to a large extent by his ability to direct and control others. At the same time, direction and control can be exercised through a wide variety of supervisory styles, and these in turn tend to elicit differing (but somewhat predictable) employee reactions. This impact of the supervisor's behavior on that of his subordinates, and therefore on their productivity, can be quite substantial.

At a large, semiautomated factory, for example, approximately 3% of all raw material is "lost" and cannot be converted into salable products because it has been ruined by incorrect processing. Management attributes approximately two thirds of this loss (that is, 2% of the factory's raw material inventory) to the tendency of employees to use shortcuts and to ignore certain routine inspections and adjustments. These "sloppy habits," in turn, have developed over a period of years because supervisors were more concerned with technical matters than with employee habits. The supervisors' failure to intervene implied a tacit approval, or at least a tolerance, of incorrect procedures. At this factory, 2% of the raw material inventory runs into tens of millions of dollars per year—a high price to pay for sloppy habits.

Impacts such as this on employee behavior derive not only from *what* the supervisor does, but *how* he does it; in other words, they derive from both the *substance* and the *style* of his actions. Ever since the Hawthorne studies, behavioral researchers have emphasized style because they have assumed, first, that it is through style that supervisors convey their estimates of their subordinates' ability and reliability and, second, that it is employees' perceptions of that estimate that produce their reactions. Thus study after study has shown that workers are more collaborative, hence more productive, under a supportive or "employee-centered" style of supervision than they are under a style implying distrust or low regard.

However, simple observation reveals that substance as well as style of supervision affect employee performance—that these two factors interact, and that neither can be ignored. At the risk of oversimplification, it might be said that *what* the supervisor does to direct and control his subordinates determines *what* they will do and that *how* he carries out these responsibilities determines the emphasis, pace, and style of their responses.

In 1973, at the request of a major food processing company, I conducted a survey of supervisory practices in its packaging plant. By following each of 12 supervisors wherever they went for an entire shift, I noted their every action in a detailed diary, and interviewed them in their rare free moments to determine the reasons for what they had done.

The following excerpts from my diaries for three of the supervisors not only give some of the flavor of factory life under high production pressure, but also demonstrate that the things to which the supervisor chooses to give his attention largely determine what his subordinates will channel their energies into. In each of the three excerpts, the supervisor's style also has its effects, of course, but, as we shall see, these are subtler.

Supervisor C: expectations and reassurances

At 2:45 in the afternoon, C was out on the packing floor, speaking to the supervisor of the preceding shift. The supervisor had had an uneventful run and was leaving C in good shape; all machines were up and the ingredients were flowing smoothly. At three minutes before the hour, there was brief confusion as the first shift streamed off the floor and those in the second, including C's department, came in from the corridors where they had just punched in on the time clock.

Spot checks

C moved down the line, quickly checking each machine visually. He also paused briefly to tell each worker how the department as a whole had performed the night before. "Good running last night," he would say. "Five hundred thirty-seven cases." Then he would grin and thrust out his hand for a quick congratulatory shake, and move on. (C gave the department's totals, not the individual's. Anyone who wanted to know his or her own record had only to glance at the meter above his machine.)

Later, C told me that his practice was to announce the previous night's results at the beginning of each shift. He shakes hands, however, only when 500 or more cases have been produced. Below that figure, he is likely to say something like, "It wasn't too bad, but we can do better."

C patrolled continually up and down the line. He was not waiting until trouble began; instead he was continually monitoring the places where trouble could start, hoping to catch it early. He checked moisture levels in the ingredient trays and pressure levels in the feed lines. If the pneumatic feed system failed, as it often had lately, he would have to bring someone in to hand-feed the premixed ingredients into the packers while the maintenance men tried to correct the problem. The alternative would be to shut down a packer, which C was reluctant to do.

From time to time, C paused briefly at the "scope," a video display unit that could be operated from a small console near his desk. This device keeps track of each machine's performance with regard to running time, rejects, weights, and so on, all on a minute-by-minute basis. With the scope, a supervisor can determine whether defects too subtle for the human eye have begun to develop, and can make an educated guess as to their cause. "That thing is kind of spooky," he confided, "but I wouldn't want to run these high-speed babies without it."

For the most part, C was no conversationalist. His contacts were brief, almost laconic. But they were also easy, with a touch of banter. For example, he seemed to have a standing joke with one operator, a lady considerably older than he was. She "wouldn't permit him" to inspect more than one pack at a time; otherwise she threatened to "slap his hand." Naturally, he pretended to grab at a second pack and she pretended to slap. Then they both giggled and he said that he was really only making sure that

"output... quality ...quota"

she was still on the ball. While his other contacts were not as demonstrative, they were equally light-hearted. C seemed to know his people well, and his manner made his inspection of their work, which after all is a control function, easier to tolerate.

Reinforcing good habits
If his contacts were brief, they were also frequent. C was constantly on the move, and in this way he would get back to any given operator in the line fairly quickly. The operators saw a lot of him, but never had to endure a concentrated dose of scrutiny. Occasionally he would point something out to them, or vice versa. Yet for the most part, he simply walked up, looked at various indicators and potential trouble spots, exchanged a few quick pleasantries, and moved on.

C was primarily interested in whether the operators were following a standard checklist of correct operating procedures; since they all knew this list as well as he did, they did follow it well. The sheer frequency of C's appearances, plus the fact that he came across as helpful rather than irritating, had the effect of reinforcing good habits. In a sense, therefore, C didn't have much to do because he handled the preventive aspect of his control responsibilities quite well.

As a matter of fact, a good run can be rather boring—nothing but the hum of the machines and the endless mechanical march of packages into the loading trough. Breakdowns provide a little variety and excitement, and operators understandably welcome it when a small army of mechanics, supervisors, and even higher management arrives on the scene. C knew this danger well. Other than relief breaks, lunch, and breakdowns, his "visits" provided the only social stimulation the machine operators got. Hence, C tried to turn his visits into welcome, if brief, respites from monotony. He even encouraged gentle ribbing and harmless jokes at his expense.

"No luck tonight"
Just before C's scheduled coffee break, the pneumatic feed did break down. The operator threw the emergency switch and stood to signal to C, but he was already on his way.

"O.K., you did the right thing," he said, reassuring the somewhat uncertain operator. "Clean up what you can and I'll get someone to hand-feed for you." He then went off to the nearest telephone to call in a maintenance crew to repair the feed line and someone from the labor pool to do the hand-feeding.

The supervisor from the next department arrived; he had been scheduled to "cover" both departments during C's break. But C waved him off. "No luck tonight," he laughed. "You drink an extra cup for me on your break." Then he headed back to the stricken machine.

Things started happening fast: a large tub was wheeled up, full of pre-mixed ingredients, and a young man arrived from the labor pool. C patiently showed him how to use a small metal scoop to hand-feed the machine. Then he instructed the operator to start up again. Glancing quickly at his watch, he noted with quiet satisfaction that the machine had been down for only four minutes.

As C checked to make sure that the machine was operating correctly, the maintenance crew arrived. C told the crew chief what had happened and then returned to the hand-feeder, making sure that the young man was properly timing his delivery of ingredients into the hopper. Before he left, he cautioned the young man: "I know you'd rather watch what those maintenance boys are doing, but I want you to keep your eyes at this level-marker in the hopper."

The maintenance crew chief emerged from the bowels of the pneumatic feed system with bad news. It might take a couple of hours to fix. C took it calmly. The hand-feeder would be disappointed; that would mean at least two hours of drudgery, with the operator constantly looking over his shoulder to make sure he kept his mind on his work. "Don't you worry, Lester," C said to the operator. "You just lost four minutes, that's all." Lester didn't seem convinced, but C kept reassuring him through the next few hours.

Preventable defect
I asked C for his opinion on why the pneumatic feed failed. He grinned and said it was a preventable defect. "But when a supervisor is running well, he doesn't want to shut down his line for preventive maintenance. It was just my turn to get caught tonight." I asked if this was because the shifts tended to compete with each other. "They're not supposed to, but they do," he replied. Everyone knows that sooner or later a piece of equipment will fail, but everyone keeps it running in hopes that it will fail on another shift.

Off at the far end of the line, a cleaning crew moved in to give one of the machines a routine swabbing. The operator and his two helpers stood aside during

this process, which took five or six minutes. "Watch that end machine," C said. The cleaning crew finished its work, and as they prepared to leave, the operator and his helpers moved right back in. They were back in operation almost before the cleaning crew had left.

"See that?" said C, with obvious pride. "They went right back into production without waiting to be told. These are good people."

I decided to probe C a bit, so I asked, "Did they do that for my benefit?"

"Hell, no," he replied, "There's no way you can run 500 cases with a lazy crew. You couldn't on this floor, anyway."

Highly rated

C is highly rated by his superiors. His shift's productivity is among the highest in the factory. This is partly due to the fact that he has a high proportion of seasoned, mature subordinates. But in large measure it is the result of the approach that he takes to supervision.

The *substance* of C's supervision is his frequent checking and his repeated demonstrations that he expects his people to follow correct procedures. C's *style* is a mixture of gentle humor and reassurance. His pride in his subordinates is genuine and not a device, and it serves to reinforce an already favorable relationship with them. Unhappily, C is not a typical supervisor, and, as one might anticipate, his easy, positive relationship with his people is not simple to attain.

Supervisor L: up and around

L is a supervisor on the night shift, from 11 p.m. to 7 a.m. This shift has certain built-in handicaps: a high proportion of inexperienced workers, a comparatively small force of maintenance men, and an almost universal desire by its employees to transfer to one of the other shifts. Thus the supervisory job on this shift is in some ways more demanding than on the other two.

Pace setter

At 10:55, L was out in the corridor near the timeclock, watching his subordinates punch in. They removed their cards from the "out" rack, inserted them into the timeclock, and placed them in the "in" rack. Promptly at 11, L pulled the remaining cards in the "out" rack—representing absentees or workers who would arrive late—and walked rapidly onto the production floor. Taking a whistle from his pocket, he blew hard to signal that production should commence. Other supervisors were also blowing whistles in other areas and for a while there was quite a din.

Then L moved quickly down the line to make sure that the people who were present were at their proper stations. He then called his superior to ask for replacements for the absentees; there were three people missing that night.

L was very energetic. He moved around a lot, and in a physical sense he worked hard. However, he was largely concerned with availability of supplies and the condition of the equipment. His concern with subordinates was primarily with regard to *where* they were; if they were in the right place, that seemed to satisfy him, and if they were not, he would insist that they return. He did very little scrutinizing of their work.

By 11:20, the "absentees" had all shown up—all were late. They didn't seem particularly sheepish about their tardiness, and L showed no reaction either, other than marking their time cards and sending their replacements back to the labor pool. Evidently, lateness was a common occurrence on this shift.

For the moment, though, everything was going well and L hung back, watching the line from a distance, alert but not directly involved. There was a certain light camaraderie among the crews on the machines. A cleaning crew was sitting on stools near some pillars, not conspicuously busy. I mentioned this to L; he replied that it was all right because the line was running well and none of the machines had got too dirty.

Names important

Now and then a worker would approach L with some information or a request. L would make a point of addressing each of them by name, and afterward he stressed to me the importance of knowing each employee's name. He also pointed to a high stool near his desk at one end of the line. The line was so long that the only way to see all of it at once would have been to perch on that stool. But L told me he sat there so seldom that his people were surprised when he did.

As we walked along the line together, L pointed to an employee whose machine had jammed. The employee was reaching into the loading trough, pulling out and discarding the packages that were stuck there. L noted that this was an incorrect procedure which had, in fact, been the subject of a recent series of meetings between supervisors and operators. The practice was unsafe and inefficient. I asked L if he was going to stop the employee, and he said no, because the jam was nearly cleared already.

Later, he returned to the subject and added two more reasons for not taking action: first, the employee had been trying to get production started again, and L had not wanted to discourage that, even if the prescribed methods were not being used. Second, the employee would only have resented it if he had been corrected, and would have found some way to "get even," probably at the expense of productivity.

Preoccupied with breakdowns

There were several breakdowns during this shift, and L spent a good deal of time at the site of each of them. He was obviously anxious to get the machines back into operation, but there wasn't a great deal he could do; the labor contract stipulated that only a union maintenance man could work on the machines.

L told me he had had grievances filed against him for such prohibited acts as tapping an out-of-line part with a hammer. Therefore he tended to hover in the background as the maintenance man worked, sometimes offering suggestions that were not necessarily followed. (The maintenance man did not report to a line supervisor, but to a maintenance supervisor who covered the entire plant at night, and who therefore showed up infrequently.)

L was greatly relieved when the machines were restored to production, and immediately resumed patrolling his line. In almost every case, he discovered trouble of one kind or another that had begun to develop while he had been preoccupied with the breakdown. I asked him if resuming his patrols as soon as he knew the maintenance man was on the job might not have been better than remaining on the scene during the entire repair. He replied that the best way to make sure the machine was repaired as quickly as possible was to stay with

the maintenance man, guaranteeing that he would not slow down or take it easy.

Beating the rush

About ten minutes before the shift ended, L was scrambling down the line, reading production meters on each machine and recording the results on a card. The operators shut down their machines after he had read their meters. They began to clean up the area or, in some cases, to chat idly with each other or with the incoming employees from the next shift. Some lined up at the time clock so as not to get caught in the rush when the shift officially ended and everyone wanted to punch out at once.

By the time L finished reading the meters, his department was completely inoperative and had about five minutes left to go on the shift. He stood at his desk, transferring the production figures from the note card to his shift report. He noted with annoyance that a few of his employees were not standing by their machines, but had drifted over to the time clocks. He said he had spoken to them about it, but that they saw no sense in standing by the machines after he had read their meters.

I asked L if he could not read their meters with one or two minutes left to go, since that is about all the time it seemed to take. He replied that it would be too confusing with the next shift coming on. Besides, his workers needed a chance to clean up.

As the bell rang to signal the end of the shift, L promptly left the floor, dropped off his shift report in his manager's office, and started for home.

Less effective

It is not surprising that L is not highly rated by management, and that his department's productivity record tends to be poor. In comparing him with C, the question inevitably arises about whether the difference in their productivity results from their supervisory methods or from other factors, such as the maturity of their workers. This is more than just a theoretical problem, since combinations like these—an effective supervisor with a mature group, a less effective supervisor with a less effective group—are not unusual. Management frequently tries to concentrate its strength to maximize productivity in certain areas, while settling for less output elsewhere.

Undoubtedly, both factors—supervisory methods and employee qualifications—are involved. But the proof that supervisory methods play a significant role is that supervisors less effective than C, working on the same shift and with essentially the same level of experience among their workers, cannot match C's sustained productive output, while more skilled supervisors than L, also on the same shift and with the same caliber of employees, consistently outproduce him.

The *substance* of L's supervision includes checking the location, but not the activity, of his subordinates, avoiding insistence on prescribed procedures, hovering around the site of a breakdown while risking loss of control of the rest of his line, and reading his meters earlier than necessary. His *style* includes the regular, albeit mechanical, use of first names in all employee contacts (most of which he does not initiate), a tendency to stay on his feet rather than sit, and much energetic rushing about.

In the sense of physical exertion, L works harder, and at the end of the day is no doubt more tired, than C. C also keeps moving, but in a more relaxed, deliberate way. L is less effective because he isn't working hard at the things that matter most—the frequent checking, repeated demonstrations, and genuine, useful manner at which C excels. Impersonal and preoccupied with production problems, L is diligent and conscientious about secondary matters, but neglects what ought to be his top priorities.

Supervisor D:
strategy and support

I met D in the supervisor's lounge at 6:45 a.m. On the way to his department, he expounded his philosophy of managing a packaging department. He stressed the importance of getting off to a good start.

"The first couple of hours pretty much set you up for the rest of the shift," he said. "You get a good start, everybody's feeling good about it, and that will carry you right to three o'clock. But you get a bad start, people start getting mad at the machines, then they get mad at each other, and then you know nothing's going to go right. You're just going to have 'one of those days,' and you'll be fighting it all the way."

I asked D what he did to ensure a good start. "First off, I talk with the supervisor from the shift before us, and I try to tell him where his people are leaving us in bad shape—things like not enough supplies on the floor or dirty machines. Sometimes his maintenance people lock up parts in their drawers to be sure they have them when they need them, which means maybe we don't have them when we need them. That supervisor, though, he's pretty good when you tell him what you want, but he gets so busy near the end of the shift, some things just get by him. And, of course, when you tell him, it's 24 hours later. Yesterday he did all right by me, but I always have my fingers crossed when I come in."

Quick diagnosis

When we arrived at D's department, the first thing he did do was talk to the preceding shift supervisor. The poor fellow looked worn out and said he had been having trouble with the machines and the pneumatic feeds. "Well," D sighed, after his predecessor left, "things are going to be a little tough this morning. When they get a lot of mechanical trouble on the second or third shift, they leave most of it with us, because we have more maintenance people."

He moved quickly into the line, watching each machine in operation. Two or three were shut down because the operators on the preceding shift had told D's operators that they weren't running right. D asked them to start up anyway so he could judge for himself how bad the machines were, and whether they could be run for a while at slower speeds or had to be shut down altogether. Since there were too many problems to handle all at once, his overall purpose was to determine where to assign his maintenance people first.

I assumed that D would assign the maintenance crews to his most serious problem right off, but, on the contrary, he sent them to the machines that could be fixed most quickly. Later he explained:

"If two machines are down, one with a big problem and one with a little problem, and you fix the big problem first, you'll have two machines down as long as it takes to fix the big problem. If you fix the little problem first, you'll have one machine back in operation fast, and the second one will be ready only a little later than if you'd done it first."

Encouragement offered
As repairs began, the operators whose machines were being fixed busied themselves with cleaning and bringing in supplies. Some of those who were operating had difficulties that would simply have to wait until the maintenance crews could get to them. D spent much of his time with these people, offering encouragement by rolling a stack of containers a short distance to where it would be needed or picking up debris. One operator seemed quite agitated, and he engaged her in a fairly lengthy discussion, out of earshot. As I watched from a distance, another operator looked up at me, smiled a bit sadly and said, "We're all running bad today." I tried to be encouraging. "Don't worry, we'll get it fixed pretty soon," I said, knowing full well I hadn't any clear notion of how long it would take. I guess he knew it, too, because his only reply to me was another sad smile.

But I could see D's point about the psychological reaction to a bad start-up. These people were facing the possibility of eight hours of unavailing effort to overcome problems they had not created. Some were depressed, some were angry, and some were grim. Certainly nobody seemed nonchalant! D was concerned that some of his people might just give up and try to get lost in the restrooms; others might sit sullenly at their machines, paying no attention to the dials and indicators, but ready to snarl at anyone who criticized them.

D returned from his lengthy discussion, and I asked him what the trouble had been. Evidently the operator had not got along with one of her helpers, and had given D an earful of her troubles.

"That's always just below the surface with her," D said, "Just takes a day like this, and it all boils over. I had to hear her out, and then I jollied her along like I always do. She'll be all right for now."

I asked why he hadn't transferred one of the two women, ending the problem that way. "I could," he said, "but then I'd have to transfer anyone else who got sore at somebody, and there'd be no end to it."

"Hang in there"
Slowly, D's department began to pull out of its slump. By working on the more easily repaired machines first, the maintenance crews began to restore some measure of productivity fairly quickly. Of course, recovery slowed as they moved on to more serious problems. But D finally had some momentum and he wanted to take advantage of it.

"We're moving again," he announced cheerily to those workers whose machines were still limping along. "Look at old number eight over there! Just hang in there, we'll get to you, too."

No one was euphoric, but at least the gloom had started to lift. D continued to spend most of his time with the operators who needed help, leaving those whose machines were repaired to their own devices and looking in on the maintenance crew only often enough to be sure that they were proceeding more or less according to his expectations.

By lunch time the line was running fairly well. D's manner of supervision reflected the change. "When we're running right," he said, "I just leave them alone." He was still very visible, moving about the floor, but with very little contact now. He spoke mainly when he was spoken to. He noted with satisfaction that some of his operators had begun to help each other in small ways, something they were not required to do.

"We could go down again at any minute," he said. "But I've got a different job now. The first four hours, I was just trying to hold everything together until we could get fixed up. Now I have to start checking all the little things to make sure we don't start sliding backwards." He was referring to the many routine checks and preventive inspections he could make to catch trouble before something got out of hand.

I asked D about his belief that a bad start meant bad running for the entire shift. "We've pulled out of the worst part," he answered. "But don't forget, we don't have any chance at all at a good run because we've lost too much production in those first few hours. You ought to be here some day when there's a real good run. That's when you'll see them all happy."

Competition between shifts
After lunch, D was already planning for the change-over to the incoming second shift, still almost three hours away. Because all of the urgent tasks had been attended to, he was ordering in supplies and putting his maintenance crew on elective or deferrable work. "I try to leave the second shift in good shape so they can get a good start," he said. I asked him about competition between shifts. "Oh, sure. We all want to be the best, but the way to do that is to have the best run you can, not to make it hard for the other shift to have its run."

With about 30 minutes to go, D proved that he meant what he said. One of his machines developed an intermittent malfunction. It would have been possible to keep it running until the end of the shift, although at the cost of discarding a higher than normal amount of substandard production. This would have maximized his own shift's production, but would have progressively worsened the problem and left the incoming shift with the task of shutting down a badly worn machine. Since repair would take an hour and his own shift couldn't complete it anyway, D could have rationalized that there was no point in shutting down.

But he resisted that temptation, shut the machine down, and set the maintenance crew to work on it. The incoming maintenance crew would relieve them, and face a partially completed job instead of the entire problem. D briefed the incoming supervisor when he arrived, and then set about thanking his subordinates for a good day's work as he passed down the line reading their meters.

Virtuoso performance

Like all other supervisors on his shift, D is vulnerable to heavy maintenance problems. Therefore his actual production record seldom matches that of a smoother running shift. On this occasion, however, he gave a virtuoso performance.

Perhaps the most important aspect of D's approach to supervision is that he has a conscious, articulated strategy that he is continually trying to implement. He has obviously thought hard about his job, and has distilled his experience into a few simple principles that guide him. Basically, he wants to get a good start, but failing that, to develop momentum as quickly as possible. He believes in allowing the natural dynamics of a successful group to govern it. His main practical problem at all times is to help that group to be genuinely successful. At no time does he try to talk his way out of his problems by telling his subordinates that the situation isn't as bad as it seems. Instead, he stresses the positive measures he has taken, and will take, to end their frustration. From past experience, they know he will make good those promises.

The *substance* of D's approach to supervision is his strategy of deferring the slower repairs so he can get back into production quickly. He concentrates his attention where he is most vulnerable: among the operators whose partially malfunctioning machines have to be kept in operation until the maintenance crews can get to them. His *style* consists of reassuring the discouraged, jollying along the angry, and leaving those who need no help pretty much alone. In brief, he gives as much support as is needed, and only where it is needed.

Restructuring the supervisor's job

Partly as a result of the study from which these episodes were excerpted, management at the packaging plant undertook to restructure the job of the supervisor. The aim was to raise employee productivity by modifying the way in which supervisors affected their behavior. Although the emphasis was clearly on substance, both substance and style were involved.

However, as with any deliberate attempt to change a culture—and the accumulated traditions of managing with certain emphases for many years is nothing less than a culture—the main difficulty was motivating supervisors to accept the change. For this reason, management used a much slower and less direct approach than might otherwise have been appropriate.

Peer analysis

Briefly, management appointed a committee of supervisors—admittedly, the brightest and best—to analyze the way they and their colleagues were actually doing their jobs. They did this by interviewing all of their peers, following a format which called for identifying actions having a significant impact on productivity that could be taken under existing company rules. The underlying strategies were: (a) to meld the collective wisdom and experience of all supervisors into a single, comprehensive approach, and (b) to build any changes around their own ideas, rather than building them around those of their superiors.

The committee sorted through the mass of data it had selected, and then chose ten factors that had clearly been mentioned most frequently. They presented this list to their colleagues to confirm that these were, indeed, their best opportunities for having an impact on productivity. Some of the ten factors were probably peculiar to this company or to the industry. Some that are generalizable are:

☐
A supervisor's reluctance to correct employees who have drifted into "sloppy habits." There was a long list of rationalizations for this, ranging from "It isn't important enough to bother with" to "It wouldn't do any good." The real reason for this reluctance is probably that acting as someone else's conscience is an extraordinarily delicate and demanding role that many supervisors prefer to avoid. This avoidance leads to a great deal of preventable downtime, with increased waste of raw materials and lower quality.
☐
An operator's tendency to continue running his machine regardless of the quality of the product being made. The employees blamed the supervisors for stressing quantity, or "cases down the chute," continually while stressing quality sporadically. This complaint was at least partially justified. Another rationalization was that quality is the responsibility of the inspector or the supervisor; the operator has his hands full just running packages through his machine. The operator's concentration on quantity was more a matter of custom than of any limitation of ability, however; and the custom was one the supervisors had tolerated and even indirectly encouraged. The result was excessive waste of raw materials, energy, and employee time. It costs just as much to produce what an inspector must reject as to produce what he can accept.
☐
The supervisors' reluctance to use electronic control devices that can make measurements of which the human eye is incapable. The ostensible reasons for this reluctance were usually that the "scopes" were unreliable or that a really expert supervisor could get along without them. The supervisors' real reasons were probably a reluctance to depend on something they did not understand, and a feeling that using the "scopes" somehow lowered their status from "experts" with a somewhat mystical, intuitive "feel" to mere readers of video displays. The results were preventable shutdowns of equipment and higher than necessary levels of wasted raw materials.
☐
A supervisor's tendency to take good work for granted and to speak to the employee chiefly when something is wrong. The rationalizations were that employees were paid to do good work, no further recognition was necessary, and that excessive praise would be embarrassing for supervisor and subordinate alike. The real reason is probably the anxiety that accountability for failures generates. This anxiety thrusts the less confident supervisors into a defensive position of constant readiness to *react* to real or potential failures. Those supervisors for

whom accountability was a less frightening experience were able to adopt a more *preventive* stance, which stressed building good habits as the best defense against the growth of bad ones. Unfortunately, the reactive stance was more common than the preventive one, with the result that employees who had been properly trained tended to drift, through lack of reinforcement, into precisely those "sloppy habits" that caused supervisors to lose control of the production process.

Videotaped lessons

Armed with these views of what their own colleagues had said was wrong about the way they supervised, the committee proceeded to write and (with professional help) produce a series of videotaped "lessons," each analyzing the effects of a current behavior pattern, exploring its causes and countering the rationalizations with which it was defended, and showing how to deal effectively with the problem.

The tapes comprise a "course" through which all supervisors are periodically put. They are animated, articulate "job descriptions" of what the supervisors themselves acknowledge their jobs should be.

The relevant and tolerable

Although it is possible to speak of substance and style as if they were separate, in reality they are inextricably intertwined. Thus there is a certain artificiality in debating which is more important than the other. Perhaps the following generalizations come closest to describing the comparative effects of both elements:

☐
When the substance of supervision consists of emphasis on preventing controllable losses—that is, when the substance is relevant to productivity—and when the style of supervision makes that substance easy to tolerate or even welcome, the effect of that supervision upon subordinate behavior is likely to lead to consistently high levels of productivity.
☐
When the substance of supervision is relevant, but the style involves minimal contact, the effect is

likely to be negligent performance with many "sloppy habits." Similarly, if the style is abrasive, the result is likely to be conformity to correct procedures only in the presence of the supervisor; at other times these procedures are likely to be flouted, more or less as a form of protest or "revenge." Thus productivity is likely to be inconsistent.
☐
When the substance of supervision is irrelevant and the style is tolerable or welcome, productivity is likely to be low. Attitudes, however, may be positive, and in this situation it is entirely too easy to conclude that the workers are being "coddled" and that what they need is firmer supervision. A change of style cannot correct a problem that is caused by irrelevant substance, but it can cause a deterioration of attitudes that could easily lead to worsened productivity.
☐
When the substance is irrelevant and the style consists of minimal contact, the result is likely to be low productivity combined with employee indifference. This might manifest itself in absenteeism, turnover, and tendencies to miss schedules, to fall short of production targets, and/or to waste materials. When the substance is irrelevant and the style is abrasive, all of the foregoing symptoms plus sabotage, frequent work interruptions, intimidation of would-be cooperative workers, theft, and other violent or near-violent manifestations are likely. Obviously, in either of these combinations, the operations are likely to be economically marginal.

Demanding role

From this analysis it follows that *both* substance and style are indispensable to effective supervision. One must, as the conventional wisdom has stressed, be able to "get along with people," but one must *also* be able to recognize what they must do to make their contribution to productivity, to make this clear to them (direction), to continually ascertain that they are performing correctly (control), and do it all in a manner that preserves their dignity.

All this adds up to a very demanding role, and perhaps that is why the ranks of first-level supervisors have seldom been filled with consistently outstanding performers. By the same token, it is why the recruitment, training, and motivation of *effective* supervisors is the single best route to sustained high productivity.

*Fernando Bartolomé
and André Laurent*

The manager:
master and servant
of power

Most managers are action oriented. As a result, many are not inclined to be introspective about how they relate to others on the job. They don't fully realize, for example, how power differences can disturb interpersonal relations at work and, consequently, undermine organizational effectiveness.

> *"Conflicts arise because managers don't understand the effects of power on behavior."*

Let's look at three typical problems:

☐   Brian Dolan and John Miller, both senior engineers in an electronics company, had worked well as colleagues in their company's R&D department. Their relationship was friendly and informal. Each felt free to drop in unannounced on the other to discuss technical problems or swap company gossip.

Then Brian was promoted to director of R&D, and shortly thereafter he called John and asked him to come to his office to discuss installation plans for the company's new computer-aided design system. The call puzzled and angered John. Brian was only two doors away. Why didn't he just drop by? After all, they were good friends. Why did he have to play the boss? When John went to Brian's office, it was all he could do to hide his irritation. Brian greeted him warmly, but John was reserved during their discussion.

Why, Brian wondered on the trip home that evening, had John acted so oddly? Was it because he had been promoted and not John? That had to be it. John was jealous. John, on the other hand, didn't understand how Brian's new position could make him insensitive to how John might react.

☐   Mary Scarpa, divisional director for a specialty steel fabricator, asked Roger Harrison, a middle manager, for his opinion on a major capital invest-

ment decision she was about to make. Roger had serious reservations about the assumptions underlying her cash flow projections. He wanted to level with her, but he also worried that honest criticism would upset her. He knew Mary could be very touchy. Although she had asked for candid feedback, Roger wasn't sure she really meant it; he sensed she really wanted reinforcement. Feeling caught in a bind, Roger conveniently "forgot" her request.

Annoyed by Roger's behavior, Mary complained to a colleague at another company about problems with her subordinates, saying they just wouldn't stick their necks out. They were afraid to give honest opinions because they were insecure, she said. On his part, Roger was insensitive to the reasons why bosses may find it risky to have subordinates challenge their judgment, even when they ask for it.

☐   Dick Rapp, vice president of production for a household appliance manufacturer, told his subordinates that his priority was quality control and cost containment. He wanted defect and scrap rates brought down. He wanted the division to be results driven, not rule driven. "If you have to bend a rule to get the job done, do it," Rapp would say.

His employees took him at his word at first and assumed that any improvement in efficiency would be welcome. But they quickly learned otherwise. Dick Rapp cared as much about style and form as he did about substance. How memos were worded and typed, for example, seemed to concern him as much as what they said. He also chewed out several plant supervisors for approving ad hoc scheduling and other changes and not going through the chain of command.

Understandably, this behavior frustrated Dick's subordinates. They faced conflicting expecta-

Mr. Bartolomé is associate professor of management at Bentley College in Waltham, Massachusetts. He is also visiting lecturer at INSEAD, the European Institute of Business Administration in Fontainebleau, France, and at the Oxford Centre for Management Studies.

Mr. Laurent is professor of organizational behavior at INSEAD, where he is doing comparative, cross-cultural management and organizational research.

tions, and they had to take time away from important tasks to meet what they considered frivolous demands. No one tried to understand, though, why bosses prefer to have things done their way and how this may be their means of heightening their feelings of being in control and reducing uncertainty. And nobody dared to explore these issues with Dick, nor could he see that he was sending mixed messages and burying people in the very red tape he wanted them to cut through.

How did these situations develop? Did Brian Dolan subconsciously need to pull rank on subordinates? Did Mary Scarpa relish putting her employees in a double bind? Did Dick Rapp enjoy tripping up his people? Were the subordinates rebellious people, unwilling to accept authority and take direction?

Such problems occur with surprising frequency in work situations. Usually they arise not because superiors are inherently insensitive or power hungry or because subordinates are naturally rebellious but because people don't understand how strongly hierarchical position affects behavior in organizations. Workplace conflicts are often attributed to personality differences, but the root of the problem is usually structural. The organization's power hierarchy can distort mutual expectations.

Power in the organization

Unevenness of power in the organization subtly influences how managers and subordinates relate to each other. Mary couldn't understand Roger's reticence. But if she had reflected on her own experiences as a subordinate, she might have realized that she too had been cautious at times about giving honest feedback to superiors. Had Brian been able to put himself in John's shoes and think of a new R&D director officiously summoning *him*, he might have better understood John's behavior.

Dick was a results-driven manager who said he cared about quality, not style. Today he works for superiors whose preference for ritualistic, by-the-book action frustrates him. Yet he can't see that he's doing the same thing. He doesn't relate his own experience as a subordinate to the feelings and behavior of the people working for him.

Brian, Mary, and Dick all had trouble putting themselves in their subordinates' shoes. In subordinate roles, on the other hand, John and Roger couldn't see how it might feel to be a boss. This lack of sensitivity on both sides can have ripple effects throughout the organization. Managers who believe

"Attention, all department heads! The buck stops there. *I've had it!"*

they are on the receiving end of unreasonable or unfair actions from their bosses, for example, may act similarly toward those below them in the organizational pyramid. And the pattern may repeat itself down the chain of command. Or relations with peers may suffer. A troubled relationship at one level can affect many other relationships.

When superiors can't see how their behavior affects their subordinates, their authority may also deteriorate. Most bosses know instinctively that their power depends more on employees' compliance than on threats or sanctions. When managers create no-win situations for people, as Mary did, or make confusing demands on workers, as did Dick, subordinates may respond by losing enthusiasm or withdrawing commitment. If workers think they've been put in impossible situations or if a superior's exaggerated need for power makes them feel inferior, they may give the company their worst rather than their best. The response could mean just going through the motions of the job or even sabotaging organizational goals.

True, managers have power. They can call on official sanctions for punishing uncooperative subordinates. But such blatant use of their clout is rarely able to restore effective working relationships. It is a weak rather than a strong pillar of authority.

There are other consequences arising from this asymmetry in power relations and role perceptions, as we can see when we look at managers as subordinates. If the danger for superiors is being insufficiently sensitive about their subordinates' potential reactions, the danger for subordinates tends to be excessive concern about superiors' potential reactions.

Managers who worry excessively about offending their bosses are much less likely to defend subordinates when higher-ups deal unfairly with them.

But if a manager doesn't defend subordinates, he or she will lose their respect. When subordinates sense that the boss won't defend them against unfairness, their morale will plummet and they will withdraw commitment to the job. A vicious circle results. As their performance deteriorates, their superior's position weakens further. The boss will receive fewer rewards and resources to dispense to subordinates, thus further undermining his or her effectiveness as distinct from merely titular authority.

It's ironic that so many managers are insensitive to this problem because almost all managers occupy a dual position in the organization. They have subordinates who report to them, and they report to superiors. Being both masters and servants of power, they should be able to understand the perspectives of the two groups of people who play the most important roles in their professional lives—namely, their superiors and subordinates.

To probe this duality of the manager's role and the sharp differences in expectations that power differences create, we recently collected questionnaires from 105 executives of major companies. We divided the people into two similar groups, matched according to age, management position, and other characteristics. We asked one group of managers to describe the expectations they had for their superiors, the second, to describe expectations for subordinates. In addition, we had conversations with a number of the executives we surveyed.

As the *Exhibit* shows, the expectations of the two groups differed sharply. Of the managers we asked to take the superior role, 78% said they are primarily concerned about subordinates' performance. A majority also said they expect subordinates to be loyal and honest. A typical comment was "I expect effective performance and loyalty even when difficult or unpleasant duties have to be performed."

The superiors we talked to view loyalty, honesty, and performance as linked. They also see honest communication and a willingness to follow orders as necessary to get the job done. But at the same time, they don't see the potential conflict that lies in demanding loyalty and desiring honesty and frankness from subordinates. Many seem unaware of the extent to which they confuse loyalty with agreement and obedience. They also seem to underestimate the difficulty subordinates have in being honest about their own problems or weaknesses with people who have so much influence on their careers.

What happens when the shoe is on the other foot?

When managers take the subordinate position, they expect leadership and good communica-

Exhibit	Comparison of role expectations	
	Desired traits	**Percentage of managers who mentioned this trait** Multiple choices were possible
What managers expect from subordinates	Good task performance	78 %
	Loyalty and obedience	60
	Honesty	53
	Initiative	31
	Other skills	26
What managers expect from superiors	Good communication and feedback	64 %
	Leadership	60
	Encouragement and support	50
	Delegation and autonomy	37
	Professional competence	21
	Information	17

tion from their superiors. A director of finance we talked to said, "I expect my superior to give me clear messages about what he expects from me." A vice president of engineering commented, "The boss should establish his requirements absolutely clearly."

Why do subordinates want clear communication and decisive leadership from their superiors? One reason is that they need reassurance that their bosses are competent. Clear communication is a good measure of competence. Subordinates also want to minimize uncertainty in their environment. Clear communication reduces guesswork. But decisiveness and clarity of communication alone aren't enough. Our interviews revealed that subordinates also want consistency.

Managers in both interview groups gave initiative and autonomy much lower ratings than we had expected. Fewer than a third of the people who took the superior role said they expect initiative from subordinates. Only 37% of those in the subordinate position said it is important for their superiors to grant them autonomy. This is odd when one considers how strongly management experts today endorse job autonomy and broad participation in decision making.

Subordinates don't want superiors to be constantly peering over their shoulders. Instead, they want enough leeway to do the jobs as they see fit. "The boss shouldn't interfere in details," a sales manager said, and "My manager should give me enough space to do my job," said an administrative officer.

Subordinates also want fair performance appraisals, support, and encouragement. Another sales manager said, "My superior should show fairness, objectivity, honesty, and a willingness to give feedback without my having to ask for it." A division manager answered, "I expect help, encouragement, and coaching, and the opportunity to learn from my mistakes." And an R&D director reported, "I expect support in conflict situations."

Managers as superiors

As bosses, managers are not only often unaware of how they misuse their power in relation to subordinates, but they are also frequently unaware of the contradictory messages they send and their motives for doing so. For example, they may tell subordinates that they expect them to be candid and to feel free to offer criticism. Yet at the same time, they communicate disapproval of candid feedback through subtle and sometimes not so subtle cues.

Managers may even confuse excessive deference (pleasing behavior) with the normal level of compliance that they feel they have a legitimate right to expect. They may not see the ways in which they signal to subordinates demands for excessively deferential behavior—and they are also often unaware of the deep resentment that these demands produce.

In the superior role, most managers say that they are more concerned about their subordinates' performance than with obedience for its own sake or with workers doing things the boss's way. Despite the overt message they send, however—"good performance is what really counts in my department"—many managers communicate subtly to subordinates that obedience and deference are just as important, if not more so. This is usually subconscious on the managers' part.

Most executives have trouble learning about the expectations their subordinates have of them simply because they are rarely forthright about how they'd like *their* bosses to behave. Actually, most subordinates work hard to adapt their behavior to what they think the boss expects. Although the chief's actions may be very frustrating to them, few will express openly their dislike of the behavior or try to persuade the boss to change—even when invited to criticize.

This reticence can lead to surprising angry outbursts when smoldering resentment suddenly surfaces. The superior ends up wondering, "Why didn't you come to me earlier with this problem?" Bosses will often deny blame and claim they've always had an open-door policy. Many apparently assume that such a policy alone is sufficient to guarantee a fully open relationship and to minimize the effects of power.

Managers as subordinates

As subordinates, managers develop an exaggerated concern over pleasing their bosses because they believe they have very little power to change the superior's behavior. Whatever the boss's rhetoric may be, they are convinced they know the real score. As a result, they spend much time scrutinizing the boss's behavior for cues that indicate approval or disapproval.

As one manager put it, "I suppose it's true: I study [my manager's] likes, dislikes, and other personal tastes; his objectives and motivations and the time pressure he may be under." One division head said of his superior, "I take into account how his thinking differs from mine, what things he is likely to view in a different way."

> *"Managers must look for subtle cues. If they do, they can create the necessary atmosphere of trust for solving problems. But they can't do it instantly."*

Managers as superiors know how much they depend on their subordinates' performance and, therefore, how much real power, as opposed to formal power, their subordinates have over them. But when bosses are subordinates, they often forget this reality of organizational life. They forget that the boss's performance depends heavily on how committed the subordinates are to their jobs and on the quality of their work. Consequently, the subordinates often seem to focus too much on accommodating their superiors' stylistic preferences and not enough on performance per se. They don't always recognize that they possess real power that they can use with their bosses to negotiate and obtain satisfaction for their legitimate needs and demands. They seem unable to transfer their experiences as bosses to their behavior as subordinates.

Because subordinates perceive themselves as being too weak to alter their superiors' behavior, managers in the subordinate role are extremely concerned with whether they have a natural match ("good chemistry") with their bosses. When relating to subordinates, on the other hand, managers don't seem concerned about compatibility. They assume that their subordinates can easily learn to conform to their expectations and that this reshaping of behavior will not harm the organization. In reality, however, having to adapt like this is likely to keep subordinates from making a full contribution. In most cases, inhibiting people this way creates resentment.

Consequences of power

When managers fail to understand how deeply the unequal distribution of power can hurt interpersonal relations and productivity, serious problems can arise for the organization. The most important and pervasive negative effect of the hierarchical structure can be summarized in the saying, "Trust flees authority." Good ideas often remain unexpressed because subordinates believe they will be punished for disagreeing with their superiors or showing too much competence. Honest feedback about the superior's managerial style is withheld because subordinates are afraid they'll be blackballed when decisions on promotions are made.

Reducing the upward flow of ideas and feedback can have many adverse consequences. Take, for example, the many MBO programs that run into difficulty. An honest contract between superiors and subordinates, based on a fair exchange of contributions and rewards between the individuals and the organization, should be at the core of an MBO program. This is only possible, however, if subordinates feel that they will not be punished for defending their interests or balking at unreasonable demands from the top. Unfair MBO agreements may work in the short term, but they will usually fail in the long haul.

When managers are dissatisfied with the contracts they have with their bosses, unfair contracts may follow at each level down the ladder. Such a pattern can damage management's credibility as well as the whole organization's authority.

What can managers do?

Nobody is to blame for these distortions of hierarchical power. The problem is inherent in organizational life because authority differences are both inevitable and also functional to a degree. The problem cannot be avoided, but it can be controlled if managers strive to link their two roles as masters and servants of power.

When they are in the superior role, they should ask themselves, "How would I feel if my boss behaved this way or demanded this of me?" For example, Brian in our first case might have stopped to think, "I need to talk to John, but if I summon him, he may think I'm trying to remind him that I got the promotion and he didn't. And why, after all, am I doing this? Can't I get the information just as well by phone? Come to think of it, I remember the time I got angry when *my* boss asked me to come running on a moment's notice."

Managers can also ask whether the tasks they assign to subordinates are truly critical to the job—as distinct from ritualistic demands motivated by an unconscious desire to show people that "rank has its privileges" or to reassure themselves that they can make people do what they want them to do. "Power: use it or lose it," as another saying goes.

The burden for getting relationships back on a healthy basis falls mainly to bosses because they have more power and because it would be unrealistic to expect subordinates to take the initiative and complain about their bosses' unreasonable or unfair conduct. Even if superiors encourage honest feedback, people rarely believe that they mean it. So, generally they won't risk testing the boss's sincerity.

When they are the superior, managers need to ask themselves, "What can I do to increase my employees' trust, or at least decrease their mistrust? What signals may indicate problems?" Managers need to learn to monitor subordinates' subtle cues. It helps to understand that it's easier for subordinates to learn about bosses' reactions and desires because superiors are more likely to express their feelings openly. By the same token, it's more difficult for bosses to find out their subordinates' real feelings; they're likely to express them indirectly and with caution.

Directly questioning subordinates rarely works when you're trying to find out what's wrong. Managers must look for subtle cues. Eventually, they can create the necessary atmosphere of trust for solving problems, but they can't do it instantly. It will come only from consistently demonstrating fairness and honesty toward the people working for them.

In the subordinate role, on the other hand, managers may find that they can more easily manage their relationships with superiors by just asking them what they want. This approach should work with competent and insightful superiors. But for some people, asking questions may not be enough; observing behavior is often equally important. Once again, the managerial subordinate should take advantage of his or her own experience as a boss and ask, "What do I care most about when I'm in the superior role?" Managers who can answer this question insightfully and realistically should be able to move ahead in the important process of understanding and managing their own superiors. ▱

Effective Daily
Management

Getting Things Done

Peter F. Drucker

How to make people decisions

There is no magic to good staffing and promotion decisions – just hard work and disciplined thought

Why is it that some managers have a golden touch when it comes to putting the right people in the right jobs? Have they mastered some abstruse method of predicting performance? Have they hit on some wondrous algorithm for personnel evaluation? Not at all, argues Peter Drucker, who draws on his long study of how effective managers operate to identify the key rules and assumptions for matching jobs with people. Instead of magic, what successful matching requires is careful understanding of the most important capabilities that a given job requires and of the strengths and weaknesses of each candidate. No mystery here, just good management.

Mr. Drucker is Clarke Professor of Social Sciences and Management at the Claremont Graduate School and professor emeritus of management at the Graduate Business School of New York University. He is the widely respected author of innumerable books and articles, including more than 20 contributions to HBR.

Executives spend more time on managing people and making people decisions than on anything else – and they should. No other decisions are so long lasting in their consequences or so difficult to unmake. And yet, by and large, executives make poor promotion and staffing decisions. By all accounts, their batting average is no better than .333: at most one-third of such decisions turn out right; one-third are minimally effective; and one-third are outright failures.

In no other area of management would we put up with such miserable performance. Indeed, we need not and should not. Managers making people decisions will never be perfect, of course, but they should come pretty close to batting 1,000 – especially since in no other area of management do we know as much.

Some executives' people decisions have, however, approached perfection. At the time of Pearl Harbor, every single general officer in the U.S. Army was overage. Although none of the younger men had been tested in combat or in a significant troup command, the United States came out of World War II with the largest corps of competent general officers any army has ever had. George C. Marshall, the army's chief of staff, had personally

chosen each man. Not all were great successes, but practically none were outright failures.

In the 40 or so years during which he ran General Motors, Alfred P. Sloan, Jr. picked every GM executive – down to the manufacturing managers, controllers, engineering managers, and master mechanics at even the smallest accessory division. By today's standards, Sloan's vision and values may seem narrow. They were. He was concerned only with performance in and for GM. Nonetheless, his long-term performance in placing people in the right jobs was flawless.

The basic principles

There is no such thing as an infallible judge of people, at least not on this side of the Pearly Gates. There are, however, a few executives who take their people decisions seriously and work at them.

Marshall and Sloan were about as different as two human beings can be, but they followed, and quite consciously, much the same principles in making people decisions:

☐ If I put a person into a job and he or she does not perform, I have made a mistake. I have no business blaming that person, no business invoking the "Peter Principle," no business complaining. I have made a mistake.

☐ "The soldier has a right to competent command" was already an old maxim at the time of Julius Caesar. It is the duty of managers to make sure that the responsible people in their organizations perform.

☐ Of all the decisions an executive makes, none are as important as the decisions about people because they determine the performance capacity of the organization. Therefore, I'd better make these decisions well.

☐ The one "don't": do not give new people new major assignments, for doing so only compounds the risks. Give this sort of assignment to someone whose behavior and habits you know and who has earned trust and credibility within your organization. Put a high-level newcomer first into an established position where the expectations are known and help is available.

Some of the worst staffing failures I have seen involved brilliant Europeans hired by U.S. companies—one based in Pittsburgh; the other, Chicago—to head up new European ventures. Dr. Hans Schmidt and M. Jean Perrin (only the names are fictitious) were hailed as geniuses when they came in. A year later they were both out, totally defeated.

No one in Pittsburgh had understood that Schmidt's training and temperament would make him sit on a new assignment for the first six or nine months, thinking, studying, planning, getting ready for decisive action. Schmidt, in turn, had never even imagined that Pittsburgh expected instant action and immediate results. No one in Chicago had known that Perrin, while a solid and doggedly purposeful man, was excitable and mercurial, flailing his arms, making speeches about trivia, and sending up one trial balloon after another. Although both men subsequently became highly successful CEOs of major European corporations, both executives were failures in companies that did not know and understand them.

Two other U.S. companies successfully established businesses for the first time in Europe during the same period (the late 1960s and early 1970s). To initiate their projects, each sent to Europe a U.S. executive who had never before worked or lived there but whom people in the head offices knew thoroughly and understood well. In turn the two managers were thoroughly familiar with their companies. At the same time, each organization hired half a dozen young Europeans and placed them in upper-middle executive jobs in the United States. Within a few years, both companies had a solid European business and a trained, seasoned, and trusted corps of executives to run it.

As Winston Churchill's ancestor, the great Duke of Marlborough, observed some three centuries ago, "The basic trouble in coalition warfare is that one has to entrust victory if not one's life, to a fellow commander whom one knows by reputation rather than by performance."

In the corporation as in the military, without personal knowledge built up over a period of time there can be neither trust nor effective communication.

The decision steps

Just as there are only a few basic principles, there are only a few important steps to follow in making effective promotion and staffing decisions:

1 **Think through the assignment.** Job descriptions may last a long time. In one large manufacturing company, for example, the job description for the position of division general manager has hardly changed since the company began to decentralize 30 years ago. Indeed, the job description for bishops in the Roman Catholic church has not changed at all since canon law was first codified in the thirteenth century. But assignments change all the time, and unpredictably.

Once in the early 1940s, I told Alfred Sloan that he seemed to spend an inordinate amount of time pondering the assignment of a fairly low-level job—general sales manager of a small accessory division—before choosing among three equally qualified candidates. "Look at the assignment the last few times we had to fill the same job," Sloan answered. To my surprise, I found that the terms of the assignment were quite different on each occasion.

When putting a man in as division commander during World War II, George Marshall always looked first at the nature of the assignment for the next eighteen months or two years. To raise a division and train it is one assignment. To lead it in combat is quite another. To take command of a division that has been badly mauled and restore its morale and fighting strength is another still.

When the task is to select a new regional sales manager, the responsible executive must first know what the heart of the assignment is: to recruit and train new salespeople because, say, the present sales force is nearing retirement age? Or is it to open up new markets because the company's products, though doing well with old-line industries in the region, have not been able to penetrate new and growing markets? Or, since the bulk of sales still comes from products that are 25 years old, is it to establish a market presence for the company's new prod-

ucts? Each of these is a different assignment and requires a different kind of person.

2 **Look at a number of potentially qualified people.** The controlling word here is "number." Formal qualifications are a minimum for consideration; their absence disqualifies the candidate automatically. Equally important, the person and the assignment need to fit each other. To make an effective decision, an executive should look at three to five qualified candidates.

3 **Think hard about how to look at these candidates.** If an executive has studied the assignment, he or she understands what a new person would need to do with high priority and concentrated effort. The central question is not "What can this or that candidate do or not do?" It is, rather, "What are the strengths each possesses and are these the right strengths for the assignment?" Weaknesses are limitations, which may, of course, rule a candidate out. For instance, a person may be excellently qualified for the technical aspects of a job; but if the assignment requires above all the ability to build a team and this ability is lacking, then the fit is not right.

But effective executives do not start out by looking at weaknesses. You cannot build performance on weaknesses. You can build only on strengths. Both Marshall and Sloan were highly demanding men, but both knew that what matters is the ability to do the assignment. If that exists, the company can always supply the rest. If it does not exist, the rest is useless.

If, for instance, a division needed an officer for a training assignment, Marshall looked for people who could turn recruits into soldiers. Every man that was good at this task usually had serious weaknesses in other areas. One was not particularly effective as a tactical commander and was positively hopeless when it came to strategy. Another had foot-in-mouth disease and got into trouble with the press. A third was vain, arrogant, egotistical, and fought constantly with his commanding officer. Never mind, could he train recruits? If the answer was yes—and especially if the answer was "he's the best"—he got the job.

In picking the members of their cabinets, Franklin Roosevelt and

Harry Truman said, in effect: "Never mind personal weaknesses. Tell me first what each of them can do." It may not be coincidence that these two presidents had the strongest cabinets in twentieth-century U.S. history.

4 **Discuss each of the candidates with several people who have worked with them.** One executive's judgment alone is worthless. Because all of us have first impressions, prejudices, likes, and dislikes, we need to listen to what other people think. When the military picks general officers or the Catholic church picks bishops, this kind of extensive discussion is a formal step in their selection process. Competent executives do it informally. Hermann Abs, the former head of Deutsche Bank, picked more successful chief executives in recent times than anyone else. He personally chose most of the top-level managers who pulled off the postwar German "economic miracle," and he checked out each of them first with three or four of the person's former bosses or colleagues.

5 **Make sure the appointee understands the job.** After the appointee has been in a new job for three or four months, he or she should be focusing on the demands of that job rather than on the requirements of preceeding assignments. It is the executive's responsibility to call that person in and say, "You have now been regional sales manager – or whatever – for three months. What do you have to do to be a success in your new job? Think it through and come back in a week or ten days and show me in writing. But I can tell you one thing right away: the things you did to get the promotion are almost certainly the wrong things to do now."

If you do not follow this step, don't blame the candidate for poor performance. Blame yourself. You have failed in your duty as a manager.

The largest single source of failed promotions – and I know of no greater waste in U.S. management – is the failure to think through, and help others think through, what a new job requires. All too typical is the brilliant former student of mine who telephoned me a few months ago, almost in tears. "I got my first big chance a year ago," he said. "My company made me engineering manager. Now they tell me that

I'm through. And yet I've done a better job than ever before. I have actually designed three successful new products for which we'll get patents."

It is only human to say to ourselves, "I must have done something right or I would not have gotten the big new job. Therefore, I had better do more of what I did to get the promotion now that I have it." It is not intuitively obvious to most people that a new and different job requires new and different behavior. Almost 50 years ago, a boss of mine challenged me four months after he had advanced me to a far more responsible position. Until he called me in, I had continued to do what I had done before. To his credit, he understood that it was his responsibility to make me see that a new job means different behavior, a different focus, and different relationships.

The high-risk decisions

Even if executives follow all these steps, some of their people decisions will still fail. These are, for the most part, the high-risk decisions that nevertheless have to be taken.

There is, for example, high risk in picking managers in professional organizations – for a research lab, say, or an engineering or corporate legal department. Professionals do not readily accept as their boss someone whose credentials in the field they do not respect. In choosing a manager of engineering, the choices are therefore limited to the top-flight engineers in the department. Yet there is no correlation (unless it be a negative one) between performance as a bench engineer and performance as a manager. Much the same is true when a high-performing operating manager gets a promotion to a staff job in headquarters or a staff expert moves into a line position. Temperamentally, operating people are frequently unsuited to the tensions, frustrations, and relationships of staff work, and vice versa. The first-rate regional sales manager may well become totally ineffective if promoted into market research, sales forecasting, or pricing.

We do not know how to test or predict whether a person's temperament will suit a new environment. We

can find this out only by experience. If a move from one kind of work to another does not pan out, the executive who made the decision has to remove the misfit, and fast. But that executive also has to say, "I made a mistake, and it is my job to correct it." To keep misfits in a job they cannot do is not being kind; it is being cruel. But there is also no reason to let the person go. A company can always use a good bench engineer, a good analyst, a good sales manager. The proper course of action – and it works most times – is to offer the misfit a return to the old job or an equivalent.

People decisions may also fail because a job has become what New England ship captains 150 years ago called a "widow maker." When a clipper ship, no matter how well designed and constructed, began to have fatal "accidents," the owners did not redesign or rebuild the ship. They broke it up as fast as possible.

Widow makers – that is, jobs that regularly defeat even good people – appear most often when a company grows or changes fast. For instance, in the 1960s and early 1970s, the job of "international vice president" in U.S. banks became a widow maker. It had always been an easy job to fill. In fact, it had long been considered a job in which banks could safely put "also rans" and could expect them to perform well. Then, suddenly, the job began to defeat one new incumbent after another. What had happened, as hindsight now tells us, is that international activity quickly and without warning became an integral part of the daily business of major banks and their corporate customers. What had been until then an easy job became, literally, a "nonjob" that nobody could do.

Whenever a job defeats two people in a row, who in their earlier assignments had performed well, a company has a widow maker on its hands. When this happens, a responsible executive should not ask the headhunter for a universal genius. Instead abolish the job. Any job that ordinarily competent people cannot perform is a job that cannot be staffed. Unless changed, it will predictably defeat the third incumbent the way it defeated the first two.

Making the right people decisions is the ultimate means of controlling an organization well. Such decisions reveal how competent management is, what its values are, and whether it takes its job seriously. No matter how hard managers try to keep their decisions a secret—and some still try hard—people decisions cannot be hidden. They are eminently visible.

Executives often cannot judge whether a strategic move is a wise one. Nor are they necessarily interested. "I don't know why we are buying this business in Australia, but it won't interfere with what we are doing here in Fort Worth" is a common reaction. But when the same executives read that "Joe Smith has been made controller in the XYZ division," they usually know Joe much better than top management does. These executives should be able to say, "Joe deserves the promotion; he is an excellent choice—just the person that division needs to get the controls appropriate for its rapid growth."

If, however, Joe got promoted because he is a politician, everybody will know it. They will all say to themselves, "Okay, that is the way to get ahead in this company." They will despise their management for forcing them to become politicians but will either quit or become politicians themselves in the end. As we have known for a long time, people in organizations tend to behave as they see others being rewarded. And when the rewards go to nonperformance, to flattery, or to mere cleverness, the organization will soon decline into nonperformance, flattery, or cleverness.

Executives who do not make the effort to get their people decisions right do more than risk poor performance. They risk losing their organization's respect. ▽

Management time: Who's got the monkey?

An analogy that underscores the value of assigning, delegating, and controlling

William Oncken, Jr. and Donald L. Wass

In any organization, the manager's bosses, peers, and subordinates—in return for their active support—impose some requirements, just as the manager imposes some requirements upon them where they are drawing upon his or her support. These demands constitute so much of the manager's time that successful leadership hinges on an ability to control this "monkey-on-the-back" input effectively.

Mr. Oncken is chairman of the board, The William Oncken Company of Texas, Inc., a management consulting firm. Mr. Wass is president of this company.

Why is it that managers are typically running out of time while their subordinates are typically running out of work? In this article, we shall explore the meaning of management time as it relates to the interaction between managers and their bosses, their own peers, and their subordinates.

Specifically, we shall deal with three different kinds of management time:

Boss-imposed time—to accomplish those activities which the boss requires and which the manager cannot disregard without direct and swift penalty.

System-imposed time—to accommodate those requests to the manager for active support from his or her peers. This assistance must also be provided lest there be penalties, though not always direct or swift.

Self-imposed time—to do those things which the manager originates or agrees to do. A certain portion of this kind of time, however, will be taken by subordinates and is called "subordinate-imposed time." The remaining portion will be his or her own and is called "discretionary time." Self-imposed time is not subject to penalty since neither the boss nor the system can discipline the manager for not doing what they did not know the manager had intended to do in the first place.

The management of time necessitates that managers get control over the timing and content of what they do. Since what their bosses and the system impose on them are backed up by penalty, managers cannot tamper with those requirements. Thus their self-imposed time becomes their major area of concern.

The managers' strategy is therefore to increase the "discretionary" component of their self-imposed time by minimizing or doing away with the "subordinate" component. They will then use the added increment to get better control over their boss-imposed and system-imposed activities. Most managers spend much more subordinate-imposed time than they even faintly realize. Hence we shall use a monkey-on-the-back analogy to examine how subordinate-imposed time comes into being and what the superior can do about it.

Where is the monkey?

Let us imagine that a manager is walking down the hall and that he notices one of his subordinates, Jones, coming up the hallway. When they are abreast of one another, Jones greets the manager with, "Good morning. By the way, we've got a problem. You see . . ." As Jones continues, the manager recognizes in this problem the same two characteristics common to all the problems his subordinates gratuitously bring to his attention. Namely, the manager knows (a) enough to get involved, but (b) not enough to make the on-the-spot decision expected of him. Eventually, the manager says, "So glad you brought this up. I'm in a rush right now. Meanwhile, let me think about it and I'll let you know." Then he and Jones part company.

Let us analyze what has just happened. Before the two of them met, on whose back was the "monkey"? The subordinate's. After they parted, on whose back was it? The manager's. Subordinate-imposed time begins the moment a monkey successfully executes a leap from the back of a subordinate to the back of his or her superior and does not end until the monkey is returned to its proper owner for care and feeding.

In accepting the monkey, the manager has voluntarily assumed a position subordinate to his subordinate. That is, he has allowed Jones to make him her subordinate by doing two things a subordinate is generally expected to do for a boss—the manager has accepted a responsibility from his subordinate, and the manager has promised her a progress report.

The subordinate, to make sure the manager does not miss this point, will later stick her head in the manager's office and cheerily query, "How's it coming?" (This is called "supervision.")

Or let us imagine again, in concluding a working conference with another subordinate, Johnson, the manager's parting words are, "Fine. Send me a memo on that."

Let us analyze this one. The monkey is now on the subordinate's back because the next move is his, but it is poised for a leap. Watch that monkey. Johnson dutifully writes the requested memo and drops it in his outbasket. Shortly thereafter, the manager plucks it from his inbasket and reads it. Whose move is it now? The manager's. If he does not make that move soon, he will get a follow-up memo from the subordinate (this is another form of supervision). The longer the manager delays, the more frustrated the subordinate will become (he'll be "spinning his wheels") and the more guilty the manager will feel (his backlog of subordinate-imposed time will be mounting).

Or suppose once again that at a meeting with a third subordinate, Smith, the manager agrees to provide all the necessary backing for a public relations proposal he has just asked Smith to develop. The manager's parting words to her are, "Just let me know how I can help."

Now let us analyze this. Here the monkey is initially on the subordinate's back. But for how long? Smith realizes that she cannot let the manager "know" until her proposal has the manager's approval. And from experience, she also realizes that her proposal will likely be sitting in the manager's briefcase for weeks waiting for him to eventually get to it. Who's really got the monkey? Who will be checking up on whom? Wheelspinning and bottlenecking are on their way again.

A fourth subordinate, Reed, has just been transferred from another part of the company in order to launch and eventually manage a newly created business venture. The manager has said that they should get together soon to hammer out a set of objectives for the new job, and that "I will draw up an initial draft for discussion with you."

Let us analyze this one, too. The subordinate has the new job (by formal assignment) and the full responsibility (by formal delegation), but the manager has the next move. Until he makes it, he will have the monkey and the subordinate will be immobilized.

Why does it all happen? Because in each instance the manager and the subordinate assume at the outset, wittingly or unwittingly, that the matter under consideration is a joint problem. The monkey in each case begins its career astride both their backs. All it has to do now is move the wrong leg, and—presto—the subordinate deftly disappears. The manager is thus left with another acquisition to his menagerie. Of course, monkeys can be trained not to move the wrong leg. But it is easier to prevent them from straddling backs in the first place.

Who is working for whom?

To make what follows more credible, let us suppose that these same four subordinates are so thoughtful and considerate of the superior's time that they are at pains to allow no more than three monkeys to leap from each of their backs to his in any one day. In a five-day week, the manager will have picked up 60 screaming monkeys—far too many to do anything about individually. So he spends the subordinate-imposed time juggling his "priorities."

Late Friday afternoon, the manager is in his office with the door closed for privacy in order to contemplate the situation, while his subordinates are waiting outside to get a last chance before the weekend to remind him that he will have to "fish or cut bait." Imagine what they are saying to each other about the manager as they wait: "What a bottleneck. He just can't make up his mind. How anyone ever got that high up in our company without being able to make a decision we'll never know."

Worst of all, the reason the manager cannot make any of these "next moves" is that his time is almost entirely eaten up in meeting his own boss-imposed and system-imposed requirements. To get control of these, he needs discretionary time that is in turn denied him when he is preoccupied with all these monkeys. The manager is caught in a vicious circle.

But time is a-wasting (an understatement). The manager calls his secretary on the intercom and instructs her to tell his subordinates that he will be unavailable to see them until Monday morning. At 7:00 p.m., he drives home, intending with firm resolve to return to the office tomorrow to get caught up over the weekend. He returns bright and early the next day only to see, on the nearest green of the golf course across from his office window, a foursome. Guess who?

That does it. He now knows *who* is really working for *whom*. Moreover, he now sees that if he actually accomplishes during this weekend what he came to accomplish, his subordinates' morale will go up so sharply that they will each raise the limit on the number of monkeys they will let jump from their backs to his. In short, he now sees, with the clarity of a revelation on a mountaintop, that the more he gets caught up, the more he will fall behind.

He leaves the office with the speed of a person running away from a plague. His plan? To get caught up on something else he hasn't had time for in years: a weekend with his family. (This is one of the many varieties of discretionary time.)

Sunday night he enjoys ten hours of sweet, untroubled slumber, because he has clear-cut plans for Monday. He is going to get rid of his subordinate-imposed time. In exchange, he will get an equal amount of discretionary time, part of which he will spend with his subordinates to see that they learn the difficult but rewarding managerial art called, "The Care and Feeding of Monkeys."

The manager will also have plenty of discretionary time left over for getting control of the timing and content not only of his boss-imposed time but of his system-imposed time as well. All of this may take months, but compared with the way things have been, the rewards will be enormous. His ultimate objective is to manage his management time.

Getting rid of the monkeys

The manager returns to the office Monday morning just late enough to permit his four subordinates to collect in his outer office waiting to see him about their monkeys. He calls them in, one by one. The purpose of each interview is to take a monkey, place it on the desk between them, and figure out together how the next move might conceivably be the subordinate's. For certain monkeys, this will take some doing. The subordinate's next move may be so elusive that the manager may decide–just for now–merely to let the monkey sleep on the subordinate's back overnight and have him or her return with it at an appointed time the next morning to continue the joint quest for a more substantive move by the subordinate. (Monkeys sleep just as soundly overnight on subordinates' backs as on superiors'.)

As each subordinate leaves the office, the manager is rewarded by the sight of a monkey leaving his office on the subordinate's back. For the next 24 hours, the subordinate will not be waiting for the manager; instead, the manager will be waiting for the subordinate.

Later, as if to remind himself that there is no law against his engaging in a constructive exercise in the interim, the manager strolls by the subordinate's office, sticks his head in the door, and cheerily asks, "How's it coming?" (The time consumed in doing this is discretionary for the manager and boss-imposed for the subordinate.)

When the subordinate (with the monkey on his or her back) and the manager meet at the appointed hour the next day, the manager explains the ground rules in words to this effect:

"At no time while I am helping you with this or any other problem will your problem become my problem. The instant your problem becomes mine, you will no longer have a problem. I cannot help a person who hasn't got a problem.

"When this meeting is over, the problem will leave this office exactly the way it came in—on your back. You may ask my help at any appointed time, and we will make a joint determination of what the next move will be and which of us will make it.

"In those rare instances where the next move turns out to be mine, you and I will determine it together. I will not make any move alone."

The manager follows this same line of thought with each subordinate until at about 11:00 a.m. he realizes that he has no need to shut his door. His monkeys are gone. They will return—but by appointment only. His appointment calendar will assure this.

Transferring the initiative

What we have been driving at in this monkey-on-the-back analogy is to transfer initiative from superior to subordinate and keep it there. We have tried to highlight a truism as obvious as it is subtle. Namely, before

developing initiative in subordinates, the manager must see to it that they *have* the initiative. Once he or she takes it back, they will no longer have it and the discretionary time can be kissed good-bye. It will all revert to subordinate-imposed time.

Nor can both manager and subordinate effectively have the same initiative at the same time. The opener, "Boss we've got a problem," implies this duality and represents, as noted earlier, a monkey astride two backs, which is a very bad way to start a monkey on its career. Let us, therefore, take a few moments to examine what we prefer to call "The Anatomy of Managerial Initiative."

There are five degrees of initiative that the manager can exercise in relation to the boss and to the system: (1) *wait* until told (lowest initiative); (2) *ask* what to do; (3) *recommend*, then take resulting action; (4) *act*, but advise at once; and (5) *act* on own, then routinely report (highest initiative).

Clearly, the manager should be professional enough not to indulge in initiatives 1 and 2 in relation either to the boss or to the system. A manager who uses initiative 1 has no control over either the timing or content of boss-imposed or system-imposed time, and thereby forfeits any right to complain about what he or she is told to do or when. The manager who uses initiative 2 has control over the timing but not over the content. Initiatives 3, 4, and 5 leave the manager in control of both, with the greatest control being at level 5.

The manager's job, in relation to subordinates' initiatives, is twofold; first, to outlaw the use of initiatives 1 and 2, thus giving subordinates no choice but to learn and master "Completed Staff Work"; then, to see that for each problem leaving the office there is an agreed-upon level of initiative assigned to it, in addition to the agreed-upon time and place of the next manager-subordinate conference. The latter should be duly noted on the manager's appointment calendar.

Care & feeding of monkeys

In order to further clarify our analogy between the monkey-on-the-back and the well-known processes of assigning and controlling, we shall refer briefly to the manager's appointment schedule, which calls for five hard and fast rules governing the "Care and Feeding of Monkeys" (violations of these rules will cost discretionary time):

Rule 1

Monkeys should be fed or shot. Otherwise, they will starve to death and the manager will waste valuable time on postmortems or attempted resurrections.

Rule 2

The monkey population should be kept below the maximum number the manager has time to feed. Subordinates will find time to work as many monkeys as he or she finds time to feed, but no more. It shouldn't take more than 5 to 15 minutes to feed a properly prepared monkey.

Rule 3

Monkeys should be fed by appointment only. The manager should not have to be hunting down starving monkeys and feeding them on a catch-as-catch-can basis.

Rule 4

Monkeys should be fed face to face or by telephone, but never by mail. (If by mail, the next move will be the manager's—remember?) Documentation may add to the feeding process, but it cannot take the place of feeding.

Rule 5

Every monkey should have an assigned "next feeding time" and "degree of initiative." These may be revised at any time by mutual consent, but never allowed to become vague or indefinite. Otherwise, the monkey will either starve to death or wind up on the manager's back.

Concluding note

"Get control over the timing and content of what you do" is appropriate advice for managing management time. The first order of business is for the manager to enlarge his or her discretionary time by eliminating subordinate-imposed time. The second is for the manager to use a portion of this new-found discretionary time to see to it that each subordinate possesses the initiative without which he or she cannot exercise initiative, and then to see to it that this initiative is in fact taken. The third is for the manager to use another portion of the increased discretionary time to get and keep control of the timing and content of both boss-imposed and system-imposed time.

The result of all this is that the manager's leverage will increase, in turn enabling the value of each hour spent in managing management time to multiply, without theoretical limit.

The woods are full of them.

Quoted by Alexander Wilson,
American Ornithology (1808),
preface

IDEAS FOR ACTION

Making Time to Manage

by ROBERT C. DORNEY

Time management is more about management than about time.

Being a naturally disorganized person, I suppose it was inevitable that I should become president of a company dedicated to helping executives organize their work and plan their time.

I am no longer president, but in the 40 years I served in that capacity, time management became an accepted technique for focusing executive energy on the most important tasks. Hewlett-Packard, AT&T, Marriott, Xerox, and a host of other companies give employees instruction in time management, particularly those moving into supervisory positions. The reason is very simple: the more responsibility people have, the more valuable their time and the more difficult the time-juggling act becomes.

The idea of time management is so widely accepted that it appears in many places. In the comics, Cathy tries it in an effort to bring order to her life. In Madonna's latest film, her suitor throws his diary into a ditch to symbolize his adoption of a more spontaneous life-style. *Money* magazine includes time management tools among the props that not-so-busy people use to create the opposite impression.

The idea goes far back in history too. Charlemagne is supposed to have used striped candles to help him apportion his time among his various duties as Holy Roman emperor. Napoleon habitually refused to answer his correspondence for six months on the assumption that it posed problems that would go away if he ignored them. Thus he saved himself untold hours solving problems for subordinates.

"Time management is a little like statistics," Stuart Smith, director of management development at Laventhal & Horwath, told me recently. "They're necessary and good, but only when linked to relevant functions. I find in teaching statistics that students cross the boredom barrier when I cross the relevance threshold. We therefore include time management in our training, but not as a separate discipline. We fold it into our curriculum of management skills. This connects it to the achievement of goals and the ordering of priorities."

Is it possible that some executives scorn time management because they fail to see its relevance? But if the achievement of goals and the ordering of priorities are managerial functions (and who would deny it?), the relevance is clear. The more valuable a person's time, the more carefully the spending of it needs scrutiny.

If asked, very few executives could say how they spend their time. Most know what they *ought* to be doing; they may even allocate blocks of time to specified tasks. But that's not the same as getting on with them.

I submit a corollary: most people don't know what their time is worth. It's simple enough to take your annual salary, add 40% or thereabouts for perks and benefits, and then divide the sum by 2,000 or some other number of hours to come up with an hourly rate. The *Exhibit* demonstrates the value—or at least the price—of executive time. Knowledge of the big numbers might encourage some executives to abandon trivial tasks and get on with running the enterprise.

Associated since 1947 with Day-Timers, Inc., a producer of self-organization systems for managers, Robert C. Dorney was president until early in 1987, when he stepped down to become senior vice president and director of product development. In 1972, Day-Timers was acquired by Beatrice Companies, then became part of E-II Holdings Inc. when that corporation was formed in 1986.

On the other hand, it might contribute to stress. An executive might say to herself anxiously, "Am I really worth $168.27 an hour when I'm reading a trade magazine?" The answer is "probably not." But I doubt that that realization would induce her to spend more time managing (whatever that means) if she were not already so disposed.

Focus on the second word

Time management is more about management than about time. Writing everything down in a planner or diary may inspire a feeling of ineffable virtue and even well-being. But if you're tracking activities you shouldn't be involved in at all, you aren't managing your time.

Unless you keep records, it's easy to think you are managing, planning, organizing, and setting goals, when in fact you may be spending most of your hours putting out fires, solving problems for subordinates, or worse, creating problems for your subordinates.

In Japan recently, I drove around Tokyo with an extremely successful Japanese businessman. Every time he had an idea, he called his office on his cellular phone. I reflected that he was not only interrupting himself but also creating chaos in his office. That this could happen in Japan, that exemplar of efficiency and enlightened management, astounded me.

As a student of Japanese business and culture, I'm emboldened to dispel my own astonishment: while the Japanese are very efficient in production, very precise in market analysis, and adept in statistical process control, they aren't very well organized. They make up for this deficiency by working extremely hard—harder, it's been noted often and with some asperity, than their American counterparts. Their keen interest in and enthusiasm for time management may have severe consequences for our trade deficit if it helps them further boost their efficiency.

Balancing act

Balancing is the most difficult part of managing one's own time. What meetings should I attend, which should I skip? Must I read all these reports? Should every important customer have access to my ear? What's important for me to know firsthand, and what can I delegate to others, is hard to pinpoint.

I used to set Saturdays aside for product development, the part of my job I liked most. So I enjoyed working Saturdays until my son started playing football at a university three hours distant. To see him play, I had to leave Friday afternoon. That ended Saturdays devoted to work. I had to rearrange my entire weekly schedule to include product de-

velopment, and that forced me to analyze where and how I was spending my time.

That analysis eventually brought me to place a value on my every activity. Some of them justified a valuation several times that of others. While product development justified five times my hourly rate, obviously I couldn't spend all my time on it. What was equally obvious, I had to limit the time I spent on less important work that didn't merit half my hourly rate.

The answer lay in allocating time to the various activities so that when I multiplied the hours devoted to each one by the hourly rate assigned to it, the total would be one that my board of directors and I could live with.

Most readers will recognize this as yet another application of Italian economist Vilfredo Pareto's 80-20 principle. Only instead of applying it to taxation of the "vital few" who pay 80% of the taxes, I apply it to the significant functions that produce 80% or more of the return while still giving the "trivial many" the time they are worth.

The arenas I operated in, besides product development, included these:

Selecting and training a
successor
Long-range planning
Short-range planning
Reviewing budgets
Conducting staff meetings
Talking with customers
Reviewing senior staff
performance
Delegating
Community activities
Facilities planning
Meeting suppliers
Reading mail
Reading professional journals
Recreation

I assigned the highest value (5) to those activities that have a

EXHIBIT	**What Is the Price of Executive Time?**				
Annual Salary	Weekly Salary	Benefits (40% of Weekly Salary)	Total Week	Value/ Hour*	Value/ Minute
$ 50,000	$ 961.54	$ 384.62	$1,346.16	$ 33.65	$0.56
60,000	1,153.85	461.54	1,615.39	40.38	0.67
75,000	1,442.31	576.93	2,019.24	50.48	0.84
100,000	1,923.08	769.23	2,692.31	67.31	1.12
250,000	4,807.70	1,923.08	6,730.78	168.27	2.80

*40-hour week

direct bearing on the company's future. They numbered only two: choosing and training my successor, and product development. Now, some might question the president's deep involvement in product development. And rightly so. But it depends on how important new products are to ensure the company's continued good health. The criterion I apply is: Can anyone else do it as well? Having settled that question with my usual modesty, I acknowledged that in an ideal world I would find and train a good engineer to direct product development.

It is a truism that many chief executives spend much of their time in their previous function. A president out of engineering tends to hang around the engineering department. A president from advertising tends to rewrite copy and fret over layouts – which is exactly where he or she should spend the least amount of time. Having expertise in the field

> **Delegating is the executive's greatest need – and greatest privilege.**

should enable the president to judge the work of that department with dispatch and precision. When an engineer-president reviews engineering, his or her expertise warrants assignment of the highest value to that time. But the instant the president sits down at a CAD terminal, the value drops to the rate paid those engaged in computer-assisted design.

And another point: the hourly value of an activity varies inversely with the amount of time spent. The reason is that as an activity takes over a president's time, it tends to become an end in itself, an activity with little or no benefit. This applies even to a CEO's most important responsibility, planning. Plans should be blueprints for action, not a way to fill a bookshelf with impressive binders without issue.

Who can do it better?

Delegating is the executive's greatest need as well as greatest privilege. Most of it, of course, should happen automatically. Reviewing a market plan, say, is a function of the marketing vice president, not that person's boss. The act of delegating rates a value of 3, and that only when applying structure to a totally new responsibility.

While marketing clearly bears directly on the company's future, the criterion for CEO involvement is not just importance. The overriding question is: Can someone do the job better? Today, even strategic planning has become a delegated function. Value factors must therefore satisfy both criteria before the chief enters the picture.

Which brings me back to balancing. How can you control the demands made on you, the interruptions, the upward delegation, the unwanted invitations? There are ways to limit your involvement. Let me give an example. My name is known to many of our customers because it appears in most of our company literature. So I get myriads of phone calls from customers with suggestions or complaints. A certain amount of time I spend that way, though I assign it a value of 1, is productive. At some point, though, its value benefit vanishes.

I have a way to satisfy the customer and spare my time. The technique is less important than the purpose, which is to assign responsibility. When I learn what's on the customer's mind, I say, "I want someone else to hear this too." I dial up a conference call, stay on for a few seconds, and then explain that Ms. So-and-So knows far more about this matter than I do and will take care of it.

The question of who can do it better also applies to the time-monitoring task. To focus on things they have identified as having the greatest impact on the future of their companies, many CEOs I have talked to keep detailed records of their daily activities. Some then dictate that record to a secretary or executive assistant. It's a laborious, boring, and time-consuming task. But they are convinced they have to do it to keep their priorities straight.

I'd go a step further. A CEO needs someone of unquestioned loyalty and discretion to monitor his or her activities against the template of differential values. I see two advantages to this tactic: it relieves the chief of the bothersome task of logging time and it offers the CEO a more detached view of how well the objective is being met.

While most companies have stated priorities and goals, it's a common lament that they are not consistently addressed. They become mere articles of faith, often repeated but not vigorously pursued.

Placing higher values on those activities that serve stated priorities and promise to achieve stated goals provides a means of measuring executive performance. Executives who consistently ask themselves, "Did I earn my salary today?" and have developed a quantitative method for answering that question should have the motivation necessary to make sure it is answered affirmatively.

Reprint 88104

How to run a meeting

Antony Jay

At critical points things may go wrong, but here are ways of putting them right

Why is it that any single meeting may be a waste of time, an irritant, or a barrier to the achievement of an organization's objectives? The answer lies in the fact, as the author says, that "all sorts of human crosscurrents can sweep the discussion off course, and errors of psychology and technique on the chairman's part can defeat its purposes." This article offers guidelines on how to right things that go wrong in meetings. The discussion covers the functions of a meeting, the distinctions in size and type of meetings, ways to define the objectives, making preparations, the chairman's role, and ways to conduct a meeting that will achieve its objectives.

Mr. Jay is chairman of Video Arts Ltd., a London-based producer of training films for industry. Currently, the company is producing a film (featuring John Cleese of Monty Python) on the subject of meetings, and this article springs from the research Mr. Jay did for that project. He has also written many TV documentaries, such as *Royal Family*, and authored several books, including *Management & Machiavelli* (Holt, Rinehart & Winston, 1968).

Drawings by Robert Osborn.

Why have a meeting anyway? Why indeed? A great many important matters are quite satisfactorily conducted by a single individual who consults nobody. A great many more are resolved by a letter, a memo, a phone call, or a simple conversation between two people. Sometimes five minutes spent with six people separately is more effective and productive than a half-hour meeting with them all together.

Certainly a great many meetings waste a great deal of everyone's time and seem to be held for historical rather than practical reasons; many long-established committees are little more than memorials to dead problems. It would probably save no end of managerial time if every committee had to discuss its own dissolution once a year, and put up a case if it felt it should continue for another twelve months. If this requirement did nothing else, it would at least refocus the minds of the committee members on their purposes and objectives.

But having said that, and granting that "referring the matter to a committee" can be a device for diluting authority, diffusing responsibility, and delaying decisions, I cannot deny that meetings fulfill a deep human need. Man is a social species. In every organization and every human culture of which we have record, people come together in small groups at regular and frequent intervals, and in larger "tribal" gatherings from time to time. If there are no meetings in the places where they work, people's attachment to the organizations they work for will be small, and they will meet in regular formal or

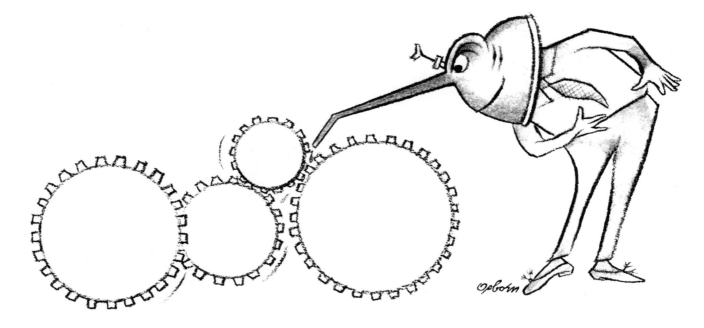

informal gatherings in associations, societies, teams, clubs, or pubs when work is over.

This need for meetings is clearly something more positive than just a legacy from our primitive hunting past. From time to time, some technomaniac or other comes up with a vision of the executive who never leaves his home, who controls his whole operation from an all-electronic, multichannel, microwave, fiber-optic video display dream console in his living room. But any manager who has ever had to make an organization work greets this vision with a smile that soon stretches into a yawn.

There is a world of science fiction, and a world of human reality; and those who live in the world of human reality know that it is held together by face-to-face meetings. A meeting still performs functions that will never be taken over by telephones, teleprinters, Xerox copiers, tape recorders, television monitors, or any other technological instruments of the information revolution.

Functions of a meeting

At this point, it may help us understand the meaning of meetings if we look at the six main functions

that meetings will always perform better than any of the more recent communication devices:

1

In the simplest and most basic way, a meeting defines the team, the group, or the unit. Those present belong to it; those absent do not. Everyone is able to look around and perceive the whole group and sense the collective identity of which he or she forms a part. We all know who we are—whether we are on the board of Universal International, in the overseas sales department of Flexitube, Inc., a member of the school management committee, on the East Hampton football team, or in Section No. 2 of Platoon 4, Company B.

2

A meeting is the place where the group revises, updates, and adds to what it knows *as a group*. Every group creates its own pool of shared knowledge, experience, judgment, and folklore. But the pool consists only of what the individuals have experienced or discussed as a group—i.e., those things which every individual knows that all the others know, too. This pool not only helps all members to do their jobs more intelligently, but it also greatly increases the speed and efficiency of all communications among them. The group knows that all special nuances and wider implications in a brief statement will be immediately clear to its members. An enormous amount of material can be left unsaid that would have to be made explicit to an outsider.

But this pool needs constant refreshing and replenishing, and occasionally the removal of impurities. So the simple business of exchanging information and ideas that members have acquired separately or in smaller groups since the last meeting is an important contribution to the strength of the group. By questioning and commenting on new contributions, the group performs an important "digestive" process that extracts what's valuable and discards the rest.

Some ethologists call this capacity to share knowledge and experience among a group "the social mind," conceiving it as a single mind dispersed among a number of skulls. They recognize that this "social mind" has a special creative power, too. A group of people meeting together can often produce better ideas, plans, and decisions than can a single individual, or a number of individuals, each working alone. The meeting can of course also produce worse outputs or none at all, if it is a bad meeting.

However, when the combined experience, knowledge, judgment, authority, and imagination of a half dozen people are brought to bear on issues, a great many plans and decisions are improved and sometimes transformed. The original idea that one person might have come up with singly is tested, amplified, refined, and shaped by argument and discussion (which often acts on people as some sort of chemical stimulant to better performance), until it satisfies far more requirements and overcomes many more objections than it could in its original form.

3
A meeting helps every individual understand both the collective aim of the group and the way in which his own and everyone else's work can contribute to the group's success.

4
A meeting creates in all present a commitment to the decisions it makes and the objectives it pursues. Once something has been decided, even if you originally argued against it, your membership in the group entails an obligation to accept the decision. The alternative is to leave the group, but in practice this is very rarely a dilemma of significance. Real opposition to decisions within organizations usually consists of one part disagreement with the decision to nine parts resentment at not being consulted before the decision. For most people on most issues, it is enough to know that their views were heard and considered. They may regret that they were not followed, but they accept the outcome.

And just as the decision of any team is binding on all the members, so the decisions of a meeting of people higher up in an organization carry a greater authority than any decision by a single executive. It is much harder to challenge a decision of the board than of the chief executive acting on his own. The decision-making authority of a meeting is of special importance for long-term policies and procedures.

5
In the world of management, a meeting is very often the only occasion where the team or group actually exists and works as a group, and the only time when the supervisor, manager, or executive is actually perceived as the leader of the team, rather than as the official to whom individuals report. In some jobs the leader does guide his team through his personal presence—not just the leader of a pit gang or construction team, but also the chef in the hotel kitchen and the maître d'hôtel in the restaurant, or the supervisor in a department store. But in large administrative headquarters, the daily or weekly meeting is often the only time when the leader is ever perceived to be guiding a team rather than doing a job.

6
A meeting is a status arena. It is no good to pretend that people are not or should not be concerned with their status relative to the other members in a group. It is just another part of human nature that we have to live with. It is a not insignificant fact that the word *order* means (a) hierarchy or pecking order; (b) an instruction or command; and (c) stability and the way things ought to be, as in "put your affairs in order," or "law and order." All three definitions are aspects of the same idea, which is indivisible.

Since a meeting is so often the only time when members get the chance to find out their relative standing, the "arena" function is inevitable. When a group is new, has a new leader, or is composed of people like department heads who are in competition for promotion and who do not work in a single team outside the meeting, "arena behavior" is likely to figure more largely, even to the point of dominating the proceedings. However, it will hardly signify with a long-established group that meets regularly.

Despite the fact that a meeting can perform all of the foregoing main functions, there is no guarantee that it will do so in any given situation. It is all too possible that any single meeting may be a waste of

time, an irritant, or a barrier to the achievement of the organization's objectives.

What sort of meeting?

While my purpose in this article is to show the critical points at which most meetings go wrong, and to indicate ways of putting them right, I must first draw some important distinctions in the size and type of meetings that we are dealing with.

Meetings can be graded by *size* into three broad categories: (1) the assembly—100 or more people who are expected to do little more than listen to the main speaker or speakers; (2) the council—40 or 50 people who are basically there to listen to the main speaker or speakers but who can come in with questions or comments and who may be asked to contribute something on their own account; and (3) the committee—up to 10 (or at the most 12) people, all of whom more or less speak on an equal footing under the guidance and control of a chairman.

We are concerned in this article only with the "committee" meeting, though it may be described as a committee, a subcommittee, a study group, a project team, a working party, a board, or by any of dozens of other titles. It is by far the most common meeting all over the world, and can perhaps be traced back to the primitive hunting band through which our species evolved. Beyond doubt it constitutes the bulk of the 11 million meetings that—so it has been calculated—take place every day in the United States.

Apart from the distinction of size, there are certain considerations regarding the *type* of meeting that profoundly affect its nature. For instance:

Frequency—A daily meeting is different from a weekly one, and a weekly meeting from a monthly one. Irregular, ad hoc, quarterly, and annual meetings are different again. On the whole, the frequency of meetings defines—or perhaps even determines—the degree of unity of the group.

Composition—Do the members work together on the same project, such as the nursing and ancillary staff on the same ward of a hospital? Do they work on different but parallel tasks, like a meeting of the company's plant managers or regional sales managers? Or are they a diverse group—strangers to each other, perhaps—united only by the meeting itself and by a common interest in realizing its objectives?

Motivation—Do the members have a common objective in their work, like a football team? Or do they to some extent have a competitive working relationship, like managers of subsidiary companies at a meeting with the chief executive, or the heads of research, production, and marketing discussing finance allocation for the coming year? Or does the desire for success through the meeting itself unify them, like a neighborhood action group or a new product design committee?

Decision process—How does the meeting group ultimately reach its decisions? By a general consensus, "the feeling of the meeting"? By a majority vote? Or are the decisions left entirely to the chairman himself, after he has listened to the facts, opinions, and discussions?

Kinds of meetings

The experienced meeting-goer will recognize that, although there seem to be five quite different methods of analyzing a meeting, in practice there is a tendency for certain kinds of meetings to sort themselves out into one of three categories. Consider:

The *daily meeting*, where people work together on the same project with a common objective and reach decisions informally by general agreement.

The *weekly* or *monthly meeting*, where members work on different but parallel projects and where there is a certain competitive element and a greater likelihood that the chairman will make the final decision himself.

The *irregular, occasional*, or *"special project" meeting*, composed of people whose normal work does not bring them into contact and whose work has little or no relationship to the others'. They are united only by the project the meeting exists to promote and motivated by the desire that the project should succeed. Though actual voting is uncommon, every member effectively has a veto.

Of these three kinds of meeting, it is the first—the workface type—that is probably the most common. It is also, oddly enough, the one most likely to be successful. Operational imperatives usually ensure that it is brief, and the participants' experience of working side by side ensures that communication is good.

The other two types are a different matter. In these meetings all sorts of human crosscurrents can sweep the discussion off course, and errors of psychology and technique on the chairman's part can defeat its purposes. Moreover, these meetings are likely to bring together the more senior people and to produce decisions that profoundly affect the efficiency, prosperity, and even survival of the whole organization. It is, therefore, toward these higher-level meetings that the lessons of this article are primarily directed.

Before the meeting

The most important question you should ask is: "What is this meeting intended to achieve?" You can ask it in different ways—"What would be the likely consequences of not holding it?" "When it is over, how shall I judge whether it was a success or a failure?"—but unless you have a very clear requirement from the meeting, there is a grave danger that it will be a waste of everyone's time.

Defining the objective

You have already looked at the six main functions that all meetings perform, but if you are trying to use a meeting to achieve definite objectives, there are in practice only certain types of objectives it can really achieve. Every item on the agenda can be placed in one of the following four categories, or divided up into sections that fall into one or more of them:

1

Informative-digestive—Obviously, it is a waste of time for the meeting to give out purely factual information that would be better circulated in a document. But if the information should be heard from a particular person, or if it needs some clarification and comment to make sense of it, or if it has deep implications for the members of the meeting, then it is perfectly proper to introduce an item onto the agenda that requires no conclusion, decision, or

action from the meeting; it is enough, simply, that the meeting should receive and discuss a report.

The "informative-digestive" function includes progress reports—to keep the group up to date on the current status of projects it is responsible for or that affect its deliberations—and review of completed projects in order to come to a collective judgment and to see what can be learned from them for the next time.

2

Constructive-originative—This "What shall we do?" function embraces all items that require something new to be devised, such as a new policy, a new strategy, a new sales target, a new product, a new marketing plan, a new procedure, and so forth. This sort of discussion asks people to contribute their knowledge, experience, judgment, and ideas. Obviously, the plan will probably be inadequate unless all relevant parties are present and pitching in.

3

Executive responsibilities—This is the "How shall we do it?" function, which comes after it has been decided what the members are going to do; at this point, executive responsibilities for the different components of the task have to be distributed around the table. Whereas in the second function the con-

tributors' importance is their knowledge and ideas, here their contribution is the responsibility for implementing the plan. The fact that they and their subordinates are affected by it makes their contribution especially significant.

It is of course possible to allocate these executive responsibilities without a meeting, by separate individual briefings, but several considerations often make a meeting desirable:

First, it enables the members as a group to find the best way of achieving the objectives.

Second, it enables each member to understand and influence the way in which his own job fits in with the jobs of the others and with the collective task.

Third, if the meeting is discussing the implementation of a decision taken at a higher level, securing the group's consent may be of prime importance. If so, the fact that the group has the opportunity to formulate the detailed action plan itself may be the decisive factor in securing its agreement, because in that case the final decision belongs, as it were, to the group. Everyone is committed to what the group decides and is collectively responsible for the final shape of the project, as well as individually answerable for his own part in it. Ideally, this sort of agenda item starts with a policy, and ends with an action plan.

4

Legislative framework: Above and around all considerations of "What to do" and "How to do it," there is a framework—a departmental or divisional organization—and a system of rules, routines, and procedures within and through which all the activity takes place. Changing this framework and introducing a new organization or new procedures can be deeply disturbing to committee members and a threat to their status and long-term security. Yet leaving it unchanged can stop the organization from adapting to a changing world. At whatever level this change happens, it must have the support of all the perceived leaders whose groups are affected by it.

The key leaders for this legislative function must collectively make or confirm the decision; if there is any important dissent, it is very dangerous to close the discussion and make the decision by decree. The group leaders cannot expect quick decisions if they are seeking to change the organization framework and routines that people have grown up with. Thus they must be prepared to leave these items unresolved for further discussion and consultation. As Francis Bacon put it—and it has never been put better—"Counsels to which time hath not been called, time will not ratify."

Making preparations

The four different functions just discussed may of course be performed by a single meeting, as the group proceeds through the agenda. Consequently, it may be a useful exercise for the chairman to go through the agenda, writing beside each item which function it is intended to fulfill. This exercise helps clarify what is expected from the discussion and helps focus on which people to bring in and what questions to ask them.

People

The value and success of a committe meeting are seriously threatened if too many people are present. Between 4 and 7 is generally ideal, 10 is tolerable, and 12 is the outside limit. So the chairman should do everything he can to keep numbers down, consistent with the need to invite everyone with an important contribution to make.

The leader may have to leave out people who expect to come or who have always come. For this job he may need tact; but since people generally preserve a fiction that they are overworked already and dislike serving on committees, it is not usually hard to secure their consent to stay away.

If the leader sees no way of getting the meeting down to a manageable size, he can try the following devices: (a) analyze the agenda to see whether everyone has to be present for every item (he may be able to structure the agenda so that some people can leave at half time and others can arrive); (b) ask himself whether he doesn't really need two separate, smaller meetings rather than one big one; and (c) determine whether one or two groups can be asked to thrash some of the topics out in advance so that only one of them needs to come in with its proposals.

Remember, too, that a few words with a member on the day before a meeting can increase the value of the meeting itself, either by ensuring that an important point is raised that comes better from the floor than from the chair or by preventing a time-wasting discussion of a subject that need not be touched on at all.

Papers

The agenda is by far the most important piece of paper. Properly drawn up, it has a power of speeding and clarifying a meeting that very few people understand or harness. The main fault is to make it unnecessarily brief and vague. For example, the phrase "development budget" tells nobody very much, whereas the longer explanation "To discuss the proposal for reduction of the 1976–1977 development budget now that the introduction of our new product has been postponed" helps all committee members to form some views or even just to look up facts and figures in advance.

Thus the leader should not be afraid of a long agenda, provided that the length is the result of his analyzing and defining each item more closely, rather than of his adding more items than the meeting can reasonably consider in the time allowed. He should try to include, very briefly, some indication of the reason for each topic to be discussed. If one item is of special interest to the group, it is often a good idea to single it out for special mention in a covering note.

The leader should also bear in mind the useful device of heading each item "For information," "For discussion," or "For decision" so that those at the meeting know where they are trying to get to.

And finally, the chairman should not circulate the agenda too far in advance, since the less organized members will forget it or lose it. Two or three days is about right—unless the supporting papers are voluminous.

Other 'paper' considerations: The order of items on the agenda is important. Some aspects are obvious—the items that need urgent decision have to come before those that can wait till next time. Equally, the leader does not discuss the budget for the reequipment program before discussing whether to put the reequipment off until next year. But some aspects are not so obvious. Consider:

☐

The early part of a meeting tends to be more lively and creative than the end of it, so if an item needs mental energy, bright ideas, and clear heads, it may be better to put it high up on the list. Equally, if there is one item of great interest and concern to everyone, it may be a good idea to hold it back for a while and get some other useful work done first. Then the star item can be introduced to carry the meeting over the attention lag that sets in after the first 15 to 20 minutes of the meeting.

☐

Some items unite the meeting in a common front while others divide the members one from another. The leader may want to start with unity before entering into division, or he may prefer the other way around. The point is to be aware of the choice and to make it consciously, because it is apt to make a difference to the whole atmosphere of the meeting. It is almost always a good idea to find a unifying item with which to end the meeting.

☐

A common fault is to dwell too long on trivial but urgent items, to the exclusion of subjects of fundamental importance whose significance is long-term rather than immediate. This can be remedied by putting on the agenda the time at which discussion of the important long-term issue will begin—and by sticking to it.

☐

Very few business meetings achieve anything of value after two hours, and an hour and a half is enough time to allocate for most purposes.

☐

It is often a good idea to put the finishing time of a meeting on the agenda as well as the starting time.

☐

If meetings have a tendency to go on too long, the chairman should arrange to start them one hour before lunch or one hour before the end of work. Generally, items that ought to be kept brief can be introduced ten minutes from a fixed end point.

☐

The practice of circulating background or proposal papers along with the minutes is, in principle, a good one. It not only saves time, but it also helps in formulating useful questions and considerations in advance. But the whole idea is sabotaged once the papers get too long; they should be brief or provide a short summary. If they are circulated, obviously the chairman has to read them, or at least must not be caught not having read them.

(One chairman, more noted for his cunning than his conscientiousness, is said to have spent 30 seconds before each meeting going through all the papers he had not read with a thick red pen, marking lines and question marks in the margins at random, and making sure these were accidentally made visible to the meeting while the subject was being discussed.)

☐

If papers are produced at the meeting for discussion, they should obviously be brief and simple, since everyone has to read them. It is a supreme folly to bring a group of people together to read six pages of closely printed sheets to themselves. The exception is certain kinds of financial and statistical papers whose function is to support and illustrate verbal points as reference documents rather than to be swallowed whole: these are often better tabled at the meeting.

☐

All items should be thought of and thought about in advance if they are to be usefully discussed. Listing "Any other business" on the agenda is an invitation to waste time. This does not absolutely preclude the chairman's announcing an extra agenda item at a meeting if something really urgent and unforeseen crops up or is suggested to him by a member, provided it is fairly simple and straightforward. Nor does it preclude his leaving time for general unstructured discussion after the close of the meeting.

☐

The chairman, in going through the agenda items in advance, can usefully insert his own brief notes of points he wants to be sure are not omitted from the discussion. A brief marginal scribble of "How much notice?" or "Standby arrangements?" or whatever is all that is necessary.

The chairman's job

Let's say that you have just been appointed chairman of the committee. You tell everyone that it is a bore or a chore. You also tell them that you have been appointed "for my sins." But the point is that you tell them. There is no getting away from it: some sort of honor or glory attaches to the chairman's role. Almost everyone is in some way pleased and proud to be made chairman of something. And that is three quarters of the trouble.

Master or servant?

Their appointment as committee chairman takes people in different ways. Some seize the opportunity to impose their will on a group that they see themselves licensed to dominate. Their chairmanship is a harangue, interspersed with demands for group agreement.

Others are more like scoutmasters, for whom the collective activity of the group is satisfaction enough, with no need for achievement. Their chairmanship is more like the endless stoking and fueling of a campfire that is not cooking anything.

And there are the insecure or lazy chairmen who look to the meeting for reassurance and support in their ineffectiveness and inactivity, so that they can spread the responsibility for their indecisiveness among the whole group. They seize on every expression of disagreement or doubt as a justification for avoiding decision or action.

But even the large majority who do not go to those extremes still feel a certain pleasurable tumescence of the ego when they take their place at the head of the table for the first time. The feeling is no sin: the sin is to indulge it or to assume that the pleasure is shared by the other members of the meeting.

It is the chairman's self-indulgence that is the greatest single barrier to the success of a meeting. His first duty, then, is to be aware of the temptation and of the dangers of yielding to it. The clearest of the danger signals is hearing himself talking a lot during a discussion.

One of the best chairmen I have ever served under makes it a rule to restrict her interventions to a single sentence, or at most two. She forbids herself ever to contribute a paragraph to a meeting she is chairing. It is a harsh rule, but you would be hard put to find a regular attender of her meetings (or anyone else's) who thought it was a bad one.

There is, in fact, only one legitimate source of pleasure in chairmanship, and that is pleasure in the achievements of the meeting—and to be legitimate, it must be shared by all those present. Meetings are *necessary* for all sorts of basic and primitive human reasons, but they are *useful* only if they are seen by all present to be getting somewhere—and somewhere they know they could not have gotten to individually.

If the chairman is to make sure that the meeting achieves valuable objectives, he will be more effective seeing himself as the servant of the group rather than as its master. His role then becomes that of assisting the group toward the best conclusion or decision in the most efficient manner possible: to interpret and clarify; to move the discussion forward; and to bring it to a resolution that everyone understands and accepts as being the will of the meeting, even if the individuals do not necessarily agree with it.

His true source of authority with the members is the strength of his perceived commitment to their combined objective and his skill and efficiency in helping and guiding them to its achievement. Control and discipline then become not the act of imposing his will on the group but of imposing the group's will on any individual who is in danger of diverting or delaying the progress of the discussion and so from realizing the objective.

Once the members realize that the leader is impelled by his commitment to their common objective, it does not take great force of personality for him to control the meeting. Indeed, a sense of urgency and a clear desire to reach the best conclusion as quickly as possible are a much more effective disciplinary instrument than a big gavel. The effective chairman can then hold the discussion to the point by indicating that there is no time to pursue a particular idea now, that there is no time for long speeches, that the group has to get through

this item and on to the next one, rather than by resorting to pulling rank.

There are many polite ways the chairman can indicate a slight impatience even when someone else is speaking—by leaning forward, fixing his eyes on the speaker, tensing his muscles, raising his eyebrows, or nodding briefly to show the point is taken. And when replying or commenting, the chairman can indicate by the speed, brevity, and finality of his intonation that "we have to move on." Conversely, he can reward the sort of contribution he is seeking by the opposite expressions and intonations, showing that there is plenty of time for that sort of idea, and encouraging the speaker to develop the point.

After a few meetings, all present readily understand this nonverbal language of chairmanship. It is the chairman's chief instrument of educating the group into the general type of "meeting behavior" that he is looking for. He is still the servant of the group, but like a hired mountain guide, he is the one who knows the destination, the route, the weather signs, and the time the journey will take. So if he suggests that the members walk a bit faster, they take his advice.

This role of servant rather than master is often obscured in large organizations by the fact that the chairman is frequently the line manager of the members: this does not, however, change the reality of the role of chairman. The point is easier to see in, say, a neighborhood action group. The question in that case is, simply, "Through which person's chairmanship do we collectively have the best chance of getting the children's playground built?"

However, one special problem is posed by this definition of the chairman's role, and it has an extremely interesting answer. The question is: How can the chairman combine his role with the role of a member advocating one side of an argument?

The answer comes from some interesting studies by researchers who sat in on hundreds of meetings to find out how they work. Their consensus finding is that most of the effective discussions have, in fact, two leaders: one they call a "team," or "social," leader; the other a "task," or "project," leader.

Regardless of whether leadership is in fact a single or a dual function, for our purposes it is enough to say that the chairman's best role is that of social leader. If he wants a particular point to be strongly advocated, he ensures that it is someone else who leads off the task discussion, and he holds back until much later in the argument. He might indeed change or modify his view through hearing the discussion, but even if he does not it is much easier for him to show support for someone else's point later in the discussion, after listening to the arguments. Then, he can summarize in favor of the one he prefers.

The task advocate might regularly be the chairman's second-in-command, or a different person might advocate for different items on the agenda. On some subjects, the chairman might well be the task advocate himself, especially if they do not involve conflict within the group. The important point is that the chairman has to keep his "social leadership" even if it means sacrificing his "task leadership." However, if the designated task advocate persists in championing a cause through two or three meetings, he risks building up quite a head of antagonism to him among the other members. Even so, this antagonism harms the group less by being directed at the "task leader" than at the "social leader."

Structure of discussion

It may seem that there is no right way or wrong way to structure a committee meeting discussion.

A subject is raised, people say what they think, and finally a decision is reached, or the discussion is terminated. There is some truth in this. Moreover, it would be a mistake to try and tie every discussion of every item down to a single immutable format.

Nevertheless, there is a logical order to a group discussion, and while there can be reasons for not following it, there is no justification for not being aware of it. In practice, very few discussions are inhibited, and many are expedited, by a conscious adherence to the following stages, which follow exactly the same pattern as a visit to the doctor:

"What seems to be the trouble?" The reason for an item being on a meeting agenda is usually like the symptom we go to the doctor with: "I keep getting this pain in my back" is analogous to "Sales have risen in Germany but fallen in France." In both cases it is clear that something is wrong and that something ought to be done to put it right. But until the visit to the doctor, or the meeting of the European marketing committee, that is about all we really know.

"How long has this been going on?" The doctor will start with a case history of all the relevant background facts, and so will the committee discussion. A solid basis of shared and agreed-on facts is the best foundation to build any decision on, and a set of pertinent questions will help establish it. For example, when did French sales start to fall off? Have German sales risen exceptionally? Has France had delivery problems, or less sales effort, or weaker advertising? Have we lost market share, or are our competitors' sales falling too? If the answers to all these questions, and more, are not established at the start, a lot of discussion may be wasted later.

"Would you just lie down on the couch?" The doctor will then conduct a physical examination to find out how the patient is now. The committee, too, will want to know how things stand at this moment. Is action being taken? Do long-term orders show the same trend? What are the latest figures? What is the current stock position? How much money is left in the advertising budget?

"You seem to have slipped a disc." When the facts are established, you can move toward a dignosis. A doctor may seem to do this quickly, but that is the result of experience and practice. He is, in fact, rapidly eliminating all the impossible or far-fetched explanations until he leaves himself with a short list. The committee, too, will hazard and eliminate a

variety of diagnoses until it homes in on the most probable—for example, the company's recent energetic and highly successful advertising campaign in Germany plus new packaging by the market leader in France.

"Take this round to the druggist." Again, the doctor is likely to take a shortcut that a committee meeting may be wise to avoid. The doctor comes out with a single prescription, and the committee, too, may agree quickly on a single course of action.

But if the course is not so clear, it is better to take this step in two stages: (a) construct a series of options—do not, at first, reject any suggestions outright but try to select and combine the promising elements from all of them until a number of thought-out, coherent, and sensible suggestions are on the table; and (b) only when you have generated these options do you start to choose among them. Then you can discuss and decide whether to pick the course based on repackaging and point-of-sale promotion, or the one based on advertising and a price cut, or the one that bides its time and saves the money for heavier new-product promotion next year.

If the item is at all complex or especially significant, it is important for the chairman not only to have the proposed course of the discussion in his own head, but also to announce it so that everyone knows. A good idea is to write the headings on an easel pad with a felt pen. This saves much of the time wasting and confusion that result when people raise items in the wrong place because they were not privy to the chairman's secret that the right place was coming up later on in the discussion.

Conducting the meeting

Just as the driver of a car has two tasks, to follow his route and to manage his vehicle, so the chairman's job can be divided into two corresponding tasks, dealing with the subject and dealing with the people.

Dealing with the subject

The essence of this task is to follow the structure of discussion as just described in the previous section. This, in turn, entails listening carefully and keeping the meeting pointed toward the objective.

At the start of the discussion of any item, the chairman should make it clear where the meeting should try to get to by the end. Are the members hoping to make a clear decision or firm recommendation? Is it a preliminary deliberation to give the members something to go away with and think about? Are they looking for a variety of different lines to be pursued outside the meeting? Do they have to approve the proposal, or merely note it?

The chairman may give them a choice: "If we can agree on a course of action, that's fine. If not, we'll have to set up a working party to report and recommend before next month's meeting."

The chairman should make sure that all the members understand the issue and why they are discussing it. Often it will be obvious, or else they may have been through it before. If not, then he or someone he has briefed before the meeting should give a short introduction, with some indication of the reason the item is on the agenda; the story so far; the present position; what needs to be established, resolved, or proposed; and some indication of lines of inquiry or courses of action that have been suggested or explored, as well as arguments on both sides of the issue.

If the discussion is at all likely to be long or complex, the chairman should propose to the meeting a structure for it with headings (written up if necessary), as I stated at the end of the section on "Structure of discussion." He should listen carefully in case people jump too far ahead (e.g., start proposing a course of action before the meeting has agreed on the cause of the trouble), or go back over old ground, or start repeating points that have been made earlier. He has to head discussion off sterile or irrelevant areas very quickly (e.g., the rights and wrongs of past decisions that it is too late to change, or distant prospects that are too remote to affect present actions).

It is the chairman's responsibility to prevent misunderstanding and confusion. If he does not follow an argument or understand a reference, he should seek clarification from the speaker. If he thinks two people are using the same word with different meanings, he should intervene (e.g., one member using *promotion* to mean point-of-sale advertising only, and another also including media publicity).

He may also have to clarify by asking people for facts or experience that perhaps influence their view but are not known to others in the meeting. And he should be on the lookout for points where an interim summary would be helpful. This device frequently takes only a few seconds, and acts like a life belt to some of the members who are getting out of their depth.

Sometimes a meeting will have to discuss a draft document. If there are faults in it, the members should agree on what the faults are and the chairman should delegate someone to produce a new draft later. The group should never try to redraft around the table.

Perhaps one of the most common faults of chairmanship is the failure to terminate the discussion early enough. Sometimes chairmen do not realize that the meeting has effectively reached an agreement, and consequently they let the discussion go on for another few minutes, getting nowhere at all. Even more often, they are not quick enough to close a discussion *before* agreement has been reached.

A discussion should be closed once it has become clear that (a) more facts are required before further progress can be made, (b) discussion has revealed that the meeting needs the views of people not present, (c) members need more time to think about the subject and perhaps discuss it with colleagues, (d) events are changing and likely to alter or clarify the basis of the decision quite soon, (e) there is not going to be enough time at this meeting to go over the subject properly, or (f) it is becoming clear that two or three of the members can settle this outside the meeting without taking up the time of the rest. The fact that the decision is difficult, likely to be disputed, or going to be unwelcome to somebody, however, is not a reason for postponement.

At the end of the discussion of each agenda item, the chairman should give a brief and clear summary of what has been agreed on. This can act as the dictation of the actual minutes. It serves not merely to put the item on record, but also to help people realize that something worthwhile has been achieved. It also answers the question "Where did all that get us?" If the summary involves action by a member of the meeting, he should be asked to confirm his acceptance of the undertaking.

Dealing with the people

There is only one way to ensure that a meeting starts on time, and that is to start it on time. Latecomers who find that the meeting has begun without them soon learn the lesson. The alternative is that the prompt and punctual members will soon realize that a meeting never starts until ten minutes after the advertised time, and they will also learn the lesson.

Punctuality at future meetings can be wonderfully reinforced by the practice of listing late arrivals (and early departures) in the minutes. Its ostensible and perfectly proper purpose is to call the latecomer's attention to the fact that he was absent when a decision was reached. Its side effect, however, is to tell everyone on the circulation list that he was late, and people do not want that sort of information about themselves published too frequently.

There is a growing volume of work on the significance of seating positions and their effect on group behavior and relationships. Not all the findings are generally agreed on. What does seem true is that:

□

Having members sit face to face across a table facilitates opposition, conflict, and disagreement, though of course it does not turn allies into enemies. But it does suggest that the chairman should think about whom he seats opposite himself.

□

Sitting side by side makes disagreements and confrontation harder. This in turn suggests that the chairman can exploit the friendship-value of the seats next to him.

□

There is a "dead man's corner" on the chairman's right, especially if a number of people are seated in line along from him (it does not apply if he is alone at the head of the table).

□

As a general rule, proximity to the chairman is a sign of honor and favor. This is most marked when he is at the head of a long, narrow table. The greater the distance, the lower the rank—just as the lower-status positions were "below the salt" at medieval refectories.

Control the garrulous

In most meetings someone takes a long time to say very little. As chairman, your sense of urgency should help indicate to him the need for brevity. You can also suggest that if he is going to take a long time it might be better for him to write a paper. If it is urgent to stop him in full flight, there is a useful device of picking on a phrase (it really doesn't matter what phrase) as he utters it as an excuse for cutting in and offering it to someone else: "Inevitable decline—that's very interesting. George, do you agree that the decline is inevitable?"

Draw out the silent

In any properly run meeting, as simple arithmetic will show, most of the people will be silent most of the time. Silence can indicate general agreement, or no important contribution to make, or the need to wait and hear more before saying anything, or too good a lunch, and none of these need worry you. But there are two kinds of silence you must break:

1

The silence of diffidence. Someone may have a valuable contribution to make but be sufficiently nervous about its possible reception to keep it to himself. It is important that when you draw out such a contribution, you should express interest and pleasure (though not necessarily agreement) to encourage further contributions of that sort.

2

The silence of hostility. This is not hostility to ideas, but to you as the chairman, to the meeting, and to the process by which decisions are being reached.

This sort of total detachment from the whole proceedings is usually the symptom of some feeling of affront. If you probe it, you will usually find that there is something bursting to come out, and that it is better out than in.

Protect the weak

Junior members of the meeting may provoke the disagreement of their seniors, which is perfectly reasonable. But if the disagreement escalates to the point of suggesting that they have no right to contribute, the meeting is weakened. So you may have to take pains to commend their contribution for its usefulness, as a pre-emptive measure. You can reinforce this action by taking a written note of a point they make (always a plus for a member of a meeting) and by referring to it again later in the discussion (a double-plus).

Encourage the clash of ideas

But, at the same time, discourage the clash of personalities. A good meeting is not a series of dialogues between individual members and the chairman. Instead, it is a crossflow of discussion and debate, with the chairman occasionally guiding, mediating, probing, stimulating, and summarizing, but mostly letting the others thrash ideas out. However, the meeting must be a contention of *ideas*, not people.

If two people are starting to get heated, widen the discussion by asking a question of a neutral member of the meeting, preferably a question that requires a purely factual answer.

Watch out for the suggestion-squashing reflex

Students of meetings have reduced everything that can be said into questions, answers, positive reactions, and negative reactions. Questions can only seek, and answers only supply, three types of response: information, opinion, and suggestion.

In almost every modern organization, it is the suggestions that contain the seeds of future success. Although very few suggestions will ever lead to anything, almost all of them need to be given every chance. The trouble is that suggestions are much easier to ridicule than facts or opinions. If people feel that making a suggestion will provoke the negative reaction of being laughed at or squashed, they will soon stop. And if there is any status-jostling going on at the meeting, it is all too easy to use the occasion of someone's making a suggestion as the opportunity to take him down a peg. It is all too easy and a formula to ensure sterile meetings.

The answer is for you to take special notice and show special warmth when anyone makes a suggestion, and to discourage as sharply as you can the squashing-reflex. This can often be achieved by requiring the squasher to produce a better suggestion on the spot. Few suggestions can stand up to squashing in their pristine state: your reflex must be to pick out the best part of one and get the other committee members to help build it into something that might work.

Come to the most senior people last
Obviously, this cannot be a rule, but once someone of high authority has pronounced on a topic, the less senior members are likely to be inhibited. If you work up the pecking order instead of down it, you are apt to get a wider spread of views and ideas. But the juniors who start it off should only be asked for contributions within their personal experience and competence. ("Peter, you were at the Frankfurt Exhibition—what reactions did you pick up there?")

Close on a note of achievement
Even if the final item is left unresolved, you can refer to an earlier item that was well resolved as you close the meeting and thank the group.

If the meeting is not a regular one, fix the time and place of the next one before dispersing. A little time spent with appointment diaries at the end, especially if it is a gathering of five or more members, can save hours of secretarial telephoning later.

Following the meeting

Your secretary may take the minutes (or better still, one of the members), but the minutes are your responsibility. They can be very brief, but they should include these facts:

☐
The time and date of the meeting, where it was held, and who chaired it.
☐
Names of all present and apologies for absence.
☐
All agenda items (and other items) discussed and all decisions reached. If action was agreed on, record (and underline) the name of the person responsible for the assignment.
☐
The time at which the meeting ended (important, because it may be significant later to know whether the discussion lasted 15 minutes or 6 hours).
☐
The date, time, and place of the next committee meeting.

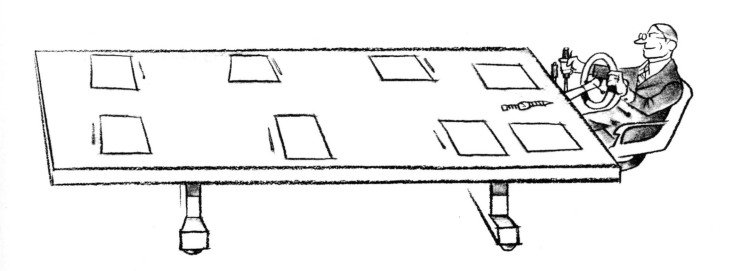

Getting Things Done

How to make a team work

Maurice Hardaker and Bryan K. Ward

In one intense session, managers set goals, accept responsibilities – and become a real team.

Anyone who has ever run a business or organized a project has discovered how hard it can be to get the whole team on board to ensure that everyone knows where the enterprise is heading and agrees on what it will take to succeed.

At IBM we've used a method for some years that helps managers do just this. The technique, which we call PQM or Process Quality Management, grew out of many studies with customers to determine their needs and from internal studies as part of IBM's business quality program. PQM has been used successfully by service companies, government agencies, and nonprofit organizations, as well as manufacturers.

In PQM, managers get back to the often overlooked basics of an endeavor. IBM has had many successes abroad by paying attention to such details.

IBM Europe's manufacturing arm relied heavily on PQM when it launched a series of changes including continuous-flow manufacturing. First the vice president of manufacturing and his team made sure they understood the task ahead. Then they focused on new priorities for the company's major materials-management processes. As a result of their decisions, changes cascaded through the manufacturing organization's work force, leading not only to better interplant logistics but also to smooth introduction of continuous-flow manufacturing among IBM's 15 European plants. As this happened, manufacturing cycle times and inventory levels improved, costs dropped, quality rose, and the company became more flexible in meeting customer demand. That may not be the end of the rainbow, but it's not bad from a two-day PQM session.

PQM has also been the starting point for many IBM customers of a host of management decisions in such areas as strategy formulation, funding, human resource management, marketing, and resource allocation for large, complex projects. Often a PQM study is undertaken because something has happened – someone sees a new opportunity, a new technology, or new competitors. But it is useful any time.

PQM does not differ radically from other planning processes: we identify goals and the activities critical to their attainment, and we provide a way to measure success. But PQM demands an intensive one- or two-day session at which *all* the key managers concerned agree on what must be done and accept specific responsibility.

There's no guarantee that a unit will achieve its mission, of course. That requires competent follow-through by the entire organization. But PQM lays the groundwork for such success. And at least all the key players start off facing in the same direction.

Gather the team

PQM begins with a person who is the leader of the management team – the boss, the one whose job depends on getting the team's mission accomplished. He or she should then involve everyone on the immediate management team and no one else – nobody missing and no hitchhikers. At most there should be 12 people, since more than that is just too unwieldy. And if even one member of the team cannot attend the study, wait. PQM requires a buy-in from everyone not only to identify what is needed but also to commit to the process.

By management team we usually mean a formal group of managers, a board of directors, say, or a divisional vice president and his or her top managers. But the team can also be a collection of individuals drawn from various sectors of the company for a specific project, like the team brought together at IBM to introduce continuous-flow manufacturing. In either case, the mission is normally too large or complex for one person, so the boss collects or inherits a team to work on it.

Maurice Hardaker is a senior consultant with IBM's International Education Centre in La Hulpe, Belgium. He has advised the boards of directors of many of IBM's customers. Most recently he has been working with senior management in IBM's program for business process quality management.

Bryan K. Ward is a senior consultant in the Systems Management Consultancy Group of IBM United Kingdom. He advises senior management of IBM customers about business planning and information technology strategy and works with senior management of IBM UK on business-related topics.

PQM demands spontaneity, so even though the boss convokes the team, a neutral outsider should lead the discussions. The leader could be a consultant or a manager or an officer from elsewhere in the company. What's important is that leaders not be the bosses' subordinates and that their livelihood should not depend on achieving the mission. Furthermore, the discussions are best held off premises; at the office, secretaries can fight their way through steel doors to deliver "urgent" messages.

Finally, and perhaps this goes without saying, the boss had better be ready to accept challenges to the status quo. We have presided at a few disasters where, despite assurances of open-mindedness, the boss turned the study into a self-justifying monologue. Fortunately, this is rare; it's a terrible waste of time.

Understand the mission

The first step in the PQM effort is to develop a clear understanding of the team's mission, what its members collectively are paid to do. *Collectively* is important. A marketing vice president and a finance vice president will have different ideas about their separate functional missions. But when they meet together as part of the management team, they should know their jobs as members of that team.

If the mission statement is wrong, everything that follows will be wrong too, so getting a clear understanding is crucial. And agreeing on a mission may not be as easy as it may at first seem. People in well-run companies and government agencies tend to know their job descriptions, the benefits package, and their own job objectives. But even at the top, their ideas about the organization's mission are often pretty vague—to make profits or something like that. In part, this reflects the nature of management teams. People are appointed, stay a while, do their jobs, and move on; each team includes long-serving members, new arrivals, and new leaders. As a group, they may never have articulated their mission to one another. A PQM study makes them stand back and ask fundamental questions like "Do we really

understand our business well enough to form a mission statement?"

Our advice is to make the mission statement explicit—nail it to the wall. It shouldn't be more than

Some managers learn their unit's true mission for the first time.

three or four short sentences. For example, the following is a mission statement for one of IBM Europe's units:

"Prepare IBM World Trade Europe Middle East Africa Corporation employees to establish their businesses.

"Organize high-level seminars for IBM customers and make a significant contribution to IBM's image in Europe.

"Demonstrate the added value of the International Education Centre through excellence in advanced education, internationalism, innovation, and cross-functional exchanges."

The unit's mission statement defines the boundaries of the business (Europe, the Middle East, and Africa) and the customer population (all IBM employees within that area plus senior people from IBM's customers). It says what has to be done and says that achievement will be measured by the unit's demonstrable impact on IBM business successes, customer satisfaction, and company image in Europe.

The mission should be clear enough to let you know when you have succeeded and are entitled to a reward. "Increase profits" is not a rewardable mission. How much of an increase? .5%? 5%? 50%? But "generate positive cash flow" might well be a rewardable mission for a management team nursing a sick company. We did a study with one IBM customer whose mission was quite simply to survive until next year. It had a well-planned strategy for the future but a rough patch to negotiate for the next 12 months.

Once a team has defined its goal or mission, it could go straight to identifying its critical success factors

(CSFs), the things it will have to do to succeed. But in our experience that's premature. At this point, few teams are relaxed enough to do the free associating needed to pinpoint their real CSFs. They are fixed on what they know and on today's problems, not on new possibilities.

To break out of old ways of thinking, we suggest a 10-minute brainstorming session in which team members list one-word descriptions of everything they believe could have an impact on achieving their mission. The usual brainstorming rules should apply:

Everyone should contribute.

Everything is fair game, no matter how crazy or outrageous.

Nobody is permitted to challenge any suggestion.

The facilitator should write everything down so the team can see the whole list.

While thinking about these dominant influences, each member should focus intently on the team's mission. Members should look inside and outside their bailiwicks, sometimes far outside to factors like national characteristics or public policy issues. The dominant influences that turned up in a brainstorming session for a Spanish company, for example, included the socialist government, the Basques, the Catalonians, regionalism, terrorism, and the mañana syndrome. Typically a team's list will contain 30 to 50 diverse items ranging from things like costs and supplier capabilities to jogging and the weather.

Spell out your goals

Now the team should be ready to identify the critical success factors, a term used for many years in corporate planning to mean the most important subgoals of a business, business unit, or project. Here we define CSFs as what the team must accomplish to achieve its mission.

Consensus on these aims is vital. In one study, the top 10 managers in 125 European companies were asked individually to identify their companies' 5 most critical objectives. The minimum number from each company would be 5; the maximum, 50. Managers of the 40 most profitable companies agreed on 6 to 12 objectives. For the 40 worst companies, the range was 26 to 43. In other words, the top executives of the poor performers had no shared vision of what they were trying to do, while just the opposite was true of the successful companies' leaders. Significantly, a few years after the managers of one worst category company had agreed on its critical objectives, the company moved into the most profitable group.[1]

Like the mission, CSFs are not the how to of an enterprise, and they are not directly manageable. Often they are statements of hope or fear. The list in the first part of the *Exhibit* is typical. In a sense, every CSF should be viewed as beginning with the words "We need..." or "We must..." to express buy-in by all ("We") and agreed-on criticality ("need" or "must").

In naming its CSFs, a team should be guided by the necessary-and-sufficient rule. That is, the group must agree that each CSF listed is *necessary* to the mission and that together they are *sufficient* to achieve the mission. This is a stringent requirement. The CSF list must reflect the absolute minimum number of subgoals that have to be achieved for the team to accomplish its mission.

The seven CSFs in the *Exhibit* are designed for a fictitious enterprise that sells consumer products in the United States. It's a mature market, and the company's market share and profitability have eroded. The CEO's mission statement for this business might read:

"Restore market share and profitability over the next two years, and prepare the company and marketplace for further profitable growth."

To accomplish that mission, the management team must achieve all seven CSFs over the next two years. That's what we mean by necessary and sufficient.

In addition, each CSF must be devoted to a single issue—pure in the elemental sense, like hydrogen or gold. The word *and* is verboten. The team has to struggle to reduce its list

honestly; it can't succumb when some creative manager says, "Why don't we combine numbers three and seven so we reduce product cost *and* improve morale?"

The list should be a mix of tactical and strategic factors. If the factors are all strategic (increase market share to 15% by 1992, for example), the business might founder while everybody concentrates on the blue skies ahead. Equally, if all are tactical (reduce the delivered cost of product ABC to $20.50 by year end), the business could kill itself on short-term success. The ratio depends on several considerations, of course, including the nature of the business unit doing the study. A regional sales office would likely have more tactical CSFs, while a corporate headquarters would have an almost entirely strategic list.

The maximum number of CSFs is eight. And if the mission is survival, four is the limit—you don't worry about whether your tie is straight when you are drowning. There is no magic about eight. It just seems to be the largest number of truly critical goals that a management team can focus on continuously.

Our rules on number and absolute consensus may be tough, but they work, and it's essential to follow them. Whenever we have been persuaded to relax either rule, we have ended up with a mess, a list of moans rather than the truly visceral issues affecting the business. If someone cries, "We can't agree, let's vote," don't do it. Insist on consensus; highly paid, experienced, businesswise people should be able to agree on what's vital to their business, after all.

Reaching agreement on the CSFs usually takes from one to three hours. The longest time we've seen was a day. In that case, the team was composed of the heads of nine quasi-independent business units and managers from headquarters. Understandably, they had a tough time reaching consensus.

Find what matters most

The third step in PQM is to identify and list what has to be done so that a company can meet its critical suc-

cess factors. This might mean being more responsive to the market, exploiting new technologies, or whatever else is essential to accomplish the CSFs.

Ask almost any management team for a list of its business activities or processes, however, and you will often get a set of bland descriptions like maintenance or sales or customer service. These aren't business processes. They don't describe what is actually done in the business.

The technique demands unanimity; all must agree to go in the same direction.

We recommend a more rigorous approach, one that draws on our necessary-and-sufficient rule. As with the CSFs' relation to the mission, each process necessary for a given CSF must be indicated, and together all those processes must be sufficient to accomplish it.

Other rules we find useful are:

Each business process description should follow a verb-plus-object sequence.

Every business process should have an owner, the person responsible for carrying out the process.

The owner should be a member of the management team that agreed to the CSFs.

No owner should have more than three or four business processes to manage.

To show how these rules work, think about the process "measure customer satisfaction," listed as P2 in the *Exhibit*. This process has an action verb and an object of the action. It can have an owner, and its quality or performance can be measured. Is this process currently being done? By whom? How often? How well? How well are competitors doing

1 "Strategy and Innovation in the Firm," an unpublished study conducted in 1973 by Charles-Hubert Heyvaert, University of Leuven, Belgium.

Exhibit Turning a mission into an agenda

Charting a project

Business processes / **Critical success factors**

Critical success factor columns:
- Best-of-breed product quality
- New products that satisfy market needs
- Excellent suppliers
- Motivated, skilled workers
- Excellent customer satisfaction
- New business opportunities
- Lowest delivered cost

Business processes	Count	Quality
P1 Research the marketplace	3	C
P2 Measure customer satisfaction	4	D
P3 Advertise products	3	B
P4 Monitor competition	6	D
P5 Measure product quality	5	C
P6 Educate vendors	4	E
P7 Train employees	6	C
P8 Define new product requirements	4	C
P9 Process customer orders	2	B
P10 Develop new products	6	B
P11 Monitor customer complaints	3	D
P12 Negotiate manufacturing designs	5	D
P13 Define future skill needs	3	C
P14 Select and certify vendors	5	C
P15 Promote the company	3	C
P16 Support installed products	3	B
P17 Monitor customer or prospect's business	3	E
P18 Announce new products	3	C

Graphing makes priorities clear

Number of critical success factor impacts

Quality →	E	D	C	B	A	impacts
						7
		P4	P7	P10		6
		P12	P5 P14			5
	P6	P2	P8			4
	P17	P11	P1 P18 P13 P15	P3 P16		3
				P9		2
						1
						0

Quality scale

Zone 1

Zone 2

Zone 3

E Embryonic stage
D Bad
C Fair
B Good
A Excellent

P = business process number

it? Since each team member shares collective responsibility for the affected CSFs, the entire team should be interested in the answers. But only one person owns that process—commitment by all, accountability by one.

"Bill customers" is another example of a business process—and it differs a lot from "invoicing," which is

In ranking objectives, the team looks beyond what it's doing now to new possibilities.

usually the title on the billing-office door. Invoicing is a simple process; bill customers describes a much richer field for disaster. Many functions contribute to billing: sales, field engineering, accounting, legal, distribution, and information services. But the person responsible for the actual invoicing is rarely one who can coordinate all the activities needed to get an accurate, understandable, complete invoice at the right time and at the lowest cost. The invoicing manager isn't likely to have a broad enough view of the business or the power to effect needed change. The result is often customer dissatisfaction, bad cash flow, a lot of arguing and finger pointing, and low morale—in other words, poor competitiveness.

Once identified as an important process, however, billing customers can be assigned to a member of the management team, who will then be responsible for its performance.

Now suppose we have a complete list of important business processes, each of which has an owner. The list is exclusive, since a process has to be important to be there. But it still needs ranking to identify the most critical processes, those whose performance or quality will have the biggest impact on the mission. This is the penultimate stage of our PQM.

First place the processes and the CSFs in random order on a matrix as shown in "Charting a project" in the Exhibit. Then focus on the first critical success factor—in our example, "best-

of-breed product quality"—and ask this question: Which business processes must be performed especially well for us to be confident of achieving this CSF? The object is to single out the processes that have a primary impact on this particular CSF. Many business activities will touch on it, of course; what you're after are the essential ones.

The facilitator fills in a box on the chart for each critical process identified for this CSF. In the Exhibit, for example, our team has listed "measure customer satisfaction," "monitor competition," "measure product quality," and seven other processes for its first CSF. Then the list must pass the sufficiency test. If all these activities are performed well, will the team achieve its first critical goal? If the team answers no, then it must identify what else is needed.

This is usually the stage at which teams begin to be really creative, looking beyond what is already being done and breaking new ground. There's a check, though, because each new process added for sufficiency must also have an owner within the management team. So it has to be important enough to feature on the matrix.

The team then repeats this process for each CSF in turn, being careful to apply the necessary-and-sufficient test before moving on to the next CSF. Then the number of CSFs that each process affects is totaled and placed in the count column on the right-hand side of the matrix.

By now the chart is a valuable document. The management team has agreed on its mission, on the subgoals, or CSFs, required to accomplish the mission, and finally, on the things that must be done to achieve those goals. Moreover, while each CSF is owned collectively by the entire team, each business process is owned by an individual member. Only one more step remains—identifying the most critical processes.

If companies had unlimited resources, each process could have equal attention for resources and management focus. But in practice, of course, managers' time and resources are always limited. So next pinpoint those activities that warrant the most attention.

Clearly, the most important processes are those that affect the most

CSFs. "Monitor competition," for example, affects six of the seven CSFs, so it is a strong candidate for scrutiny. But to get a meaningful ranking for management's attention, we also need to know how well each process is being performed.

In our PQM studies, we use a subjective ranking, which is entered in the quality column on the matrix. A = excellent performance, B = good performance, C = fair performance, D = bad performance, and E = informal or embryonic performance or indicates a process that's not performed at all. It may seem surprising, but we hear very few arguments about process quality. By this stage in the PQM process, the managers are really working as a team.

"Graphing makes priorities clear," the second part of the Exhibit, shows the best way we've found to help the team translate its rankings into an action plan. The quality of each process is plotted horizontally and the number of CSFs the process impacts is plotted vertically. Then the team divides the graph into zones to create groups of processes. We can see immediately that Zone 1 contains the most critical processes. All the processes are important, by definition. But the higher risk (or higher opportunity) processes are found in Zone 1. These activities need the team's closest attention if the company is to improve market share and profitability within two years.

Follow-through

That's the PQM process—one way to conduct what is, in truth, a never-ending journey to zero defects.

But as we said up front, PQM requires follow-through. Decide the nature of the improvement needed, and establish relevant process measurements. Then apply the needed resources for the appropriate improvements.

We cannot stress follow-through enough. The decisions reached by the management team must cascade throughout the organization. And always there are surprises. During one PQM process, it was discovered that not only was the process "define management responsibilities" one of the most critical at that time, it was also agreed that it was just not being done. This is the kind of function that everyone assumes is being done and someone else is doing it. Yet its poor performance (or nonexistence) can be a major inhibitor to success. The CEO immediately accepted ownership of that process and responsibility for its quality improvement.

We recommend revisiting the CSF list about once a year or whenever a significant change has taken place in a team's mission, its makeup, or the marketplace. In a year's time, the mission usually stays the same, but the critical success factors and the most critical processes usually don't. Some of the processes will have moved from Zone 1 to Zone 2; others will be newly critical.

If a company's CSFs remained constant while all of its business processes were being attended to, it would end up with zero-defect processes—and a justified reputation as a highly competitive company. But all kinds of things can alter a company's mission and goals: government, competitors, reorganization, new technology, new opportunities, the marketplace. And when you change the CSFs, you necessarily change the grid.

The next time a new matrix is produced, however, the business should be stronger and more flexible. If PQM has been applied, fewer existing processes will fall in quality category D or C. The average quality of business activities will be higher, and the biggest focus will be on new categories, the E processes, that the new CSFs demand. Eventually, you may even find that all your basic business activities are clustered in category A. Then the only changes a new CSF list will provoke are those responding to a changing environment. Such adaptability is the ultimate goal of PQM.

But does this mean the list of important processes is getting longer and longer and the matrix deeper and deeper? Not necessarily. Over time, what was once a most critical process will become sufficiently stable and well performed to allow its ownership to be delegated. And that's as it should be. ▽

Overcoming group warfare

How should you go about reconciling the differences between groups that need to cooperate but that already have swords drawn?

Robert R. Blake and Jane S. Mouton

The company you run stands on the threshold of success. The competition's new product has serious flaws, and all you need do to take giant strides toward controlling market share is to hit the market with your new product. Nothing stands in your way except, of course, that pesky misunderstanding between the product design group and manufacturing. They just can't seem to get along, and it does look as if you may have to push the start-up date back a little. You realize suddenly that if the battle between the two groups doesn't end, the product may not get to market in time to take advantage of the space your competitor has left.

What should you do? The authors of this article present two very different approaches to resolving conflicts between embattled groups. In one method, a neutral facilitator tries to mediate between the two groups by offering compromises and trying to get each group to see the other's point of view. In the other method, the groups form their own views of what their ideal relationship should be and a neu-

tral administrator helps them go through steps to achieve it. Examining two cases of conflict in detail, the authors show how the two approaches work, discuss the outsider's role in each, and offer guidelines for deciding when one approach is likely to work better than the other.

Robert R. Blake and Jane S. Mouton are directors of Scientific Research, Inc., a consulting firm located in Austin, Texas. They are well-known for their work in organization development, especially for developing the "managerial grid," which they wrote about with Louis B. Barnes and Larry E. Greiner in HBR exactly 20 years ago in the November-December 1964 issue (see "Breakthrough in Organization Development"). This is their first HBR article since then. It is adapted from their book, Solving Costly Organizational Conflicts: Achieving Intergroup Trust, Cooperation, and Teamwork *(Jossey-Bass, 1984).*

While many people worried about the absence of experienced air traffic controllers after the Professional Air Traffic Controllers Organization went on strike in 1981, they also wondered why it was so difficult for the FAA and PATCO to come to terms before the strike was called. Important groups that need to cooperate can often overcome their difficulties and continue working together, but sometimes they can't. Over the years disputants in the transportation and coal industries have had skirmishes that have resulted in open warfare. Even when the battles are not waged so publicly or fiercely, the human and material costs organizations pay can be staggering.

We have identified two strategies for resolving intergroup conflicts, each with variations. What we have come to call the *interpersonal facilitator approach* relies on a neutral person to provide a bridge to help disputing parties find common ground. The facilitator does this by identifying areas of agreement as well as disagreement so that the latter can be reduced and resolution achieved.

In what we call the *interface conflict-solving approach,* disputants deal with each other directly as members of whole groups. A neutral person helps the groups go through a program of steps that aids principal members of both groups to identify and resolve their differences.

Line managers and internal consultants who are respected and neutral may serve as facilitators or administrators of the step program. The person selected should be of a rank comparable to or higher than that of the highest-ranking member in either of the groups in conflict. A neutral of lesser rank is likely to be brushed aside by a higher-ranking member in a group bent on attack. When the conflict is between headquarters and a subsidiary or when top management is involved in both groups, as in a merger, the groups should consider calling in an outsider who will have no stake in the outcome.

In the first approach, the facilitator on occasion becomes involved in the discussions themselves and carries messages and proposals from one side to the other. In the second approach, the spokesperson or administrator is uninvolved in the content of discussions and acts principally as a guide to the process.

These two models are quite different, and any reader who wishes to use one or the other approach needs to understand their pros and cons. In what follows, we present two actual but disguised cases that illuminate the benefits and pitfalls of the two models and show how each works. The first case involves a long-term conflict between central engineering and plant management in a large industrial complex. The second case is a union-management conflict of long standing.

Trouble at the Elco Corporation

In this description of how the interpersonal facilitator approach worked at the Elco Corporation, we present the events chronologically through a month of negotiations.

The story & the players

The president of Elco, Stewart McFadden, had been frustrated for a long time by reports of constant bickering and poor cooperation between central engineering and plant management. Among the many things McFadden told Jim Craig when hiring him as vice president of human resources, was, "This is a nasty situation. I'd like you to take a look at it."

About a month later, when it came up again, Craig said to the president, "I've met several people from both central engineering and plant management, and it looks like quite a one-sided problem to me. The people in central engineering aren't involved that much. They feel this problem is one of those inevitable tensions in organization life, and they are trying to be patient. But the people in plant management are up in arms. They are furious."

"It's hopeless," said McFadden.

"That depends," said Craig, "on whether the problem is one of competence or of communication. If it's the former, yes, it's hopeless. If it's the latter, it's not."

"Competence? No way. They are the cream of the crop—upper 10% of graduating classes, all

of them. So it's not competence. Can you help?" McFadden asked.

"Well, I've been through a lot of hang points with unions, and in principle this situation is no different. They realize I'm a newcomer with no ax to grind. Possibly I can get them together to talk it out. At least it's worth a try."

"Anything," said McFadden. "I'm so sick of it. What do you propose?"

"I'd like to get the principals of both groups together for a day or two to get the facts out on the table. Then we'll see what can be done," said Craig.

"You've got my blessing. I look forward to whatever happens, even if you have to bang a few heads together to get their attention."

Later that week, Craig, Walt Reeves, vice president of engineering, and Jack Lewis, central coordinator of the plant management group, set up the meetings. They agreed that the purpose of the meetings was to study how the groups might cooperate. Reeves wanted Craig to take part in any negotiations as a full partner, speaking for Elco headquarters, and Lewis wanted Craig to mediate the discussions but not to formulate and present substantive proposals.

By offering the services of his office, Craig made it appropriate that he implement his own strategy. He planned for the two groups to meet initially as one large group. Craig saw himself as a facilitator. "My thought was," he reported later, "that both groups would come to know and understand each other better in a constructive atmosphere and that they would trust me to be honest and fair in my role as moderator, mediator, and, if necessary, active negotiator. I also thought that without an established agenda, the main issues would surface."

Accompanying Walt Reeves from central engineering were four of his key personnel. With Jack Lewis from the plant management group were five others—two from the plant in question and three from different plants. Craig himself was joined by other senior personnel, including the human resources advisors assigned to central engineering and to plant management. From time to time, depending on the issue, the group consulted other senior people.

Mutual trust & respect

The first meeting was held in a large room that didn't have a table. To break up a "we-they" seating arrangement and help each person participate according to his or her own convictions rather than follow a party line, Craig placed the chairs at spaced intervals around the room.

Craig, seated near the center, opened the meeting. "As you know, the president has long been concerned about how to get your groups to cooperate. He asked me to see if I could help. This meeting has no agenda beyond what the problem is and how we can solve it. Anyone is free to speak, but to keep things moving forward, I will moderate the discussion. Who'd like to start?"

"I'll tell you the problem," a member from central engineering said. "Each engineering discipline, not to mention emerging new materials and construction techniques, is becoming more complex. Plus we've got rapid changes in requirements from EPA, the Nuclear Regulatory Commission, OSHA, and half a dozen other agencies. The heavy fines for operations that violate requirements are bound to teach us all a lesson we should have learned long ago. On these scores, we've got to keep ourselves risk free. There's no option but to centralize engineering."

"That's not the problem at all," a member of plant management shot back. "We're qualified engineers, every one of us, but we are treated like children who can't be trusted to build a derrick with an erector set. It's demeaning. We manage millions in operating expenses, but we can't spend $100 on an air conditioning duct."

The meeting thereupon broke down into mutual recriminations. Later, trying a new tack, Craig stopped trying to moderate discussion between the two groups and held meetings with the two leaders instead.

From the very beginning, Craig had felt that Walt Reeves and Jack Lewis didn't trust or respect each other, and he thought that if he could get them into an informal setting, things would ease between them. He thought it was important for Reeves and Lewis to know each other better before he brought the two groups together again.

Craig wanted to accentuate the positive. He cautioned Lewis not to overreact when he first heard Reeves's formal statement about central engineering being responsible for 100% of engineering and plant management for 100% of operations.

After the first meeting between Reeves and Lewis, Craig reported that "the meeting did produce a buildup of tensions. Reeves's fixed position in regard to the 100% engineering concept was the primary reason. I already knew this to be entirely unacceptable to Lewis. We didn't make much progress, and another session was scheduled."

At this point Craig was not free to reveal to Lewis what Reeves had told him in confidence. Later Craig said, "I felt Reeves was ready to make immediate, even if minor, modifications," such as recommending an increase in the amount plant managers could authorize for small projects. Craig also knew that Reeves deeply distrusted Lewis's reasons for wanting to do "gut" engineering. He tried to help Reeves appreciate Lewis's motives.

Craig used the same strategy again and again: "When we got under way, I stepped back from the discussions because I wanted them to speak to each other directly. Soon they refrained from talking to me or even attempting to draw me into the conversation. Their talk was full of accusations and counteraccusations. Their faces became flushed. The niceties of diplomatic protocol slipped away. They had almost forgotten I was there, while I just continued taking notes.

"Eventually, the argument bogged down when each began to repeat himself and to ignore the other. By the end they were both talking at once. My attempts to change the subject were futile. As they moved toward the door, I got in front of them to block the way. I urged them not to stop these conversations but to give me another chance to use my influence. I said, 'If you have no confidence in me, then these tensions will remain.'

"Lewis agreed readily. I looked Reeves in the eye, and finally he nodded agreement. They left without speaking to each other. During the 30 or so days this effort took, I spent a lot of time preventing the sessions from being interrupted or terminated and in defending and explaining each of them to the other."

During the next few meetings, Craig took a more active role: "I began acting as a referee and made efforts to put the discussion back on track, occasionally explaining what I thought someone meant when the other person seemed to misinterpret it. After one of these sessions, when they were going back to their offices, Reeves drew me aside and said, 'Look, I don't want to talk to that SOB anymore. If you want to talk to him, you can represent my point of view, but I've had it up to here. Tell me about any progress you make, and I promise to be as constructive as possible in meeting their criticisms of us. I want you to understand the issue is not one of simply dividing engineering up in a 25-75 or a 50-50 way. Just to give them *some* will not solve the problem.' "

With this breakdown, it was no longer possible to bring the two men together to discuss their fixed positions. Craig summarized his feelings at the time this way: "I did not know where to go from there. We had accomplished little, except to name the difficult issues and to recognize the depth of disagreements. There was little or no commonality between them as men, and almost every discussion deteriorated into an unproductive argument that reopened old wounds. The final meeting ended with Reeves and Lewis casting accusations at each other."

Craig now shifted to the go-between strategy, which became the arrangement for the remainder of the month. He proposed that he be an intermediary who formulated positions. "I asked them to give me the opportunity to devise my own compromise proposals and to present my views to both of them."

As he continued to work with various individuals and subgroups within both departments, Craig drafted proposals. Then he met again with each principal to solicit reactions to his ideas. He expressed his intention to each as follows: "This proposal is drafted with the idea that neither side will alter it substantially. I've tried to keep in mind what your group wants and needs. My commitment is to continue to try to represent your interests and to negotiate for you."

Better times

The turning point in Reeves's attitude came after he and Craig had slipped into a win-lose argument about the necessity for central engineering to accept some local engineering on small-plant projects. The hot, unpleasant, and repetitive argument deteriorated until Craig stood up to leave and accused Reeves of being willing to give up peace with plant management because of an unrealistic, rigid position. Craig explained what had happened: "My strong statement made me appear tilted to the plant's perspective and therefore less trustworthy.

"In a final effort to persuade Reeves to continue these negotiations," Craig continued, "I explained the serious consequences of unilaterally breaking off. This action would harm the relationship between central engineering, the personnel function, and the corporate offices. He would be violating his promises to me, and the onus of failure would be on him. Also, I described how headquarters might give up and simply realign assignments by edict."

Reeves saw the seriousness of the situation and realized that even though he wasn't convinced about Lewis's motives or whether concessions would satisfy him, he would have to be less rigid himself.

Ultimately, the relationship between Reeves and Lewis improved, but the division of responsibility for engineering and operations did not change. Three central engineering people now provide liaison engineering. They are located so that they can quickly communicate and troubleshoot as well as provide the plant employees firsthand knowledge of in-plant engineering activities. The liaisons have reduced tensions and improved services in a variety of ways—removing bottlenecks, solving priority issues, and enabling engineering to do more realistic, functional design work. A gray area that allows plant managers to do a few functions in the name of maintenance, which in fact do involve some engineering, now exists between construction and maintenance.

What Craig did

Jim Craig's role during the negotiations shifted often. When pushed to the wall, for instance, on occasion Craig himself would become confrontational. He too became angry and fearful of disastrous consequences if something didn't change. But he kept discussion moving with many intervention techniques:

Building anticipation. Before the meetings Craig told Lewis that Reeves was coming forward with the strongest statement about a 100% to a 0% engineering-operations proposal and the reasons why. He also reported to Reeves that Lewis had no plans beyond trying to work with the situation as it developed.

Controlling discussion. When the going got tough, Craig authorized who should speak to whom and in what order, particularly in the three-way discussions: "I asked Reeves to begin—I then asked Lewis to respond—" and so forth.

Reversing antagonists' roles. Craig helped each participant clarify his understanding of the other's position by asking, "Would you repeat what Reeves just said?" and asking for confirmation: "Is that a fair statement?"

Relieving tension. After Reeves's strong initial presentation, Craig ended the strained silence by saying, "Perhaps it's appropriate now for Jack to accept the position as stated and send a memo around to that effect."

Transmitting information. Craig passed information between the two principals to prevent the process from breaking down: "I conveyed Lewis's position to Reeves by saying, 'Lewis sincerely wants to continue to explore how to make use of plant engineers to do local engineering.' "

Formulating proposals. From the beginning, Craig saw part of his job as drafting possible solutions and proposing them to the principals.

Near the end of the process, as he shuttled back and forth, Craig kept coming up with new ideas. He suggested that central engineering perform a check-and-balance function when the people in the plants did some engineering on their own. Although things do not always run smoothly at Elco, enough of the conflict has been resolved that the disagreements between engineering and plant management are not constant thorns in McFadden's side. Jim Craig continues to shuttle, keeping sparks from becoming fires.

The Hillside strike

Another, though less familiar, approach also works effectively in dealing with conflict between groups. Underlying this approach is the assumption that key leaders and their staffs in whole groups can resolve win-lose conflicts through direct confrontation.

The Hillside facility, a large modern plant serving the paper products industry, was wracked by an unresolved management-union conflict. Like true enemies, both parties had placed themselves in peril to deprive the other of a "victory."

After months of conflict, Jeff O'Hare, plant manager, said, "We are on a collision course toward a contract expiration date only months away. If a positive, productive relationship can't be established, it means another head-on clash. I'm not sure how we'd survive another shutdown as a viable economic entity, but I am sure that when and if we start up again, this plant won't be operated by the same people who are managing and operating it now."

Relationship-building strategy

Hal Floyd, corporate employee relations manager, proposed to Jeff O'Hare that they try solving their problems with the union face to face. Floyd had read about a situation similar to Hillside's in which a union and management had used the interface approach. O'Hare reluctantly agreed.

Floyd explored the possibility with the president of the local union, Rick Keenan, and then both made a joint pitch to the international union representative, Bruce Boyd. Boyd was as pessimistic and doubtful as O'Hare had been but agreed, saying, "I don't want to be accused of causing a strike because I wouldn't respond to a constructive gesture." Since no one in the company or the union could be regarded as neutral, Floyd contracted with an outsider to act as administrator.

Six members of top management and six union officials made up the two groups participating in the meetings. Because its members sat together, each group kept its feeling of solidarity. The administrator, Bob, started the sessions by reviewing goals.

"Our goal for this session is to answer the question, Can these two groups shift from a destructive relationship based on fear and suspicion to a problem-solving relationship based on respect?"

Bob explained the procedure: "As a first step, each group is to meet separately to prepare descriptions of what a sound union-management relationship would be for Hillside. You should record these on large sheets so that we can compare them at a joint session. Each group should select a spokesperson to present its conclusions in the next general session. The spokesperson may be the designated leader, but since O'Hare and Keenan have faced one another so many times in the past, it may be better to ask someone else to give your reports.

"The rest of you should try to avoid taking spontaneous potshots. They don't produce useful insights and often just cause counterattacks, which only make things worse. If you feel something important needs to be said, ask the spokesperson if you may speak. After you finish, you'll identify the similarities and differences in your separately produced descriptions to develop a consolidated model to which both groups can be committed."

He continued: "The next step is to describe the actual conditions that characterize the here and now. You'll later consolidate these into a joint statement of union-management problems at Hillside. You can then identify steps you can take to move away from the antagonistic situation to a cooperative one, with specific plans for follow-up, review, and reevaluation.

"To keep track of what's going on," he said, "I'll be in and out of both rooms, but I don't expect to take an active part. I'll be happy to answer any questions about the procedure."

Visualizing a sound relationship

At first, management seemed unable to concentrate on trying to formulate the ideal sound relationship. The session began with O'Hare questioning Keenan's, the union president's, motivations.

"I wonder what Keenan means by 'recognition'?" said O'Hare, referring to a remark Keenan had made in the joint meeting.

"Special treatment for the union president is my guess," Mike Barret, general foreman, replied. "We know they want to run the plant."

"Give 'em an inch," Allen, head of maintenance, commented supportively, "I've seen it over and over—they'll squeeze this plant dry, even dryer than it already is."

"I can't respect Keenan or his tactics," Sam Kobel, the manufacturing supervisor, said. "Maybe we'd be better off with somebody else as union president. He's a political animal. He doesn't care about the plant or the people. He just wants to move up the union ladder."

Management knew that Keenan wielded considerable influence over the membership. Wayne, the personnel manager, said, "When he person-

Exhibit I	Perceptions of actual relationship at Hillside		
	Management's view	**Union's view**	**Consolidated view**
	We have an adversary relationship. It's we versus they.	Hopelessness; a shutdown is necessary to bring them to their senses. We're ready for the shutdown.	Our adversary relationship promotes readiness for win-lose clashes; a strike is preferable to perpetual humiliation.
	There's mistrust on both sides. Cooperation means consenting to union demands. The union wants comanagement.	Cooperation is one-sided: it means doing what the company says. Hopelessness extends to all workers. Dignity is lost in a guard-prisoner relationship.	Mistrust prevails; cooperation is misinterpreted by the company as compliance and by the union as the company conceding to union demands.
	The union does not give its members a true picture of management's position. Cooperation is lacking in the promotion of efficiency and economy. Use outsiders to resolve internal issues.	Management cares only for production; people be damned. Management destroys people's incentive.	Without measuring the consequences, management concentrates on production, and the union conveys this attitude to its members.
	Management acknowledges low credibility with union members; the union president has low credibility with management.	Management blames past regimes for problems; it sees no deficiency in itself. This plant is our home for life but management's hotel until the next round of promotions.	Leaders have not earned credibility from one another; they do not make the relationship viable as a long-term investment.
	Management is only enforcing existing rules and agreement interpretation but is seen by the union as inflexible and enforcing the contract to the hilt in order to be provocative.	The union can't get its foot in the door to solve the problems.	The union accepts the exercise of initiative as a management prerogative, but management sees the union's offers of help through informal testing before decisions are finalized as comanagement.

ally favors a management proposal, he presents it at the union hall in a straightforward, positive way. If he wants a proposal rejected, he twists it to emphasize negative implications and works to see it defeated."

After venting their anger, which often participants must do before they can take a more constructive approach, management concentrated on identifying the elements of a sound relationship: mutual trust, honesty, effective communication, problem solving, and consistency. The union also started on a negative note before producing its list, which was similar to management's.

Walking toward the general session room, O'Hare overheard Melton, the shop steward, muttering to Keenan, "We'll see this kind of relationship with those buzzards when hell freezes over." Keenan nodded to the apparent truth in Melton's remark.

O'Hare shot back, "It wouldn't take long for us to agree on that, would it?" Bob, the administrator, noted this exchange but said nothing since it was not a part of the formal meetings.

When they convened in a general session to exchange their separately developed statements, the spokespersons chosen by each group made their presentations and questioned one another's meaning. The ideal relationship each proposed seemed so remote from actuality that neither the union nor management viewed it as realistic. Before sending them off to separate meeting places, Bob asked the two

groups to rate each statement in the other's report on a four-point scale:

1   "We agree with the statement as written."

2   "We agree with the statement as rewritten in the following way."

3   "We wish to ask the following questions for further clarification."

4   "We disagree with the statement for the following reasons."

He stated that each group could ask the other's spokesperson to explain the numbers and reasons for the ratings. As the two groups converted the 4's, 3's, and 2's into 1's, reflecting mutual agreement, the statements became part of the consolidated ideal model.

Getting down to brass tacks

The next step in the process is for each group to describe as objectively as possible the present reality. The members of the groups should explore specific factors that have shaped and influenced the relationship as well as the barriers that have stifled progress. At Hillside, management and the union were so preoccupied with the details of recent conflict and perceived injustice that they were anxious to begin describing actual conditions – where the real battle-ground was.

From management's perspective, the union was usurping authority and responsibility, thereby justifying to management its distrust and disrespect.

The union maintained that while it did not want to "run" the plant, it had much to contribute to productivity and efficiency but would withhold effort until members were treated with dignity and respect. *Exhibit I* shows how management and the union viewed the situation.

When each side revealed its view of the situation, both parties seemed stunned at the depth of the cleavage and each other's unhappiness. Recognizing that both groups had agreed to the properties of a sound relationship, management was particularly shaken by the union's conviction that, given prevailing attitudes and behavior, progress was impossible. With the plant's future on the line, along with their careers, the top managers could not reconcile themselves to giving up.

At this point each group was asked to return to its team room to digest the implications of the other's input and to apply the four-point method to the other's perception of the situation.

The tipover

The first shift in position occurred when management began comparing the two descriptions of the actual relationship, particularly the two views of "cooperation," and saw how far apart they were.

"How could two groups work in the same plant, grappling with the same problems, and see each other with such diametrically opposed viewpoints?" O'Hare asked the management group. "What do they mean, 'Cooperation is one-sided – it means doing what the company says'? During the past ten years we've given away more valuable clauses in the name of co-operation and lost more management prerogatives than any other plant in our area of competition."

"As far as I can see," said Kobel, manufacturing supervisor, "when you say 'given away,' literally that is what it's been. We've given away paragraph after paragraph and have gotten nothing in return."

"You can say that again," piped up Allen, maintenance director. "I'm so fed up with some people sitting on their fannies waiting for other people to work. If one could give a helping hand to the other, they could get the job done in half the time. We keep falling further behind."

"I propose," said Bruce Wayne, the personnel manager, "that we give this item a 4. We just flatly disagree with it."

"Hold it, fellas," said Mike Barret. "Let's look at what's been going on in the past few weeks and see how these guys could say such a thing. Any of you heard them say things in meetings you've had with them?"

"Well," said Wayne, "they think we're trying to erode the contract. They think we're putting unreasonable interpretations on various clauses and challenging them to file grievances, to which we say, 'Arbitrate.' They say this is our search-and-destroy technique."

As they continued, discussion kept returning to the first item on the union's list, "hopelessness." The contradiction between what management expected – that is, "militancy" – and what it observed – "despair and hopelessness" – compelled management to reexamine in a candid way how it could have the expectations it did.

"Does Keenan really speak for the membership when he says a strike is inevitable," O'Hare asked, "or is he just trying to shake us up?"

"It doesn't matter," Floyd said. "If he wants a strike, he can convince the people."

"And," said Mike Barret, "they know it."

"What are you hearing," questioned O'Hare, "when you talk outside the plant? Is there talk in the community about a strike? Are spouses unhappy?"

"Keenan has the strike vote in his pocket as far as I can tell," Wayne said. "He can get them riled up. If he doesn't have complete support now, he will by May. He and his cronies can convince the rest that a strike will ultimately be to their advantage. Make no mistake, he's a strong leader."

Surprised by Wayne's report of the union's reaction to what it called "unreasonable interpretations that pushed members to file grievances," O'Hare said, "Maybe we'd better look at ourselves more objectively before pointing any more fingers at them. How have you seen me relating to Keenan and the others?" he asked.

"I see you coming across as strong and hard-nosed," Allen said.

"I think you're open, forthright, and honest to the point of being naive," Floyd observed. "You've had a good reputation as a production and people man. Lately, though, I've seen you change to using force – no discussion, no alternatives, no involvement, pure force."

Wayne added, "In the past I've seen you as open, honest, fair. You listen well and take good advice. But I think you're shifting toward a tough attitude."

"I haven't seen much of a change since you've been here," Barret said. "It seems you've always been direct and aggressive."

Kobel spoke last. "I don't have much to add," he said. "Basically, I agree with what's been said. O'Hare is fair, but firm—to the point of being stubborn, I guess."

Having heard the others, O'Hare summed up his own feelings. "You're right," he said. "I think I'm so determined to turn this thing around, I've become unreasonable. It's much easier to blame our problems on my predecessors or to dump them on Keenan and his cohorts. I thought I'd kept a pretty open mind, but if my attitudes seem rigid to you, they probably seem even more so to them."

The management group then examined each member's attitude toward the union in turn. While individual differences were present, the management team shared similar attitudes, and each recognized how destructive his own actions had become. Allen ended the discussion by saying, "It's clear that we're the ones who are going to have to change."

"It won't be easy," Barret said.

"We've described the kind of relationship we want in the ideal," O'Hare said. "Now we need to decide how to get there."

"Look at what we've done in the past few months," Allen remarked. "We've created the image that we're only out for production—that we care nothing for people. They say we've destroyed the incentive for people to make any input at all."

O'Hare responded, "We don't have any choice but to try for the best relationship we can."

"I feel that's an important first step," Floyd commented. "It isn't going to be easy to turn around years of antagonism, frustration, and disappointment, and your recognition of the hard work involved is a positive sign."

"What about the rest of you?" O'Hare asked. "What do you think?"

"What other option do we have?" Kobel responded, and the others nodded affirmatively.

"What should we do now—communicate our feelings to the union?" asked Allen.

"What else is there to do?" O'Hare said.

"Okay, then, let's prepare a summary of our quandary and present it," Barret suggested.

Management made a list of five statements describing its thoughts and feelings at the time. While management grappled with its own contribution to the current conflict, the union members collected evidence of management's refusal to deal constructively.

"It's no use trying to help," they concluded. "Management sees only what it wants to, and it wants to see us as responsible for all its problems and

Exhibit II	Hillside management's description of its thoughts and feelings
1	We recognize that we have a deep win-lose orientation toward the union.
2	We want to change!
3	We have challenges to meet: to convince the union we want to change, to convince ourselves we have the patience and skill and conviction to change.
4	We're responsible for bringing the rest of management on board.
5	We recognize the risk but want to resist the temptation to revert to a win-lose stance when things get tough.

failures. What it never seems to realize is that for management Hillside is an assignment. Two, three, or four years and they're gone. For us, it's a lifetime. Do we want a plant that's not a profit maker? Nothing could be dumber. But we're not twentieth-century slaves either. We can't work overtime just to cover up their goof-offs. We can go the last mile, but to go beyond destroys our self-respect."

After each group had had the opportunity to formulate a response to the other's assessment of the actual relationship, the two groups met again to share their reactions.

Convergence of convictions

O'Hare went to Bob and said, "Look, I want to speak my own feelings, which the others agree to. Don't worry about my polarizing it."

Bob started the session by saying, "O'Hare has asked to begin by telling about management's self-study description."

O'Hare introduced the group's self-study by saying, "I guess we were concerned and angry with you in the beginning. There was a lot of blaming and finger pointing until we began really to look at ourselves." He then presented the five items shown in *Exhibit II*.

"I'd like your reactions," O'Hare said.

"Speaking for the union," Boyd, the international union representative, replied, "this comes as a total surprise, given the way things have been building up. We're really pleased that you're willing to take these steps. Both sides stand to benefit. We don't want a caucus, but we do want to go back and talk a moment among ourselves."

Leaving the room, Melton commented to Keenan, "I never believed it was possible."

O'Hare, who overheard the remark, said, "I suppose this means 'hell has frozen over'?"

"No," said Keenan, "it doesn't mean that at all."

Exhibit III **Comparison of two approaches to intergroup problem solving**

Issue	Interpersonal facilitator model	Interface conflict-solving model
Composition	Nominal group attendance but top leaders "lead"; top leaders only	Top group plus representatives of major other constituencies who need to be involved
Contact between groups	Primarily with or through facilitator	Through spokespersons in general sessions with group integrity maintained
Facilitator or administrator to deal with	Leaders (and others) usually on a one-to-one basis	All as members of whole groups
Meetings	Exchange of entry positions	Monitoring and validation of design integrity
	Formulation of proposals and counter-proposals on a one-to-one basis by facilitator or intermediary	Ideal and actual relationship modeling on an element-by-element basis; consolidation through the four points
Communication between groups or individuals	Message-passing through facilitator	Exchanges through spokespersons, not necessarily leaders, both oral and written
	Exchange of written positions	
	Proposals made by facilitator	
Initial agenda	Perceived tensions and antagonisms	Thinking through the elements of an ideal sound relationship
Role of expert	Go-between	Procedural design administrator
	Message carrier	Not a spokesperson for other group
	Spokesperson for other group	No content role
	Solution proposer	Not a solution proposer
Tactics for dealing with an impasse	Exerting influence on members of group one to one, starting with easiest to persuade	Direct interchanges through spokespersons
	Use of acceptance and rejection to induce movement	
	Fear-provoking remarks	
Time required	Three days to one week (often longer)	Four to five days; follow-up usually months later

When the groups reconvened, Melton spoke for the union: "Our reaction is that your self-study is a giant step. We recognize it must have been hard for you to face up to the need for such drastic change. We can't tell you how welcome it is. We'll cooperate in any way to bring about the change."

Because both management and the union saw the possibility of pursuing a shared goal, each contributing from the standpoint of what was in the best interest of the plant, the tension underlying the relationship broke. This positive attitude led to a desire to get to specifics. Once the two groups gave up their antagonistic stance, they found that agreement was possible in areas where they had been deadlocked for months. For instance, at one point in the discussion of certain problems, O'Hare and Keenan were looking together at the 77 grievances that had been filed. Keenan commented, "I'm sure we've filed a number of grievances more for their annoyance value than for the merit of the issues involved."

O'Hare quickly responded, "And we've dilly-dallied in answering them and have opted for no action whenever it was legally reasonable to do so."

"We can withdraw those that have annoyance value only, identify the real issues, and clear up the situation," Keenan said.

"You won't get a no from me on that," O'Hare responded.

Smooth sailing

Several years have passed since the day O'Hare and Keenan sat down together to look at the list of grievances. How has the plant changed since the union-management meeting? In the final step of the program, ten union-management task forces grappled with problems or groups of problems. Each brought proposed solutions to the plant manager, who considered the recommendations and either approved or modified them or provided a full and satisfactory explanation for why he could not. The union has not called a strike during this time, and both union and management judge this plant to be tops in problem solving. Before the union and management got together, the plant was eleventh in the financial performance of the company's plants; today it is number one.

Bob's role

The administrator of this five-step program makes many contributions to ensure that the interface conflict-solving approach is effective. This person:

Sets expectations. Bob described the objectives and activities involved in each step of the program.

Establishes ground rules for the general sessions. Bob made sure, for instance, that up to the point where tempers quieted only the spokespersons for each group were to speak.

Determines sequence. Bob established which spokesperson would speak first. This arrangement is preferable to group members volunteering to speak first.

Monitors for candor. The design administrator monitors teams to ensure openness on a within-group basis.

Curbs open expression of hostile attitudes between groups. Bob intervened to let participants who made snide remarks know that they were breaking the ground rules.

Avoids evaluation. Bob didn't evaluate the progress or quality of group efforts, nor did he respond to inquiries regarding content or the issues being discussed.

Introduces procedures to reduce disagreements. When the group reached an impasse, Bob suggested procedures for breaking the deadlock, such as the four-point rating method.

Ensures understanding. When each spokesperson had finished speaking, Bob made sure that the other spokesperson had no further questions and that answers were to the point.

Follows up. After the meetings, Bob helped set follow-up schedules to ensure that the changes were implemented.

Which model should you use?

The interpersonal facilitator model has many adherents. The concept is inherent in the idea of the honest broker and is present when a lawyer seeks an out-of-court settlement between conflicting parties.

Exhibit IV	When to use each model

Use the interpersonal facilitator model when:	Use the interface conflict-solving model when:
Only two people are involved.	Support of group members will strengthen implementation of any change.
Personal chemistry blocks direct discussion between the principals.	Personal chemistry problems are not sufficient to prevent participation.
The leader's agreeing to change has no adverse consequences for his or her acceptability as a leader.	The leader's agreeing to change places his or her leadership in jeopardy with those who are being led.
The leaders know the depth and scope of the problem.	The leaders do not know the depth and scope of the problem.
The change can be implemented on the basis of compliance or without agreement about its soundness.	The change can best be implemented by agreement and understanding of its soundness.
A deadline is near and decisions, even though imperfect, are necessary to prevent a total breakdown.	Sufficient time is available to develop basic solutions.
A multiplicity of views exists in both groups and therefore there is no common point of view or shared feeling.	The interface problem is deeply embedded in the culture of both groups.

In each case the objective is to create a meeting of minds without dictating the terms or the outcome.

In our experience, however, the prospect of success in relieving tensions between adversary groups is much greater when managers use the interface conflict-solving approach rather than the interpersonal facilitator model. While the latter has become a more or less standard approach, it has severe limitations.

In *Exhibit III* we compare the two models in regard to some important factors such as who should comprise the groups and what the expert's role is.

Exhibit IV offers guidelines for judging which approach stands the greatest likelihood of resolving conflicts between opposing parties that impede organizational success.

The facilitator approach tends to be most successful when the outcome produced constitutes a compromise of differences and is a mutually acceptable solution to both parties, neither side feeling it has won or lost. But when membership of two or more groups is involved, that kind of compromise is hard to achieve.

Part of the power of the interface conflict-solving approach comes from the participants' lifting their thinking above the status quo to envision a model of a sound relationship. Doing so, they see the relationship in a different light and recognize the possibility of creating a new relationship rather than merely diminishing the negative aspects of the present one.

A second strength of the problem-solving approach is that it forces members of the same group to confront each other. At Hillside, Wayne challenged O'Hare to look at how management had come to use the contract as a weapon rather than as guidance for cooperation.

The reader may well ask, "Why are participants prepared to risk exposure by being open with each other, particularly when they may place themselves in jeopardy?" In many organizations, smoothly operating interfaces, say between management and the union, are crucial. When the pain it suffers from the frustration of being unable to get the job done is greater than the pain it associates with frankness, then management brings itself to the level of candor essential for focusing on the real issues.

Another compelling motivation is the rationality of problem solving. When people see something that is faulty, they want to set it right. The program of steps focuses attention on the contradictions between the sound solution and existing arrangements. When all those who feel a sense of responsibility for solving the problem see that both parties agree about what the relationship should be, they share a desire to see the problem solved.

Any executive who is involved in a conflict between groups or who is responsible for groups in dispute should seriously consider which of these two models would work in given situations. The more central and serious the issue is to the relationship between the groups, the greater the likelihood of success using the interface conflict-solving approach has. If the issue is not crucial or serious, the greater the likelihood that it can be resolved through third-party facilitation.

Beyond that, managers can always apply the facilitator model should the conflict-solving model fail, but the reverse is less likely to be true. If the facilitator approach fails, key leaders are not likely to want to try another approach, whereas if the conflict-solving model should fail, the leaders themselves may be ready to continue to seek agreement with the help of a facilitator. ▽

The indirect rewards

Conflict...is a theme that has occupied the thinking of man more than any other, save only God and love. In the vast output of discourse on the subject, conflict has been treated in every conceivable way. It has been treated descriptively, as in history and fiction; it has been treated in an aura of moral approval, as in epos; with implicit resignation, as in tragedy; with moral disapproval, as in pacifistic religions. There is a body of knowledge called military science, presumably concerned with strategies of armed conflict. There are innumerable handbooks, which teach how to play specific games of strategy. Psychoanalysts are investigating the genesis of "fight-like" situations within the individual, and social psychologists are doing the same on the level of groups and social classes....

I suspect that the most important result of a systematic and many-sided study of conflict would be the changes which such a study could effect in ourselves, the conscious and unconscious, the willing and unwilling participants in conflicts. Thus, the rewards to be realistically hoped for are the indirect ones, as was the case with the sons who were told to dig for buried treasure in the vineyard. They found no treasure, but they improved the soil.

From
Fights, Games, and Debates
by Anatol Rapoport
(Ann Arbor: University of
Michigan Press, 1960)
pp. 11, 360.
Reprinted with the permission
of the publisher.

HBR Classic

Paul R. Lawrence

How to deal with resistance to change

*The real problem is not technical change
but the human changes that
often accompany technical innovations*

Foreword

This "HBR Classic," one of a series of articles from the past with retrospective commentary, was first published in the May-June 1954 issue of HBR. It has been used and reused by executives and managers ever since; request for reprints, for instance, have continued steadily to this day—evidence that the author's analysis of the problems and of how to deal with them continues to be valid. Mr. Lawrence is still associated with the Harvard Business School, where he is now Wallace Brett Donham Professor of Organizational Behavior.

One of the most baffling and recalcitrant of the problems which business executives face is employee resistance to change. Such resistance may take a number of forms—persistent reduction in output, increase in the number of "quits" and requests for transfer, chronic quarrels, sullen hostility, wildcat or slowdown strikes, and, of course, the expression of a lot of pseudological reasons why the change will not work. Even the more petty forms of this resistance can be troublesome.

All too often when executives encounter resistance to change, they "explain" it by quoting the cliché that "people resist change" and never look further. Yet changes must continually occur in industry. This applies with particular force to the all-important "little" changes that constantly take place—changes in work methods, in routine office procedures, in the location of a machine or a desk, in personnel assignments and job titles.

No one of these changes makes the headlines, but in total they account for much of our increase in productivity. They are not the spectacular once-in-a-lifetime technological revolutions that involve mass layoffs or the obsolescence of traditional skills, but they are vital to business progress.

Does it follow, therefore, that business management is forever saddled with the onerous job of "forcing" change down the throats of resistant people? My answer is *no*. It is the thesis of this article that people do *not* resist technical change as such and that most of the resistance which does occur is unnecessary. I shall discuss these points, among others:

1. A solution which has become increasingly popular for dealing with resistance to change is to get the people involved to "participate" in making the change. But as a practical matter "participation" as a device is not a good way for management to think about the problem. In fact, it may lead to trouble.

2. The key to the problem is to understand the true nature of resistance. Actually, what employees resist is usually not technical change but social change—the change in their human relationships that generally accompanies technical change.

3. Resistance is usually created because of certain blind spots and attitudes which staff special-

ists have as a result of their preoccupation with the technical aspects of new ideas.

4. Management can take concrete steps to deal constructively with these staff attitudes. The steps include emphasizing new standards of performance for staff specialists and encouraging them to think in different ways, as well as making use of the fact that signs of resistance can serve as a practical warning signal in directing and timing technological changes.

5. Top executives can also make their own efforts more effective at meetings of staff and operating groups where change is being discussed. They can do this by shifting their attention from the facts of schedules, technical details, work assignments, and so forth, to what the discussion of these items indicates in regard to developing resistance and receptiveness to change.

Let us begin by taking a look at some research into the nature of resistance to change. There are two studies in particular that I should like to discuss. They highlight contrasting ways of interpreting resistance to change and of coping with it in day-to-day administration.

Is participation enough?

The first study was conducted by Lester Coch and John R.P. French, Jr. in a clothing factory.[1] It deserves special comment because, it seems to me, it is the most systematic study of the phenomenon of resistance to change that has been made in a factory setting. To describe it briefly:

The two researchers worked with four different groups of factory operators who were being paid on a modified piece-rate basis. For each of these four groups a minor change in the work procedure was installed by a different method, and the results were carefully recorded to see what, if any, problems of resistance occurred. The four experimental groups were roughly matched with respect to efficiency ratings and degree of cohesiveness; in each group the proposed change modified the established work procedure to about the same degree.

The work change was introduced to the first group by what the researchers called a "no-participation" method. This small group of op-

erators was called into a room where some staff people told the members that there was a need for a minor methods change in their work procedures. The staff people then explained the change to the operators in detail, and gave them the reasons for the change. The operators were then sent back to the job with instructions to work in accordance with the new method.

The second group of operators was introduced to the work change by a "participation-through-representation" method—a variation of the approach used with the third and fourth groups which turned out to be of little significance.

The third and fourth groups of operators were both introduced to the work change on a "total-participation" basis. All the operators in these groups met with the staff people concerned. The staff people dramatically demonstrated the need for cost reduction. A general agreement was reached that some savings could be effected. The groups then discussed how existing work methods could be improved and unnecessary operations eliminated. When the new work methods were agreed on, all the operators were trained in the new methods, and all were observed by the time-study people for purposes of establishing a new piece rate on the job.

Research findings: The researchers reported a marked contrast between the results achieved by the different methods of introducing this change:

▽ *No-participation group*—The most striking difference was between Group #1, the no-participation group, and Groups #3 and #4, the total-participation groups. The output of Group #1 dropped immediately to about two thirds of its previous output rate. The output rate stayed at about this level throughout the period of 30 days after the change was introduced. The researchers further reported:

"Resistance developed almost immediately after the change occurred. Marked expressions of aggression against management occurred, such as conflict with the methods engineer, . . . hostility toward the supervisor, deliberate restriction of production, and lack of cooperation with the supervisor. There were 17% quits in the first 40 days. Grievances were filed about piece rates;

1. See Lester Coch and John R.P. French, Jr., "Overcoming Resistance to Change," *Human Relations*, Vol. 1, No. 4, 1948, p. 512.

but when the rate was checked, it was found to be a little 'loose.' "

△ *Total-participation groups* — In contrast with this record, Groups #3 and #4 showed a smaller initial drop in output and a very rapid recovery not only to the previous production rate but to a rate that exceeded the previous rate. In these groups there were no signs of hostility toward the staff people or toward the supervisors, and there were no quits during the experimental period.

Appraisal of results: Without going into all the researchers' decisions based on these experiments, it can be fairly stated that they concluded that resistance to methods changes could be overcome by *getting the people involved in the change to participate in making it.*

This was a very useful study, but the results are likely to leave the manager of a factory still bothered by the question, "Where do we go from here?" The trouble centers around that word "participation." It is not a new word. It is seen often in management journals, heard often in management discussions. In fact, the idea that it is a good thing to get employee participation in making changes has become almost axiomatic in management circles.

But participation is not something that can be conjured up or created artificially. You obviously cannot buy it as you would buy a typewriter. You cannot hire industrial engineers and accountants and other staff people who have the ability "to get participation" built into them. It is doubtful how helpful it would be to call in a group of supervisors and staff people and exhort them, "Get in there and start participation."

Participation is a feeling on the part of people, not just the mechanical act of being called in to take part in discussions. Common sense would suggest that people are more likely to respond to the way they are customarily treated—say, as people whose opinions are respected because they themselves are respected for their own worth—rather than by the stratagem of being called to a meeting or being asked some carefully calculated questions. In fact, many

supervisors and staff have had some unhappy experiences with executives who have read about participation and have picked it up as a new psychological gimmick for getting other people to think they "want" to do as they are told—as a sure way to put the sugar coating on a bitter pill.

So there is still the problem of how to get this thing called participation. And, as a matter of fact, the question remains whether participation was the determining factor in the Coch and French experiment or whether there was something of deeper significance underlying it.

Resistance to what?

Now let us take a look at a second series of research findings about resistance to change. . . . While making some research observations in a factory manufacturing electronic products, a colleague and I had an opportunity to observe a number of incidents that for us threw new light on this matter of resistance to change.[2] One incident was particularly illuminating:

☐ We were observing the work of one of the industrial engineers and a production operator who had been assigned to work with the engineer on assembling and testing an experimental product that the engineer was developing. The engineer and the operator were in almost constant daily contact in their work. It was a common occurrence for the engineer to suggest an idea for some modification in a part of the new product; he would then discuss his idea with the operator and ask her to try out the change to see how it worked. It was also a common occurrence for the operator to get an idea as she assembled parts and to pass this idea on to the engineer, who would then consider it and, on occasion, ask the operator to try out the idea and see if it proved useful.

A typical exchange between these two people might run somewhat as follows:

Engineer: "I got to thinking last night about that difficulty we've been having on assembling the x part in the last few days. It occurred to me

that we might get around that trouble if we washed the part in a cleaning solution just prior to assembling it."

Operator: "Well, that sounds to me like it's worth trying."

Engineer: "I'll get you some of the right kind of cleaning solution, and why don't you try doing that with about 50 parts and keep track of what happens."

Operator: "Sure, I'll keep track of it and let you know how it works."

With this episode in mind, let us take a look at a second episode involving the same production operator. One day we noticed another engineer approaching the production operator. We knew that this particular engineer had had no previous contact with the production operator. He had been asked to take a look at one specific problem on the new product because of his special technical qualifications. He had decided to make a change in one of the parts of the product to eliminate the problem, and he had prepared some of these parts using his new method. Here is what happened:

☐ He walked up to the production operator with the new parts in his hand and indicated to her by a gesture that he wanted her to try assembling some units using his new part. The operator picked up one of the parts and proceeded to assemble it. We noticed that she did not handle the part with her usual care. After she had assembled the product, she tested it and it failed to pass inspection. She turned to the new engineer and, with a triumphant air, said, "It doesn't work."

The new engineer indicated that she should try another part. She did so, and again it did not work. She then proceeded to assemble units using all of the new parts that were available. She handled each of them in an unusually rough manner. None

2. For a complete report of the study, see Harriet O. Ronken and Paul R. Lawrence, *Administering Changes: A Case Study of Human Relations in a Factory* (Boston, Division of Research, Harvard Business School, 1952).

of them worked. Again she turned to the engineer and said that the new parts did not work.

The engineer left, and later the operator, with evident satisfaction, commented to the original industrial engineer that the new engineer's idea was just no good.

Social change: What can we learn from these episodes? To begin, it will be useful for our purposes to think of change as having both a technical and a social aspect. The *technical* aspect of the change is the making of a measurable modification in the physical routines of the job. The *social* aspect of the change refers to the way those affected by it think it will alter their established relationships in the organization.

We can clarify this distinction by referring to the two foregoing episodes. In both of them, the technical aspects of the changes introduced were virtually identical: the operator was asked to use a slightly changed part in assembling the finished product. By contrast, the social aspects of the changes were quite different.

In the first episode, the interaction between the industrial engineer and the operator tended to sustain the give-and-take kind of relationship that these two people were accustomed to. The operator was used to being treated as a person with some valuable skills and knowledge and some sense of responsibility about her work; when the engineer approached her with his idea, she felt

she was being dealt with in the usual way. But, in the second episode, the new engineer was introducing not only a technical change but also a change in the operator's customary way of relating herself to others in the organization. By his brusque manner and by his lack of any explanation, he led the operator to fear that her usual work relationships were being changed. And she just did not like the new way she was being treated.

The results of these two episodes were quite different also. In the first episode there were no symptoms of resistance to change, a very good chance that the experimental change would determine fairly whether a cleaning solution would improve product quality, and a willingness on the part of the operator to accept future changes when the industrial engineer suggested them. In the second episode, however, there were signs of resistance to change (the operator's careless handling of parts and her satisfaction in their failure to work), failure to prove whether the modified part was an improvement or not, and indications that the operator would resist any further changes by the engineer. We might summarize the two contrasting patterns of human behavior in the two episodes in graphic form; see *Exhibit I.*

It is apparent from these two patterns that the variable which determines the result is the *social* aspect of the change. In other words, the

operator did not resist the technical change as such but rather the accompanying change in her human relationships.

Confirmation: This conclusion is based on more than one case. Many other cases in our research project substantiate it. Furthermore, we can find confirmation in the research experience of Coch and French, even though they came out with a different interpretation.

Coch and French tell us in their report that the procedure used with Group #1, i.e., the no-participation group, was the usual one in the factory for introducing work changes. And yet they also tell us something about the customary treatment of the operators in their work life. For example, the company's labor relations policies are progressive, the company and the supervisors place a high value on fair and open dealings with the employees, and the employees are encouraged to take up their problems and grievances with management. Also, the operators are accustomed to measuring the success and failure of themselves as operators against the company's standard output figures.

Now compare these *customary* work relationships with the way the Group #1 operators were treated when they were introduced to this particular work change. There is quite a difference. When the management called them into the room for indoctrination, they were treated as if they had no useful knowledge of their own jobs. In effect, they were told that they were not the skilled and efficient operators they had thought they were, that they were doing the job inefficiently, and that some "outsider" (the staff expert) would now tell them how to do it right. How could they construe this experience *except* as a threatening change in their usual working relationship? It is the story of the second episode in our research case all over again. The results were also the same, with signs of resistance, persistently low output, and so on.

Now consider experimental Groups #3 and #4, i.e., the total-participation groups. Coch and French referred

Exhibit I. Two contrasting patterns of human behavior

	Change		
	Technical aspect	Social aspect	Results
Episode 1	Clean part prior to assembly	Sustaining the customary work relationship of operator	1. No resistance 2. Useful technical result 3. Readiness for more change
Episode 2	Use new part in assembly	Threatening the customary work relationship of operator	1. Signs of resistance 2. No useful technical result 3. Lack of readiness for more change

to management's approach in their case as a "new" method of introducing change; but, from the point of view of the *operators* it must not have seemed new at all. It was simply a continuation of the way they were ordinarily dealt with in the course of their regular work. And what happened? The results—reception to change, technical improvement, better performance—were much like those reported in the first episode between the operator and the industrial engineer.

So the research data of Coch and French tend to confirm the conclusion that the nature and size of the technical aspect of the change does not determine the presence or absence of resistance nearly so much as does the social aspect of the change.

Roots of trouble

The significance of these research findings, from management's point of view, is that executives and staff experts need not expertness in using the devices of participation but a real understanding, in depth and detail, of the specific social arrangements that will be sustained or threatened by the change or by the way in which it is introduced.

These observations check with everyday management experience in industry. When we stop to think about it, we know that many changes occur in our factories without a bit of resistance. We know that people who are working closely with one another continually swap ideas about short cuts and minor changes in procedure that are adopted so easily and naturally that we seldom notice them or even think of them as change. The point is that because these people work so closely with one another, they intuitively understand and take account of the existing social arrangements for work and so feel no threat to themselves in such everyday changes.

By contrast, management actions leading to what we commonly label "change" are usually initiated outside the small work group by staff people. These are the changes that we notice and the ones that most frequently bring on symptoms of resistance. By the very nature of their work, most of our staff specialists in industry do not have the intimate contact with operating groups that allows them to acquire an intuitive understanding of the complex social arrangements which their ideas may affect. Neither do our staff specialists always have the day-to-day dealings with operating people that lead them to develop a natural respect for the knowledge and skill of these people. As a result, all too often the men behave in a way that threatens and disrupts the established social relationships. And the tragedy is that so many of these upsets are inadvertent and unnecessary.

Yet industry must have its specialists—not only many kinds of engineering specialists (product, process, maintenance, quality, and safety engineers) but also cost accountants, production schedulers, purchasing agents, and personnel people. Must top management therefore reconcile itself to continual resistance to change, or can it take constructive action to meet the problem?

I believe that our research in various factory situations indicates why resistance to change occurs and what management can do about it. Let us take the "why" factors first.

Self-preoccupation: All too frequently we see staff specialists who bring to their work certain blind spots that get them into trouble when they initiate change with operating people. One such blind spot is "self-preoccupation." The staff specialists get so engrossed in the technology of the change they are interested in promoting that they become wholly oblivious to different kinds of things that may be bothering people. Here are two examples:

☐ In one situation the staff people introduced, with the best of intentions, a technological change which inadvertently deprived a number of skilled operators of much of the satisfaction that they were finding in their work. Among other things, the change meant that, whereas formerly the operators' outputs had been placed beside their work positions where they could be viewed and appreciated by everyone, they were now being carried away immediately from their work positions. The workers did not like this.

The sad part of it was that there was no compelling cost or technical reason why the output could not be placed beside the work position as it had been formerly. But the staff people who had introduced the change were so literal-minded about their ideas that when they heard complaints on the changes from the operators, they could not comprehend what the trouble was. Instead, they began repeating all the logical arguments why the change made sense from a cost standpoint. The final result here was a chronic restriction of output and persistent hostility on the part of the operators.

☐ An industrial engineer undertook to introduce some methods changes in one department with the notion firmly in mind that this assignment presented her with an opportunity to "prove" to higher management the value of her function. She became so preoccupied with her personal desire to make a name for her particular techniques that she failed to pay any attention to some fairly obvious and practical considerations which the operating people were calling to her attention but which did not show up in her time-study techniques. As could be expected, resistance quicky developed to all her ideas, and the only "name" that she finally won for her techniques was a black one.

Obviously, in both of these situations the staff specialists involved did not take into account the social aspects of the change they were introducing. For different reasons they got so preoccupied with the technical aspects of the change that they literally could not see or understand what all the fuss was about.

We may sometimes wish that the validity of the technical aspect of the change were the sole determinant of its acceptability. But the fact remains that the social aspect is what determines the presence or absence of resistance. Just as ignoring this fact is the sure way to trouble, so taking advantage of it can lead to positive results. We must not forget that these same social arrangements which at times seem so bothersome are essential for the performance of work. Without a network of established social relationships a factory would be populated with a collection of people who had no idea of how to work with one another in an organized fashion. By working *with* this network instead of *against* it, management's staff representatives can give new technological ideas a better chance of acceptance.

Know-how of operators overlooked: Another blind spot of many staff specialists is to the strengths as well as to the weaknesses of firsthand production experience. They do not recognize that the production foreman and the production operator are in their own way specialists themselves—specialists in actual experience with production problems. This point should be obvious, but it is amazing how many staff specialists fail to appreciate the fact that even though they themselves may have a superior knowledge of the technology of the production process involved, the foreman or the operators may have a more practical understanding of how to get daily production out of a group of workers and machines.

The experience of the operating people frequently equips them to be of real help to staff specialists on at least two counts: (1) The operating people are often able to spot practical production difficulties in the ideas of the specialists—and iron out those difficulties before it is too late; (2) the operating people are often able to take advantage of their intimate acquaintance with the existing social arrangements for getting work done. If given a chance, they can use this kind of knowledge to help detect those parts of the change that will have undesirable social consequences. The staff experts can then go to work on ways to avoid the trouble area without materially affecting the technical worth of the change.

Further, some staff specialists have yet to learn the truth that, even after the plans for a change have been carefully made, it takes *time* to put the change successfully into produc-

tion use. Time is necessary even though there may be no resistance to the change itself. The operators must develop the skill needed to use new methods and new equipment efficiently; there are always bugs to be taken out of a new method or piece of equipment even with the best of engineering. When staff people begin to lose patience with the amount of time that these steps take, the workers will begin to feel that they are being pushed; *this* amounts to a change in their customary work relationships, and resistance will start building up where there was none before.

The situation is aggravated if the staff specialist mistakenly accuses the operators of resisting the idea of the change, for there are few things that irritate people more than to be blamed for resisting change when actually they are doing their best to learn a difficult new procedure.

Management action

Many of the problems of resistance to change arise around certain kinds of *attitudes* that staff people are liable to develop about their jobs and their own ideas for introducing change. Fortunately, management can influence these attitudes and thus deal with the problems at their source.

Broadening staff interests: It is fairly common for staff members to work so hard on an idea for change that they come to identify themselves with it. This is fine for the organization when the staff person is working on the idea alone or with close colleagues; the idea becomes "his baby," and the company benefits from this complete devotion to work.

But when, for example, a staff member goes to some group of operating people to introduce a change, his very identification with his ideas tends to make him unreceptive to any suggestions for modification. He just does not feel like letting anyone else tamper with his pet ideas. It is easy to see, of course, how this attitude is interpreted by the operating people as a lack of respect for their suggestions.

This problem of staff peoples' extreme identification with their work is one which, to some extent, can

only be cured by time. But here are four suggestions for speeding up the process:

1. Managers can often, with wise timing, encourage the staff's interest in a different project that is just starting.

2. Managers can also, by "coaching" as well as by example, prod the staff people to develop a healthier respect for the contributions they can receive from operating people; success in this area would, of course, virtually solve the problem.

3. It also helps if staff people can be guided to recognize that the satisfaction they derive from being productive and creative is the same satisfaction they deny the operating people by resisting them. Experience shows that staff people can sometimes be stimulated by the thought of finding satisfaction in sharing with others in the organization the pleasures of being creative.

4. Sometimes, too, staff people can be led to see that winning acceptance of their ideas through better understanding and handling of human beings is just as challenging and rewarding as giving birth to an idea.

Using understandable terms: One of the problems that must be overcome arises from the fact that most staff people are likely to have the attitude that the reasons why they are recommending any given change may be so complicated and specialized that it is impossible to explain them to operating people. It may be true that the operating people would find it next to impossible to understand some of the staff specialists' analytical techniques, but this does not keep them from coming to the conclusion that the staff specialists are trying to razzle-dazzle them with tricky figures and formulas—insulting their intelligence—if they do not strive to their utmost to translate their ideas into terms understandable to the operators. The following case illustrates the importance of this point:

□ A staff specialist was temporarily successful in "selling" a change based on a complicated mathematical formula to a foreman who really did not understand it. The whole thing backfired, however, when the foreman tried to sell it to his operating people. They asked him a couple of sharp questions that he could not answer. His embarrassment about this led him to resent and resist the change so much that eventually the whole proposition fell through. This was unfortunate in terms not only of human relations but also of technological progress in the plant.

There are some very good reasons, both technical and social, why staff people should be interested in working with the operating people until their recommendations make "sense." (This does not mean the the operating people need to understand the recommendations in quite the same way or in the same detail that the staff people do, but that they should be able to visualize the recommendations in terms of their job experiences.) Failure of the staff person to provide an adequate explanation is likely to mean that a job the operators had formerly performed with understanding and satisfaction will now be performed without understanding and with less satisfaction.

This loss of satisfaction not only concerns the individual involved but also is significant from the standpoint of the company that is trying to get maximum productivity from the operating people. People who do not have a feeling of comprehension of what they are doing are denied the opportunity to exercise that uniquely human ability—the ability to use informed and intelligent judgment on what they do. If the staff person leaves the operating people with a sense of confusion, they will also be left unhappy and less productive.

Top line and staff executives responsible for the operation should make it a point, therefore, to know how the staff person goes about installing a change. They can do this by asking discerning questions about staff reports, listening closely to reports of employee reaction, and, if they have the opportunity, actually watching the staff specialist at work. At times they may have to take such drastic action as insisting that the time of installation of a proposed change be postponed until the operators are ready for it. But, for the most part, straight-forward discussions with the staff specialist evaluating that person's approach should help the staffer over a period of time, to learn what is expected in relationships with operating personnel.

New look at resistance: Another attitude that gets staff people into trouble is the *expectation* that all the people involved will resist the change. It is curious but true that the staff person who goes into a job with the conviction that people are going to resist any new idea with blind stubbornness is likely to find them responding just the way the staff specialist thinks they will. The process is clear: whenever the people who are supposed to buy new ideas are treated as if they were bullheaded, the way they are used to being treated changes; and they *will* be bullheaded in resisting *that* change!

I think that staff people—and management in general—will do better to look at it this way: When resistance *does* appear, it should not be thought of as something to be *overcome.* Instead, it can best be thought of as a useful red flag—a signal that something is going wrong. To use a rough analogy, signs of resistance in a social organization are useful in the same way that pain is useful to the body as a signal that some bodily functions are getting out of adjustment.

The resistance, like the pain, does not tell what is wrong but only that something *is* wrong. And it makes no more sense to try to overcome such resistance than it does to take a pain killer without diagnosing the bodily ailment. Therefore, when resistance appears, it is time to listen carefully to find out what the trouble is. What is needed is not a long harangue on the logics of the new recommendations but a careful exploration of the difficulty.

It may happen that the problem is some technical imperfection in the change that can be readily corrected. More than likely, it will turn out that the change is threatening and upsetting some of the established social arrangements for doing work. Whether the trouble is easy or difficult to correct, management will at least know what it is dealing with.

New job definition: Finally, some staff specialists get themselves in trouble because they assume they have the answer in the thought that people will accept a change when they have participated in making it. For example:

☐ In one plant we visited, an engineer confided to us (obviously because we, as researchers on human relations, were interested in psychological gimmicks!) that she was going to put across a proposed production layout change of hers by inserting in it a rather obvious error, which others could then suggest should be corrected. We attended the meeting where this stunt was performed, and superficially it worked. Somebody caught the error, proposed that it be corrected, and our engineer immediately "bought" the suggestion as a very worthwhile one and made the change. The group then seemed to "buy" his entire layout proposal.

It looked like an effective technique—oh, so easy—until later, when we became better acquainted with the people in the plant. Then we found out that many of the engineer's colleagues considered her a phony and did not trust her. The resistance they put up to her ideas was very subtle, yet even more real and difficult for management to deal with.

Participation will never work so long as it is treated as a device to get other people to do what you want them to. Real participation is based on respect. And respect is not acquired by just trying; it is acquired when the staff people face the reality that they need the contributions of the operating people.

If staff people define their jobs as not just generating ideas but also getting those ideas into practical operation, they will recognize their real dependence on the contributions of the operating people. They will ask the operators for ideas and suggestions, not in a backhanded way to get compliance, but in a straightforward way to get some good ideas and avoid some unnecessary mistakes. By this process staff people will be treating the operating people in such a way that their behavior will not be perceived as a threat to customary work relationships. It will be possible to discuss, and accept or reject, the ideas on their own merit.

The staff specialist who looks at the process of introducing change and at resistance to change in the manner outlined in the preceding pages may not be hailed as a genius, but can be counted on in installing a steady flow of technical changes that will cut costs and improve quality without upsetting the organization.

Role of the administrator

Now what about the way top executives go about their *own* jobs as they involve the introduction of change and problems of resistance?

One of the most important things an executive can do, of course, is to deal with staff people in much the same way that the staff members should deal with the operators. An executive must realize that staff people resist social change, too. (This means, among other things, that par-

ticular rules should not be prescribed to staff on the basis of this article!)

But most important, I think, is the way the administrators conceive of their job in coordinating the work of the different staff and line groups involved in a change. Does an administrator think of these duties *primarily* as checking up, delegating and following through, applying pressure when performance fails to measure up? Or does the executive think of them *primarily* as facilitating communication and understanding between people with different points of view—for example, between a staff engineering group and a production group who do not see eye to eye on a change they are both involved in? An analysis of management's actual experience—or, at least, that part of it which has been covered by our research—points to the latter as the more effective concept of administration.

I do not mean that executives should spend their time with the different people concerned discussing the

human problems of change as such. They *should* discuss schedules, technical details, work assignments, and so forth. But they should also be watching closely for the messages that are passing back and forth as people discuss these topics. Executives will find that people—themselves as well as others—are always implicitly asking and making answers to questions like: "How will she accept criticism?" "How much can I afford to tell him?" "Does she really get my point?" "Is he playing games?" The answers to such questions determine the degree of candor and the amount of understanding between the people involved.

When administrators concern themselves with these problems and acts to facilitate understanding, there will be less logrolling and more sense of common purpose, fewer words and better understanding, less anxiety and more acceptance of criticism, less griping and more attention to specific problems—in short, better performance in putting new ideas for technological change into effect.

Readers of this article may be interested in the following other *HBR Classics:*

Business Leadership and a Creative Society, by Abram T. Collier
January-February 1968, No. 68103

The Foreman: Master and Victim of Double Talk, by
F. J. Roethlisberger
September-October 1965, No. 65511

How to Choose a Leadership Pattern, by Robert Tannenbaum and
Warren H. Schmidt
May-June 1973, No. 73311

Marketing Myopia, by Theodore Levitt
September-October 1975, No. 75507

Pricing Policies for New Products, by Joel Dean
November-December 1976, No. 76604

Problems of a New Executive, by Edmund P. Learned
July-August 1966, No. 66407

Skills of an Effective Administrator, by Robert L. Katz
September-October 1974, No. 74509

'*Skyhooks*,' by O.A. Ohmann
January-February 1970, No. 70106

An Uneasy Look at Performance Appraisal, by Douglas McGregor
September-October 1972, No. 72507

Managing your boss

*A compatible relationship
with your superior is
essential to being
effective in your job*

John J. Gabarro and John P. Kotter

Good managers recognize that a relationship with a boss involves mutual dependence and that, if it is not managed well, they cannot be effective in their jobs. They also recognize that the boss-subordinate relationship is not like the one between a parent and a child, in that the burden for managing the relationship should not and cannot fall entirely on the boss. Bosses are only human; their wisdom and maturity are not always greater than their subordinates'. Effective managers see managing the relationship with the boss as part of their job. As a result, they take time and energy to develop a relationship that is consonant with both persons' styles and assets and that meets the most critical needs of each.

Mr. Gabarro is professor of organizational behavior at the Harvard Business School. His main area of research is how executives build effective working relationships. His most recent publication is *Interpersonal Behavior* (Englewood Cliffs, N.J.: Prentice-Hall, 1978), which he coauthored with Anthony G. Athos. Mr. Kotter is associate professor of organizational behavior at the Harvard Business School. This is his third article in HBR, the most recent being "Choosing Strategies for Change," March-April 1979, coauthored by Leonard A. Schlesinger.

Drawings by Arnie Levin.

Reprint number 80104

To many the phrase *managing your boss* may sound unusual or suspicious. Because of the traditional top-down emphasis in organizations, it is not obvious why you need to manage relationships upward—unless, of course, you would do so for personal or political reasons. But in using the expression *managing your boss*, we are not referring to political maneuvering or apple polishing. Rather, we are using the term to mean the process of consciously working with your superior to obtain the best possible results for you, your boss, and the company.

Recent studies suggest that effective managers take time and effort to manage not only relationships with their subordinates but also those with their bosses.[1] These studies show as well that this aspect of management, essential though it is to survival and advancement, is sometimes ignored by otherwise talented and aggressive managers. Indeed, some managers who actively and effectively supervise subordinates, products, markets, and technologies, nevertheless assume an almost passively reactive stance vis-à-vis their bosses. Such a stance practically always hurts these managers and their companies.

If you doubt the importance of managing your relationship with your boss or how difficult it is to do so effectively, consider for a moment the following sad but telling story:

Frank Gibbons was an acknowledged manufacturing genius in his industry and, by any profitability standard, a very effective executive. In 1973, his

---

1. See, for example, John J. Gabarro, "Socialization at the Top: How CEOs and Their Subordinates Develop Interpersonal Contracts," *Organizational Dynamics*, Winter 1979; and John P. Kotter, *Power in Management*, AMACOM, 1979.

strengths propelled him into the position of vice president of manufacturing for the second largest and most profitable company in its industry. Gibbons was not, however, a good manager of people. He knew this, as did others in his company and his industry. Recognizing this weakness, the president made sure that those who reported to Gibbons were good at working with people and could compensate for his limitations. The arrangement worked well.

In 1975, Philip Bonnevie was promoted into a position reporting to Gibbons. In keeping with the previous pattern, the president selected Bonnevie because he had an excellent track record and a reputation for being good with people. In making that selection, however, the president neglected to notice that, in his rapid rise through the organization, Bonnevie himself had never reported to anyone who was poor at managing subordinates. Bonnevie had always had good-to-excellent bosses. He had never been forced to manage a relationship with a difficult boss. In retrospect, Bonnevie admits he had never thought that managing his boss was a part of his job.

Fourteen months after he started working for Gibbons, Bonnevie was fired. During that same quarter, the company reported a net loss for the first time in seven years. Many of those who were close to these events say that they don't really understand what happened. This much is known, however: while the company was bringing out a major new product—a process that required its sales, engineering, and manufacturing groups to coordinate their decisions very carefully—a whole series of misunderstandings and bad feelings developed between Gibbons and Bonnevie.

For example, Bonnevie claims Gibbons was aware of and had accepted Bonnevie's decision to use a new type of machinery to make the new product; Gibbons swears he did not. Furthermore, Gibbons claims he made it clear to Bonnevie that introduction of the product was too important to the company in the short run to take any major risks.

As a result of such misunderstandings, planning went awry: a new manufacturing plant was built that could not produce the new product designed by engineering, in the volume desired by sales, at a cost agreed on by the executive committee. Gibbons blamed Bonnevie for the mistake. Bonnevie blamed Gibbons.

Of course, one could argue that the problem here was caused by Gibbons's inability to manage his subordinates. But one can make just as strong a case that the problem was related to Bonnevie's inability to manage his boss. Remember, Gibbons was

not having difficulty with any other subordinates. Moreover, given the personal price paid by Bonnevie (being fired and having his reputation within the industry severely tarnished), there was little consolation in saying the problem was that Gibbons was poor at managing subordinates. Everyone already knew that.

We believe that the situation could have turned out differently had Bonnevie been more adept at understanding Gibbons and at managing his relationship with him. In this case, an inability to manage upward was unusually costly. The company lost $2 to $5 million, and Bonnevie's career was, at least temporarily, disrupted. Many less costly cases like this probably occur regularly in all major corporations, and the cumulative effect can be very destructive.

Misreading the boss-subordinate relationship

People often dismiss stories like the one we just related as being merely cases of personality conflict. Because two people can on occasion be psychologically or temperamentally incapable of working together, this can be an apt description. But more often, we have found, a personality conflict is only a part of the problem—sometimes a very small part.

Bonnevie did not just have a different personality from Gibbons, he also made or had unrealistic assumptions and expectations about the very nature of boss-subordinate relationships. Specifically, he did not recognize that his relationship to Gibbons involved *mutual dependence* between two *fallible* human beings. Failing to recognize this, a manager typically either avoids trying to manage his or her relationship with a boss or manages it ineffectively.

Some people behave as if their bosses were not very dependent on them. They fail to see how much the boss needs their help and cooperation to do his or her job effectively. These people refuse to acknowledge that the boss can be severely hurt by their actions and needs cooperation, dependability, and honesty from them.

Some see themselves as not very dependent on their bosses. They gloss over how much help and information they need from the boss in order to perform their own jobs well. This superficial view is particularly damaging when a manager's job and decisions affect other parts of the organization, as

was the case in Bonnevie's situation. A manager's immediate boss can play a critical role in linking the manager to the rest of the organization, in making sure the manager's priorities are consistent with organizational needs, and in securing the resources the manager needs to perform well. Yet some managers need to see themselves as practically self-sufficient, as not needing the critical information and resources a boss can supply.

Many managers, like Bonnevie, assume that the boss will magically know what information or help their subordinates need and provide it to them. Certainly, some bosses do an excellent job of caring for their subordinates in this way, but for a manager to expect that from all bosses is dangerously unrealistic. A more reasonable expectation for managers to have is that modest help will be forthcoming. After all, bosses are only human. Most really effective managers accept this fact and assume primary responsibility for their own careers and development. They make a point of seeking the information and help they need to do a job instead of waiting for their bosses to provide it.

In light of the foregoing, it seems to us that managing a situation of mutual dependence among fallible human beings requires the following:

> That you have a good understanding of the other person and yourself, especially regarding strengths, weaknesses, work styles, and needs.

> That you use this information to develop and manage a healthy working relationship—one which is compatible with both persons' work styles and assets, is characterized by mutual expectations, and meets the most critical needs of the other person. And that is essentially what we have found highly effective managers doing.

Understanding the boss & yourself

Managing your boss requires that you gain an understanding of both the boss and his context as well as your own situation and needs. All managers do this to some degree, but many are not thorough enough.

The boss's world

At a minimum, you need to appreciate your boss's goals and pressures, his or her strengths and weaknesses. What are your boss's organizational and personal objectives, and what are the pressures on him, especially those from his boss and others at his level? What are your boss's long suits and blind spots? What is his or her preferred style of working? Does he or she like to get information through memos, formal meetings, or phone calls? Does your boss thrive on conflict or try to minimize it?

Without this information, a manager is flying blind when dealing with his boss, and unnecessary conflicts, misunderstandings, and problems are inevitable.

Goals & pressures

In one situation we studied, a top-notch marketing manager with a superior performance record was hired into a company as a vice president "to straighten out the marketing and sales problems." The company, which was having financial difficulties, had been recently acquired by a larger corporation. The president was eager to turn it around and gave the new marketing vice president free rein—at least initially. Based on his previous experience, the new vice president correctly diagnosed that greater market share was needed and that strong product management was required to bring that about. As a result, he made a number of pricing decisions aimed at increasing high-volume business.

When margins declined and the financial situation did not improve, however, the president increased pressure on the new vice president. Believing that the situation would eventually correct itself as the company gained back market share, the vice president resisted the pressure.

When by the second quarter margins and profits had still failed to improve, the president took direct control over all pricing decisions and put all items on a set level of margin, regardless of volume. The new vice president began to find himself shut out by the president, and their relationship deteriorated. In fact, the vice president found the president's behavior bizarre. Unfortunately, the president's new pricing scheme also failed to increase margins, and by the fourth quarter both the president and the vice president were fired.

What the new vice president had not known until it was too late was that improving marketing and sales had been only *one* of the president's goals. His most immediate goal had been to make the company more profitable—quickly.

Nor had the new vice president known that his boss was invested in this short-term priority for personal as well as business reasons. The president had been a strong advocate of the acquisition with-

in the parent company, and his personal credibility was at stake.

The vice president made three basic errors. He took information supplied to him at face value, he made assumptions in areas where he had no information, and—most damaging—he never actively tried to clarify what his boss's objectives were. As a result, he ended up taking actions that were actually at odds with the president's priorities and objectives.

Managers who work effectively with their bosses do not behave this way. They seek out information about the boss's goals and problems and pressures. They are alert for opportunities to question the boss and others around him to test their assumptions. They pay attention to clues in the boss's behavior. Although it is imperative they do this when they begin working with a new boss, effective managers also do this on an ongoing basis because they recognize that priorities and concerns change.

Strengths, weaknesses & work style
Being sensitive to a boss's work style can be crucial, especially when the boss is new. For example, a new president who was organized and formal in his approach replaced a man who was informal and intuitive. The new president worked best when he had written reports. He also preferred formal meetings with set agendas.

One of his division managers realized this need and worked with the new president to identify the kinds and frequency of information and reports the president wanted. This manager also made a point of sending background information and brief agendas for their discussions. He found that with this type of preparation their meetings were very useful. Moreover, he found that with adequate preparation his new boss was even more effective at brainstorming problems than his more informal and intuitive predecessor had been.

In contrast, another division manager never fully understood how the new boss's work style differed from that of his predecessor. To the degree that he did sense it, he experienced it as too much control. As a result, he seldom sent the new president the background information he needed, and the president never felt fully prepared for meetings with the manager. In fact, the president spent much of his time when they met trying to get information that he felt he should have had before his arrival. The boss experienced these meetings as frustrating and inefficient, and the subordinate often found himself thrown off guard by the questions that the president asked. Ultimately, this division manager resigned.

The difference between the two division managers just described was not so much one of ability or even adaptability. Rather, the difference was that one of the men was more sensitive to his boss's work style than the other and to the implications of his boss's needs.

You & your needs

The boss is only one-half of the relationship. You are the other half, as well as the part over which you have more direct control. Developing an effective working relationship requires, then, that you know your own needs, strengths and weaknesses, and personal style.

Your own style
You are not going to change either your basic personality structure or that of your boss. But you can become aware of what it is about you that impedes or facilitates working with your boss and, with that awareness, take actions that make the relationship more effective.

For example, in one case we observed, a manager and his superior ran into problems whenever they disagreed. The boss's typical response was to harden his position and overstate it. The manager's reaction was then to raise the ante and intensify the forcefulness of his argument. In doing this, he channeled his anger into sharpening his attacks on the logical fallacies in his boss's assumptions. His boss in turn would become even more adamant about holding his original position. Predictably, this escalating cycle resulted in the subordinate avoiding whenever possible any topic of potential conflict with his boss.

In discussing this problem with his peers, the manager discovered that his reaction to the boss was typical of how he generally reacted to counterarguments—but with a difference. His response would overwhelm his peers, but not his boss. Because his attempts to discuss this problem with his boss were unsuccessful, he concluded that the only way to change the situation was to deal with his own instinctive reactions. Whenever the two reached an impasse, he would check his own impatience and suggest that they break up and think about it before getting together again. Usually when they renewed their discussion, they had digested their differences and were more able to work them through.

Gaining this level of self-awareness and acting on it are difficult but not impossible. For example, by reflecting over his past experiences, a young manager learned that he was not very good at dealing with difficult and emotional issues where people were involved. Because he disliked those issues and realized that his instinctive responses to them were seldom very good, he developed a habit of touching base with his boss whenever such a problem arose. Their discussions always surfaced ideas and approaches the manager had not considered. In many cases, they also identified specific actions the boss could take to help.

Dependence on authority figures

Although a superior-subordinate relationship is one of mutual dependence, it is also one in which the subordinate is typically more dependent on the boss than the other way around. This dependence inevitably results in the subordinate feeling a certain degree of frustration, sometimes anger, when his actions or options are constrained by his boss's decisions. This is a normal part of life and occurs in the best of relationships. The way in which a manager handles these frustrations largely depends on his or her predisposition toward dependence on authority figures.

Some people's instinctive reaction under these circumstances is to resent the boss's authority and to rebel against the boss's decisions. Sometimes a person will escalate a conflict beyond what is appropriate. Seeing the boss almost as an institutional enemy, this type of manager will often, without being conscious of it, fight with the boss just for the sake of fighting. His reactions to being constrained are usually strong and sometimes impulsive. He sees the boss as someone who, by virtue of his role, is a hindrance to progress, an obstacle to be circumvented or at best tolerated.

Psychologists call this pattern of reactions counterdependent behavior. Although a counterdependent person is difficult for most superiors to manage and usually has a history of strained relationships with superiors, this sort of manager is apt to have even more trouble with a boss who tends to be directive or authoritarian. When the manager acts on his or her negative feelings, often in subtle and nonverbal ways, the boss sometimes *does* become the enemy. Sensing the subordinate's latent hostility, the boss will lose trust in the subordinate or his judgment and behave less openly.

Paradoxically, a manager with this type of predisposition is often a good manager of his own people. He will often go out of his way to get support for them and will not hesitate to go to bat for them.

At the other extreme are managers who swallow their anger and behave in a very compliant fashion when the boss makes what they know to be a poor decision. These managers will agree with the boss even when a disagreement might be welcome or when the boss would easily alter his decision if given more information. Because they bear no relationship to the specific situation at hand, their responses are as much an overreaction as those of counterdependent managers. Instead of seeing the boss as an enemy, these people deny their anger—the other extreme—and tend to see the boss as if he or she were an all-wise parent who should know best, should take responsibility for their careers, train them in all they need to know, and protect them from overly ambitious peers.

Both counterdependence and overdependence lead managers to hold unrealistic views of what a boss is. Both views ignore that most bosses, like everyone else, are imperfect and fallible. They don't have unlimited time, encyclopedic knowledge, or extrasensory perception; nor are they evil enemies. They have their own pressures and concerns that are sometimes at odds with the wishes of the subordinate—and often for good reason.

Altering predispositions toward authority, especially at the extremes, is almost impossible without intensive psychotherapy (psychoanalytic theory and research suggest that such predispositions are deeply rooted in a person's personality and upbringing). However, an awareness of these extremes and the range between them can be very useful in understanding where your own predispositions fall and what the implications are for how you tend to behave in relation to your boss.

If you believe, on the one hand, that you have some tendencies toward counterdependence, you can understand and even predict what your reactions and overreactions are likely to be. If, on the other hand, you believe you have some tendencies toward overdependence, you might question the extent to which your overcompliance or inability to confront real differences may be making both you and your boss less effective.

Developing & managing the relationship

With a clear understanding of both your boss and yourself, you can—usually—establish a way of working together that fits both of you, that is characterized by unambiguous mutual expectations, and that helps both of you to be more productive and effec-

tive. We have already outlined a few things such a relationship consists of, which are itemized in the *Exhibit*, and here are a few more.

Compatible work styles

Above all else, a good working relationship with a boss accommodates differences in work style. For example, in one situation we studied, a manager (who had a relatively good relationship with his superior) realized that during meetings his boss would often become inattentive and sometimes brusque. The subordinate's own style tended to be discursive and exploratory. He would often digress from the topic at hand to deal with background factors, alternative approaches, and so forth. His boss, instead, preferred to discuss problems with a minimum of background detail and became impatient and distracted whenever his subordinate digressed from the immediate issue.

Recognizing this difference in style, the manager became terser and more direct during meetings with his boss. To help himself do this, before meetings with the boss he would develop brief agendas that he used as a guide. Whenever he felt that a digression was needed, he explained why. This small shift in his own style made these meetings more effective and far less frustrating for them both.

Subordinates can adjust their styles in response to their bosses' preferred method for receiving information. Peter Drucker divides bosses into "listeners" and "readers." Some bosses like to get information in report form so that they can read and study it. Others work better with information and reports presented in person so that they can ask questions. As Drucker points out, the implications are obvious. If your boss is a listener, you brief him in person, *then* follow it up with a memo. If your boss is a reader, you cover important items or proposals in a memo or report, *then* discuss them with him.

Other adjustments can be made according to a boss's decision-making style. Some bosses prefer to be involved in decisions and problems as they arise. These are high-involvement managers who like to keep their hands on the pulse of the operation. Usually their needs (and your own) are best satisfied if you touch base with them on an ad hoc basis. A boss who has a need to be involved will become involved one way or another, so there are advantages to including him at your initiative. Other bosses prefer to delegate—they don't want to be involved. They expect you to come to them with major problems and inform them of important changes.

Creating a compatible relationship also involves drawing on each other's strengths and making up for each other's weaknesses. Because he knew that his boss—the vice president of engineering—was not very good at monitoring his employees' problems, one manager we studied made a point of doing it himself. The stakes were high: the engineers and technicians were all union members, the company worked on a customer-contract basis, and the company had recently experienced a serious strike.

The manager worked closely with his boss, the scheduling department, and the personnel office to ensure that potential problems were avoided. He also developed an informal arrangement through which his boss would review with him any proposed changes in personnel or assignment policies before taking action. The boss valued his advice and credited his subordinate for improving both the performance of the division and the labor-management climate.

Mutual expectations

The subordinate who passively assumes that he or she knows what the boss expects is in for trouble. Of course, some superiors will spell out their expectations very explicitly and in great detail. But most do not. And although many corporations have systems that provide a basis for communicating expectations (such as formal planning processes, career planning reviews, and performance appraisal reviews), these systems never work perfectly. Also, between these formal reviews expectations invariably change.

Ultimately, the burden falls on the subordinate to find out what the boss's expectations are. These expectations can be both broad (regarding, for example, what kinds of problems the boss wishes to be informed about and when) as well as very specific (regarding such things as when a particular project should be completed and what kinds of information the boss needs in the interim).

Getting a boss who tends to be vague or nonexplicit to express his expectations can be difficult. But effective managers find ways to get that information. Some will draft a detailed memo covering key aspects of their work and then send it to their bosses for approval. They then follow this up with a face-to-face discussion in which they go over each item in the memo. This discussion often surfaces virtually all of the boss's relevant expectations.

Exhibit
Managing the relationship with your boss

Make sure you understand your boss and his context, including:

His goals and objectives

The pressures on him

His strengths, weaknesses, blind spots

His preferred work style

Assess yourself and your needs, including:

Your own strengths and weaknesses

Your personal style

Your predisposition toward dependence on authority figures

Develop and maintain a relationship that:

Fits both your needs and styles

Is characterized by mutual expectations

Keeps your boss informed

Is based on dependability and honesty

Selectively uses your boss's time and resources

Other effective managers will deal with an inexplicit boss by initiating an ongoing series of informal discussions about "good management" and "our objectives." Still others find useful information more indirectly through those who used to work for the boss and through the formal planning systems in which the boss makes commitments to his superior. Which approach you choose, of course, should depend on your understanding of your boss's style.

Developing a workable set of mutual expectations also requires that you communicate your own expectations to the boss, find out if they are realistic, and influence the boss to accept the ones that are important to you. Being able to influence the boss to value your expectations can be particularly important if the boss is an overachiever. Such a boss will often set unrealistically high standards that need to be brought into line with reality.

A flow of information

How much information a boss needs about what a subordinate is doing will vary significantly depending on the boss's style, the situation he is in, and the confidence he has in the subordinate. But it is not uncommon for a boss to need more information than the subordinate would naturally supply or for the subordinate to think the boss knows more than he really does. Effective managers recognize that they probably underestimate what the boss needs to know and make sure they find ways to keep him informed through a process that fits his style.

Managing the flow of information upward is particularly difficult if the boss does not like to hear about problems. Although many would deny it, bosses often give off signals that they want to hear only good news. They show great displeasure—usually nonverbally—when someone tells them about a problem. Ignoring individual achievement, they may even evaluate more favorably subordinates who do not bring problems to them.

Nevertheless—for the good of the organization, boss, and subordinate—a superior needs to hear about failures as well as successes. Some subordinates deal with a good-news-only boss by finding indirect ways to get the necessary information to him, such as a management information system in which there is no messenger to be killed. Others see to it that potential problems, whether in the form of good surprises or bad news, are communicated immediately.

Dependability & honesty

Few things are more disabling to a boss than a subordinate on whom he cannot depend, whose work he cannot trust. Almost no one is intentionally undependable, but many managers are inadvertently so because of oversight or uncertainty about the boss's priorities. A commitment to an optimistic delivery date may please a superior in the short term but be a source of displeasure if not honored. It's difficult for a boss to rely on a subordinate who repeatedly slips deadlines. As one president put it (describing a subordinate): "When he's great, he's terrific, but I can't depend on him. I'd rather he be more consistent even if he delivered fewer peak successes—at least I could rely on him."

Nor are many managers intentionally dishonest with their bosses. But it is so easy to shade the truth a bit and play down concerns. Current concerns often become future surprise problems. It's almost impossible for bosses to work effectively if they cannot rely on a fairly accurate reading from their subordinates. Because it undermines credibility, dishonesty is perhaps the most troubling trait a subordinate can have. Without a basic level of trust in a subordinate's word, a boss feels he has to check all of a subordinate's decisions, which makes it difficult to delegate.

Good use of time & resources

Your boss is probably as limited in his store of time, energy, and influence as you are. Every request you make of him uses up some of these resources. For this reason, common sense suggests drawing on these resources with some selectivity. This may sound obvious, but it is surprising how many managers use up their boss's time (and some of their own credibility) over relatively trivial issues.

In one instance, a vice president went to great lengths to get his boss to fire a meddlesome secretary in another department. His boss had to use considerable effort and influence to do it. Understandably, the head of the other department was not pleased. Later, when the vice president wanted to tackle other more important problems that required changes in the scheduling and control practices of the other department, he ran into trouble. He had used up many of his own as well as his boss's blue chips on the relatively trivial issue of getting the secretary fired, thereby making it difficult for him and his boss to meet more important goals.

Whose job is it?

No doubt, some subordinates will resent that on top of all their other duties, they also need to take time and energy to manage their relationships with their bosses. Such managers fail to realize the importance of this activity and how it can simplify their jobs by eliminating potentially severe problems. Effective managers recognize that this part of their work is legitimate. Seeing themselves as ultimately responsible for what they achieve in an organization, they know they need to establish and manage relationships with everyone on whom they are dependent, and that includes the boss.▽

The subordinate's predicaments

Subordinates can overcome their tendency to react self-defensively to superiors' efforts to assert power

Eric H. Neilsen and
Jan Gypen

How can subordinates improve relations with their superiors? And how can superiors help their subordinates feel comfortable in what is often a tense relationship? These questions have usually been dealt with only indirectly in management circles. Yet the relationship is so threatening to many subordinates that they react in ways that are damaging to themselves and their organizations. Drawing heavily on the work of psychologist Erik Erikson, the authors present dilemmas that commonly confront the subordinate. They point out that being aware of these dilemmas can make them more manageable and then offer advice to superiors to aid subordinates in handling such situations.

Mr. Neilsen is associate professor in the Department of Organizational Behavior at the School of Management of Case Western Reserve University. He is the author of numerous articles on the organization and development of groups and a coauthor (with Dexter C. Dunphy, David Fraser, and Ricardo Zuniga) of *The Primary Group: A Handbook for Analysis and Field Research* (Appleton-Century-Crofts, 1972). Mr. Gypen is a Ph.D. candidate in organizational behavior at Case Western Reserve University. Before starting his research there, he served as a consultant at the Management Development Center at the University of Leuven, Belgium.

Drawings by Geoffrey Moss.

Nearly everyone in the administrative world is subordinate to someone else. Thus getting along with superiors is critical to career success.

Managers, however, tend to approach the topic only tangentially by talking about effective leadership (the other half's responsibility in the relationship) or by striving to get out of the subordinate's role and into the superior's. Ignored is the fact that most managers will always be working under someone else and that being an effective subordinate is just as important a professional task as being an effective superior.

But being a subordinate means dealing with special tensions that often result in debilitating self-protective responses, as the following examples illustrate:

☐ A senior manager of a major retailing company returns to the home office after spending 15 years developing new divisions all around the country. He is made executive vice president and told that he will succeed to the presidency within a couple of years. But after a year at headquarters, he comes to realize that his mentor has no intention of retiring and, more important, deals with people in a manipulative and domineering way. His inability to confront his boss creates discomfort and finally an emotional crisis. He takes a position at another business and leaves the retailing company without an heir apparent.

☐ A former army officer is hired as an administrator by a large company because of his experience in managing large-scale projects. Although his competence is valued, he clings to a bureaucratic style that served him well in the army. The more informal system his new boss prefers makes him so uncomfortable he refuses to adapt to it, and eventually he is dismissed.

☐ A project manager of a research group feels threatened when his boss assigns to the group's staff someone who is both talented and competitive. When asked how the new man is fitting in, the manager compliments him but fails to discuss the newcomer's weaknesses and the concerns the manager has about his own future. Eventually he resigns out of fear that the new man will soon replace him. The boss cannot explain what has happened. He was just about to assign the new man to another project and had no intention of replacing the project manager at all.

One might argue that all three cases are examples of ineffective subordinates whom superiors should be happily rid of. But in another sense, each of the subordinates' actions is quite understandable as an attempt to maintain personal integrity, remain competent, or prevent embarrassment. What superior would not admit that these are legitimate needs in professional life?

How to meet the organization's need for an appropriate amount of hierarchy and at the same time meet the subordinate's need for protecting his own identity has always been a problem in organizations. Recent research on power dynamics suggests that a subordinate's effort to be self-protective is a natural consequence of hierarchy itself. That is, the power the superior holds frequently leads him or her to attempt to manipulate the subordinate and to lose sight of the fact that the subordinate has important feelings and emotions, not to mention important abilities.

The research indicates that this manipulation happens because of the structure of the superior-subordinate relationship, not because of the personalities of the superiors.[1]

Indeed, what manager acting as a superior has not had the experience of looking at a project in retrospect and admitting, if only to himself, that his role was not as critical as he felt at the time and that his subordinates' contributions were probably greater than he has cared to recognize? And what manager acting as a subordinate has not felt that a superior has not given due credit for effort and that looking out for oneself is a necessary, though perhaps degrading, fact of organization life?

Dilemmas of self-protection

If one admits that hierarchy can corrupt superiors but assumes that hierarchy is necessary to organization life, one must also accept the premise that subordinates are justified in becoming self-protective. The issue for those concerned with the effective management of the organization as a whole, then, is not to try to rid subordinates of self-protectiveness but instead to create an environment that reduces their need to protect themselves.

A first step in this direction is to clarify the ways in which self-protectiveness is evoked. Few managers acting as superiors or subordinates are aware of just how pervasive the self-protective urge is and, therefore, of how many aspects of the superior-subordinate relationship it affects. We suggest that the situation be conceived of as a series of dilemmas that subordinates must resolve in dealing with superiors, as follows:
> Alliance vs. competition.
> Clarifying expectations vs. second guessing.
> Initiative vs. dependence.
> Competence vs. inferiority.
> Differentiation vs. identification.
> Relating personally vs. relating impersonally.
> Mutual concern vs. self-interest.
> Integrity vs. denial.

We have derived these dilemmas largely from the theory of individual development formulated by Erik Erikson, the pioneering psychologist who wrote *Childhood and Society* and other books on human development.[2] Our contention is that the same issues which, according to Erikson, every individual must face in finding a meaningful role in society are recreated in the superior-subordinate relationship. The superior in a sense represents what Erikson describes as the pressures of society.[3]

In each dilemma, we shall first consider the consequences of the subordinate's choosing either option and then examine situations in which the dilemma tends to be most important.

1. See David Kipnis, "Does Power Corrupt?" *Journal of Personality and Social Psychology*, January 1972, p. 33; and Philip G. Zimbardo, Craig Harvey, W. Curtis Banks, and David Jaffe, "A Pirandellian Prison: The Mind is a Formidable Jailer," *New York Times Magazine*, April 3, 1973, p. 38.

2. New York: Norton, 1964.

3. Erik Erikson summarizes his theory in *Identity and the Life Cycle* (New York: International University Press, 1959).

Alliance vs. competition

To view the superior as a trustworthy ally or as a competitor to be on guard against.

How a subordinate handles this dilemma is especially important because the consequences of a poor choice can be disastrous. Distrusting the superior when he or she is really well-intentioned can lead to hurt feelings and missed opportunities for all concerned. Of course, trusting the superior and then being taken advantage of can create difficulties as well because the subordinate's lower position makes retaliating difficult.

Obviously, the superior also has to make a choice about whether to view a subordinate as an ally or as a competitor, but a superior can redress a poor choice fairly easily because of his power.

This dilemma arises frequently for subordinates, regardless of an organization's dominant management philosophy, as we found recently in a company with a reputation for being sensitive to its employees' needs. A female personnel manager reporting directly to a male division head had risen rapidly through the ranks to become one of the organization's senior female managers. Although she had worked effectively to remove sexual bias in pro-

motion, she sensed that she had not been totally successful.

Her feelings were confirmed when the company passed-over a woman and promoted a male candidate to fill a management position. The woman who was not promoted complained to her superiors, and so they called a meeting of the managers involved in the case. The female personnel manager felt that the complaining woman was justified in feeling discriminated against; nevertheless, the boss asked the manager to defend the division's promotion practices at the meeting.

Should she voice her convictions at this meeting and risk generating the wrath of her superior? Or should she go to him directly and share her concerns with him? Either choice might reduce her chances of successfully documenting her case and supporting her female colleague if her superior proved to be unsympathetic or unwilling to examine the issue objectively.

After much agonizing, she chose to confide in her boss. Her superior was sympathetic to her concerns and after further consideration decided to support her position.

The same sort of choice arises when, in order to test the waters, a superior asks a subordinate to advocate a controversial position that the superior has yet to support publicly, when a subordinate is assigned the task of defending an unpopular cause, or when a subordinate is asked to sign papers and relay messages he or she does not really understand. Such situations abound in the day-to-day life of organizations. No one gets hurt as long as there is mutual trust up and down the hierarchy. Nonetheless, events like these place the subordinate at a disadvantage if the superior proves untrustworthy and if, at the time of the act itself, it is the subordinate who must make the critical choice.

Clarifying expectations vs. second-guessing

To seek explanations of what the superior wants or to stay uncertain about the superior's expectations and to risk misinterpretation.

Delegating authority so that both the superior and the subordinate are comfortable is critical to the overall relationship. Even then, a certain amount of tension can be expected to reappear because conditions frequently change. The accessibility of each party to the other may change as one person begins to travel more or moves to a new office. New projects may lend themselves to different patterns of delegation.

The subordinate who copes with these changes by regularly seeking clarification of what the superior expects increases his ability to sense what results the superior really wants. The subordinate can thus develop clear ideas about what to do when unforeseen events arise. He can enjoy open-ended assignments and at the same time feel good about taking issues to a superior that either cannot or should not be handled alone.

Seeking clarification about expectations as conditions change can, however, be a threatening process for a subordinate. New conditions may cause the superior to demand more delegation than the subordinate is ready for, triggering anxiety and self-doubt, which can lead to ineffective job performance. Certain situations may cause the superior to tighten control, leaving an independently inclined subordinate with a sense of being boxed in. Thus second-guessing the superior's changing expectations and avoiding direct clarification may be seen as the best available strategy. The most common results of such an approach are misunderstandings that lead to poor performance and misgivings on the part of all concerned.

The earlier example of the executive vice president who left his company rather than confront

his mentor about his retirement date and operating style is a case in which several important changes occurred concerning delegation that were not dealt with effectively. When the subordinate was out establishing new divisions, communication was sporadic and focused on critical results. When he returned to headquarters, however, communication was continuous and dealt with operating details. Out in the field he had been delegated clear-cut matters involving technology and costs. Back at headquarters, where differences in the management styles of the two men were more apparent, the president also monitored and controlled the vice president's operating style.

While the subordinate was in the field, he was still a young manager on the way up. On his return, he was in his fifties and eager to take the reins, but his mentor was in his seventies and becoming concerned about hanging on to control. Clearly, each man's personal growth and changing developmental needs were adding fuel to the fire. The various changes led to a situation in which the subordinate thought his autonomy unfairly reduced, and yet he was unwilling in the end to confront his superior about this.

The fact that the subordinate in the example left the company when he was so near the top and after such a long career shows how this dilemma can linger throughout a manager's career. The clarification of expectations is inevitably an imperfect process. Superiors do not always know what they want. Often they find out too late. What a superior wants and how well a subordinate understands it are rarely in perfect balance. At some point, however, the subordinate must clear the air or face the consequences.

Initiative vs. dependence

To suggest and promote ways to achieve the organization's goals and enhance one's own development or to wait for the superior to take charge and modify personal aspirations.

Most managers value initiative in their subordinates for achieving the organization's goals and developing as individual contributors, but they vary considerably in how they distinguish between initiative that supports their work and initiative that is competitive. The latter breeds competition in return, and unless the subordinate has other powerful supporters, he or she is likely to lose out because of the superior's power.

A subordinate who works at taking the initiative until he finds areas where it is welcome can feel free to make suggestions that will fit in with his own aspirations without fear of being blocked.

When he fears that taking the initiative will be fruitless or will invoke retaliation, the subordinate is likely to shy away from such behavior and also to take the blame for failures that arise from poor guidance. This pattern may heighten his feelings of dependence and encourage him to refrain from making suggestions when he could indeed be helpful. The superior thus sets the direction without the benefit of the subordinate's input.

Deciding whether to take the initiative or to rely on the superior for setting new directions is especially difficult for a subordinate whose talents are rapidly developing and who many people are beginning to identify as a valuable resource. Then the risks of arousing competitive feelings in the superior and the chances of finding new opportunities the subordinate would like to exploit are both on the rise. Consider the case of a personnel manager who had completed a training program in organization development and was just putting his new skills to work:

"As soon as I completed the diagnosis for the data processing group and word got out that the

managers involved were really pleased, I started getting phone calls from other department heads. Within three weeks, I had lined up enough work to keep me busy for a year.

"But then my boss got cold feet. He knows about organization development, but I think he's basically afraid of it. He made me cancel almost all of the jobs because, he said, he wanted me to develop the rest of the EEOC program. I think the real reason was that he didn't want us to become known as an OD group. Then he would have had to play the expert, which he knows he isn't, or rely on me,

which he's not about to do, or get more training, which he's afraid of."

Whenever a subordinate has an opportunity to increase his own status at the expense of the superior, this dilemma arises, yet change and innovation on the part of both are critical to the success of any organization.

Competence vs. inferiority

To feel capable in one's work given one's experience and training or to feel inept and out of step with one's colleagues.

Subordinates who view their own skills as adequate compared with the skills of others at their level are likely to learn from feedback concerning their performance. They can also feel free to ask for feedback at appropriate times. They welcome challenging new tasks and expect rewards for good performance. Their interest in how the superior views their skills encourages collaboration on mapping out career development steps.

Subordinates who have doubts about their skills are apt to avoid feedback, to misinterpret performance criteria, and to be devastated by critical evalu-

ations. They are also unlikely to initiate new activities that would improve their skills. The subordinate's desire to retrace steps or elect safe courses of action for fear of falling farther behind adversely affects the relationship with the superior.

The decision about how open to be with the superior about competence comes up whenever subordinates face yearly reviews, budget analyses, contract decisions, progress meetings, or major promotion points. These periods are especially stressful because of the rewards and punishments that can result. Viewing oneself as competent and being open to evaluation and feedback facilitates indepth review, but poor evaluations can harm an entire career. Classifying oneself as out of the running beforehand or as not in a position to be given a fair hearing can save face with colleagues and reduce emotional turmoil, but the chances of being seen as unwilling to cooperate may also be heightened.

Unfortunately, this dilemma is frequently complicated by organization politics. While avoiding negative evaluation is sometimes legitimate, it can become intertwined with avoiding evaluation by those whom subordinates incorrectly assume are biased against them.

Consider the case of a project leader in an engineering firm who developed a very close relationship with the senior partner, the person most responsible for hiring him. Aware that several others had opposed his selection, the project leader generally avoided contact with them but invited evaluation from the partner. Shortly before a major promotion decision, the senior partner died of a heart attack. The other partners felt quite justified in passing the project leader over because of their past relationship with him.

Being passed over put the manager at a disadvantage with competing colleagues. His relationship with the other partners never did improve, and his performance declined. Eventually he left the company for another position.

Differentiation vs. identification

To come across as being very different from the superior in terms of skills, aspirations, values, and professional concerns or to identify with the superior as someone to emulate.

One critical task facing every subordinate is deciding what kind of image to project vis-à-vis the superior. This task is addressed partly by the ways in which the previously discussed dilemmas are resolved.

The subordinate's dilemma whether to define himself as similar in approach and outlook to the superior or as uniquely different hinges on the extent to which the superior is an attractive role model.

Unlike the other dilemmas, we do not see any of the choices in this dilemma as necessarily ideal for the organization. A distinctly different identity for the subordinate compared with the superior's may be just as valuable to the organization as a highly similar one, depending on the circumstances. Likewise, neither choice is necessarily ideal for the subordinate. At one point in his career, he may find it especially beneficial to identify with his superior and to use him as an important role model. At other times, the subordinate may find that differentiating himself clearly from his superior is important for improving his own self-image.

Nonetheless, the dilemma is an important one because its resolution can affect the overall tone of the relationship. To see oneself as different from the superior encourages an emphasis on contrast. To identify with the superior emphasizes like-mindedness and invites a teacher-student type of relation-

ship. What is important for the subordinate is to clarify his choice early in the relationship so that he can make the most out of it and resist pulls in the opposite direction.

The identity issue comes to the foreground every time a manager gets a new leader. Frequently managers entering midcareer use such leadership changes as opportunities to strike out on their own. Here is what a 37-year-old production superintendent said about his change in bosses:

"I moved into this position when Bill was division manager. He had held my position previously and that, along with our similarities in backgrounds, made it easy for me to use him as a model. I did to the fullest. People used to tell me that I even answered the phone the way he did, used the same phrases, and told the same jokes. More important, when I was in a tight spot, I would often ask myself what he would do in my shoes.

"When Roger took over from Bill, I made an important decision. Roger is a very charismatic manager. It would have been easy for me to use him as a model in the same way as I did Bill. But I chose not to. I needed time to figure out on my own who I am.

"I talked with Roger about my career interests, and he has been quite supportive in helping me tie them into his own objectives without pressuring me to adopt his style."

Relating personally vs. relating impersonally

To view the superior as a fellow human facing similar problems in managing family and career and in developing friendships or to view the superior's world as different and distant and thus to relate to him or her on a utilitarian basis only.

Our business culture has a bias against close friendships among managers, especially in large corporations. The bias appears to stem from fears that non-job-related ties might jeopardize objectivity and also from frequent transfers, which discourage people from developing close ties to a place.

Nonetheless, taking the time to inquire into family life, share nonjob concerns, and listen to each other's personal problems are types of intimacy that are becoming more permissible in today's management world.

Deciding whether to treat a superior as a fellow human or as just a functionary in a business role is difficult for subordinates who have been unable to resolve the previously discussed dilemmas satisfactorily. Relating to the superior as an individual opens the door to expressing one's feelings of competition, self-doubt, dependence, and inferiority. But owning up to these feelings in a business relationship could easily be interpreted as a sign of weakness.

Even when the preceding dilemmas have been resolved satisfactorily, the choice to relate personally or impersonally has important consequences. Subordinates must recognize that few superiors act strictly as role players all the time. They have temper tantrums, playful moments, idiosyncrasies, and periods of depression or elation because of what is happening in their personal lives. Any of these states can intimidate, confuse, or frustrate a subordinate who chooses to relate on strictly impersonal terms.

Subordinates who treat their superiors as adults with common interests and problems can tolerate their superiors' moods and idiosyncrasies, resist their irrational behavior without fear of permanently damaging the relationship, and accept whatever friendship develops.

Relating personally can help a subordinate understand the interplay between the superior's emotional needs and his or her business behavior. Consider the case of an engineer in a large manufacturing plant:

"I had had 18 years of experience in industrial engineering when I came on board here, and when I first began to work with Howard, my superior, things were very rocky. I could see right away that I had a lot of things to contribute, but every time I suggested something, Howard would turn me down. Somehow I was always wrong. He'd tell me the idea had been tried before and hadn't worked, or the cost of doing this was not worth the effort, or production people wouldn't buy that.

"It wasn't until I got to know him that I realized Howard says no to everything the first time. He does it in management meetings. He does it with his secretary. He did it with his kids when I was having drinks at his house.

"Two things eventually became clear. First, Howard doesn't forget. He'll bring your idea back to you if he's interested, and he'll give you credit for it and help you act on it. Second, I realized I didn't like starting out with a no. I confronted him, and he's improved a lot. I can see him catching himself when he starts to be negative, and we joke about it. Sometimes he does it anyway, but now I get along pretty well with him because we both know it's 'just his way.'"

Mutual concern vs. self-interest

To keep the superior's welfare and development seriously in mind or to be totally preoccupied with one's own success.

Superiors are frequently rewarded for how well they develop their subordinates, but the reverse tends not to be true. And yet, subordinates who can look beyond their self-interest and aid their superiors' performance can help their relationships and themselves. Superiors are likely to work at developing subordinates who willingly share their expertise in areas where the superior is weak and who show concern about the company's welfare.

The risk is, of course, that few formally sanctioned rewards exist for helping develop a superior, and the chance always remains that the superior will exploit the relationship by taking undue credit for something that the subordinate has actually accomplished.

Nonetheless, we have found that superiors respond positively to subordinates who have something important to contribute to their superiors' development and who are willing to share it. For example, while interviewing a white marketing executive about his key subordinates, we found he was closest to a black product manager. When we asked him why this particular relationship had worked out so well, he explained that for the first time he had found a black manager who was willing to share the day-to-day experiences of being black in a white-dominated organization. The insights helped the white superior evaluate his own behavior, deal with black colleagues more effectively, and identify important problems in race relations within the company.

Thus we suspect that the most successful superior-subordinate relationships are those in which both parties can identify and use important resources in each other. These resources can be skills, knowledge, charisma, or simply the capacity to help in articulating commonly held values.

Integrity vs. denial

To accept the relationship with its limitations or to reject or misrepresent it.

Toward the end of one's life, according to Erikson, one must decide how the whole affair has come off.

To pass the later years with a sense of integrity is to accept the past for what it has been, to admit to both the good and the bad, and to appreciate one's total experience as something that cannot, need not, and should not be changed. Wisdom is gained from emotionally integrating what has happened and from faithfully passing on one's ideas to the next generation. The lack of such integration leads to despair. People caught in despair become bitter and attempt to rewrite their histories by engaging in new ventures that are impossible to complete.

Most subordinates do not come to grips with this dilemma until they retire, but on a smaller scale it comes up every time a subordinate moves on to another position or undergoes evaluation. He can treat the relationship with his superior either with a sense of integrity or with a sense of denial, which is the counterpart of despair.

Subordinates who are honest with themselves accept the relationship for what it is and has been. In discussions with others, such subordinates are candid about both the strengths and weaknesses they see in the superior, but they are also likely to consider the superior's experience and to evaluate the implications for their own futures. Subordinates with this turn of mind see the facts of the past as a sound framework for understanding the present and envisioning the future.

For example, a manager who had just left an employer of many years described the meeting at which he announced his decision to leave:

"Kenneth is often short on words. When I told him I was leaving, he said only three. First, he smiled and said, 'That's great!' Then he paused for a minute, looked at me with a sad face, and said, 'Nuts!' That was all he needed to say. We had both been working to get me a promotion within the company that would fit my talents and interests. The right slot simply wasn't available. We both knew I was valuable in my old position, but it was clear that I couldn't stay there forever. So this was a good move. Kenneth was a good boss."

Subordinates who are unrealistic about their relationships with superiors are often unwilling to accept the responsibility for what has occurred. They see the relationships as having been unsuccessful or at least as not having lived up to their expectations. In their eyes, failure lies mostly with the superiors. It is the superiors who should have been wiser or more caring, more sharing, more competent.

From the viewpoint of a third party, there might be a grain of truth in these accusations. The superior is indeed more powerful than the subordinate and can have a greater impact on their relationship.

Nevertheless, it takes two people to make a relationship.

Certainly a subordinate has some responsibility to confront a superior who does not live up to the subordinate's expectations. This is not to say that continuous confrontation around all the dilemmas we have discussed is the best way of relating to a superior. But a subordinate who wishes to maintain a sense of integrity must accept personal responsibility for failing to face a difficult situation.

Taking action

Simply recognizing the various dilemmas that subordinates face is a first step in dealing with the problem of self-protection. A second step is to use the dilemmas as a tool for discussing problems and concerns. Of course, the nature and outcome of such discussions partly depend on how both subordinates and superiors have previously resolved the dilemmas.

Subordinates who see their superiors as competitors are unlikely to be candid with them. Those who lack self-confidence will be preoccupied with what the superior wants to hear. Those who are afraid of taking the initiative will not speak from their hearts. Those who feel inferior will steer the conversation toward trivial issues. Those who rely on their superiors to define their identities will be unable to take consistent positions. Those who insist on maintaining a strictly task-oriented relationship will reject the exercise as out of place in the work setting or will fail to grasp its relevance to the total situation. Those who are self-centered will not listen to the superior's needs, and those who lack integrity will paint pretty pictures of themselves and place the total burden for change on the powerful superior.

Superiors who have similarly failed to resolve the dilemmas are likely to respond in kind, despite their more protected positions. The dialogue is likely to end up being a lot of talking about talking that leaves nothing resolved.

While the dilemmas are actually the subordinate's, it is the superior who has the greater power to act, and so we feel it appropriate at this point to address him with several suggestions.

Introspection: Keep the dilemmas in mind when dealing with a subordinate. What kinds of self-pro-

tective behavior are you most likely encouraging, however inadvertently, by your actions? A subordinate will appreciate your sensitivity and will thus be able to make known his concerns.

Empathy: Let your subordinate know how you would react if your own superior were discussing the same important issues with you. While you and your subordinate may be very different, letting the subordinate know you have thought the issues out in such a way is a sign of your respect for him or her, which is likely to encourage open discussion.

Preparedness: Occasionally, discuss issues of self-protection directly at training sessions or retreats, after mutually shared successes, or at the beginning and end of major tasks. Make the most of such occasions by clarifying to yourself in advance what you think the most important issues are and how you might begin discussing them.

Commitment: Once dialogue about an issue has started, do not let it drop until some resolution has been reached. Important issues can rarely be resolved in one session. Take the time to follow up and to consider new approaches. Failing to follow up can be just as damaging as initially failing to confront an issue.

Hope: Interpersonal relationships are rarely ideal from both parties' perspectives simultaneously. Unless you can accept and share the fact that both of you are working for an unachievable ideal and are willing to accept that premise, both of you are bound to become disillusioned.

The need for self-protection is an enduring consequence of the superior-subordinate relationship. The need cannot be eliminated, but each party can examine the costs of self-protective reactions to the other and can make choices that reflect the stake they have in the larger organization.▽

MANAGEMENT COMMUNICATION
and the Grapevine

❧ No administrator in his right mind would ever try to abolish the management grapevine. It is as permanent as humanity is. It should be recognized, analyzed, and consciously used for better communication.

By Keith Davis

Communication is involved in all human relations. It is the "nervous system" of any organized group, providing the information and understanding necessary for high productivity and morale. For the individual company it is a continuous process, a way of life, rather than a one-shot campaign. Top management, therefore, recognizes the importance of communication and wants to do something about it. But what? Often, in its frustration, management has used standard communication "packages" instead of dealing situationally with its individual problems. Or it has emphasized the means (communication techniques) rather than the ends (objectives of communication).

One big factor which management has tended to overlook is communication *within its own group.* Communication to the worker and from the worker is dependent on effective management communication; and clearly this in turn requires informal as well as formal channels.

The Grapevine

A particularly neglected aspect of management communication concerns that informal channel, the grapevine. There is no dodging the fact that, as a carrier of news and gossip among executives and supervisors, the grapevine often affects the affairs of management. The proof of this is the strong feelings that different executives have about it. Some regard the grapevine as an evil — a thorn in the side which regularly spreads rumor, destroys morale and reputations, leads to irresponsible actions, and challenges authority. Some regard it as a good thing because it acts as a safety valve and carries news fast. Others regard it as a very mixed blessing.

Whether the grapevine is considered an asset or a liability, it is important for executives to try to understand it. For one thing is sure: although no executive can absolutely control the grapevine, he can *influence* it. And since it is here to stay, he should learn to live with it.

Perspective

Of course, the grapevine is only part of the picture of communication in management. There is also formal communication — via conferences, reports, memoranda, and so on; this provides the basic core of information, and many administrators rely on it almost exclusively because they think it makes their job simpler to have everything reduced to explicit terms — as if that were possible! Another important part of the picture is the expression of attitudes, as contrasted with the transmission of information (which is what we will be dealing with in this article). Needless to say, all these factors influence the way the grapevine works in a given company, just as the grapevine in turn influences them.

In this article I want to examine (a) the significance, character, and operation of management communication patterns, with particular emphasis on the grapevine; and (b) the influence that various factors, such as organization and the chain of procedure, have upon such patterns. From this analysis, then, it will be possible to point up (c) the practical implications for management.

As for the research basis of the analysis, the major points are these:

1. *Company studied* — The company upon which the research is based is a real one. I shall refer to it as the "Jason Company." A manufacturer of leather goods, it has 67 people in the management group (that is, all people who supervise the work of others, from top executives to foremen) and about 600 employees. It is located in a rural town of 10,000 persons, and its products are distributed nationally.

In my opinion, the pattern of management communication at the Jason Company is typical of that in many businesses; there were no special conditions likely to make the executives and supervisors act differently from their counterparts in other companies. But let me emphasize that this is a matter of judgment, and hence broader generalizations cannot be made until further research is undertaken.

As a matter of fact, one of the purposes of this article is to encourage businessmen to take a close look at management communication in their own companies and to decide for themselves whether it is the same or different. In many companies, men in the management group now follow the popular practice of examining and discussing their problems of communicating with workers, but rarely do they risk the embarrassment of appraising their communications with each other.

2. *Methodology* — The methods used to study management communication in the Jason Company are new ones. Briefly, the basic approach was to learn from each communication recipient how he first received a given piece of information and then to trace it back to its source. Suppose D and E said they received it from G; G said he received it from B; and B from A. All the chains or sequences were plotted in this way — A to B to G to D and E — and when the data from all recipients were assembled, the pattern of the flow of communication emerged. The findings could be verified and developed further with the help of other data secured from the communication recipients.

This research approach, which I have called "ecco analysis," is discussed in detail elsewhere.[1]

Significant Characteristics

In the Jason Company many of the usual grapevine characteristics were found along with others less well known. For purposes of this discussion, the four most significant characteristics are these:

1. *Speed of transmission* — Traditionally the grapevine is fast, and this showed up in the Jason Company.

For example, a certain manager had an addition to his family at the local hospital at 11 o'clock at night, and by 2:00 p.m. the next day 46% of the whole management group knew about the event. The news was transmitted only by grapevine and mostly by face-to-face conversation, with an occasional interoffice telephone call. Most communications occurred immediately before work began, during "coffee hour," and during lunch hour. The five staff executives who knew of the event learned of it during "coffee hour," indicating that the morning rest period performed an important social function for the staff as well as providing relaxation.

2. *Degree of selectivity* — It is often said that the grapevine acts without conscious direction or thought — that it will carry anything, any time, anywhere. This viewpoint has been epitomized in the statement that "the grapevine is without conscience or consciousness." But flagrant grapevine irresponsibility was not evident in the Jason Company. In fact, the grapevine here showed that it could be highly selective and discriminating.

For example, the local representative of the company which carried the employee group insurance contract planned a picnic for company executives. The Jason Company president decided to invite 36 executives, mostly from higher executive levels. The grapevine immediately went to work spreading this information, but it was carried to *only two of the 31 executives not invited.* The grapevine communicators thought the news was confidential, so they had told only those who they thought would be invited (they had to guess, since they did not have access to the invitation list). The two uninvited executives who knew the information were foremen who were told by their invited superintendent; he had a very close working relationship with them and generally kept them well informed.

Many illustrations like the above could be gathered to show that the grapevine can be discriminating. Whether it may be *counted on* in that respect,

[1] Keith Davis, "A Method of Studying Communication Patterns in Organizations," to be published in *Personnel Psychology*, Fall 1953.

however, is another question. The answer would of course differ with each case and would depend on many variables, including other factors in the communication picture having to do with attitudes, executive relationships, and so forth.

3. *Locale of operation* — The grapevine of company news operates mostly at the place of work.

Jason managers were frequently in contact with each other after work because the town is small; yet grapevine communications about company activities predominantly took place at the plant, rather than away from it. It was at the plant that executives and supervisors learned, for instance, that the president was taking a two weeks' business trip, that the style designer had gone to Florida to study fashion trends, and that an executive had resigned to begin a local insurance business.

The significance of at-the-company grapevines is this: since management has some control over the work environment, it has an opportunity to influence the grapevine. By exerting such influence the manager can more closely integrate grapevine interests with those of the formal communication system, and he can use it for effectively spreading more significant items of information than those commonly carried.

4. *Relation to formal communication* — Formal and informal communication systems tend to be jointly active, or jointly inactive. Where formal communication was inactive at the Jason Company, the grapevine did not rush in to fill the void (as has often been suggested [2]); instead, there simply was lack of communication. Similarly, where there was effective formal communication, there was an active grapevine.

Informal and formal communication may supplement each other. Often formal communication is simply used to confirm or to expand what has already been communicated by grapevine. Thus in the case of the picnic, as just described, management issued formal invitations even to those who already knew they were invited. This necessary process of confirmation results partly because of the speed of the grapevine, which formal systems fail to match, partly because of its unofficial function, and partly because of its transient nature. Formal communication needs to come along to stamp "Official" on the news and to put it "on the record," which the grapevine cannot suitably do.

Spreading Information

Now let us turn to the actual operation of the grapevine. How is information passed along?

[2] For example, see National Industrial Conference Board, *Communicating with Employees*, Studies in Personnel Policy, No. 129 (New York, 1952), p. 34.

What is the relationship among the various people who are involved?

Human communication requires at least two persons, but each person acts independently. Person A may talk or write, but he has not *communicated* until person B receives. The individual is, therefore, a basic communication unit. That is, he is one "link" in the communication "chain" for any bit of information.

EXHIBIT I. TYPES OF COMMUNICATION CHAINS

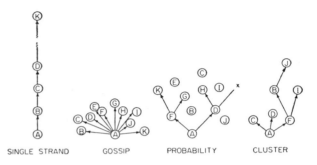

The formal communication chain is largely determined by the chain of command or by formal procedures, but the grapevine chain is more flexible. There are four different ways of visualizing it, as EXHIBIT I indicates:

1. *The single-strand chain* — A tells B, who tells C, who tells D, and so on; this makes for a tenuous chain to a distant receiver. Such a chain is usually in mind when one speaks of how the grapevine distorts and filters information until the original item is not recognizable.

2. *The gossip chain* — A seeks and tells everyone else.

3. *The probability chain* — A communicates randomly, say, to F and D, in accordance with the laws of probability; then F and D tell others in the same manner.

4. *The cluster chain* — A tells three selected others; perhaps one of them tells two others; and then one of these two tells one other. This was virtually the only kind of chain found in the Jason Company, and may well be the normal one in industry generally.

Active Minority

The predominance of the cluster chain at the Jason Company means that only a few of the persons who knew a unit of information ever transmitted it — what Jacobson and Seashore call the "liaison" individuals.[3] All others who

[3] Eugene Jacobson and Stanley E. Seashore, "Communication Practices in Complex Organizations," *The Journal of Social Issues*, Vol. VII, No. 3, 1951, p. 37.

received the information did not transmit it; they acted merely as passive receivers.

For example, when a quality-control problem occurred, 68% of the executives received the information, but only 20% transmitted it. Again, when an executive planned to resign to enter the insurance business, 81% of the executives knew about it, but only 11% passed the news on to others. Those liaison individuals who told the news to more than one other person amounted to less than 10% of the 67 executives in each case.

These active groups varied in membership. There was no evidence that any one group consistently acted as liaison persons; instead, different types of information passed through different liaison persons. However, as will be shown later, some individuals were invariably communication "isolates"; they received and transmitted information poorly or not at all.

The above findings indicate that if management wants more communication, it should increase the number and/or effectiveness of its liaison individuals. This appears to be a large order, but it is entirely possible. Liaison individuals tend to act in a predictable way. If an individual's unit of information concerns a job function in which he is interested, he is likely to tell others. If his information is about a person with whom he is associated socially, he also is likely to tell others. Furthermore, the sooner he knows of an event after it happened, the more likely he is to tell others. If he gets the information late, he does not want to advertise his late receipt of it by telling it to others.

In other words, three well-known communication principles which are so often mentioned in relation to attitudes also have a major influence on the spread of information by liaison individuals:

(1) Tell people about what will affect them (job interest).

(2) Tell people what they want to know, rather than simply what you want them to know (job and social interest).

(3) Tell people soon (timing).

Organizational Effects

The way an organization is divided horizontally into organizational levels and vertically into functions, such as production and sales, obviously has effects on management communication, for it cuts each company's over-all administrative function into small work assignments, or jobs, and sets each management person in certain relationships to others in his company.

Horizontal Levels

Organizational levels are perhaps the more dramatic in effect because they usually carry authority, pay increases, and status. From the communication point of view, they are especially important because of their number. In a typical firm there are usually several management levels, but only one or two worker levels; furthermore, as the firm grows, the management levels increase in number, while the worker levels remain stationary.

Communication problems are aggravated by these additional levels because the chain of communication is lengthened and complicated. Indeed, just because of this, some companies have been led to try to reduce the number of intermediate management levels. Our concern here is with the patterns of communication among individuals at the different levels.

At the Jason Company, executives at *higher* levels communicated more often and with more people than did executives at *lower* levels. In other words, the predominant communication flow was downward or horizontal. When an event happened at the bottom level, usually the news did reach a high level; but a single line of communication sufficed to carry it there, and from that point it went downward and outward in the same volume and manner (cluster chain) as if it had originated at the top.

Accordingly, the higher an executive was in the organizational hierarchy (with the exception of nonresident executives), the greater was his knowledge of company events. This was true of events which happened both above his level and below his level. Thus, if the president was out of town, a greater proportion at the fourth level knew of it than at the sixth level. Or — and this is less to be expected — if a foreman at the sixth level had an accident, a larger proportion of executives at the third level knew of it than at the fourth level, or even than at the sixth level where the accident happened. The more noteworthy the event, of course, the more likely it was to be known at upper levels — but, in a company of this size, it had to be quite trivial indeed before it failed to reach the ears of top executives.

The converse follows that in terms of communications transmitted and received the sixth and lowest level of supervision, the foreman level, was largely isolated from all other management. The average foreman was very hesitant to communicate with other members of management; and on the rare occasions when he did, he usually chose someone at his own level and preferably in his own department. Members of this group tended to be the last links in management communication, regardless of whether the chains were formal or informal.

A further significant fact concerns the eight departmental superintendents at the fourth level. Six of them supervised foremen directly; two others, with larger departments, each had a single line assistant between him and his foremen. The two who had line assistants were much more active in the communication chains than were the six others; indeed, all but one of the six appeared to have little to do with their foremen except in a formal way.

Perhaps the clue is that, with increased organizational levels, those at the higher (and hence further removed) levels both recognize a greater need for communication and have more time to practice it!

Functional Groups

Functionalization, the second important way in which an organization is "cut up," also has a significant impact on communication in management. The functions which are delegated to a manager help to determine the people he contacts, his relationships with them, his status, and, as a result, the degree to which he receives and transmits information. More specifically, his role in communication is affected (a) by his position in the chain of command and (b) by his position in the chain of procedure, which involves the sequence of work performance and cuts across chains of command, as when a report goes from the superintendent in one chain of command to the chief engineer in another chain of command and to the controller in still another.

In the Jason Company the effects of functionalization showed up in three major ways:

1. *Staff men "in the know"* — More staff executives than line men usually knew about any company event. This was true at each level of management as well as for the management group as a whole. For example, when the president of the company made a trip to seek increased governmental allotments of hides to keep the line tannery operating at capacity, only 4% of the line

executives knew the purpose of the trip, but 25% of the staff men did. In another case, when a popular line superintendent was awarded a hat as a prize in a training program for line superintendents, within six days a larger proportion of the staff executives than of the line executives knew about this event.

The explanation is not just that, with one staff executive to every three line executives, there were more line executives to be informed. More important is the fact that the *chain of procedure* usually involved more staff executives than line executives. Thus, when the superintendent was awarded his hat, a line executive had approved the award, but a staff personnel executive had processed it and a staff accounting executive had arranged for the special check.

Also the staff was more *mobile* than the line. Staff executives in such areas as personnel and control found that their duties both required and allowed them to get out of their offices, made it easy for them to walk through other departments without someone wondering whether they were "not working," to get away for coffee, and so on — all of which meant they heard more news from the other executives they talked with. (In a larger company staff members might be more fixed to their chairs, but the situation in the Jason Company doubtless applies to a great many other businesses.)

Because of its mobility and its role in the chain of procedure, the staff not only received but also transmitted communications more actively than did the line. Most of these communications were oral; at least in this respect, the staff was not the "paper mill" it is often said to be. It seems obvious that management would do well to make conscious use of staff men as communicators.

2. *Cross-communication* — A second significant effect of functionalization in the Jason Company was that the predominant flow of information for events of general interest was between the four large areas of production, sales, finance and office, and industrial relations, rather than within them. That is, if a production executive had a bit of news of general interest, he was more likely to tell a sales, finance, or personnel executive than another production executive.

Social relationships played a part in this, with executives in the various groups being lodge brothers, members of the same church, neighbors, parents of children in the same schools, and so on. In these relationships the desire to make an impression was a strong motivation for cross-communication, since imparting information to executives outside his own area served to make a man feel that the others would consider him "in the know."

Procedural relationships, discussed earlier, also encouraged the executives to communicate across functional lines.

Since communications tended not to stay within an area, such as production, they tended even less to follow chains of command from boss to sub-boss to sub-sub-boss. Indeed, the chain of command was seldom used in this company except for very formal communications. Thus EXHIBIT II reproduces a communication chain concerning a quality control problem in production, first brought to the attention of a group sales manager in a letter from a customer. Although it was the type of problem that could have been communicated along the chain of command, the exhibit shows that, of 14 communications, only 3 were within the chain of command and only 6 remained within one functional area — sales — where the information was first received.

chains. Also, there were other groups which received information but did not transmit it, and thus contributed to the same problem — the uneven spread of information through the company. Here are three examples at the foreman level illustrating different degrees of failure to participate in the communication process and different reasons for this failure:

(a) The foremen in one group were generally left out of communication chains. These men were of a different nationality from that of the rest of the employees, performed dirty work, and worked in a separate building. Also, their work fitted into the manufacturing process in such a way that it was seldom necessary for other executives to visit their work location.

(b) Another group often was in a communication chain but on the tail end of it. They were in a separate building some distance from the main

EXHIBIT II.   COMMUNICATION CHAIN FOR A QUALITY CONTROL PROBLEM

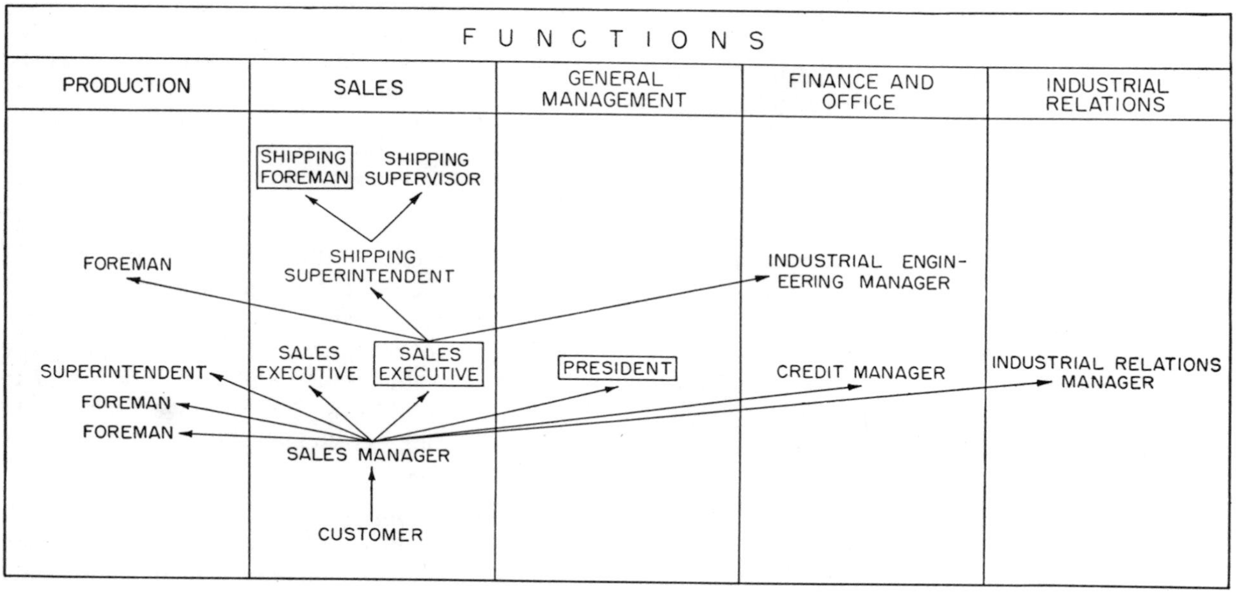

NOTE: Executives in boxes received chain-of-command communications.

The fact that the chain of command may affect management communication patterns less than procedural and social influences — which has shown up in other companies too [4] — means that management needs to devote considerably more attention to the problems and opportunities of cross-communication.

3. *Group isolation* — The research in the Jason Company revealed that some functional groups were consistently isolated from communication

[4] See Carroll L. Shartle, "Leadership and Executive Performance," *Personnel*, March 1949, pp. 377-378.

manufacturing area, their function was not in the main manufacturing procedure, and they usually received information late. They had little chance or incentive to communicate to other executives.

(c) A third group both received and transmitted information, but transmitted only within a narrow radius. Although they were in the midst of the main work area, they failed to communicate with other functional groups because their jobs required constant attention and they felt socially isolated.

In sum, the reasons for group isolation at the Jason Company were: geographical separation; work association (being outside the main procedures or at the end of them); social isolation; and organizational level (the lower the level of a group, the greater its tendency to be isolated).

Obviously, it is not often feasible for management to undertake to remove such causes of group isolation as geographical or social separation. On the other hand, it may well be possible to compensate for them. For example, perhaps the volume of formal communication to men who happen to be in a separate building can be increased, or arrangements can be made for a coffee break that will bring men who are isolated because of the nature of their work or their nationality into greater contact with other supervisors. In each situation management should be able to work out measures that would be appropriate to the individual circumstances.

Conclusion

The findings at the Jason Company have yet to be generalized by research in other industries, but they provide these starting points for action:

(1) If management wants more communication among executives and supervisors, one way is to increase the number and effectiveness of the liaison individuals.

(2) It should count on staff executives to be more active than line executives in spreading information.

(3) It should devote more attention to cross-communication — that is, communication between men in different departments. It is erroneous to consider the chain of command as *the* communication system because it is only one of many influ-ences. Indeed, procedural and social factors are even more important.

(4) It should take steps to compensate for the fact that some groups are "isolated" from communication chains.

(5) It should encourage further research about management grapevines in order to provide managers with a deeper understanding of them and to find new ways of integrating grapevine activities with the objectives of the firm.

(6) "Ecco analysis," the recently developed research approach used at the Jason Company, should be useful for future studies.

If management wants to do a first-class communication job, at this stage it needs fewer medicines and more diagnoses. Communication analysis has now passed beyond "pure research" to a point where it is immediately useful to top management in the individual firm. The patterns of communication that show up should serve to indicate both the areas where communication is most deficient and the channels through which information can be made to flow most effectively.

In particular, no administrator in his right mind would try to abolish the management grapevine. It is as permanent as humanity is. Nevertheless, many administrators have abolished the grapevine from *their own minds*. They think and act without giving adequate weight to it or, worse, try to ignore it. This is a mistake. The grapevine is a factor to be reckoned with in the affairs of management. The administrator should analyze it and should consciously try to influence it.

ABCs of Job Interviewing

Preparation, via a scenario, is the key.

by James M. Jenks and Brian L.P. Zevnik

Your organization is looking over several candidates for a vacancy in its managerial ranks, and you have the final say in the decision. You are getting ready to interview the applicants.

Are you well prepared for this task? Poorly conducted interviews can come back to haunt you – you may hire someone who doesn't work out or reject someone with star potential. Or in these litigious days, you may risk being slapped with a lawsuit and hauled into court.

Unlike your human resources people, you interview applicants only occasionally. You don't catch that duty often enough to hone your skills. The candidates themselves are likely to be more adroit than you. Often they have received careful instructions from the recruiting firms that sent them your way. Recent experience on the job trail may have taught them all the right things to ask and say.

Then there are the personal attributes that you bring to the interview. The aggressive characteristics that helped put you in an executive position also put obstacles in your way to becoming an expert interviewer – learning how to ask, to watch, and to listen. The take-charge attitude of many top executives makes it hard for them to keep their ears open and mouths shut – two critical characteristics of the expert interviewer.

On the other hand, you know the job and the qualities you're looking for. Furthermore, your concern over having a good fit between individual and organization is your greatest advantage: with the proper preparation, it will give you an edge in the interview.

Prepping for the interviews

Before the interviews begin, write out a job profile based on the job description. The purpose is to translate duties and responsibilities into the personal characteristics the manager must have to do the job.

Take the job description for a national sales manager for a life insurance company. One duty is, "Reviews data to calculate sales potential and customer desires and to recommend prices and policies to meet sales goals." From that you distill these requirements for your profile: powers of analysis, managerial skills, commitment. Another duty, "Prepares periodic sales reports showing potential sales and actual results," calls for skill in writing and in oral communication.

Now you get down to specifics. For every duty or responsibility, you list the characteristics or qualities your candidate must possess to do the job. For instance, regarding powers of analysis: "Finds information in such publications as *Insurance and Tax News* and interprets it to show how sales agents can use tax law changes to sell life insurance policies." And concerning written communication: "Writes copy for advertising department to prepare new sales brochures for agents describing benefits of various types of life insurance for young singles, young newly marrieds, and mature empty nesters."

Naturally, you'll find that many requirements for different jobs are alike. Your human resources department can help in determining the most important characteristics and otherwise preparing you for the interviews.

Once you've listed the job requirements, put them in black and white: prepare a written interview guide. Using such a guide doesn't mean that you lack verbal facility, smoothness in meeting people, or deftness in leading a discussion; rather, it contributes substantially to a wise assessment of applicants with whom you must go one-on-one.

Here is a checklist of items as a basis for an interview guide:
☐ Consult the applicant's résumé and application for jobs, experience, accomplishments that are most relevant to your job requirements.
☐ Plan questions touching on the qualities you are looking for. In the interviews with applicants for insur-

James M. Jenks is chairman of the Alexander Hamilton Institute, which has purveyed employment relations information to organizations for 80 years. Brian L.P. Zevnik is its editor-in-chief. Jointly they wrote Managers Caught in the Crunch *(Franklin Watts, 1988).*

ance company national sales manager, if you know that a candidate indeed reads journals like *Insurance and Tax News*, you might probe: "Tell me how you've interpreted information from such publications for sales purposes."

☐ Prepare a step-by-step scenario of how to present the position.

☐ Do the same for your company, division, and department.

☐ Seek examples of behavior by focusing on what the applicant has done, not on what he or she might do. Of the life insurance sales manager applicant, you might ask: "Can you show me samples of brochures, sales letters, or articles you've developed?"

An interview guide will help you to be consistent and focused in your questioning, thus ensuring each applicant a fair shake, steering you clear of improper questions, and preventing you from putting applicants on the defensive. Moreover, an interview guide keeps you in control of the conversation.

Past performance

It has long been established that a person's past behavior is the surest guide to future performance. To determine an applicant's fit with the people in your company (including you) requires questions that uncover personality characteristics.

How can you make a judgment as to whether an applicant will do the job and fit in well? You are looking for a particular kind of behavior for every critical requirement you've listed for the job. The question to keep in mind is, What has this candidate done in the past to meet these requirements? So make a list of questions that are relevant to your concerns about them.

The following examples illustrate the kinds of questions that reveal willingness to do the job as well as style and personality:

Your concern: In this era of DINK (double income, no kids) couples, you may wonder about the prospective employee's motivation to work. Will this person put in the hours necessary to get the job done?

Faulty question: "Is your spouse employed?"

Comment: Such a question makes for amiable conversation, but it doesn't meet your concern. It has little to do with the candidate's motivation to work.

Improved questions: "Can you tell me about any project you had to

---

The executive's take-charge bent isn't conducive to effective interviewing.

---

tackle where you had to meet a hard deadline? What did you do to get the work out on time?"

When the individual you seek is one who can make an appreciable difference in the company, simply meeting the position's technical qualifications is not enough. You're not just filling a slot, you're hiring someone who is flexible, who will do what the job requires.

Your concern: How well this candidate will meet the demands of the position.

Faulty question: "Did you ever drop the ball on your last job and get bawled out by your boss?"

Comment: There are several problems with this question. For one thing, it can be answered with a single word—"yes" or "no." And a single-word answer (whichever it is) does nothing to get at your concern. Secondly, you're asking for a confession of failure, which is difficult for anyone to make. Finally, the question is unrelated to any requirement of the position and therefore gives you no behavioral matches.

Improved question: "Tell me about a task you took on in your previous job that would prepare you for handling the requirements we're discussing here."

Naturally, you want to consider how well the applicant will get along with colleagues as well as top executives—if the job opening is at a high level.

Your concern: How well the candidate will fit in your organization.

Faulty questions: "You need a lot of personal PR in this position. Do

you get along well with people? What clubs do you belong to?"

Comment: No matter how strong the candidates or how expert in their fields, if they don't work well in your particular environment, they'll fail. Some interviewers ask about hobbies and clubs to ascertain fit. But such questions stray into irrelevant areas. What does being a good tennis player have to do with getting along with peers or superiors?

Improved question: "Tell me about any incident in your last job that caused a conflict with another manager; what did you do to smooth things out?"

Assessment of how well candidates have mastered human relations skills is difficult. Interviewers often ask questions about activities that are at best only dimly connected to the position's requirements.

Your concern: On paper, your candidate for a professional position is well qualified. But the person selected will also direct a staff that includes several supervisors, so you need to find a candidate with good people-managing skills.

Faulty question: "What do you do on your own time, say, with clubs, associations, or groups of people?"

Comment: This question is designed to find out if the candidate is congenial and well rounded, but it promises to uncover nothing valuable about the candidate's behavior.

Improved questions: "We all run into instances where two people disagree on how to get a job done. Can you tell me how you handled a particular argument or disagreement about operations that came up among the people you managed in your last job? How about disputes between colleagues?"

Wrong and right tacks

Doing your homework thoroughly will help you maintain control of the dialogue and avoid pitfalls that interviewers often run into. Here are some "don'ts" in the art of interviewing.

Don't telegraph the response you're seeking. Suppose you are exploring the candidate's ability to work with departments that he or she would have no control over. "Do

Shooting the Rapids

The principle of fairness in employment, which has become the law of the land, does not ignore the seemingly straightforward job interview. Not only must you be sure that your hiring practices conform to legal specs but you must also take great care in your questions.

The dangerous questions aren't those that reflect overt discrimination. In any case, the law and its enforcers are more concerned with the effects of employers' actions than with their intentions. The dangerous questions are those meant to discover something interviewers *think* they need to know, something it would be *nice* to know, or even something intended to put the applicant at ease, like questions about family or nationality.

Executives ask irrelevant questions because they reason that the information may be useful should the job seeker become an employee. Questions that can be asked after hire, concerning age and marital status, for example, may be illegal during pre-employment interviews. (Technically, a question

by itself usually isn't illegal. It's when the answers are improperly used that the *gendarmes* swarm in.)

Suppose an executive asks a female applicant this seemingly innocuous question: "What kind of work does your husband do?" He wants to put her at ease and at the same time get an inkling about how long the candidate might want to stay on the job. But the question is patently discriminatory because it is seldom asked of males. Moreover, it is irrelevant to the job requirements or the person's qualifications.

Our society seems intent on using the courts as the first resort, not the last, to redress suffering. Corporations and executives are being dragged into court with dismaying frequency, and juries are awarding enormous sums—even into the millions—against both "deep pockets" corporations and individual executives.

The key to preventing discrimination claims lies in one simple policy. If a question is not directly related to the hiring decision and relevant to the job, don't ask it.

to be at work by 8 A.M. At unscheduled times each month, you'll have to come to executive committee meetings beginning at 5 P.M. and lasting several hours. How do you feel about that kind of unpredictable schedule?"

Don't get into a joust. Some people revel in one-upmanship or competitive tilting. You wonder whether this candidate is willing to work what are usually leisure hours to complete projects within deadline, so you ask, "Would you work weekends and holidays when necessary?" Your applicant fires back, "Absolutely. I can keep up with anybody else's schedule."

Implicit in this thrust is the claim that he or she can do anything you can do. Feel your hackles rising? Avoid that kind of behavior with straightforward business questions. Keep your feelings in check and your combativeness on a short leash. A better tack would be, "How do you plan your week's activities? Tell me what you do in your current job when you can't meet your planned schedule."

Finally, don't get uptight if the applicant gets uptight. You control the situation, it's your show. Part of your job is to make the interview an informative meeting, not a trip to the dentist's chair. Remember too that part of your task is to sell your organization to a top-notch candidate. You do that with convincing descriptions of the position, the opportunities, and the organization itself; also by how you come across—natural, prepared, professional. Furthermore, if you get uptight, you're liable to do too much talking and not enough listening.

Hiring is like a contest, especially when you're engaging skillful players who are the kind you always want on your managerial team. Choosing the right applicants for important management slots is a key to achieving exceptional results for you and your company. Behavioral-match, performance-oriented questions, buttressed by careful preparation, give you the best chance of finding talented candidates who will do more than just fill those slots well.⊟

Reprint 89408

you think you'll be able to get cooperation from managers in other areas of the company?" you ask. The applicant smoothly replies, "No problem. I get along with everybody."

Your question not only allows a sharp interviewee to give you the response you want to hear but also gives you zero help in finding out what you really want to know. We suggest something like: "Tell me about a time when you had to gain the cooperation of a group you had no authority over. What did you do?"

Don't get defensive if an interviewee directs a tough question right back at you. You may be concerned,

for example, about the person's steady availability. So you ask, "Do you have any small children at home?" She replies easily, "I think you'll agree that my experience and education clearly show I'm qualified. I'm not at all sure why you asked that question. Can you explain?" The applicant has neatly lobbed the ball back into your court and put you on the defensive. (And since the question is rarely asked of males, it borders on illegality anyway. See the insert "Shooting the Rapids.")

A better approach would be: "I don't know if you're aware of this, but we need managers at your level

People and
Organizations

We don't need flat organizations. We need layers of accountability and skill.

In Praise of Hierarchy

by Elliott Jaques

At first glance, hierarchy may seem difficult to praise. Bureaucracy is a dirty word even among bureaucrats, and in business there is a widespread view that managerial hierarchy kills initiative, crushes creativity, and has therefore seen its day. Yet 35 years of research have convinced me that managerial hierarchy is the most efficient, the hardiest, and in fact the most natural structure ever devised for large organizations. Properly structured, hierarchy can release energy and creativity, rationalize productivity, and actually improve morale. Moreover, I think most managers know this intuitively and have only lacked a workable structure and a decent intellectual justification for what they have always known could work and work well.

As presently practiced, hierarchy undeniably has its drawbacks. One of business's great contemporary problems is how to release and sustain among the people who work in corporate hierarchies the thrust, initiative, and adaptability of the entrepreneur. This problem is so great that it has become fashionable to call for a new kind of organization to put in place of managerial hierarchy, an organization that will better meet the requirements of what is variously called the Information Age, the Services Age, or the Post-Industrial Age.

As vague as the description of the age is the definition of the kind of new organization required to suit it. Theorists tell us it ought to look more like a symphony orchestra or a hospital or perhaps the British raj. It ought to function by means of primus groups or semiautonomous work teams or matrix overlap groups. It should be organic or entrepreneurial or tight-loose. It should hinge on skunk works or on management by walking around or perhaps on our old friend, management by objective.

All these approaches are efforts to overcome the perceived faults of hierarchy and find better ways to improve morale and harness human creativity. But the theorists' belief that our changing world requires an alternative to hierarchical organization is simply wrong, and all their proposals are based on an inadequate understanding of not only hierarchy but also human nature.

Hierarchy is not to blame for our problems. Encouraged by gimmicks and fads masquerading as insights, we have burdened our managerial systems with a makeshift scaffolding of inept structures and attitudes. What we need is not simply a new, flatter organization but an understanding of how managerial hierarchy functions—how it relates to the complexity of work and how we can use it to achieve a more effective deployment of talent and energy.

The reason we have a hierarchical organization of work is not only that tasks occur in lower and higher degrees of complexity—which is obvious—but also that there are sharp discontinuities in complexity that separate tasks into a series of steps or categories—which is not so obvious. The same discontinuities occur with respect to mental work and to the breadth and duration of accountability. The hierarchical kind of organization we call bureaucracy did not emerge accidentally. It is the only form of

> **Managerial hierarchy has never been properly described or adequately used.**

organization that can enable a company to employ large numbers of people and yet preserve unambiguous accountability for the work they do. And that is why, despite its problems, it has so doggedly persisted.

Elliott Jaques, currently visiting research professor in management science at George Washington University, has been studying hierarchy and organizational structure for 40 years. His most recent book is Requisite Organization: The CEO's Guide to Creative Structure and Leadership *(Cason Hall/Gower, 1989).*

Hierarchy has not had its day. Hierarchy never did have its day. As an organizational system, managerial hierarchy has never been adequately described and has just as certainly never been adequately used. The problem is not to find an alternative to a system that once worked well but no longer does; the problem is to make it work efficiently for the first time in its 3,000-year history.

What Went Wrong...

There is no denying that hierarchical structure has been the source of a great deal of trouble and inefficiency. Its misuse has hampered effective management and stifled leadership, while it's track record as a support for entrepreneurial energy has not been exemplary. We might almost say that successful businesses have had to succeed despite hierarchical organization rather than because of it.

One common complaint is excessive layering — too many rungs on the ladder. Information passes through too many people, decisions through too many levels, and managers and subordinates are too close together in experience and ability, which smothers effective leadership, cramps accountability, and promotes buck passing. Relationships grow stressful when managers and subordinates bump elbows, so to speak, within the same frame of reference.

Another frequent complaint is that few managers seem to add real value to the work of their subordinates. The fact that the breakup value of many large corporations is greater than their share value shows pretty clearly how much value corporate managers can *subtract* from their subsidiary businesses, but in fact few of us know exactly what managerial added value would look like as it was occurring.

Many people also complain that our present hierarchies bring out the nastier aspects of human behavior, like greed, insensitivity, careerism, and self-importance. These are the qualities that have sent many behavioral scientists in search of cooperative, group-oriented, nonhierarchical organizational forms. But are they the inevitable companions of hierarchy, or perhaps a product of the misuse of hierarchy that would disappear if hierarchy were properly understood and structured?

...And What Continues to Go Wrong

The fact that so many of hierarchy's problems show up in the form of individual misbehavior has led to one of the most widespread illusions in business, namely, that a company's managerial leadership can be significantly improved solely by doing psychotherapeutic work on the personalities and attitudes of its managers. Such methods can help individuals gain greater personal insight, but I doubt that individual insight, personality matching, or even exercises in group dynamics can produce much in the way of organizational change or an overall improvement in leadership effectiveness. The problem is that our managerial hierarchies are so badly designed as to defeat the best efforts even of psychologically insightful individuals.

Solutions that concentrate on groups, on the other hand, fail to take into account the real nature of employment systems. People are not employed in groups. They are employed individually, and their employment contracts — real or implied — are individual. Group members may insist in moments of great esprit de corps that the group as such is the author of some particular accomplishment, but once the work is completed, the members of the group look for individual recognition and individual progression in

> No one ever holds groups accountable for their work. Who ever heard of promoting a group — or firing one?

their careers. And it is not groups but individuals whom the company will hold accountable. The only true group is the board of directors, with its corporate liability.

None of the group-oriented panaceas face this issue of accountability. All the theorists refer to group authority, group decisions, and group consensus, none of them to group accountability. Indeed, they avoid the issue of accountability altogether, for to hold a group accountable, the employment contract would have to be with the group, not with the individuals, and companies simply do not employ groups as such.

To understand hierarchy, you must first understand employment. To be employed is to have an ongoing contract that holds you accountable for doing work of a given type for a specified number of hours per week in exchange for payment. Your specific tasks within that given work are assigned to you by a person called your manager (or boss or supervisor), who *ought to be held accountable* for the work you do.

If we are to make our hierarchies function properly, it is essential to place the emphasis on *accountability for getting work done.* This is what hierarchical systems ought to be about. Authority is a secondary issue and flows from accountability in the sense that there should be just that amount of authority needed to discharge the accountability. So if a group is to be given authority, its members must be held accountable as a group, and unless this is done, it is very hard to take so-called group decisions seriously. If the CEO or the manager of the group is held accountable for outcomes, then in the final analysis, he or she will have to agree with group decisions or have the authority to block them, which means that the group never really had decision-making power to begin with. Alternatively, if groups are allowed to make decisions without their manager's seal of approval, then accountability as such will suffer, for if a group does badly, the group is never fired. (And it would be shocking if it were.)

In the long run, therefore, group authority *without* group accountability is dysfunctional, and group authority *with* group accountability is unacceptable. So images of organizations that are more like symphony orchestras or hospitals or the British raj are surely nothing more than metaphors to express a desired feeling of togetherness—the togetherness produced by a conductor's baton, the shared concern of doctors and nurses for their patients, or the apparent unity of the British civil service in India.

In employment systems, after all, people are not mustered to play together as their manager beats time. As for hospitals, they are the essence of everything bad about bureaucratic organization. They function in spite of the system, only because of the enormous professional devotion of their staffs. The Indian civil service was in many ways like a hospital, its people bound together by the struggle to survive in a hostile environment. Managers do need authority, but authority based appropriately on the accountabilities they must discharge.

Why Hierarchy?

The bodies that govern companies, unions, clubs, and nations all employ people to do work, and they all organize these employees in managerial hierarchies, systems that allow organizations to hold people accountable for getting assigned work done. Unfortunately, we often lose sight of this goal and set up the organizational layers in our managerial hierarchies to accommodate pay brackets and facilitate career development instead. If work happens to get done as well, we consider that a useful bonus.

But if our managerial hierarchical organizations tend to choke so readily on debilitating bureaucratic practices, how do we explain the persistence and continued spread of this form of organization for more than 3,000 years? And why has the determined search for alternatives proved so fruitless?

The answer is that managerial hierarchy is and will remain the *only* way to structure unified working systems with hundreds, thousands, or tens of thousands of employees, for the very good reason that managerial hierarchy is the expression of two fundamental characteristics of real work. First, the tasks we carry out are not only more or less complex but they also become more complex as they separate out into discrete categories or types of complexity. Second, the same is true of the mental work that people do on the job, for as this work grows more complex, it too separates out into distinct categories or types of mental activity. In turn, these two characteristics permit hierarchy to meet four of any organization's fundamental needs: to add real value to work as it moves through the organization, to identify and nail down accountability at each stage of the value-adding process, to place people with the necessary competence at each organizational layer, and to build a general consensus and acceptance of the managerial structure that achieves these ends.

Hierarchical Layers

The complexity of the problems encountered in a particular task, project, or strategy is a function of the variables involved—their number, their clarity or ambiguity, the rate at which they change, and, overall, the extent to which they are distinct or tangled. Obviously, as you move higher in a managerial hierarchy, the most difficult problems you have to contend with become increasingly complex. The biggest problems faced by the CEO of a large corporation are vastly more complex than those encountered on the shop floor. The CEO must cope not only with a huge array of often amorphous and constantly changing data but also with variables so tightly interwoven that they must be disentangled before they will yield useful information. Such variables might include the cost of capital, the interplay of corporate cash flow, the structure of the international competitive market, the uncertainties of Europe after 1992, the future of Pacific Rim development, social developments with respect to labor, political developments in Eastern Europe, the Middle East, and the Third World, and technological research and change.

That the CEO's and the lathe operator's problems are different in quality as well as quantity will come as no surprise to anyone. The question is—and always has been—where does the change in quality occur? On a continuum of complexity from the bottom of the structure to the top, where are the discontinuities that will allow us to identify layers of hierarchy that are distinct and separable, as different as ice is from water and water from steam? I spent years looking for the answer, and what I found was somewhat unexpected.

My first step was to recognize the obvious, that the layers have to do with manager-subordinate relationships. The manager's position is in one layer and the subordinate's is in the next layer below. What then sets the necessary distance between? This question cannot be answered without knowing just what it is that a manager does.

The managerial role has three critical features. First, and *most* critical, every manager must be held accountable not only for the work of subordinates but also for adding value to their work. Second, every manager must be held accountable for sustaining a team of subordinates capable of doing this work. Third, every manager must be held accountable for setting direction and getting subordinates to follow willingly, indeed enthusiastically. In brief, every manager is accountable for work and leadership.

In order to make accountability possible, managers must have enough authority to ensure that their subordinates can do the work assigned to them. This authority must include at least these four elements: (1) the right to veto any applicant who, in the manager's opinion, falls below the minimum standards of ability; (2) the power to make work assignments; (3) the power to carry out performance appraisals and, within the limits of company policy, to make decisions—not recommendations—about raises and merit rewards; and (4) the authority to initiate removal—at least from the manager's own team—of anyone who seems incapable of doing the work.

But defining the basic nature of the managerial role reveals only part of what a managerial layer means. It cannot tell us how wide a managerial layer should be, what the difference in responsibility should be between a manager and a subordinate, or, most important, where the break should come between one managerial layer and another. Fortunately, the next step in the research process supplied the missing piece of the puzzle.

Responsibility and Time

This second step was the unexpected and startling discovery that the level of responsibility in any organizational role—whether a manager's or an individual contributor's—can be objectively measured in terms of the target completion time of the *longest* task, project, or program assigned to that role. The more distant the target completion date of the longest task or program, the heavier the weight of responsibility is felt to be. I call this measure the responsibility time span of the role. For example, a supervisor whose principal job is to plan tomorrow's production assignments and next week's work schedule but who also has ongoing responsibility for uninterrupted production supplies for the month ahead has a responsibility time span of one month. A foreman who spends most of his time riding herd on

> Hierarchical layers depend on jumps in responsibility that depend in turn on how far ahead a manager must think and plan.

this week's production quotas but who must also develop a program to deal with the labor requirements of next year's retooling has a responsibility time span of a year or a little more. The advertising vice president who stays late every night working on next week's layouts but who also has to begin making contingency plans for the expected launch of two new local advertising media campaigns three years hence has a responsibility time span of three years.

To my great surprise, I found that in all types of managerial organizations in many different countries over 35 years, people in roles at the same time span experience the same weight of responsibility and declare the same level of pay to be fair, regardless of their occupation or actual pay. The time-span range runs from a day at the bottom of a large corporation to more than 20 years at the top, while the felt-fair pay ranges from $15,000 to $1 million and more.

Armed with my definition of a manager and my time-span measuring instrument, I then bumped into the second surprising finding—repeatedly confirmed—about layering in managerial hierarchies: the boundaries between successive managerial layers occur at certain specific time-span increments, just as ice changes to water and water to steam at certain specific temperatures. And the fact that everyone in the hierarchy, regardless of status, seems to see these boundaries in the same places suggests that the boundaries reflect some universal truth about human nature.

The illustration "Managerial Hierarchy in Fiction and in Fact" shows the hierarchical structure of

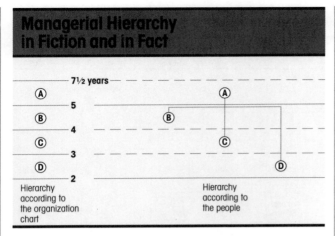

Managerial Hierarchy in Fiction and in Fact

part of a department at one company I studied, along with the approximate responsibility time span for each position. The longest task for manager A was more than five years, while for B, C, and D, the longest tasks fell between two and five years. Note also that according to the organization chart, A is the designated manager of B, B of C, and C of D.

In reality, the situation was quite different. Despite the managerial roles specified by the company, B, C, and D all described A as their "real" boss. C complained that B was "far too close" and "breathing down my neck." D had the same complaint about C. B and C also admitted to finding it very difficult to manage their immediate subordinates, C and D respectively, who seemed to do better if treated as colleagues and left alone.

In short, there appeared to be a cutoff at five years, such that those with responsibility time spans of less than five years felt they needed a manager with a responsibility time span of more than five years. Manager D, with a time span of two to three years, did not feel that C, with a time span of three to four, was distant enough hierarchically to take orders from. D felt the same way about B. Only A filled the bill for *any* of the other three.

As the responsibility time span increased in the example from two years to three to four and approached five, no one seemed to perceive a qualitative difference in the nature of the responsibility that a manager discharged. Then, suddenly, when a manager had responsibility for tasks and projects that exceeded five years in scope, everyone seemed to perceive a difference not only in the scope of responsibility but also in its quality and in the kind of work and worker required to discharge it.

I found several such discontinuities that appeared consistently in more than 100 studies. Real managerial and hierarchical boundaries occur at time spans of three months, one year, two years, five years, ten years, and twenty years.

These natural discontinuities in our perception of the responsibility time span create hierarchical strata that people in different companies, countries, and circumstances all seem to regard as genuine and acceptable. The existence of such boundaries has important implications in nearly every sphere of organizational management. One of these is performance appraisal. Another is the capacity of managers to add value to the work of their subordinates.

The only person with the perspective and authority to judge and communicate personal effectiveness is an employee's accountable manager, who, in most cases, is also the only person from whom an employee will accept evaluation and coaching. This accountable manager must be the supervisor one real layer higher in the hierarchy, not merely the next higher employee on the pay scale.

As I suggested earlier, part of the secret to making hierarchy work is to distinguish carefully between hierarchical layers and pay grades. The trouble is that companies need two to three times as many pay grades as they do working layers, and once they've established the pay grades, which are easy to describe and set up, they fail to take the next step and set up a different managerial hierarchy based on responsibility rather than salary. The result is too many layers.

My experience with organizations of all kinds in many different countries has convinced me that effective value-adding managerial leadership of subordinates can come only from an individual one category higher in cognitive capacity, working one category higher in problem complexity. By contrast, wherever managers and subordinates are in the same layer – separated only by pay grade – subordinates see the boss as too close, breathing down their necks, and they identify their "real" boss as the next manager at a genuinely higher level of cognitive and task complexity. This kind of overlayering is what produces the typical symptoms of bureaucracy in its worst form – too much passing problems up and down the system, bypassing, poor task setting, frustrated subordinates, anxious managers, wholly inadequate performance appraisals, "personality problems" everywhere, and so forth.

Layering at Company X

Companies need more than seven pay grades – as a rule, many more. But seven hierarchical layers is enough or more than enough for all but the largest corporations.

Let me illustrate this pattern of hierarchical layering with the case of two divisions of Company X, a corporation with 32,000 employees and annual sales of $7 billion. As shown in "Two Divisions of Corporation X," the CEO sets strategic goals that look ahead as far as 25 years and manages executive vice presidents with responsibility for 12- to 15-year development programs. One vice president is accountable for several strategic business units, each with a president who works with critical tasks of up to 7 years duration.

One of these units (Y Products) employs 2,800 people, has annual sales of $250 million, and is engaged in the manufacture and sale of engineering products, with traditional semiskilled shop-floor production at Layer I. The other unit (Z Press) publishes books and employs only 88 people. Its funding and negotiations with authors are in the hands of a general editor at Layer IV, assisted by a small group of editors at Layer III, each working on projects that may take up to 18 months to complete.

So the president of Y Products manages more people, governs a greater share of corporate resources, and earns a lot more money for the parent company than does the president of Z Press. Yet the two presidents occupy the same hierarchical layer, have similar authority, and take home comparable salaries. This is neither coincidental nor unfair. It is natural, correct, and efficient.

It is the level of responsibility, *measured in terms of time span*, that tells you how many layers you need in an enterprise—not the number of subordinates or the magnitude of sales or profits. These factors may have a marginal influence on salary; they have no bearing at all on hierarchical layers.

Changes in the Quality of Work

The widespread and striking consistency of this underlying pattern of true managerial layers leads naturally to the question of why it occurs. Why do people perceive a sudden leap in status from, say, four-and-a-half years to five and from nine to ten?

The answer goes back to the earlier discussion of complexity. As we go higher in a managerial hierarchy, the most difficult problems that arise grow in-

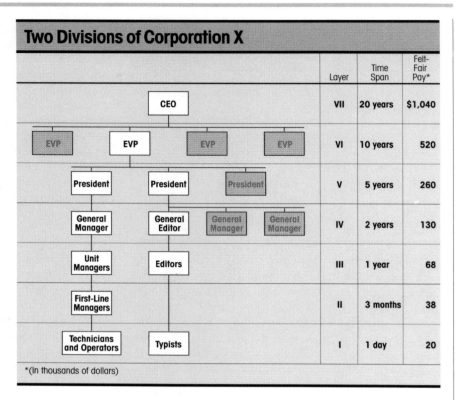

Two Divisions of Corporation X

	Layer	Time Span	Felt-Fair Pay*
CEO	VII	20 years	$1,040
EVP	VI	10 years	520
President	V	5 years	260
General Manager / General Editor	IV	2 years	130
Unit Managers / Editors	III	1 year	68
First-Line Managers	II	3 months	38
Technicians and Operators / Typists	I	1 day	20

*(In thousands of dollars)

creasingly complex, and, as the complexity of a task increases, so does the complexity of the mental work required to handle it. What I found when I looked at this problem over the course of ten years was that this complexity, like responsibility time span, also occurs in leaps or jumps. In other words, the most difficult tasks found within any given layer are all characterized by the same type or category of complexity, just as water remains in the same liquid state from 0° to 100° Celsius, even though it ranges from very cold to very hot. (A few degrees cooler or hotter and water changes in state, to ice or steam.)

It is this suddenly increased level of necessary mental capacity, experience, knowledge, and mental stamina that allows managers to add value to the work of their subordinates. What they add is a new perspective, one that is broader, more experienced, and, most important, one that extends further in time. If, at Z Press, the editors at Layer III find and develop manuscripts into books with market potential, it is their general editor at Layer IV who fits those books into the press's overall list, who thinks ahead to their position on next year's list and later allocates resources to their production and marketing, and who makes projections about the publishing and book-buying trends of the next two to five years.

It is also this sudden change in the quality, not just the quantity, of managerial work that subordinates accept as a natural and appropriate break in the continuum of hierarchy. It is why they accept the boss's authority and not just the boss's power.

So the whole picture comes together. Managerial hierarchy or layering is the only effective organizational form for deploying people and tasks at complementary levels, where people can do the tasks assigned to them, where the people in any given layer can add value to the work of those in the layer below them, and, finally, where this stratification of management strikes everyone as necessary and welcome.

What we need is not some new kind of organization. What we need is managerial hierarchy that understands its own nature and purpose. Hierarchy is the best structure for getting work done in big organizations. Trying to raise efficiency and morale without first setting this structure to rights is like trying to lay bricks without mortar. No amount of exhortation, attitudinal engineering, incentive planning, or even leadership will have any permanent effect unless we understand what hierarchy is and why and how it works. We need to stop casting about fruitlessly for organizational Holy Grails and settle down to the hard work of putting our managerial hierarchies in order.

Reprint 90107

"Let's not panic until we see how the Fed reacts."

How one unorthodox company makes money by avoiding decisions, rules, and executive authority.

Managing Without Managers

by Ricardo Semler

In Brazil, where paternalism and the family business fiefdom still flourish, I am president of a manufacturing company that treats its 800 employees like responsible adults. Most of them—including factory workers—set their own working hours. All have access to the company books. The vast majority vote on many important corporate decisions. Everyone gets paid by the month, regardless of job description, and more than 150 of our management people set their own salaries and bonuses.

This may sound like an unconventional way to run a business, but it seems to work. Close to financial disaster in 1980, Semco is now one of Brazil's fastest growing companies, with a profit margin in 1988 of 10% on sales of $37 million. Our five factories produce a range of sophisticated products, including marine pumps, digital scanners, commercial dishwashers, truck filters, and mixing equipment for everything from bubble gum to rocket fuel. Our customers include Alcoa, Saab, and General Motors. We've built a number of cookie factories for Nabisco, Nestlé, and United Biscuits. Our multinational competitors include AMF, Worthington Industries, Mitsubishi Heavy Industries, and Carrier.

Management associations, labor unions, and the press have repeatedly named us the best company in Brazil to work for. In fact, we no longer advertise jobs. Word of mouth generates up to 300 applications for every available position. The top five managers—we call them counselors—include a former human resources director of Ford Brazil, a 15-year veteran Chrysler executive, and a man who left his job as president of a larger company to come to Semco.

When I joined the company in 1980, 27 years after my father founded it, Semco had about 100 employees, manufactured hydraulic pumps for ships, generated about $4 million in revenues, and teetered on the brink of catastrophe. All through 1981 and 1982, we ran from bank to bank looking for loans, and we fought persistent, well-founded rumors that the company was in danger of going under. We often stayed through the night reading files and searching the desk drawers of venerable executives for clues about contracts long since privately made and privately forgotten.

Most managers and outside board members agreed on two immediate needs: to professionalize and to diversify. In fact, both of these measures had been discussed for years but had never progressed beyond wishful thinking.

For two years, holding on by our fingertips, we sought licenses to manufacture other companies' products in Brazil. We traveled constantly. I remember one day being in Oslo for breakfast, New York for lunch, Cincinnati for dinner, and San Francisco for the night. The obstacles were great. Our company lacked an international reputation—and so did

Late at night, we searched the desks of elderly executives for forgotten contracts.

our country. Brazil's political eccentricities and draconian business regulations scared many companies away.

Still, good luck and a relentless program of beating the corporate bushes on four continents finally paid off. By 1982, we had signed seven license agreements. Our marine division—once the entire company—was now down to 60% of total sales. Moreover, the managers and directors were all professionals with no connection to the family.

Ricardo Semler, 30, is president of Semco S/A, Brazil's largest marine and food-processing machinery manufacturer, and his book, Turning the Tables, *has been on Brazil's best-seller list for 60 weeks. He is vice president of the Federation of Industries of Brazil and a board member of SOS Atlantic Forest, Brazil's foremost environmental defense organization.*

With Semco back on its feet, we entered an acquisitions phase that cost millions of dollars in expenditures and millions more in losses over the next two or three years. All this growth was financed by banks at interest rates that were generally 30% above the rate of inflation, which ranged from 40% to 900% annually. There was no long-term money in Brazil at that time, so all those loans had maximum terms of 90 days. We didn't get one cent in government financing or from incentive agencies either, and we never paid out a dime in graft or bribes.

How did we do it and survive? Hard work, of course. And good luck—fundamental to all business success. But most important, I think, were the drastic changes we made in our concept of management. Without those changes, not even hard work and good luck could have pulled us through.

Semco has three fundamental values on which we base some 30 management programs. These values—democracy, profit sharing, and information—work in a complicated circle, each dependent on the other two. If we eliminated one, the others would be meaningless. Our corporate structure, employee freedoms, union relations, factory size limitations—all are products of our commitment to these principles.

It's never easy to transplant management programs from one company to another. In South America, it's axiomatic that our structure and style cannot be duplicated. Semco is either too small, too big, too far away, too young, too old, or too obnoxious.

We may also be too specialized. We do cellular manufacturing of technologically sophisticated products, and we work at the high end on quality and price. So our critics may be right. Perhaps nothing we've done can be a blueprint for anyone else. Still, in an industrial world whose methods show obvious signs of exhaustion, the merit of sharing experience is to encourage experiment and to plant the seeds of conceptual change. So what the hell.

Participatory Hot Air

The first of Semco's three values is democracy, or employee involvement. Clearly, workers who control their working conditions are going to be happier than workers who don't. Just as clearly, there is no contest between the company that buys the grudging compliance of its work force and the company that enjoys the enterprising participation of its employees.

But about 90% of the time, participatory management is just hot air. Not that intentions aren't good. It's just that implementing employee involvement is so complex, so difficult, and, not uncommonly, so frustrating that it is easier to talk about than to do.

We found four big obstacles to effective participatory management: size, hierarchy, lack of motivation, and ignorance. In an immense production unit, people feel tiny, nameless, and incapable of exerting influence on the way work is done or on the final profit made. This sense of helplessness is underlined by managers who, jealous of their power and prerogatives, refuse to let subordinates make any decisions for themselves—sometimes even about going to the bathroom. But even if size and hierarchy can be overcome, why should workers *care* about productivity and company profits? Moreover, even if you can get them to care, how can they tell when they're doing the right thing?

As Antony Jay pointed out back in the 1950s in *Corporation Man*, human beings weren't designed to work in big groups. Until recently, our ancestors were hunters and gatherers. For more than five million years, they refined their ability to work in groups of no more than about a dozen people. Then along comes the industrial revolution, and suddenly workers are trying to function efficiently in factories that employ hundreds and even thousands. Organizing those hundreds into teams of about ten members each may help some, but there's still a limit to how many small teams can work well together. At Semco, we've found the most effective production unit to consist of about 150 people. The exact number is open to argument, but it's clear that several thousand people in one facility makes individual involvement an illusion.

When we made the decision to keep our units small, we immediately focused on one facility that had more than 300 people. The unit manufactured commercial food-service equipment—slicers, scales, meat grinders, mixers—and used an MRP II system hooked up to an IBM mainframe with dozens of terminals all over the plant. Paperwork often took two days to make its way from one end of the factory to the other. Excess inventories, late delivery, and quality problems were common. We had tried various worker participation programs, quality circles, kanban systems, and motivation schemes, all of which got off to great starts but lost their momentum within months. The whole thing was just too damn big and complex; there were too many managers in too many layers holding too many meetings. So we decided to break up the facility into three separate plants.

To begin with, we kept all three in the same building but separated everything we could—entrances, receiving docks, inventories, telephones, as well as certain auxiliary functions like personnel, management information systems, and internal controls. We also scrapped the mainframe in favor of three independent, PC-based systems.

The first effect of the breakup was a rise in costs due to duplication of effort and a loss in economies of scale. Unfortunately, balance sheets chalk up items like these as liabilities, all with dollar figures attached, and there's nothing at first to list on the asset side but airy stuff like "heightened involvement" and "a sense of belonging." Yet the longer term results exceeded our expectations.

Within a year, sales doubled; inventories fell from 136 days to 46; we unveiled eight new products that had been stalled in R&D for two years; and overall quality improved to the point that a one-third rejection rate on federally inspected scales dropped to less than 1%. Increased productivity let us reduce the work force by 32% through attrition and retirement incentives.

I don't claim that size reduction alone accomplished all this, just that size reduction is essential for putting employees in touch with one another so they can coordinate their work. The kind of distance we want to eliminate comes from having too many people in one place, but it also comes from having a pyramidal hierarchy.

Pyramids and Circles

The organizational pyramid is the cause of much corporate evil, because the tip is too far from the base. Pyramids emphasize power, promote insecurity, distort communications, hobble interaction, and make it very difficult for the people who plan and the people who execute to move in the same direction. So Semco designed an organizational *circle*. Its greatest advantage is to reduce management levels to three—one corporate level and two operating levels at the manufacturing units.

It consists of three concentric circles. One tiny, central circle contains the five people who integrate the company's movements. These are the counselors I mentioned before. I'm one of them, and except for a couple of legal documents that call me president, counselor is the only title I use. A second, larger circle contains the heads of the eight divisions—we call them partners. Finally, a third, huge circle holds all the other employees. Most of them are the people we call associates; they do the research, design, sales, and manufacturing work and have no one reporting to them on a regular basis. But some of them are the permanent and temporary team and task leaders we call coordinators. Counselors, partners, coordi-

nators, and associates. Four titles. Three management layers.

The linchpins of the system are the coordinators, a group that includes everyone formerly called foreman, supervisor, manager, head, or chief. The only people who report to coordinators are associates. No coordinator reports to another coordinator—that feature of the system is what ensures the reduction in management layers.

Like anyone else, we value leadership, but it's not the only thing we value. In marine pumps, for exam-

Our people often make higher salaries than their bosses.

ple, we have an applications engineer who can look at the layout of a ship and then focus on one particular pump and say, "That pump will fail if you take this thing north of the Arctic Circle." He makes a lot more money than the person who manages his unit. We can change the manager, but this guy knows what kind of pump will work in the Arctic, and that's worth more. Associates often make higher salaries than coordinators and partners, and they can increase their status and compensation without entering the "management" line.

Managers and the status and money they enjoy—in a word, hierarchy—are the single biggest obstacle to participatory management. We had to get the managers out of the way of democratic decision making, and our circular system does that pretty well.

But we go further. We don't hire or promote people until they've been interviewed and accepted by all their future subordinates. Twice a year, subordinates evaluate managers. Also twice a year, everyone in the company anonymously fills out a questionnaire about company credibility and top management competence. Among other things, we ask our employees what it would take to make them quit or go on strike.

We insist on making important decisions collegially, and certain decisions are made by a company-wide vote. Several years ago, for example, we needed a bigger plant for our marine division, which makes pumps, compressors, and ship propellers. Real estate agents looked for months and found nothing. So we asked the employees themselves to help, and over the first weekend they found three factories for sale, all of them nearby. We closed up shop for a day, piled everyone into buses, and drove out to inspect the three buildings. Then the workers voted—and they chose a plant the counselors didn't really want. It was an interesting situation—one that tested our commitment to participatory management.

The building stands across the street from a Caterpillar plant that's one of the most frequently struck factories in Brazil. With two tough unions of our own, we weren't looking forward to front-row seats for every labor dispute that came along. But we accepted the employees' decision, because we believe that in the long run, letting people participate in the decisions that affect their lives will have a positive effect on employee motivation and morale.

We bought the building and moved in. The workers designed the layout for a flexible manufacturing system, and they hired one of Brazil's foremost artists to paint the whole thing, inside and out, including the machinery. That plant really belongs to its employees. I feel like a guest every time I walk in.

I don't mind. The division's productivity, in dollars per year per employee, has jumped from $14,200 in 1984 – the year we moved – to $37,500 in 1988, and for 1989 the goal is $50,000. Over the same period, market share went from 54% to 62%.

Employees also outvoted me on the acquisition of a company that I'm still sure we should have bought. But they felt we weren't ready to digest it, and I lost the vote. In a case like that, the credibility of our management system is at stake. Employee involvement must be real, even when it makes management uneasy. Anyway, what is the future of an acquisition if the people who have to operate it don't believe it's workable?

Hiring Adults

We have other ways of combating hierarchy too. Most of our programs are based on the notion of giving employees control over their own lives. In a word, we hire adults, and then we treat them like adults.

Think about that. Outside the factory, workers are men and women who elect governments, serve in the army, lead community projects, raise and educate families, and make decisions every day about the future. Friends solicit their advice. Salespeople court them. Children and grandchildren look up to them for their wisdom and experience. But the moment they walk into the factory, the company transforms them into adolescents. They have to wear badges and name tags, arrive at a certain time, stand in line to punch the clock or eat their lunch, get permission to go to the bathroom, give lengthy explanations every time they're five minutes late, and follow instructions without asking a lot of questions.

One of my first moves when I took control of Semco was to abolish norms, manuals, rules, and regulations. Everyone knows you can't run a large organization without regulations, but everyone also knows that most regulations are poppycock. They rarely solve problems. On the contrary, there is usually some obscure corner of the rule book that justifies the worst silliness people can think up. Common sense is a riskier tactic because it requires personal responsibility.

It's also true that common sense requires just a touch of civil disobedience every time someone calls attention to something that's not working. We had to free the Thoreaus and the Tom Paines in the factory and come to terms with that fact that civil disobedience was not an early sign of revolution but a clear indication of common sense at work.

So we replaced all the nitpicking regulations with the rule of common sense and put our employees

> **We wanted our workers to act like adults, so we stopped treating them like adolescents.**

in the demanding position of using their own judgment.

We have no dress code, for example. The idea that personal appearance is important in a job – any job – is baloney. We've all heard that salespeople, receptionists, and service reps are the company's calling cards, but in fact how utterly silly that is. A company that needs business suits to prove its seriousness probably lacks more meaningful proof. And what customer has ever canceled an order because the receptionist was wearing jeans instead of a dress? Women and men look best when they feel good. IBM is not a great company because its salespeople dress to the special standard that Thomas Watson set. It's a great company that also happens to have this quirk.

We also scrapped the complex company rules about travel expenses – what sorts of accommodations people were entitled to, whether we'd pay for a theater ticket, whether a free call home meant five minutes or ten. We used to spend a lot of time discussing stuff like that. Now we base everything on common sense. Some people stay in four-star hotels and some live like spartans. Some people spend $200 a day while others get by on $125. Or so I suppose. No one checks expenses, so there is no way of knowing. The point is, we don't care. If we can't trust people with our money and their judgment, we sure as hell shouldn't be sending them overseas to do business in our name.

We have done away with security searches, storeroom padlocks, and audits of the petty-cash accounts

Ricardo Semler's Guide to Stress Management

There are two things all managers have in common—the 24-hour day and the annoying need to sleep. Without the sleeping, 24 hours might be enough. With it, there is no way to get everything done. After years of trying to vanquish demon sleep and the temptation to relax, I tried an approach suggested by my doctor, who put it this way: "Slow down or kiss yourself good-bye."

Struck by this imagery, I learned to manage my time and cut my work load to less than 24 hours. The first step is to overcome five myths:

1. *Results are proportional to efforts.* The Brazilian flag expresses this myth in a slightly different form. "Order and Progress," it says. Of course, it ought to say, "Order *or* Progress," since the two never go together.

2. *Quantity of work is more important than quality.* Psychologically, this myth may hold water. The executive who puts in lots of hours can always say, "Well, they didn't promote me, but you can see how unfair that is. Everyone knows I get here at 8 A.M. and that my own children can't see me without an appointment."

3. *The present restructuring requires longer working hours temporarily.* We think of ourselves as corks on a mountain stream headed for Lake Placid. But the lake ahead is Loch Ness. The present, temporary emergency is actually permanent. Stop being a cork.

4. *No one else can do it right.* The truth is, you *are* replaceable, as everyone will discover within a week of your funeral.

5. This *problem is urgent.* Come on. The real difference between "important" and "urgent" is the difference between thoughtfulness and panic.

Those are the myths. The second step is to master my eight cures:

1. Set an hour to leave the office and obey it blindly. If you normally go home at 7:00, start leaving at 6:00. If you take work home on weekends, give yourself a month or two to put a stop to this pernicious practice.

2. Take half a day, maybe even an entire Saturday, to rummage through that mountain of paper in your office and put it in three piles.

Pile A: Priority items that require your personal attention and represent matters of indisputable importance. If you put more than four or five documents in this category and are not currently the president of your country, start over.

Pile B: Items that need your personal attention, but not right away. This pile is very tempting; everything fits. But don't fall into the trap. Load this stuff on your subordinates, using the 70% test to help you do it. Ask yourself: Is there someone on my staff who can do this task at least 70% as well as I can? Yes? Then farm it out. Whether or not your subordinates are overworked should not weigh in your decision. Remember, control of your time is an exercise in selfishness.

Pile C: Items that fall under the dubious rubric "a good idea to look at." One of the most egregious executive fallacies is that you have to read a little of everything in order to stay well-informed. If you

of veteran employees. Not that we wouldn't prosecute a genuinely criminal violation of our trust. We just refuse to humiliate 97% of the work force to get our hands on the occasional thief or two-bit embezzler.

We encourage—we practically insist on—job rotation every two to five years to prevent boredom. We try hard to provide job security, and for people over 50 or who've been with the company for more than three years, dismissal procedures are extra complicated.

On the more experimental side, we have a program for entry-level management trainees called "Lost in Space," whereby we hire a couple of people every year who have no job description at all. A "godfather" looks after them, and for one year they can do anything they like, as long as they try at least 12 different areas or units.

By the same logic that governs our other employee programs, we have also eliminated time clocks. People come and go according to their own schedules—even on the factory floor. I admit this idea is hard to swallow; most manufacturers are not ready for factory-floor flextime. But our reasoning was simple.

First, we use cellular manufacturing systems. At our food-processing equipment plant, for example, one cell makes only slicers, another makes scales, another makes mixers, and so forth. Each cell is self-contained, so products—and their problems—are segregated from each other.

Second, we assumed that all our employees were trustworthy adults. We couldn't believe they would come to work day after day and sit on their hands because no one else was there. Pretty soon, we figured, they would start coordinating their work hours with their coworkers.

limit the number of newspapers, magazines, and internal communications that you read regularly, you'll have more time to do what's important—like think. And remember to keep your reading timely; information is a perishable commodity.

3. In dealing with Pile A, always start with the most difficult or the most time-consuming. It also helps to have a folder for the things that *must* be done before you go home that day and to make a list of the things that simply cannot go undone for more than a few days or a week. Everything else is just everything else.

4. Buy another wastepaper basket. I know you already have one. But if you invited me to go through that pile of papers on your desk, I could fill both in a trice. To help you decide what to toss and what to save, ask yourself the question asked by the legendary Alfred P. Sloan, Jr.: "What is the worst that can happen if I throw this out?" If you don't tremble, sweat, or grow faint when you think of the consequences, toss it.

This second wastebasket is a critical investment, even though you'll never be able to fill both on a regular basis. Keep it anyway. It has a symbolic value. It will babysit your in-basket and act like a governess every time you wonder why you bought it.

5. Ask yourself Sloan's question about every lunch and meeting invitation. Don't be timid. And practice these three RSVPs:

"Thanks, but I just can't fit it in."

"I can't go, but I think X can." (If you think someone should.)

"I'm sorry I can't make it, but do let me know what happened."

Transform meetings into telephone calls or quick conversations in the hall. When you hold a meeting in your office, sit on the edge of your desk, or when you want to end the discussion, stand up from behind your desk and say, "OK, then, that's settled." These tricks are rude but almost foolproof.

6. Give yourself time to think. Spend half a day every week away from your office. Take your work home, or try working somewhere else—a conference room in another office, a public library, an airport waiting room—any place you can concentrate, and the farther away from your office the better. The point is, a fresh environment can do wonders for productivity. Just make sure you bring along a healthy dose of discipline, especially if you're working at home.

7. About the telephone, my practical but subversive advice is: Don't return calls. Or rather, return calls only to people you want to talk to. The others will call back. Better yet, they'll write, and you can spend ten seconds with their letter and then give it to the governess.

Two ancillary bits of phone advice: Ask your assistants to take detailed messages. Ask them always to say you cannot take the call at the moment. (Depending on who it is, your assistants can always undertake to see if you can't be interrupted.)

8. Close your door. Oh, I know you have an open-door policy, but don't be so literal.

And that's exactly what happened, only more so. For example, one man wanted to start at 7 A.M., but because the forklift operator didn't come until 8, he couldn't get his parts. So a general discussion arose, and the upshot was that now everyone knows how to operate a forklift. In fact, most people can now do several jobs. The union has never objected because the initiative came from the workers themselves. It was their idea.

Moreover, the people on the factory floor set the schedule, and if they say that this month they will build 48 commercial dishwashers, then we can go play tennis, because 48 is what they'll build.

In one case, one group decided to make 220 meat slicers. By the end of the month, it had finished the slicers as scheduled—except that even after repeated phone calls, the supplier still hadn't produced the motors. So two employees drove over and talked to the supplier and managed to get delivery at the end of that day, the 31st. Then they stayed all night, the whole work force, and finished the lot at 4:45 the next morning.

When we introduced flexible hours, we decided to hold regular follow-up meetings to track problems and decide how to deal with abuses and production interruptions. That was years ago, and we haven't yet held the first meeting.

Hunting the Woolly Mammoth

What makes our people behave this way? As Antony Jay points out, corporate man is a very recent animal. At Semco, we try to respect the hunter that dominated the first 99.9% of the history of our species. If you had to kill a mammoth or do without supper, there was no time to draw up an organization chart, assign tasks, or delegate authority. Basically, the person who saw the mammoth from farthest away was the Official Sighter, the one who ran fastest was the Head Runner, whoever threw the most accurate spear was the Grand Marksman, and the person all others respected most and listened to was the Chief. That's all there was to it. Distributing little charts to produce an appearance of order would have been a waste of time. It still is.

What I'm saying is, put ten people together, don't appoint a leader, and you can be sure that one will emerge. So will a sighter, a runner, and whatever else the group needs. We form the groups, but they find their own leaders. That's not a lack of structure, that's just a lack of structure imposed from above.

But getting back to that mammoth, why was it that all the members of the group were so eager to do their share of the work – sighting, running, spearing, chiefing – and to stand aside when someone else could do it better? Because they all got to eat the thing once it was killed and cooked. What mattered was results, not status.

Corporate profit is today's mammoth meat. And though there is a widespread view that profit sharing is some kind of socialist infection, it seems to me that few motivational tools are more capitalist. Everyone agrees that profits should belong to those who risk their capital, that entrepreneurial behavior deserves reward, that the creation of wealth should enrich the creator. Well, depending on how you define capital and risk, all these truisms can apply as much to workers as to shareholders.

Still, many profit-sharing programs are failures, and we think we know why. Profit sharing won't motivate employees if they see it as just another management gimmick, if the company makes it difficult for them to see how their own work is related to profits and to understand how those profits are divided.

> **After the hunt, primitive people shared their kill. Today's mammoth meat is profits.**

In Semco's case, each division has a separate profit-sharing program. Twice a year, we calculate 23% of after-tax profit on each division income statement and give a check to three employees who've been elected by the workers in their division. These three invest the money until the unit can meet and decide – by simple majority vote – what they want to do with it. In most units, that's turned out to be an equal distribution. If a unit has 150 workers, the total is divided by 150 and handed out. It's that simple. The guy who sweeps the floor gets just as much as the division partner.

One division chose to use the money as a fund to lend out for housing construction. It was a pretty close vote, and the workers may change their minds next year. In the meantime, some of them have already received loans and have begun to build themselves houses. In any case, the employees do what they want with the money. The counselors stay out of it.

Semco's experience has convinced me that profit sharing has an excellent chance of working when it crowns a broad program of employee participation, when the profit-sharing criteria are so clear and simple that the least gifted employee can understand them, and, perhaps most important, when employees have monthly access to the company's vital statistics – costs, overhead, sales, payroll, taxes, profits.

Transparency

Lots of things contribute to a successful profit-sharing program: low employee turnover, competitive pay, absence of paternalism, refusal to give consolation prizes when profits are down, frequent (quarterly or semiannual) profit distribution, and plenty of opportunity for employees to question the management decisions that affect future profits. But nothing matters more than those vital statistics – short, frank, frequent reports on how the company is doing. Complete transparency. No hocus-pocus, no hanky-panky, no simplifications.

On the contrary, all Semco employees attend classes to learn how to read and understand the numbers, and it's one of their unions that teaches the course. Every month, each employee gets a balance sheet, a profit-and-loss analysis, and a cash-flow statement for his or her division. The reports contain about 70 line items (more, incidentally, than we use to run the company, but we don't want anyone to think we're withholding information).

Many of our executives were alarmed by the decision to share monthly financial results with all employees. They were afraid workers would want to know everything, like how much we pay executives. When we held the first large meeting to discuss these financial reports with the factory committees and the leaders of the metalworkers' union, the first question we got was, "How much do division managers make?" We told them. They gasped. Ever since, the factory workers have called them "maharaja."

But so what? If executives are embarrassed by their salaries, that probably means they aren't earning them. Confidential payrolls are for those who cannot look themselves in the mirror and say with conviction, "I live in a capitalist system that remunerates on a geometric scale. I spent years in school, I have years of experience, I am capable and dedicated and intelligent. I deserve what I get."

I believe that the courage to show the real numbers will always have positive consequences over the long term. On the other hand, we can show only the numbers we bother to put together, and

> **If executives are embarrassed by what they make, they probably aren't earning it.**

there aren't as many as there used to be. In my view, only the big numbers matter. But Semco's accounting people keep telling me that since the only way to get the big numbers is to add up the small ones, producing a budget or report that includes every tiny detail would require no extra effort. This is an expensive fallacy, and a difficult one to eradicate.

A few years ago, the U.S. president of Allis-Chalmers paid Semco a visit. At the end of his factory tour, he leafed through our monthly reports and budgets. At that time, we had our numbers ready on the fifth working day of every month in super-organized folders, and were those numbers comprehensive! On page 67, chart 112.6, for example, you could see how much coffee the workers in Light Manufacturing III had consumed the month before. The man said he was surprised to find such efficiency in a Brazilian company. In fact, he was so impressed that he asked his Brazilian subsidiary, an organization many times our size, to install a similar system there.

For months, we strolled around like peacocks, telling anyone who cared to listen that our budget system was state-of-the-art and that the president of a Big American Company had ordered his people to copy it. But soon we began to realize two things. First, our expenses were always too high, and they never came down because the accounting department was full of overpaid clerks who did nothing but compile them. Second, there were so damn many numbers inside the folder that almost none of our managers read them. In fact, we knew less about the company then, with all that information, than we do now without it.

Today we have a simple accounting system providing limited but relevant information that we can

Ricardo Semler's Guide to Compensation

Employers began hiring workers by the hour during the industrial revolution. Their reasons were simple and rapacious. Say you ran out of cotton thread at 11:30 in the morning. If you paid people by the hour, you could stop the looms, send everyone home, and pay only for hours actually worked.

You couldn't do such a thing today. The law probably wouldn't let you. The unions certainly wouldn't let you. Your own self-interest would argue strongly against it. Yet the system lives on. The distinction between wage-earning workers and salaried employees is alive but not well, nearly universal but perfectly silly. The new clerk who lives at home and doesn't know how to boil an egg starts on a monthly salary, but the chief lathe operator who's been with the company 38 years and is a master sergeant in the army reserve still gets paid by the hour.

At Semco, we eliminated Frederick Winslow Taylor's segmentation and specialization of work. We ended the wage analyst's hundred years of solitude. We did away with hourly pay and now give everyone a monthly salary. We set the salaries like this:

A lot of our people belong to unions, and they negotiate their salaries collectively. Everyone else's salary involves an element of self-determination.

Once or twice a year, we order salary market surveys and pass them out. We say to people, "Figure out where you stand on this thing. You know what you do; you know what everyone else in the company makes; you know what your friends in other companies make; you know what you need; you know what's fair. Come back on Monday and tell us what to pay you."

When people ask for too little, we give it to them. By and by, they figure it out and ask for more. When they ask for too much, we give that to them too—at least for the first year. Then, if we don't feel they're worth the money, we sit down with them and say, "Look, you make x amount of money, and we don't think you're making x amount of contribution. So either we find something else for you to do, or we don't have a job for you anymore." But with half a dozen exceptions, our people have always named salaries we could live with.

We do a similar thing with titles. Counselors are counselors, and partners are partners; these titles are always the same. But with coordinators, it's not quite so easy. Job titles still mean too much to many people. So we tell coordinators to make up their own titles. They know what signals they need to send inside and outside the company. If they want "Procurement Manager," that's fine. And if they want "Grand Panjandrum of Imperial Supplies," that's fine too.

grasp and act on quickly. We pared 400 cost centers down to 50. We beheaded hundreds of classifications and dozens of accounting lines. Finally, we can see the company through the haze.

(As for Allis-Chalmers, I don't know whether it ever adopted our old system in all its terrible completeness, but I hope not. A few years later, it began to suffer severe financial difficulties and eventually lost so much market share and money that it was broken up and sold. I'd hate to think it was our fault.)

In preparing budgets, we believe that the flexibility to change the budget continually is much more important than the detailed consistency of the initial numbers. We also believe in the importance of comparing expectations with results. Naturally, we compare monthly reports with the budget. But we go one step further. At month's end, the coordinators in each area make guesses about unit receipts, profit margins, and expenses. When the official numbers come out a few days later, top managers compare them with the guesses to judge how well the coordinators understand their areas.

What matters in budgets as well as in reports is that the numbers be few and important and that people treat them with something approaching passion. The three monthly reports, with their 70 line items, tell us how to run the company, tell our managers how well they know their units, and tell our employees if there's going to be a profit. Everyone works on the basis of the same information, and everyone looks forward to its appearance with what I'd call fervent curiosity.

And that's all there is to it. Participation gives people control of their work, profit sharing gives them a reason to do it better, information tells them what's working and what isn't.

Letting Them Do Whatever the Hell They Want

So we don't have systems or staff functions or analysts or anything like that. What we have are people who either sell or make, and there's nothing in between. Is there a marketing department? Not on your life. Marketing is everybody's problem. Everybody knows the price of the product. Everybody knows the cost. Everybody has the monthly statement that says exactly what each of them makes, how much bronze is costing us, how much overtime we paid, all of it. And the employees know that 23% of the after-tax profit is theirs.

We are very, very rigorous about the numbers. We want them in on the fourth day of the month so we can get them back out on the fifth. And because we're so strict with the financial controls, we can be extremely lax about everything else. Employees can paint the walls any color they like. They can come to work whenever they decide. They can wear whatever clothing makes them comfortable. They can do whatever the hell they want. It's up to them to see the connection between productivity and profit and to act on it.

Reprint 89509

HBR CASE STUDY

Dominion-Swann management acquires technology to support employees — or control them?

The Case of the Omniscient Organization

by Gary T. Marx

The following is an excerpt from Dominion-Swann Industries' 1995 Employee Handbook. DS is a $1 billion diversified company, primarily in the manufacture of electrical components for automobiles. This section of the handbook was prepared by the corporate director of personnel, in consultation with the human resource management firm Sciex-Plan Inc.

Dominion-Swann's new workplace: Hope for industry through technology

We are a technology-based company. We respect our employees, whose knowledge is the core of the technological enterprise. We care about the DS community. We value honesty, informed consent, and unfettered scientific inquiry. Our employees understand company strategy. They are free to suggest ways to improve our performance. We offer handsome rewards for high productivity and vigorous participation in the life of our company. Committed to science, we believe

in careful experimentation and in learning from experience.

Since 1990, we have instituted changes in our work environment. The reasons for change were clear enough from the start. In 1990, DS faced an uncertain future. Our productivity and quality were not keeping pace with overseas competition. Employee turnover was up, especially in the most critical part of our business — automotive chips, switches, and modules. Health costs and work accidents were on the rise. Our employees were demoralized. There were unprecedented numbers of thefts from plants and offices and leaks to competitors about current research. There was also a sharp rise in drug use. Security personnel reported unseemly behavior by company employees not only in our parking lots and athletic fields but also in restaurants and bars near our major plants.

In the fall of 1990, the company turned to SciexPlan Inc., a specialist in employee-relations management in worldwide companies, to help de-

velop a program for the radical restructuring of the work environment. We had much to learn from the corporate cultures of overseas competitors and were determined to benefit from the latest advances in work-support technology. The alternative was continued decline and, ultimately, the loss of jobs.

Frankly, there was instability while the program was being developed and implemented. Some valued employees quit and others took early retirement. But widespread publicity about our efforts drew to the program people who sincerely sought a well-ordered, positive environment. DS now boasts a clerical, professional, and factory staff which understands how the interests of a successful company correspond with the interests of individual employees. To paraphrase psychologist William James, "When the community dies, the individual withers." Such sentiments, we believe, are as embedded in Western traditions as in Eastern; they are the foundation of world community. They are also a fact of the new global marketplace.

The fundamentals

Since 1990, productivity per worker is up 14%. Sales are up 23%, and the work force is down 19%. Employees' real income is up 18%, due in large part to our bonus and profit-sharing plans. Many of these efficiencies can be attributed to reform of our factories' production technologies. But we can be proud to have been ahead of our time in the way we build our corporate spirit and use social technologies.

At DS four principles underlie work-support restructuring:

1. Make the company a home to employees. Break down artificial and alienating barriers between work and home. Dissolve, through company initiative, feelings of isolation. Great companies are made by great people; all employee behavior and self-development counts.

Gary T. Marx is professor of sociology at Massachusetts Institute of Technology. He is author of Undercover: Police Surveillance in America *(University of California Press, 1988).*

2. Hire people who will make a continuing contribution. Bring in people who are likely to stay healthy and successful, people who will be on the job without frequent absences. Candor about prospective employees' pasts may be the key to the company's future.

3. Technical, hardware-based solutions are preferable to supervision and persuasion. Machines are cheaper, more reliable, and fairer than managers. Employees want to do the right thing; the company wants nothing but this and will give employees all the needed technical assistance. Employees accept performance evaluation from an impartial system more readily than from a superior and appreciate technical solutions that channel behavior in a constructive direction.

4. Create accountability through visibility. Loyal employees enjoy the loyalty of others. They welcome audits, reasonable monitoring, and documentary proof of their activities, whether of location, business conversations, or weekly output. Once identified, good behavior can be rewarded, inappropriate behavior can be improved.

These principles have yielded an evolving program that continues to benefit from the participation and suggestions of our employees. The following summary is simply an introduction. The personnel office will be pleased to discuss any aspect of community performance or breaches of company policy in detail with employees. (You may call for an appointment during normal business hours at X-2089.)

Entry-level screening

As a matter of course and for mutual benefit, potential employees are screened and tested. We want to avoid hiring people whose predictive profile—medications, smoking, obesity, debt, high-risk sports, family crises—suggests that there will be serious losses to our community's productivity in the future.

Job applicants volunteer to undergo extensive medical and psychological examinations and to provide the company with detailed personal information and records, including background information about the health, lifestyle, and employment of parents, spouses, siblings, and close friends. Company associates seek permission to make discreet searches of various databases, including education, credit, bankruptcy and mortgage default, auto accident, driver's license suspension, insurance, health, worker's compensation, military, rental, arrest, and criminal activity.

The company opposes racial and sexual discrimination. DS will not check databases containing the names of union organizers or those active in controversial political causes (whether on the right or the left). Should the company's inquiry unwittingly turn up such information, it is ignored. We also use a résumé verification service.

Since our community is made up of people, not machines, we have found it useful to compare physiological, psychological, social, and demographic factors against the profiles of our best employees. Much of this analysis has been standardized. It is run by SciexPlan's expert system, INDUCT.

Community health

We want employees who are willing to spend their lives with the company, and we care about their long-term health. The company administers monthly pulmonary tests in behalf of the zero-tolerance smoking policy. Zero tolerance means lower health insurance premiums and improved quality of life for all employees.

In cooperation with Standar-Hardwick, one of the United States's most advanced makers of medical equipment and a valued customer, we've developed an automated health monitor. These new machines, used in a private stall and activated by employee thumbprint, permit biweekly urine analysis and a variety of other tests (blood pressure, pulse, temperature, weight) without the bother of having to go to a health facility. This program has received international attention: at times, it has been hailed; at times, severely criticized. People at DS often express surprise at the fuss. Regular monitoring of urine means early warning against diabetes and other potentially catastrophic diseases—and also reveals pregnancy. It also means that we can keep a drug-free, safe environment without subjecting people to the in-

DRAWINGS BY CHUCK MORRIS

dignities of random testing or the presence of an observer.

The quality environment

Drawing on SciexPlan's research, our company believes that the physical environment is also important to wellness and productivity. Fragrant aromas such as evergreen may reduce stress; the smell of lemon and jasmine can have a rejuvenating effect. These scents are introduced to all work spaces through the air-conditioning and heating systems. Scents are changed seasonally.

Music is not only enjoyable to listen to but can also affect productivity. We continually experiment with the impact of different styles of music on an office's or plant's aggregate output. Since psychologists have taught us that the most serious threat to safety and productivity is stress, we use subliminal messages in music such as "safety pays," "work rapidly but carefully," and "this company cares." Personal computers deliver visual subliminals such as "my world is calm" or "we're all on the same team."

At the start of each month, employees are advised of message content. Those who don't want a message on their computers may request that none be transmitted—no questions asked. On the whole, employees who participate in the program feel noticeably more positive about their work. Employees may borrow from our library any one of hundreds of subliminal tapes, including those that help the listener improve memory, reduce stress, relax, lose weight, be guilt-free, improve self-confidence, defeat discouragement, and sleep more soundly.

On the advice of SciexPlan's dieticians, the company cafeteria and dining room serve only fresh, wholesome food prepared without salt, sugar, or cholesterol-producing substances. Sugar- and caffeine-based, high-energy snacks and beverages are available during breaks, at no cost to employees.

Work monitoring

Monitoring system performance is our business. The same technologies that keep engines running at peak efficiency can keep the companies that make engine components running efficiently too. That is the double excitement of the information revolution.

At DS, we access more than 200 criteria to assess productivity of plant employees and data-entry personnel. These criteria include such things as the quantity of keystroke activity, the number of errors and corrections made, the pressure on the assembly tool, the speed of work, and time away from the job. Reasonable productivity standards have been established. We are proud to say that, with a younger work force, these standards keep going up, and the incentive pay of employees who exceed standards is rising proportionately.

Our work units are divided into teams. The best motivator to work hard is the high standards of one's peers. Teams, not individuals, earn prizes and bonuses. Winning teams have the satisfaction of knowing they are doing more than their share. Computer screens abound with productivity updates, encouraging employees to note where their teams stand and how productive individuals have been for the hour, week, and month. Computers send congratulatory messages such as "you are working 10% faster than the norm" or messages of concern such as "you are lowering the team average."

Community morale

There is no community without honesty. Any community must take reasonable precautions to protect itself from dishonesty. Just as we inspect the briefcases and purses of visitors exiting our R&D division, the company reserves the right to call up and inspect without notice all data files and observe work-in-progress currently displayed on employees' screens. One random search discovered an employee using the company computer to send out a curriculum vitae seeking employment elsewhere. In another, an employee was running a football pool.

Some companies try to prevent private phone calls on company time by invading their employees' privacy. At DS, encroachments on employees' privacy are obviated by telecommunications programs that block inappropriate numbers (dial-a-joke, dial-a-prayer) and unwanted incoming calls. In addition, an exact record of all dialing behavior is recorded, as is the number from which calls are received. We want our employees to feel protected against any invalid claims against them.

Video and audio surveillance too protects employees from intruders in hallways, parking lots, lounges, and work areas. Vigilance is invaluable in protecting our community from illegal behavior or actions that violate our safety and high commitment to excellence. All employees, including managers, check in and out of various workstations—including the parking lot, main entrance, elevator, floors, office, and even the bathroom—by means of an electronic entry card. In one case, this surveillance probably saved the life of an employee who had a heart attack in the parking lot: when he failed to check into the next workstation after five minutes, security personnel were sent to investigate.

Beyond isolation

Our program takes advantage of the most advanced telecommunications equipment to bind employees to one another and to the company. DS vehicles are equipped with onboard computers using satellite transponders. This offers a tracking service and additional two-way communication. It helps our customers keep inventories down and helps prevent hijacking, car theft, and improper use of the vehicles. Drivers save time since engines are checked electronically. They also drive more safely, and vehicles are better maintained since speed, gear shifts, and idling time are measured.

In addition to locator and paging devices, all managers are given fax machines and personal computers for their homes. These are connected at all times. Cellular telephones are provided to selected employees who commute for more than half an hour or for use while traveling.

Instant communication is vital in today's international economy. The global market does not function only from 9 to 5. Modern technology can greatly increase productivity by ensuring instant access and communication. Periodic disruptions to vacations or sleep are a small price to pay for the tremendous gains to be won in worldwide competition. DS employees share in these gains.

Great companies have always unleashed the power of new technology for the social welfare, even in the face of criticism. During the first industrial revolution, such beloved novelists as Charles Dickens sincerely opposed the strictures of mass production. In time, however, most of the employees who benefited from the wealth created by new factories and machines came to take progress for granted and preferred the modern factory to traditional craft methods. Today we are living through a Second Industrial Revolution, driven by the computer.

Advanced work-support technology is democratic, effective, and anti-hierarchical. DS's balance sheet and the long waiting list of prospective employees indicate how the new program has helped everybody win. To recall the phrase of journalist Lincoln Steffens, "We have been over into the future, and it works." We are a company of the twenty-first century.

HBR's cases are derived from the experiences of real companies and real people. As written, they are hypothetical, and the names used are fictitious.

Dominion-Swann Industries wants its employees to be productive, happy, and safe. Are they?

Four experts on technology and human resource management discuss Dominion-Swann's work-support technology.

Nothing is wrong with Dominion-Swann's admirable goals except their priority.

Like many companies, Dominion-Swann seeks to protect and maximize two vital resources critical to its ongoing success: the vast investment of the company in technology

JOSEPH MODEROW *is senior vice president and general counsel of United Parcel Service. He also serves on UPS's Technology Steering Committee.*

and its employees. Nothing is wrong with these admirable goals except their priority. People come second at DS, even in the handbook title which points to technology as the hope for industry and the centerpiece of Dominion-Swann's new workplace.

DS management informs employees that necessary changes in the work environment have been instituted and justifies these changes with a trail of failures rather than a vision of success. But it lacks the curiosity—not to mention wisdom—to explore the causes of its workers' demoralized state.

Despite DS's disturbing actions, competitive companies do have the right to determine, direct, and even measure how employees perform their responsibilities. Anyone who has seen recent UPS commercials will likely identify us with the phrase "We run the tightest ship in the shipping business." When you observe the urgency and determination of our delivery drivers, you may be led to believe that we achieved such efficiency through a corporate culture like that of DS. That is not the case. UPS succeeds because of its conviction that control and efficiency must not be achieved at the cost of employee commitment.

Much of UPS's success is attributable to continuous effort to optimize the efficient use and allocation of people, facilities, equipment, and technology. We do utilize work measurement programs in which drivers are given specific quantitative goals to achieve. This is a valuable tool in properly allocating resources and reflects the fundamental philosophy of "A fair day's wage for a fair day's work." This scientific management is, however, balanced by our commitment to communications programs that allow for an open exchange with employees on matters affecting the work environment, including direct participation in forming and applying company policies.

The DS handbook is not the basic product of managers addressing the needs of the employees they work with; it is primarily the product of a consulting firm charged with developing a "radical restructuring of the work environment." This clinical work follows a well-organized but unjustified pattern. Each instituted change is preceded by an explanation intended to gain employees' understanding and consensus on the action taken. Theft is a problem; therefore the solution is employee monitoring. Poor attitudes have adversely affected production; therefore scents, music, and subliminal messages will alter the workers' perspective of the work environment. Closer scrutiny of any of the justifications reveals obvious self-serving motives for the imposed practices that undermine Dominion-Swann's credibility.

There are three underlying themes in the handbook that undermine its long-term viability as a workable tool to affect employee attitudes and conduct positively.

1. The handbook attempts to establish a model whereby existing and future employees will fit neatly into a "scientifically" developed mold. The baseline of this mold is the "physiological, psychological, social, and demographic factors" of DS's *best* employees, as determined by Sciex-Plan's expert INDUCT system. Such standardization does not allow sufficient latitude for a diverse work force where creativity can flourish. Corporate mavericks – not corporate clones – bring vitality and diversity to managerial work.

2. The scope of the handbook is particularly disturbing. There seems to be no limit to the areas of an employee's life that are not invaded by personnel practices. On the job, there is continuous monitoring and surveillance of virtually every movement. The camera watches even in the lounge. Leaving work does not provide the refuge of privacy either. Employees are required to be "connected at all times" to the company through the umbilical cord of paging devices, fax machines, and personal computer modems. Disruptions of vacations and sleep become part of the norm in the company's quest for competitive gain. With ever-tightening standards of performance and personal conduct, both on and off the job, a diminishing portion of employees will be able to "measure up," resulting in eroding morale and, probably, open challenges to the strict employment practices and rules.

3. Finally, and most troubling, is the removal of the human element of management and evaluation. This principle is clearly enunciated in the handbook, which establishes that "technical, hardware-based solutions are preferable to supervision and persuasion." It goes on to conclude that "machines are fairer than managers." While we must admit to a computer's edge in accuracy, can we accept that machines make fairer evaluations of people than people do? I think not.

In the final analysis, we are all human and make mistakes, especially when measured with unrelenting scrutiny against the strictest of standards. Under such conditions, I want someone managing me who shares some of my own human frailties and imperfections. A machine suffers only mechanical failures but lacks the spark of human imagination.

Dominion-Swann already exists. Some elements of its organizational strategy have been practiced for over 100 years.

SHOSHANA ZUBOFF *is associate professor at the Harvard Business School and author of* In the Age of the Smart Machine: The Future of Work and Power *(Basic Books, 1988).*

The future creeps in on small feet. Change in the contours of lives and things is incremental and fragmented. We do not awaken suddenly to a brave new world. Ten years ago, our lives *were* different – no PCs, no fax machines. But even as these inventions and the uses we put them to renovate our world, we continue to wake up in the same beds, drive the same routes to work, and look forward to turkey on Thanksgiving. In consequence, the future gets away with a lot, making itself at home in our lives before we've had a chance to say no thank you.

Dominion-Swann Industries sounds like a futuristic workplace, where life is saturated with comput-

ers that measure everything from your productivity to your heartbeat, where dreams of a perfectly ordered, clockwork world, shorn of human conflict, can come true. But DS already exists. Its technology strategy is widely adhered to. Some elements of its organizational strategy have been practiced for over 100 years. Others have been implemented and perfected throughout the 1980s.

Dominion-Swann of 1995 rose from the ashes of its managers. Somehow, its managers had lost their authority. There appears to have been, in the late 1980s, a rupture in their relationship with the work force. This was probably because maintaining constructive relationships with workers is demanding. It requires the kind of face-to-face interaction that builds trust, shared values, and reciprocity.

The failure of authority at DS is clear from the symptoms that have made it into the official history – and note that it is the symptoms that were reported, not their causes. Thus we are told about falling levels of productivity, quality, and morale. Employee turnover was on the rise, as were accidents, theft, drug use, and "unseemly behavior."

What to do when authority fails? How do those in power ensure that their commands will be obeyed if they detect that others may doubt their right to leadership? What good is a command if no one takes it seriously? Let's look at the options DS management faced back in 1990. It could have thrown in the towel, liquidated its assets, been taken over. Or it could have chosen to renew and reinvigorate management's authority by creating a workplace based on a new sharing of knowledge and power, where people are entrusted to do the work they know best, and managers are educators, guiding the development of value creation. It could have shown some faith in human beings, could have striven for growth and learning in every employee. It could have demonstrated its belief in the enterprise of management and in the skills and untapped wisdom of the managerial group.

In 1990, there was a growing number of corporate models for such an approach, as many businesses throughout the United States, Europe, and Japan achieved unprecedented economic success pioneering new, more progressive and humane forms of organization—setting new standards for quality, service, and the development of human potential. We will never know why DS leaders chose not to take this approach, but we can guess. Such an approach takes leaders who confront problems when they see them, who believe that human ingenuity and integrity, combined with technical prowess, are our last, best hope for sustained competitiveness.

Instead, DS managers decided that the key to renewal lay in information technology and in so doing tapped into an ancient response to the age-old problem of failed leadership. DS's managers, like other rulers before them, established techniques of control as a fail-safe system to guard against the frailties of their uncertain authority. Feudal kings used to take hostages from a noble's family, just in case he might want to raise a fuss over paying taxes. States employ radar traps, in case someone doesn't obey a speed limit. It was for just such a purpose that DS turned to information technology. As their handbook puts it: "Technical hardware-based solutions are preferable to supervision and persuasion." The means are at hand to shape behavior through monitoring, surveillance, and detection without even the slightest managerial effort.

Technology itself is not to blame for this state of affairs. In fact, information technologies, which represent a radical discontinuity in industrial history, could well lead to more reciprocity in the workplace, not less. Earlier generations of machines were designed to do essentially what human bodies could, only faster, more reliably, and at less cost. With machines, work required less human intervention and, overall, fewer human skills. This process has come to be known as automation. The ideal of automation is the self-diagnosing, self-correcting machine system that runs perfectly without human assistance.

Information technology can be used to automate all sorts of work in factories and offices. But unlike other tools of automation, information technology simultaneously registers data about the conversion processes it governs. Take the example of an industrial robot. It looks like a classic piece of automation, but the same microprocessors embedded in the robot that tell it what to do are also registering data about its activities. That slice of the production process is logged in a very precise way, as the robot supplies data on dozens of variables that could never have been defined or measured without it.

Multiply this effect across a highly automated manufacturing process and what you get is not only a complex machine system doing its job *but also an enormous, dynamic, fluid electronic text*, displayed on video screens and in computer printouts, full of numbers, charts, words, and symbols that portray total plant functioning in a way that never existed—indeed, never could have been imagined—before. The same effect is present in the office environment where we see connections being made between transaction systems, communication systems, management information systems, financial systems, customer and supplier systems, EPOS systems, scanner systems, and imaging systems.

As the time frames in which data are collected and presented become more accelerated, as more sectors of data are integrated, and as access to the systems becomes more widely distributed, the business is rendered transparent, as never before, through a dynamic electronic text. Moreover, anybody with the wit to access the data can discern patterns and dynamics, anticipate problems and opportunities, and make connections.

When information technology works to create this new kind of transparency, it is doing far more than automating—it is performing a second function that I call *informating*. The informated business invites the whole work force to think strategically.

All of which brings us back to Dominion-Swann. For the potential

of the informated workplace to be fulfilled, two conditions are critical: an organizational strategy that emphasizes learning and a leadership vision that understands how technology and the organization are integrated to generate more participatory approaches to value creation. The informated business redistributes authority, turns managers into educators, and devolves responsibility on those at the front line of the organization to use information quickly and creatively, where and when it counts.

Has DS created transparency? You bet. But transparency of what? For what? The short answer is transparency of human behavior for the purposes of total control. DS has tapped into the technology's informating power: almost every aspect of employee performance and behavior has been translated into and is displayed in the form of electronic data. But it is a transparency that allows unseen senior managers (the few who survived the demise of management) to monitor and control people and processes down to the tiniest detail, to shape behavior by recording everything and detecting all variances.

Does DS represent a brave new world of organizational trends? Ask Jeremy Bentham, who founded the utilitarian movement at the turn of nineteenth century, and also worried about the unproductive and "unseemly" behavior of workers, paupers, and convicts. Bentham conceived the "Panopticon," a polygonal structured prison-factory, consisting of a central tower from which rows of glass-walled cells emanated. With the use of mirrors fixed around the center tower, it was possible for an observer to see into each cell while remaining invisible to the cells' inhabitants. ("Universal transparency" was the term he liked.)

The assurance of permanent visibility, Bentham thought, would elicit "good behavior" from the inmates. The architecture itself was the guarantee of conformity. It promised observation but eliminated any way for workers or convicts to know for sure if they were being watched. In much the same way, DS relies on the certainty of panoptic power. Transparency is achieved, not through the architecture of a building but rather through the architecture of information systems. In DS language, this is "accountability through visibility." All optimum solutions are decided a priori by the few remaining managers. The only real challenges, they think, are to find a docile work force and design systems that will monitor everything.

In the end, the British government refused to build the Panopticon, and paid Bentham off—some £23,000. Dominion-Swann might have done better to pay off SciexPlan, for as history shows, most people will not remain docile for long. In subtle ways, they begin to develop techniques of defense as countermeasures to the techniques of control with which they must contend. For example, those knowledgeable about software will attempt to confound the systems operations in several ways. They may try to block the system's ability to monitor their behavior or attempt to "snow the computer" by finding ways to alter data traveling upward in the organization. Those with fewer computer skills are more likely to practice passive resistance. They will simply ignore what the computer tells them or blame it when their performance is not up to standard.

For others, the pressure of visibility is enough to reorganize behavior at its roots. Their coping strategy is what I call "anticipatory conformity." These employees so want to avoid the embarrassment of being singled out as a source of variance that they will go out of their way to conform to standards rather than risk detection. Don't count on these employees to figure out how to solve a customer's problem or initiate an improvement in the production process. They are simply too fearful to take any risks.

Finally, there is the intimidating rush of "objective" data about their work with which employees cannot argue and which, at times, they do not even understand. An individual's views count for less than the force of truth that shines through all these real-time facts.

Some humility is, of course, necessary for learning. But humiliation will cause people to give up. Don't count on these employees to detect errors or anticipate problems. It's not that they have stopped thinking but rather that they have ceased to value what they think.

Are things at Dominion-Swann as rosy as they seem? We have only the word of DS managers. And, for all we know, the handbook was itself written by consultants.

DS has failed to capitalize on the full potential offered by its investment in automation.

BILL HOWARD is vice president of information technology at Bechtel Corporation.

The date on Dominion-Swann's handbook should read 1895, not 1995. Rather than a company of the twenty-first century, DS brings to mind an organization firmly rooted in the first industrial revolution, one that has applied twenty-first century technology to nineteenth century management practice. Computers are used in much the same way as the tools of the late nineteenth and twentieth centuries: to monitor, audit, replace, deskill, and dehumanize staff and supervision, rather than to empower workers and management to realize a quantum leap in productivity.

In its effort to make the company a home to employees, DS has used computers and telecommunications to produce the modern-day equivalent of the company town or the company store. Every move is logged, monitored, and evaluated— even the bathroom at work and the bedroom at home. Privacy and individualism are severely impaired. The company uses technology to tie the employee to the company but fails to use technology to stimulate individuals to greater creativity and productivity.

The entry-level screening and community health programs capitalize on the vast amounts of information in databases around the country and the capabilities of medical monitoring equipment. DS is pushing the limits of society's tolerance for this type of inquiry and information gathering. It appears to be effective for DS, but management should not be surprised when market opportunities are missed and increasing legislative restrictions in this area of inquiry and discrimination start to appear. And, by its careful selection techniques, DS creates a mediocre and homogeneous group of followers. It also misses the opportunity to include the ideas and values of those creative contributors who fall outside the norm.

Teamwork and suggestions by employees for improved performance are encouraged by DS. But my perception of the DS team is more like a swim team made up of individual performers trying for "personal bests" to aggregate the maximum team score rather than the highly successful work team of the 1990s, which operates more like a basketball team made up of skilled performers who improvise together to capitalize on opportunities as they arise. Interaction is more important than the sum of the individual player's actions. A supervisor serves as the coach rather than as the commander.

For Dominion-Swann to fully exploit the potential of the latest advances in work-support technology, I would suggest.

1. Establish a dialogue among the human resource department, the information technology organization,

and representatives of all parts of the company affected by the use of information technology to sort out which systems enhance productivity and which systems or practices should be modified or abandoned because they induce fear or privacy concerns. All new systems should be planned and implemented with employees' involvement.

2. Use information technology to enhance the power of the individual to participate and to contribute his or her ideas to work rather than simply as monitoring tools. Promote interactive discussions and analysis in a team environment with participation of multiple disciplines at various levels of the organization. Develop systems that allow management to serve as coach or mentor rather than critic or enforcer.

3. Use information technology to establish closer links with business partners outside the company. Extend the reach of DS to a broader team concept that includes suppliers and the all-important customer.

4. Design systems to span across functional boundaries so that teams can be organized electronically to solve problems and contribute to productivity.

5. Train, train, train employees in the use of information systems, and use technology to enhance training so that workers and supervisors can fully understand and buy into delivering the full potential offered by the technology.

6. Encourage a new leadership model that is attuned to technology and that recognizes the need to change the organization and processes to match the tools of the twenty-first century. Identify managers who recognize the interdependence of the various business units and operating functions and who can bridge those boundaries to deliver crossfunctional solutions. Automating old processes and functions without taking into account the powerful capability of the new tools assures that the anticipated payback will not be realized.

7. Continue to reward performance of teams rather than individuals, provide technology to key players to eliminate the barriers of time and distance, encourage healthful lifestyles, reduce middle management layers that merely serve as switches and filters, assure that the company strategy continues to be understood at all levels.

8. Fire SciexPlan, Inc.

Some may be impressed with the five-year gains in worker productivity, employee income, and sales. However, in my view, sales, productivity, and performance in all areas must be measured against the best performers in industry to ensure maintaining a competitive position. I believe Dominion-Swann has failed to capitalize on the full potential offered by its investment in automation and will fall behind more enlightened competition in the last half of the 1990s. But it has no way of knowing that. Dominion-Swann is an underachieving organization because it has failed to see the true potential in information technology: to empower workers to deliver competitive solutions that were not possible without the information tools of the Second Industrial Revolution.

Not only are employees rejecting surveillance techniques, but the courts are too.

KAREN NUSSBAUM *is the executive director of 9 to 5, National Association of Working Women, and president of District 925, Service Employees International Union.*

What's wrong with this picture? Dominion-Swann Industries cares about its employees. DS is committed to its employees. Here's how managers show it:

☐ They weed out the old and infirm and those with family problems.

☐ They use highly personal information on employees and their families and friends to keep out those who don't fit the "norm."

☐ They test urine, check fingerprints, run data checks, inspect files, conduct video surveillance, track movements, monitor.

☐ They control minds, control movement, control substances, control association.

Does that sound like love? DS's policies are discriminatory, invasive, and counterproductive. And though few companies implement such an impressive package of organizational and technological measures, all of these policies exist in one form or another in American businesses—with poor results. I will reflect on a few of them.

Weeding the work force. Dominion-Swann's method for upgrading the work force is to screen for imperfections. Justifiable caution becomes an ugly effort to create an Aryan nation of employees when you start to ask questions about parents' health and lifestyle. In any case, advanced-selection processes are a shortsighted way to respond to a diverse work force in a tight labor market. We are entering an era marked by a shortage of skilled workers. Employers need to adapt to the needs of a variety of new workers—workers who are old, handicapped, foreign, female—instead of just culling the "best." Successful employers will learn how to be strengthened by diversity, instead of hiring only in their own image. Besides, it is still *illegal* to discriminate in hiring on the basis of age and handicap, as well as race, sex, and national origin.

Is there a boss under my bed? DS's surveillance, testing, control, and data-check methods keep tabs on employees round-the-clock, cradle-to-grave, and home-to-office. But what's the point? Most of the information is not very useful to the employers, and I've yet to find the worker who *likes* surveillance. Let's take monitoring, for example. A study by the Office of Technology Assessment (aptly titled *Electronic Supervisor*) said this about monitoring: "The knowledge that one's every move is being watched, without an ability to watch the watcher, can create feelings that one's privacy is being invaded and that one is an object under close scrutiny. Being subject to close scrutiny without an ability to confront the observer may mean the

loss of a feeling of autonomy....The employee may feel powerless and exposed under the gaze of electronic monitoring." In a word, fear.

Take the case of the United Airlines reservation clerk who was disciplined for comments she made to a coworker. She was courteous to an obnoxious customer and handled him well—management had no quarrel with her there. But after this three-minute call, which was monitored, she complained to a coworker. Management, listening in, put her on probation for her remark, then sent her to the company psychiatrist when she complained, and ultimately fired her.

An ad for networking software in the March 13, 1989 issue of *PC Week* makes the following claim: "Close-Up LAN brings you a level of control never before possible. It connects PCs on your network giving you the versatility to instantly share screens and keyboards....You decide to look in on Sue's computer screen....Sue won't even know you are there!...All from the comfort of your chair." Another airline employee got into trou-

ble because her monitoring system strictly enforced a 12-minute limit on bathroom breaks. When she went over by 2 minutes, she was disciplined, and ultimately quit in emotional crisis. A data processor in New York told me that her screen periodically flashed "You're not working as fast as the person next to you." A secretary from Florida told me that the thing she found most offensive about her (generally abusive) boss was that he calls up on *his* VDT the work she's doing, while she's doing it. This is "work support"?

Not just workers. The "higher professions" are being hit too. One reporter told me that as she was typing in her story, her computer flashed "I don't like that lead." A surreptitious editor was butting in on a first draft. This kind of thing makes one feel humiliated, harassed, and under the gun. A leading maker of monitoring software programs says, "Monitoring helps employees. It's the only way we can get everything on the permanent record." But I've never met even one highly poised professional who appreciates this kind of "feedback."

Not only are employees rejecting surveillance techniques, but the courts are too. Legal challenges to employer access to databases of personal information are expected to grow. And workers are filing privacy suits against their employers in unprecedented numbers. Between 1984 and 1987, *20 times* as many workplace privacy suits were decided by U.S. courts than in the three years before. Jury verdicts in favor of workers averaged $316,000—compared with 1979 and 1980 when no workers won compensation.

Why were they doing this anyway? If for no other reason, I'd advise managers not to follow Dominion-Swann's example because their policies are counterproductive. Studies repeatedly show that monitoring and surveillance of employees lead to high levels of stress, and stress-related diseases are now the most common occupational illness for workers under 40, costing U.S. business hundreds of millions of dollars each year. Even if you start with the Wheaties class

of employees, as DS has tried to do, after a period of increased productivity, workers will simply burn out.

Monitoring expert Alan Westin of Columbia University describes Federal Express's "people first" approach to office automation, which was supposed to downplay quantitative measures (recorded through monitoring) and elevate nine "quality" elements. However, the manager of customer service in one regional office, in contradiction to the organizational policy, enforced a campaign designed to "get the handle time down!" Before corrective actions raised quality back to where it had been, the staff experienced high rates of physical and psychological ill-health. Incidentally, once these corrective changes were in place, average handle time dropped below its level under the coercive regime.

And DS will be disappointed if its goal is to bring employees closer to management and create a "homey" team. A survey by the Massachusetts Coalition on New Office Technology shows deep alienation among monitored workers.

Corporate culture does need retooling. There are real problems facing employers, but substituting control and fear for supervision and training is not the answer. Dominion-Swann's new policies are the marks of the *failure* of management, not its crowning achievement. I endorse the call for commitment and professionalization of the workplace. To get there, we need education, training, and respect.

Reprint 90209

Solving Managerial Dilemmas

Skilled incompetence

Chris Argyris

"Managers who are skilled communicators may also be good at covering up real problems."

The ability to get along with others is always an asset, right? Wrong. By adeptly avoiding conflict with coworkers, some executives eventually wreak organizational havoc. And it's their very adeptness that's the problem. The explanation for this lies in what I call skilled incompetence, whereby managers use practiced routine behavior (skill) to produce what they do not intend (incompetence). We can see this happen when managers talk to each other in ways that are seemingly candid and straightforward. What we don't see so clearly is how managers' skills can become institutionalized and create disastrous side effects in their organizations. Consider this familiar situation:

The entrepreneur-CEO of a fast-growing medium-sized company brought together his bright, dedicated, hardworking top managers to devise a new strategic plan. The company had grown at about 45% per year, but fearing that it was heading into deep administrative trouble, the CEO had started to rethink his strategy. He decided he wanted to restructure his organization along more rational, less ad hoc, lines. As he saw it, the company was split between the sales-oriented people who sell off-the-shelf products and the people producing custom services who are oriented toward professionals. And each group was suspicious of the other. He wanted the whole group to decide what kind of company it was going to run.

His immediate subordinates agreed that they must develop a vision and make some strategic decisions. They held several long meetings to do this. Although the meetings were pleasant enough and no

Chris Argyris is the James Bryant Conant Professor of Education and Organizational Behavior at the Harvard University Graduate School of Education. His studies have focused on how people learn and have resulted in a long list of articles—many of which have appeared in HBR—and books, the latest of which is Strategy, Change, and Defensive Routines *(Ballinger, 1985).*

one seemed to be making life difficult for anyone else, they concluded with no agreements or decisions. "We end up compiling lists of issues but not deciding," said one vice president. Another added, "And it gets pretty discouraging when this happens every time we meet." A third worried aloud, "If you think we are discouraged, how do you think the people below us feel who watch us repeatedly fail?"

This is a group of executives who are at the top, who respect each other, who are highly committed, and who agree that developing a vision and strategy is critical. Yet whenever they meet, they fail to create the vision and the strategy they desire. What is going on here? Are the managers really so incompetent? If so, why?

What causes incompetence

At first, the executives in the previous example believed that they couldn't formulate and implement a good strategic plan because they lacked sound financial data. So they asked the financial vice president to reorganize and reissue the data. Everyone agreed he did a superb job.

But the financial executive reported to me, "Our problem is *not* the absence of financial data. I can flood them with data. We lack a vision of what kind of company we want to be and a strategy. Once we produce those, I can supply the necessary data." The other executives reluctantly agreed.

After several more meetings in which nothing got done, a second explanation emerged. It had to do with the personalities of the individuals and the way they work with each other. The CEO explained, "This is a group of lovable guys with very strong egos. They are competitive, bright, candid, and dedicated. But when we meet, we seem to go in circles; we are not prepared to give in a bit and make the necessary compromises."

Is this explanation valid? Should the top managers become less competitive? I'm not sure. Some management groups are not good at problem solving and decision making precisely because the participants have weak egos and are uncomfortable with competition.

If personality were really the problem, the cure would be psychotherapy. And it's simply not true that to be more effective, executives need years on the couch. Besides, pinpointing personality as the issue hides the real culprit.

The culprit is skill

Let's begin by asking whether counterproductive behavior is also natural and routine. Does everyone seem to be acting sincerely? Do things go wrong even though the managers are not being destructively manipulative and political?

For the executive group, the answer to these questions is yes. Their motives were decent, and they were at their personal best. Their actions were spontaneous, automatic, and unrehearsed. They acted in milliseconds; they were skilled communicators.

How can skillful actions be counterproductive? When we're skillful we usually produce what we intend. So, in a sense, did the executives. In this case, the skilled behavior—the spontaneous and automatic responses—was meant to avoid upset and conflict at the meetings. The unintended by-products are what cause trouble. Because the executives don't say what they really mean or test the assumptions they really hold, their skills inhibit a resolution of the important intellectual issues embedded in developing the strategy. Thus the meetings end with only lists and no decisions.

This pattern of failure is not only typical for this group of managers. It happens to people in all kinds of organizations regardless of age, gender, educational background, wealth, or position in the hierarchy. Let me illustrate with another example that involves the entire organizational culture at the upper levels. Here we'll begin to see how people's tendency to avoid conflict, to duck the tough issues, becomes institutionalized and leads to a culture that can't tolerate straight talk.

Where the skillful thrive

The top management of a large, decentralized corporation was having difficulty finding out what some of its division presidents were up to. Time and time again the CEO would send memos to the presidents asking for information, and time and time again they'd send next to nothing in return. But other people at headquarters accepted this situation as normal. When asked why they got so little direct communication from their division heads, they'd respond, "That's the way we do things around here."

Here is an organization that isn't talking to itself. The patterns that managers set up among themselves have become institutionalized, and what were once characteristic personal exchanges have now become organizational defensive routines. Before I go on to describe what these routines look like, let's look at how this situation arose.

Built into decentralization is the age-old tug between autonomy and control: superiors want no surprises, subordinates want to be left alone. The subordinates push for autonomy; they assert that by leaving them alone, top management will show its trust from a distance. The superiors, on the other hand, try to keep control through information systems. The subordinates see the control devices as confirming their suspicions—their superiors don't trust them.

Many executives I have observed handle this tension by pretending that the tension is not there. They act as if everyone were in accord and trust that no one will point out disagreements and thereby rock the boat. At the same time, however, they do feel the tension and can't help but soft-pedal their talk. They send mixed messages. (See the insert on chaos.)

The CEO in this example kept saying to his division presidents, "I mean it—you run the show down there." The division presidents, wanting to prove their mettle, believed him until an important issue came up. When it did the CEO, concerned about the situation and forgetting that he wanted his division chiefs to be innovative, would make phone calls and send memos seeking information.

Defensive routines emerge

One of the most powerful ways people deal with potential embarrassment is to create "organizational defensive routines." I define these as any action or policy designed to avoid surprise, embarrassment, or threat. But they also prevent learning and

Four easy steps to chaos

How does a manager send mixed messages? It takes skill. Here are four rules:

1

Design a clearly ambiguous message. For example, "Be innovative and take risks, but be careful" is a message that says in effect, "Go, but go just so far" without specifying how far far is. The ambiguity and imprecision cover the speaker who can't know ahead of time what is too far.

The receiver, on the other hand, clearly understands the ambiguity and imprecision. Moreover, he or she knows that a request for more precision would likely be interpreted as a sign of immaturity or inexperience. And the receivers may also need an out some day and may want to keep the message imprecise and ambiguous. Receivers don't want "far" defined any more clearly than the senders do.

2

Ignore any inconsistencies in the message. When people send mixed messages, they usually do it spontaneously and with no sign that the message is mixed. Indeed, if they did appear to hesitate, they would defeat their purpose of maintaining control. Even worse, they might appear weak.

3

Make the ambiguity and inconsistency in the message undiscussable. The whole point of sending a mixed message is to avoid dealing with a situation straight on. The sender does not want the message's mixedness exposed. An executive is not about to send a mixed message and then ask, "Do you find my message inconsistent and ambiguous?" The executive also renders the message undiscussable by the very natural way of sending it. To challenge the innocence of the sender is to imply that the sender is duplicitous — not a likely thing for a subordinate to do.

4

Make the undiscussability also undiscussable. One of the best ways to do this is to send the mixed message in a setting that is not conducive to open inquiry, such as a large meeting or a group where people of unequal organizational status are present. No one wants to launder linen in public. While they are sending mixed messages during a meeting, people rarely reflect on their actions or talk about how the organizational culture, including the meeting, makes discussing the undiscussable difficult.

thereby prevent organizations from investigating or eliminating the underlying problems.

Defensive routines are systemic in that most people within the company adhere to them. People leave the organization and new ones arrive, yet the defensive routines remain intact.

To see the impact of the defensive routines and the range of their effects, let's return to the division heads who are directed by mixed messages. They feel a lack of trust and are suspicious of their boss's intentions but they must, nonetheless, find ways to live with the mixed messages. So they "explain" the messages to themselves and to their subordinates. These explanations often sound like this:

> "Corporate never *really* meant decentralization."

> "Corporate is willing to trust divisions when the going is smooth, but not when it's rough."

> "Corporate is more concerned about the stock market than about us."

Of course, the managers rarely test their hypotheses about corporate motives with top executives. If discussing mixed messages among themselves would be uncomfortable, then public testing of the validity of these explanations would be embarrassing.

But now the division heads are in a double bind. On the one hand, if they go along unquestioningly, they may lose their autonomy and their subordinates will see them as having little influence with corporate. On the other, if the division executives do not comply with orders from above, headquarters will think they are recalcitrant, and if noncompliance continues, disloyal.

Top management is in a similar predicament. It senses that division managers have suspicions about headquarters' motives and are covering them up. If headquarters makes its impression known, though, the division heads may get upset. If the top does not say anything, the division presidents could infer full agreement when there is none. Usually, in the name of keeping up good relations, the top covers up its predicament.

Soon, people in the divisions learn to live with their binds by generating further explanations. For example, they may eventually conclude that openness is a strategy that top management has devised intentionally to cover up its unwillingness to be influenced.

Since this conclusion is based on the assumption that people at the top are covering up, managers won't test it either. Since neither headquarters nor division executives discuss or resolve the attributions or the frustrations, both may eventually stop communicating regularly and openly. Once in place, the climate of mistrust makes it more likely that the issues become undiscussable.

Now both headquarters and division managers have attitudes, assumptions, and actions that create self-fulfilling and self-sealing processes that each sees the other as creating.

"It's an interesting invention, but because of some irregularities, the elders have decided to have it recalled."

———————————

Under these conditions, it is not surprising to find that superiors and subordinates hold both good and bad feelings about each other. For example, they may say about each other: "They are bright and well intentioned but they have a narrow, parochial view"; or "They are interested in the company's financial health but they do not understand how they are harming earnings in the long run"; or "They are interested in people but they pay too little attention to the company's development."

My experience is that people cannot build on their appreciation of others without first overcoming their suspicions. But to overcome what they don't like, people must be able to discuss it. And this requirement violates the undiscussability rule embedded in the organizational defensive routines.

Is there any organization that does not have these hang-ups and problems? Some people suggest that getting back to basics will open lines of communication. But the proffered panacea does not go far enough; it does not deal with the underlying patterns. Problems won't be solved by simply correcting one isolated instance of poor performance.

When CEOs I have observed declared war against organizational barriers to candor and demanded that people get back to basics, most often they implemented the new ideas with the old skills. People changed whatever they could and learned to cover their asses even more skillfully. The freedom to question and to confront is crucial, but it is inadequate. To overcome skilled incompetence, people have to learn new skills—to ask the questions behind the questions.

Defensive routines exist. They are undiscussable. They proliferate and grow underground. And the social pollution is hard to identify until something occurs that blows things open. Often that something is a glaring error whose results cannot be hidden. The recent space shuttle disaster is an example. Only after the accident occurred were the mixed messages and defensive routines used during the decision to launch exposed. The disaster made it legitimate for outsiders to require insiders to discuss the undiscussable. (By the way, writing a tighter set of controls and requiring better communication won't solve the problem. Tighter controls will only enlarge the book of rules that William Rogers, chairman of the president's committee to investigate the Challenger disaster, acknowledged can be a cure worse than the illness. He pointed out that in his Navy years, when the players went by the book, things only got worse.)

Managers do not have the choice to ignore the organizational problems that these self-sealing loops create. They may be able to get away with it today, but they're creating a legacy for those who will come after them.

How to become unskilled

The top management group I described at the beginning of this article decided to learn new skills by examining the defenses they created in their own meetings.

First, they arranged a two-day session away from the office for which they wrote a short case beforehand. The purpose of these cases was twofold. First, they allowed the executives to develop a collage of the problems they thought were critical. Not surprisingly, in this particular group at least half wrote on issues related to the product versus custom service conflict. Second, the cases provided a kind of window into the prevailing rules and routines the executives used. The form of the case was as follows:

1   In one paragraph describe a key organizational problem as you see it.

2   In attacking the problem, assume you could talk to whomever you wish. Describe, in a paragraph or so, the strategy you would use in this meeting.

3   Next, split your page into two columns. On the right-hand side, write how you would begin the meeting: what you would actually say. Then write

what you believe the other(s) would say. Then write your response to their response. Continue writing this scenario for two or so double-spaced typewritten pages.

4   In the left-hand column write any of your ideas or feelings that you would not communicate for whatever reason.

The executives reported that they became engrossed in writing the cases. Some said that the very writing of their case was an eye-opener. Moreover, once the stories were distributed, the reactions were jocular. They enjoyed them: "Great, Joe does this all the time"; "Oh, there's a familiar one"; "All salespeople and no listeners"; "Oh my God, this is us."

What is the advantage of using the cases? Crafted and written by the executives themselves, they become vivid examples of skilled incompetence. They illustrate the skill with which each executive sought to avoid upsetting the other while trying to change the other's mind. The cases also illustrate their incompetence. By their own analysis, what they did upset the others, created suspicion, and made it less likely that their views would prevail.

The cases are also very important learning devices. During a meeting, it is difficult to slow down behavior produced in milliseconds, to reflect on it, and to change it. For one thing, it's hard to pay attention to interpersonal actions and to substantive issues at the same time.

A collage from several cases appears in the *Exhibit*. It was written by executives who believed the company should place a greater emphasis on custom service.

The cases written by individuals who supported the product strategy did not differ much. They too were trying to persuade, sell, or cajole their fellow officers. Their left-hand columns were similar.

In analyzing their left-hand columns, the executives found that each side blamed the other for the difficulties, and they used the same reasons. For example, each side said:

"If you insist on your position, you'll harm the morale I've built."

"Don't hand me that line. You know what I'm talking about."

"Why don't you take off your blinders and wear a company hat?"

"It upsets me when I think of how they think."

"I'm really trying hard, but I'm beginning to feel this is hopeless."

Exhibit	Case of the custom-service advocate	
	Thoughts and feelings	**Actual conversation**
	He's not going to like this topic, but we have to discuss it. I doubt that he will take a company perspective, but I should be positive.	**I:** Hi Bill. I appreciate having the opportunity to talk with you about this custom service versus product problem. I'm sure that both of us want to resolve it in the best interests of the company.
		Bill: I'm always glad to talk about it, as you well know.
	I better go slow. Let me ease in.	**I:** There are a rising number of situations where our clients are asking for custom service and rejecting the off-the-shelf products. I worry that your salespeople will play an increasingly peripheral role in the future.
		Bill: I don't understand. Tell me more.
	Like hell you don't understand. I wish there was a way I could be more gentle.	**I:** Bill, I'm sure you are aware of the changes [I explain].
		Bill: No, I don't see it that way. My salespeople are the key to the future.
	There he goes, thinking like a salesman and not like a corporate officer.	**I:** Well, let's explore that a bit.

These cases effectively illustrate the influence of skilled incompetence. In crafting the cases, the executives were trying not to upset the others and at the same time were trying to change their minds. This process requires skill. Yet the skill they used in the cases has the unintended side effects I talked about. In the cases, the others became upset and dug in their heels without changing their minds.

Here's a real problem. These executives and all the others I've studied to date can't prevent the counterproductive consequences until and unless they learn new skills. Nor will it work to bypass the skilled incompetence by focusing on the business problems, such as, in this case, developing a business strategy.

The answer is unlearning

The crucial step is for executives to begin to revise how they'd tackle their case. At their two-day seminar each manager selected an episode he wished to redesign so that it would not have the unhappy result it currently produced.

In rewriting their cases, the managers realized that they would have to slow things down. They could not produce a new conversation in the milliseconds in which they were accustomed to speak. This troubled them a bit because they were impatient to learn. They had to keep reminding themselves that learning new skills meant they had to slow down.

Each manager took a different manager's case and crafted a new conversation to help the writer of the episode. After five minutes or so, they showed their designs to the writer. In the process of discussing these new versions, the writer learned a lot about how to redesign his words. And, as they discovered the bugs in their suggestions and the way they made them, the designers also learned a lot.

The dialogues were constructive, cooperative, and helpful. Typical comments were:

"If you want to reach me, try it the way Joe just said."

"I realize your intentions are good, but those words push my button."

"I understand what you're trying to say, but it doesn't work for me. How about trying it this way?"

"I'm surprised at how much my new phrases contain the old messages. This will take time."

Practice is important. Most people require as much practice to overcome skilled incompetence as to play a not-so-decent game of tennis. But it doesn't need to happen all at once. Once managers are committed to change, the practice can occur in actual business meetings where executives set aside some time to reflect on their actions and to correct them.

But how does unlearning skilled incompetence lead to fewer organizational snafus? The first step is to make sure executives are aware of defensive routines that surround the organizational problems that they are trying to solve. One way to do this is to observe them in the making. For example, during a meeting of the top line and corporate staff officers in our large decentralized organization, the CEO asked why the line and staff were having problems working effectively. They identified at least four causes:

The organization's management philosophy and policies are inadequate.

Corporate staff roles overlap and lead to confusion.

Staff lacks clear-cut authority when dealing with line.

Staff has inadequate contact with top line officers.

The CEO appointed two task forces to come up with solutions. Several months later, the entire group met for a day and hammered out a solution that was acceptable to all.

This story has two features that I would highlight. First, the staff-line problems are typical. Second, the story has a happy ending. The organization got to the root of its problems.

But there is a question that must be answered in order to get at the organizational defensive routines. Why did all the managers—both upper and lower—adhere to, implement, and maintain inadequate policies and confusing roles in the first place?

Why open this can of worms if we have already solved the problem? Because defensive routines prevent executives from making honest decisions. Managers who are skilled communicators may also be good at covering up real problems. If we don't work hard at reducing defensive routines, they will thrive—ready to undermine this solution and cover up other conflicts. ▽

There is great skill in knowing how to conceal one's skill.

La Rochefoucauld

The abrasive personality

Sharp-tongued yet blunt young executives who irritate others on their way to the top probably will not make it despite their intelligence and passion for hard work

Harry Levinson

Not everyone who rises quickly in a company and has good analytical skills and a lot of energy is abrasive, nor are all abrasive people in high management levels, but when the two do coincide, top management has a real problem. The problem is simply how to keep the extraordinarily talented person in a position where he or she can be most effective, and at the same time not sacrifice the feelings and aspirations of the people who work with and for this person. According to this author, managers can cope with this dilemma by helping their abrasive subordinates to understand the negative consequences of their personalities. This method takes time and patience, but it is most likely the only way managers can save such people for the organization.

Mr. Levinson is very well-known to HBR readers. This is his fourteenth article in HBR, the most recent being "Appraisal of What Performance," which appeared in the July-August 1976 issue. Mr. Levinson is the author of many books on what motivates executives including *The Exceptional Executive* (Harvard University Press, 1968) and *The Great Jackass Fallacy* (Harvard University Press, 1973), and is president of the Levinson Institute. He is also a lecturer at The Harvard University Medical School.

Reprint 78307

The corporate president stared out the window of his skyscraper office. His forehead was furrowed in anger and puzzlement. His fingers drummed the arm of his chair with a speed that signified intense frustration. The other executives in the room waited expectantly. Each had said his piece. Each had come to his and her own conclusion about the problem.

Darrel Sandstrom, vice president of one of the corporation's major divisions, was the problem. Sandstrom was one of those rare young men who had rocketed to the division vice presidency at an age when most of his peers were still in lower-middle management. "He is sharp," his peers said, "but watch out for his afterburn. You'll get singed as he goes by." And that, in a phrase, was the problem.

There was no question that Sandstrom was well on his way to the top. Others were already vying for a handhold on his coattails. He had a reputation for being a self-starter. Give him a tough problem, like a failing division, and he would turn it around almost before anyone knew what had happened. He was an executive who could quickly take charge, unerringly get to the heart of a problem, lay out the steps for overcoming it, bulldoze his way through corporate red tape, and reorganize to get the job done. All that was well and good. Unfortunately, that was not all there was to it.

In staff discussions and meetings with his peers Sandstrom would ask pointed questions and make incisive comments. However, he would also brush his peers' superfluous words aside with little tact, making them fearful to offer their thoughts in his presence. Often he would get his way in meetings because of the persuasiveness of his arguments and his commanding presentations, but just as often those who were responsible for following up the conclusions of a meeting would not do so.

In meetings with his superiors, his questions were appropriate, his conclusions correct, and his insights important assets in examining problems. But he would antagonize his superiors by showing little patience with points and questions that to him seemed irrelevant or elementary. Unwilling to compromise, Sandstrom was an intellectual bully with little regard for those of his colleagues who could not keep up with him.

There were complaints from subordinates too. Some resented his controlling manner. Fearing his wrath, they spoke up at meetings only when they knew it to be safe. They knew he would not accept mediocrity and so they strived to attain the perfection he demanded of them. When he said they had done a good job, they knew they had earned his compliments, though many felt he did not really mean what he said.

His meetings were not noted for their liveliness, in fact he did not have much of a sense of humor. On the golf course and tennis courts he was equally humorless and competitive. Playing as intensely as he worked, he did not know what a game was.

And now here he was. The division presidency was open and the corporate president was in a dilemma. To promote Sandstrom was to perpetuate in a more responsible position what seemed to many a combination of Moshe Dayan, General George Patton, and Admiral Hyman Rickover. Sandstrom would produce; no question about that. But at what cost? Could the corporation afford it? If Sandstrom did not get the job, the likelihood was that he would quit. The company could ill afford that either, for his division's bottom line was a significant portion of its bottom line.

Around the table the opinion was divided. "Fire him now," some said; "you'll have to do it sooner or later." "Be gentle with him," others said; "if you hurt him, he'll lose his momentum." "He'll mature with age," said others. Still others commented, "When he gets to be president, he'll relax." And there were those who said, "What difference does it make? He's bringing in the bucks." The corporate president faced the dilemma; Sandstrom could not be promoted but neither could he be spared. None of the options presented gave him a way out; none of them could.

Darrel Sandstrom epitomizes people who puzzle, dismay, frustrate, and enrage others in organizations—those who have an abrasive personality. Men and women of high, sometimes brilliant, achievement who stubbornly insist on having their own way, and are contemptuous of others, are the bane of bosses, subordinates, peers, and colleagues.

In the long run, they are a bane to themselves as well; when they fail, their failure is usually due to their abrasive personalities. Because of their value to their organizations, however, their superiors frequently go to great lengths to help them fit in the organization. In fact, top executives probably refer more managers with abrasive personalities to psychologists and psychiatrists, and human relations training programs in order to rescue them, than any other single classification of executives.

In this article I describe the abrasive personality, trace its origins, and suggest what managers might do to both help and cope with such people.

A profile

Like the proverbial porcupine, an abrasive person seems to have a natural knack for jabbing others in an irritating and sometimes painful way. But that knack masks a desperation worse than that of those who receive the jabs, namely, a need to be perfect. (For a closer look at how a need to be perfect drives a person to the point where he alienates and causes significant stress to most people around him, see the ruled insert on page 29). The person who becomes a Darrel Sandstrom however, is not just someone who needs perfection. He has other characteristics which, combined with that need, create the behavior others find so offensive.

Such a person is most usually extremely intelligent. With a passion for perfection, accuracy, and completeness, he pushes himself very hard, and can be counted on to do a job well, often spectacularly. He tends to want to do the job himself, however, finding it difficult to lean on others who he feels will not do it to his standards, on time, or with the required finessse. He has, therefore, great difficulty delegating even $25 decisions. Such complete thoroughness, however, no matter how good for the company as a whole, tends to leave others figura-

tively breathless, making them feel that they cannot compete in the same league.

He is often keenly analytical, capable of cutting through to the nub of a problem, but with his need for constant achievement, he is impatient with those who cannot think as quickly or speak as forthrightly as he can. Thus his capacity for analysis tends not to be matched by equal skill as a leader to implement the answers he has deduced.

On a one-to-one basis he is often genial and helpful to people he is not supervising. But despite what he says, he is usually not a good developer of people for, frequently, they feel too inadequate when they have to compare themselves with him. Also, the abrasive person's intense rivalry with others often leads him to undercut them, even though he himself may not be aware of doing so.

When his competitive instincts overwhelm his judgment, an abrasive person will sometimes crudely raise issues others are reluctant to speak about, leaving himself a scapegoat for his own forthrightness. In groups he tends to dominate others, treating all differences as challenges to be debated and vanquished. At the same time that he is domineering to his subordinates, he is fawning to his superiors. If he feels himself to be exceptionally competent, however, he may try to dominate his superiors also.

Though often in imaginative pursuit of bigger and broader achievements for which he frequently gets many accolades, he may well leave his bosses and those around him with no sense of having any input to the task or project. He moves so fast and ranges so widely that even when he has good ideas, his boss will tend to turn him down fearing that if he gives an inch, the subordinate will take a mile. The boss feels there will be no catching him, no containing him, and no protecting the stellar subordinate, himself, or higher management from any waves that may be created, the backwash from which might overwhelm them all.

Once reined in by his boss, the abrasive person feels that he has been let down, that his efforts have been in vain. Feeling unjustly treated, he becomes angry because he was asked to do something and it did not end well. Therefore, he reasons, he is being penalized because other people are jealous, rivalrous, or do not want to undertake anything new. Seeing his boss as somebody to be outflanked, rather than as somebody whose step-by-step involvement is necessary for a project's success, he is politically insensitive and often righteously denies the need for such sensitivity.

Although others often perceive him as both grandiose and emotionally cold, the abrasive person has a strong and very intense emotional interest in himself. Needing to see himself as extraordinary, he acts sometimes as if he were a privileged person—indeed, as if he had a right to be different or even inconsiderate.

At times he sees others as mere devices for his self-aggrandizement, existing as extensions of himself, rather than as full-fledged, unique adults with their own wishes, desires, and aspirations. To inflate his always low sense of self-worth, he competes intensely for attention, affection, and applause. At the same time, he seems to expect others to accept his word, decision, or logic just because it is his. When disappointed in these expectations, he becomes enraged.

To such a person, self-control is very important, as is control of others, which he makes total if possible. Thus he overorganizes, and copes with imperfections in others by oversupervising them. To him, losing a little control is the same as losing total control. To prevent that, he is rigid, constricted, and unable to compromise. In fact, for him, making a compromise is the same as giving in to lower standards. He therefore has little capacity for the necessary give and take of organizational political systems. This inflexibility is especially apparent around issues of abstract values which, for him, become specifically concrete.

To others the same control makes him appear emphatically right, self-confident, and self-assured. In contrast, those who are not so sure of what they believe or of the clarity of an issue, feel inadequate and less virtuous.

The abrasive person, appearing to have encyclopedic knowledge, is often well read, and, with already a good academic background, strives for more. While subordinates and even peers may strive as well to meet the high expectations of such a person, and some may reach extraordinary heights, many ultimately give up, especially if he beats them down. Thus the legendary Vince Lombardi drove the Green Bay Packers to great success, but all of its members, recognizing that he was the key to their success, felt that the better and more competent he was the less adequate they were. When such a person dies or leaves an organization, those left behind are de-

The need to be perfect

If a person's ultimate aspiration, his ego ideal, is perfection, then he is always going to fall short of it—by astronomical distances. And if this person's self-image is already low, the distance between where he perceives himself to be and the omnipotence he wants to attain will be constantly increasing as the feeling of failure continues. He must, therefore, push himself ever harder—all the time. Others who are or may be viewed as competitors threaten his self-image even further; if they win, by his own definition, he loses. His intense need to be perfect then becomes translated into intense rivalry.

If a person is always pushing himself toward impossible aspirations and is never able to achieve them, there are two consequences for his emotions. The greater the gap between his ego ideal and self-image, the greater will be both his guilt and anger with himself for not achieving the dream. And the angrier a person is with himself the more likely he is to attack himself or drive himself to narrow the gap between his ideal and his present self-image. Only in narrowing the gap can he reduce his feelings of anger, depression, and inadequacy.

However, as the unconscious drive for perfection is irrational, no degree of conscious effort can possibly achieve the ideal nor decrease the self-punishment such a person brings down on himself for not achieving it. The anger and self-hatred are never ending, therefore, and build up to the point where they spill over in the form of hostile attacks on peers and subordinates, such as treating them with contempt and condescension.

These feelings may also spill over onto spouses, children, and even pets. In fact, the abrasive person's need for self-punishment may be so great that he may take great, albeit neurotic, pleasure in provoking others who will subsequently reject, that is, punish him. In effect, he acts as if he were his own parent, punishing himself as well as others. In Anna Freud's words, he becomes a good hater.[1]

---

[1] Anna Freud, "Comments on Aggression," *International Journal of Psychoanalysis*, vol. 53, no. 2, 1972, p. 163.

moralized because they have no self-confidence. Usually they will feel that they have not been able to measure up and indeed, frequently, they cannot.

If they are compelled to retire, abrasive people will have difficulty. If they are not compelled to retire, they tend to hold on to the very end, and with age, their judgment is usually impaired. In their view, they have less and less need to adapt to people and circumstances, or to change their way of doing things. Thus they become more and more tangential to the main thrust of the business. If they are entrepreneurs, they may frequently destroy organizations in an unconscious effort to keep somebody else from taking over their babies. J. Edgar Hoover, a case in point, ultimately corrupted and very nearly destroyed the reputation of the FBI out of his own self-righteousness.

Solving the dilemma

Given that you, the reader, have a subordinate who fits the profile I have drawn, what can you do? Corrective effort occurs in stages, and takes time and patience on everybody's part.

First-stage techniques

The following steps can be used with any employee who is having a behavior problem, but they are particularly effective in introducing an abrasive person to the consequences of his or her behavior:

☐

Recognize the psychological axiom that each person is always doing the best he can. Understanding that abrasive, provocative behavior springs from an extremely vulnerable self-image, a hunger for affection, and an eagerness for contact, do not become angry. Instead, initiate frequent discussion with this person.

☐

In such discussions, uncritically report your observations of his abrasive behavior. Describe what you see, especially the more subtle behavior to which people react automatically. Ask how he thinks others feel when he says or does what you describe. How does he think they are likely to respond? Is that the result he wants? If not, what would you do differently to get the response he wants? How would he respond if someone else said or did what he does?

☐

Point out that you recognize his desire to achieve and that you want to help. But tell him that if he wants to advance in the company, he needs to take others into account, and that his progress along these lines has implications for his future. Ensure him also that everyone experiences defeats and disappointments along the way.

☐

When, as is likely to be the case, his provocative behavior ultimately irritates you, try to avoid both impulsively attacking back on the one hand and being critical of yourself for not responding in kind on the other. Explain to him that although you understand his need to do or be the best, that he made you angry and that others he works with must feel the same. Tell him you get irritated and annoyed, particularly with hostile, depreciating, or controlling tactics. After all, you can say, you are

only human, too, even if he thinks he is not. Let him know how frequently such behavior occurs.
☐
If he challenges, philosophizes, defends, or tries to debate your observations, or accuses you of hostility to him, do not counterattack. Tell him you are not interested in arguing. Merely report your observations of what he is doing or misinterpreting *at that moment.* Keep his goal the point of your discussion; does he want to make it or not?
☐
If your relationship is strong enough, you might ask why he must defend or attack in situations that are not combat. Point out that to be part of a critical examination of a problem is one thing; to turn such a situation into a win-lose argument is another.
☐
Expect to have to repeat this process again and again, pointing out legitimate achievements about which he can be proud. Explain that goals are achieved step by step, that compromise is not necessarily second best, that the all-or-none principle usually results in futile disappointment, and that perfection is not attainable.

Much good talent can be saved if managers employ these steps with their abrasive subordinates. Of course, some people are less abrasive than others and may be able to modulate their behavior voluntarily and cope consciously with their abrasive tendencies. For those who cannot, however, more drastic measures may be needed.

Further steps

Sometimes people with unconscious drives cannot see reality despite repeated attempts to show them. Perhaps they are too busy thinking up defensive arguments or are preoccupied with their own thoughts. Whatever, if they do not respond to the gentle counseling I have described, then they should be confronted with what their arrogant, hostile, and controlling behavior is costing them.

Such people must be told *very early on* how their behavior undermines them. All too often afraid to do this, their bosses quickly become resentful and withdraw, leaving their subordinates uncomfortable, but not knowing why. Feeling anxious, the abrasive subordinate then attempts to win back the regard and esteem of the boss in the only way he knows, by intensifying this behavior. That only makes things worse.

Abrasive persons can make significant contributions to an organization, but managers need to steer them again and again into taking those political steps that will enable them to experience success rather than rejection. Rather than corral such people, who tend to figuratively butt their heads against restrictions, managers do better to act like sheepdogs, gently nudging them back into position when they stray.

Highly conscientious people, who need to demonstrate their own competence by doing things themselves, are likely to have had to prove themselves against considerable odds in the past. Their demonstration of competence has had to be in terms of what they, themselves, could do as individuals. Thus they need political guidance and instruction in teamwork, as well as support from a superior who will tell them the consequences of their behavior in straightforward terms.

These people will often need frequent feedback on each successive step they take in improving their political relationships. As they move slowly in such a process, or at least more slowly than they are accustomed to, they will experience increasing anxiety. While not demonstrating their individual competence, such people may feel that they are not doing well, and get so anxious that they may indeed fail. When they have such feelings, they then tend to revert to their old unilateral way of doing things.

However, if despite the boss's best efforts the subordinate does not respond, the manager must tell him *in no uncertain terms* that his behavior is abrasive and therefore unsatisfactory. Managers should not assume that their subordinates know this, but should tell them and tell them repeatedly, and in written form. Being told once or twice during a performance appraisal should be enough. My experience is, however, that most superiors are very reluctant to tell people, particularly abrasive ones, the effects of their behavior during performance appraisals.

In one instance, when I was asked to see such a manager, he did not know why he had been referred to me. When I told him, he was dismayed. Showing me his performance appraisal, he complained that his boss had not told him. Rather his boss had commented favorably on all his qualities and assets, and in one sentence had written that his behavior with people was improving. In reality, the boss was so enraged with his subordinate's behavior that he was not promoting him as far as he would have wished.

When the steps I have outlined have been followed to no avail, when the subordinate clearly knows, and he or she is unable to respond by changing his or her behavior, when repeated words to the person and even failures to be promoted have produced no significant improvement, there are two likely consequences. First, the abrasive person will feel unfairly treated, unrecognized for his or her skills and competence, and unappreciated for what he or she could bring to the organization. Second, the superior is usually desperate, angry, and at his wit's end.

If by this point the abrasive person has not already been referred to a competent psychologist or psychiatrist for therapy, he should be. *Nothing else will have a significant effect*, and even therapy may not. Whether it does will depend on the severity of the problem and the skill of the therapist. This is not a problem that will be solved in a T-group, or a weekend encounter, or some other form of confrontation.

The manager should make sure the subordinate understands that when a person is referred to a psychologist, there are two implications. The first is that the person is so competent, skilled, or capable in some dimension of his role that his superiors would not only hate to lose him, but also have reason to expect that the person could flower into a mature executive who can assume greater responsibility. The second is that despite his talent, the subordinate is so unable to get along with other people that he cannot be promoted beyond his present role. Both points should be made emphatically.

These same principles apply equally in dealing with any ineffective or dysfunctional behavior on the job. Some people cannot seem to get their work done. Others have a habit of getting in their own way as well as that of others. Still others manage to stumble their way to work late each morning or produce incomplete or inadequate work. Whatever the case, steps in treating them are essentially the same.

Other problem situations

What do you do if the abrasive person is your boss, your peer, someone you are interviewing, or, hardest to face of all, yourself? What recourse do you have then?

The boss

Let us assume that you are relatively new or inexperienced in a particular area and need a certain amount of time to achieve your own competence. Chances are that because of his knowledge and competence, your abrasive boss will have much to teach. Since his high standards will ensure that the model he provides will be a good one, there will be sufficient reason for you to tolerate his abrasiveness.

But after two years, or whenever you establish your own competence, you will begin to chafe under the rigid control. As you push for your own freedom, your boss is likely to become threatened with loss of control and feel that you are becoming rivalrous. He is then likely to turn on you, now no longer a disciple, and, in sometimes devious ways, get back at you. Your memos will lie on his desk, unanswered. Information being sent through channels will be delayed. Complaints, suggestions, requests will either be rejected outright or merely tabled. Sometimes he will reorganize the unit around you, which will fence you in and force you to deal with decoys—nominal bosses who have no real power.

If you are in a safe position, you might tell the boss how he appears to you, and his effect on subordinates. If he is at a high level, it will usually do little good to go above his head. Certainly, you should check out how much concern his superiors have about him, how much they are willing to tolerate, and how able they are to face him in a confrontation. Few at higher management levels are willing to take on a bright, combative, seemingly self-confident opponent—especially if he has a record of achievement, and there is little concrete evidence of the negative effects of his behavior.

In short, after you have learned what you can from such a person, it is probably time to get out from under him.

The peer

If you are the peer of an abrasive person, do not hesitate to tell him if his behavior intimidates you. Speaking of your irritation and anger and that of others, you might tell him you do not think he wants to deliberately estrange people or be self-defeating. He might become angry, but if approached in a kindly manner, he is more likely to be contrite and may even ask for more feedback on specific occasions.

Do you have an abrasive personality?

You might ask yourself these questions. Then ask them of your spouse, your peers, your friends — and even your subordinates:

1
Are you condescendingly critical? When you talk of others in the organization, do you speak of "straightening them out" or "whipping them into shape"?

2
Do you need to be in full control? Does almost everything need to be cleared with you?

3
In meetings, do your comments take a disproportionate amount of time?

4
Are you quick to rise to the attack, to challenge?

5
Do you have a need to debate? Do discussions quickly become arguments?

6
Are people reluctant to discuss things with you? Does no one speak up? When someone does, are his or her statements inane?

7
Are you preoccupied with acquiring symbols of status and power?

8
Do you weasel out of responsibilities?

9
Are you reluctant to let others have the same privileges or perquisites as yourself?

10
When you talk about your activities, do you use the word "I" disproportionately?

11
Do your subordinates admire you because *you* are so strong and capable or because, in your organization, *they* feel so strong and capable — and supported?

12
To your amazement do people speak of you as cold and distant when you really want them to like you?

13
Do you regard yourself as more competent than your peers, than your boss? Does your behavior let them know that?

The candidate

What should you look for during an interview to avoid hiring someone who will turn out to be abrasive?

Pay attention to the charming personality. Not all charming persons are self-centered, but many are. Some preen themselves, dress to perfection, and in other ways indicate that they give an inordinate amount of attention to themselves. The more exhibitionistic the person, the more a person needs approval, the less he or she can be thoughtful of others. Also pay special attention to precision in speech or manner. Clarity is a virtue, but a need for exactness indicates a need to control.

Find out how the person gets things done by having him or her describe past projects and activities. How much does he report starting and finishing tasks all by himself, even to the surprise of his superiors? To do so is not necessarily bad; in fact, it may be good for a person to be a self-starter. But repeated singular achievement might indicate a problem in working as part of a team. How often does he use "I"? How closely did he have to check the work of subordinates? How important was it for him to have control of what was happening? How did he talk to people about their mistakes? How did he go about coaching them?

How did he view the limits and inadequacies of others, as human imperfections or as faults? How much better does he think things could have been done? Why were they not done better? Why could he not do better? What did his bosses say about him in performance appraisals?

You, yourself

Finally, what if you are abrasive? If you ask yourself the questions in the ruled insert on this page and find that you answer three of them in the affirmative, the chances are that your behavior is abrasive to the people around you. If you answer six or more affirmatively, it takes no great insight to recognize that you have more problems than are good for your career. Of course, none of these questions taken by itself is necessarily indicative of anything, but enough affirmative answers may reveal an abrasive profile.

If you are the problem and it troubles you, you can work at self-correction. Most often, however, you need the help of a third person—your spouse, a friend, your boss, or a professional. If your behavior causes you serious problems on the job, then a professional is indicated. Managers and executives with naturally heavy orientations to control, need to check themselves carefully for this kind of behavior lest unconsciously they defeat their own ends.

Sally Seymour

The case of the mismanaged Ms.

It started out as one of those rare quiet mornings when I could count on having the office to myself. The Mets had won the World Series the night before, and most of the people in the office had celebrated late into the night at a bar across the street. I'm a fan too, but they all like to go to one of those bars where the waitresses dress like slave girls and the few women customers have to run a mine field of leers when they go to a ladies' room labeled "Heifers." Instead, I watched the game at home with my husband and escaped a hangover.

Before I could say good morning, she demanded to know what business it was of the company who she slept with and why.

So I was feeling pretty good, if a little smug, when Ruth Linsky, a sales manager here at Triton, stormed past my secretary and burst into my office. Before I could say good morning, she demanded to know what business it was of the company who she slept with and why. I didn't know what she was talking about, but I could tell it was serious. In fact, she was practically on the verge of tears, but I knew she wasn't the type to fly off the handle.

Ruth had been with the company for three years, and we all respected her as a sensible and intelligent woman. She had been top in her class at business school and we recruited her hard when she graduated, but she didn't join us for a couple of years. She's since proved to be one of our best people in sales, and I didn't want to lose her. She fumed around the

Sally Seymour is on the faculty of the Harvard Business School, where she teaches management communication.

room for a while, not making much sense, until I talked her into sitting down.

"I've had it with this place and the way it treats women!" she shouted.

I allowed her to let off some more steam for a minute or two, and then I tried to calm her down. "Look, Ruth," I said, "I can see you're upset, but I need to know exactly what's going on before I can help you."

"I'm not just upset, Barbara," she said, "I'm damned mad. I came over to Triton because I thought I'd get more chances to advance here, and I just found out that I was passed over for director of the marketing division and Dick Simon got it instead. You know that I've had three outstanding years at the company, and my performance reviews have been excellent. Besides, I was led to believe that I had a pretty good shot at the job."

"What do you mean, 'led to believe'?"

"Steve heard through the grapevine that they were looking for a new marketing director, and he suggested I put in my name," she said. "He knows my work from when we worked together over at Forge Techtronics, and he said he'd write a letter in support. I wouldn't have even known they were looking for someone if Steve hadn't tipped me off."

Steve Baines is vice president of manufacturing. He's certainly a respected senior person in the company and he pulls some weight, but he doesn't have sole control of the marketing position. The hierarchy doesn't work that way, and I tried to get Ruth to see that. "Okay, so Steve wrote a letter for you, but he's only one of five or six VPs who have input in executive hiring decisions. Of course it helps to have his support, but lots of other factors need to be considered as well."

"Come off it, Barbara," Ruth snapped. "You know as well as I do there's only one thing that really matters around here and that's whether you're one of the boys. I've got a meeting this afternoon with my lawyer, and I'm going to file a sexual discrimination suit, a sexual harassment suit, and whatever other kind of suit she can come up with. I've had it with this old-boy crap. The only reason I'm here is that, as human resources director, you should know what's going on around here."

So the stakes were even higher than I had thought; not only did it look like we might lose Ruth, but we also might have a lawsuit on our hands. And to top it off, with the discrimination issue Ruth might be trying to get back at us for promoting Dick. I felt strongly about the importance of this legal remedy, but I also knew that using it frivolously would only undermine women's credibility in legitimate cases.

"Ruth," I said, "I don't doubt your perceptions, but you're going to need some awfully strong evidence to back them up."

"You want evidence? Here's your evidence. Number one: 20% of the employees in this company are women. Not one is on the board of directors, and not one holds an executive-level position. You and I are the only two in mid-level positions. Number two: there's no way for women to move into the mid-level positions because they never know when they're

---

Every time I go to a sales meeting, I feel like I've walked into a locker room.

---

available. When a vacancy comes up, the VPs — all men, of course — decide among themselves who should fill it. And then, over and over again I hear that some guy who hasn't worked half as hard as most of the women at his level has been given the plum. Number three: there are plenty of subtle and sometimes not-so-subtle messages around here that women are less than equal."

"Ruth, those are still pretty vague accusations," I interrupted. "You're going to have to come up with something more specific than feelings and suppositions."

"Don't worry, Barbara. Just keep listening and maybe you'll learn something about how this company you think so highly of operates. From the day Ed Coulter took over as vice president of marketing and became my boss, he's treated me differently from the male sales managers. Instead of saying good morning, he always has some comment about my looks — my dress is nice, or my hair looks pretty, or the color of my blouse brings out my eyes. I don't want to hear that stuff. Besides, he never comments on a guy's eyes. And then there's that calendar the sales reps have in their back office. Every time I go in there for a sales meeting, I feel like I've walked into a locker room."

So far, this all seemed pretty harmless to me, but I didn't want Ruth to feel I wasn't sympathetic. "To tell you the truth, Ruth, I'm not so sure all women here find compliments like that insulting, but

maybe you can give me other examples of discriminatory treatment."

"You bet I can. It's not just in the office that these things happen. It's even worse in the field. Last month Ed and I and Bill, Tom, and Jack went out to Dryden Industries for a big project meeting. I'll admit I was a little nervous because there were some heavy hitters in the room, so I kept my mouth shut most of the morning. But I was a team member and I wanted to contribute.

"So when Ed stumbled at one point, I spoke up. Well, it was like I had committed a sacrilege in church. The Dryden guys just stared at me in surprise, and then they seemed actually angry. They ignored me completely. Later that afternoon, when I asked Ed why I had gotten that reaction, he chuckled a little and explained that since we hadn't been introduced by our specific titles, the Dryden guys had assumed I was a research assistant or a secretary. They thought I was being presumptuous. But when Ed explained who I was, they admitted that I had made an important point.

"But that wasn't all," she went on. "The next day, when we explained to them that I would be interviewing some of the factory foremen for a needs assessment, one of the executives requested that someone else do it because apparently there's a superstition about women on the factory floor bringing bad luck. Have you ever heard of anything so stupid? But that's not the worst of it. Ed actually went along with it. After I'd pulled his bacon out of the fire the day before. And when I nailed him for it, he had the gall to say 'Honey, whatever the client wants, the client gets.'

"Well, we got the contract, and that night we all went out to dinner and everything was hurray for our team. But then, when I figured we'd all go back to the hotel for a nightcap, Ed and the guys just kind of drifted off."

"Drifted off?" I asked.

"Yeah. To a bar. They wanted to watch some basketball game."

"And you weren't invited?"

"I wasn't invited and I wasn't disinvited," she said. "They acted like they didn't know what to say."

By this point Ruth had cooled down quite a bit, and although she still seemed angry, she was forthright in presenting her case. But now her manner changed. She became so agitated that she got up from her chair to stare out the window. After a few minutes, she sort of nodded her head, as if she had come to some private, difficult decision, and then crossed the room to sit down again. Looking at her lap and twisting a paper clip around in her hands, she spoke so softly that I had to lean forward to hear her.

"Barbara," she began, "what I'm going to tell you is, I hope, in confidence. It's not easy for me to talk about this because it's very personal and private,

"If I have any say about it, when the history of this company is written, it will be a pack of lies."

but I trust you and I want you to understand my position. So here goes. When Steve Baines and I were both at Forge, we had a brief affair. I was discreet about it; it never interfered with business, and we ended it shortly after we both came to work here. But we're still very close friends, and occasionally we have dinner or a drink together. But it's always as friends. I think Ed found out about it somehow. The day after I notified the head office that I wanted to be considered for the director position, Ed called me into his office and gave me a rambling lecture about how we have to behave like ladies and gentlemen these days because of lawsuits on sexual harassment.

"At the time, I assumed he was referring somehow to one of our junior sales reps who had gotten drunk at the Christmas party and made a fool of himself with a couple of secretaries; but later I began to think that the cryptic comment was meant for me. What's more, I think Ed used that rumor about my relationship with Steve to block my promotion. And that, Barbara, is pure, sexist, double-standard hypocrisy because I can name you at least five guys at various levels in this company who have had affairs with colleagues and clients, and Ed is at the top of the list."

I couldn't deny the truth of Ruth's last statement, but that wasn't the point, or not yet. First I had to find out which, if any, of her accusations were true. I told her I needed some time and asked if she could give me a week before calling in a lawyer. She said no way. Having taken the first step, she was anxious to take the next, especially since she didn't believe things would change at Triton anyway. We dickered back and forth, but all I could get from her was a promise to hold off for 24 hours. Not much of a concession, but it was better than nothing.

Needless to say, I had a lot to think about and not very much time to do it in. It was curious that this complaint should come shortly after our organization had taken steps to comply with affirmative action policies by issuing a companywide memo stating that we would continue to recruit, employ, train, and promote individuals without regard to race, color, religion, sex, age, national origin, physical or mental handicap, or status as a disabled veteran or veteran of the Vietnam era. And we did this to prevent any problems in the future, not because we'd had trouble in the past. In fact, in my five years as HRM director, I'd never had a sexual discrimination or harassment complaint.

But now I was beginning to wonder whether there had never been grounds for complaint or whether the women here felt it was useless or even dangerous to complain. If it was the latter, how had I contributed to allowing that feeling to exist? And this thought led me to an even more uncomfortable one: Had I been co-opted into ignoring injustices in a system that, after all, did pretty well by me? Was I afraid to slap the hand that buttered my bread?

Questioning one's own motives may be enlightening, but it's also time consuming, and I had more pressing matters to deal with before I could indulge in what would likely be a painful self-analysis. I asked my secretary to find George Drake, CEO of Triton, and get him on the phone. In the meantime, I wrote down as much as I could remember of what Ruth had just told me. When George finally called, I told him I knew his schedule was full but we had an emergency of sorts on our hands and I needed an hour of his time this morning. I also asked that Ed Coulter be called into the meeting. George told me I had the hour.

When I got to George's office, Ed and George were already waiting. They were undoubtedly curious about why I had called this meeting, but as I've seen people do in similar situations, they covered their anxiety with chitchat about ball games and hangovers. I was too impatient for these rituals, so I cut the conversation short and told them that we were going to have a serious lawsuit on our hands in a matter of days if we didn't act very quickly. That got their attention, so I proceeded to tell Ruth's story. When I began, George and Ed seemed more surprised than anything else, but as I built up Ruth's case their surprise turned to concern. When I finished, we all sat in silence for I don't know how long and then George asked Ed for comments.

"Well, George," Ed said, "I don't know what to say. Ruth certainly was a strong contender for the position, and her qualifications nearly equaled Dick's, but it finally came down to the fact that Dick had the seniority and a little more experience in the industrial sector. When you've got two almost equally qualified candidates, you've got to distinguish them somehow. The decision came down to the wire, which in this case was six months seniority and a few more visits to factory sites."

"Were those the only criteria that made a difference in the decision?" George wanted to know.

"Well, not exactly. You know as well as I do that we base hiring decisions on a lot of things. On one hand, we look at what's on paper: years at the company, education, experience, recommendations. But we also rely on intuition, our feel for the situation. Sometimes, you don't know exactly why, but you just feel better about some people than others, and I've learned that those gut reactions are pretty reliable. The other VPs and I all felt good about Dick. There's something about him—he's got the feel of a winner. You know? He's confident—not arrogant—but solid and really sharp. Bruce had him out to the club a couple of times, and I played squash with him all last winter. We got to know him and we liked what we saw; he's a family man, kids in school here, could use the extra money, and is looking to stick around for a while. None of these things mean a lot by themselves, of course, but together they add up.

We've got lawsuits if we don't advance Dick and lawsuits if we don't advance Ruth.

"Don't get me wrong. I like Ruth too. She's very ambitious and one of our best. On the other hand, I can't say that I or any of the VPs know her as well as we know Dick. Of course, that's not exactly Ruth's fault, but there it is."

I had to be careful with the question I wanted Ed to respond to next because Ruth had asked for my confidence about the affair. I worded it this way: "Ed, did any part of your decision take into account Ruth's relationship with anyone else at the company?"

The question visibly disturbed Ed. He walked across the room and bummed a cigarette from me—he had quit last week—before answering: "Okay, I didn't want to go into this, but since you brought it up .... There's a rumor—well it's stronger than a rumor—that Ruth is more than professionally involved with Steve Baines—I mean she's having an, ah, sexual affair

with him. Now before you tell me that's none of my business, let me tell you about some homework I did on this stuff. Of course it's real tricky. It turns out there are at least two court cases that found sexual discrimination where an employer involved in a sexual relationship with an employee promoted that person over more qualified candidates.

"So here's what that leaves us with: we've got Steve pushing his girlfriend for the job. You saw the letter he wrote. And we've got Dick with seniority. So if we go with Ruth, what's to keep Dick from charging Steve and the company on two counts of sexual discrimination: sexual favoritism because Ruth is Steve's honey and reverse discrimination because we pass over a better qualified man just to get a woman into an executive position. So we're damned if we do and damned if we don't. We've got lawsuits if we don't advance Dick, and, so you tell me, lawsuits if we don't advance Ruth!"

We let that sink in for a few seconds. Then George spoke up: "What evidence do you have, Ed, that Steve and Ruth are having an affair?" he asked.

"Look, I didn't hire some guy to follow them around with a camera, if that's what you mean," Ed said. "But come on, I wasn't born yesterday; you can't keep that kind of hanky-panky a secret forever. Look at the way she dresses; she obviously enjoys men looking at her, especially Steve. In fact, I saw them having drinks together at Dino's the other night and believe me, they didn't look like they were talking business. All that on top of the rumors, you put two and two together."

Well, that did it for me. I'd been trying to play the objective observer and let Ed and George do all the talking, but Ed's last comment, along with some budding guilt about my own blindness to certain things at Triton that Ruth had pointed out, drove me out in the open. "Come off it, Ed," I said. "That's not evidence, that's gossip."

Now Ed turned on me: "Look," he shouted, "I didn't want to talk about this, but now that you've brought it up, I'll tell you something else. Even if we didn't have to worry about this sexual discrimination business, I still wouldn't back Ruth for the director's job." He calmed down a bit. "No offense, Barbara, but I just don't think women work out as well as men in certain positions. Human resources is one thing. It's real soft, person-to-person stuff. But factories are still a man's world. And I'm not talking about what I want it to be like. I'm talking facts of life.

"You see what happens when we send a woman out on some jobs, especially in the factories. To be any good in marketing you have to know how to relate to your client; that means getting to know him, going out drinking with him, talking sports, hunting, whatever he's interested in. A lot of our clients feel uncomfortable around a woman in business. They know how to relate to their wives, mothers, and girlfriends, but when a woman comes to the office and wants to talk a deal on industrial drills—well, they don't know what to do.

"And then there's the plain fact that you can't depend on a woman the way you can on a guy. She'll get married and her husband will get transferred, or she'll have a baby and want time off and not be able to go on the road as much. I know, Barbara, you probably think I'm a pig, or whatever women's libbers call guys like me these days. But from where I'm sitting, it just made good business sense to choose Dick over Ruth."

I saw them having drinks together, and they didn't look like they were talking business.

"Ed, I don't believe it," I said. "The next thing you'll tell me is that women ought to stay at home, barefoot and pregnant." There was a long silence after that—my guess was that I had hit on exactly what Ed thought. At least he didn't deny it. Ed stared at the rug, and George frowned at his coffee cup. I tried to steer the conversation back to the subject at hand, but it dwindled into another silence. George took a few notes and then told Ed he could go back to work. I assumed I was excused too, but as I started to leave, George called me back.

"Barbara, I'm going to need your help thinking through this mess," he said. "Of course we've got to figure out how we can avoid a lawsuit before the day is out, but I also want to talk about what we can do to avoid more lawsuits in the future. While Ed was talking I took some notes, and I've got maybe four or five points I think we ought to hash out. I'm not saying we're going to come up with all the answers today, but it'll be a start. You ready?"

"Shoot."

"Okay, let's do the big one first," he began. "What should I have done or not done to avoid this situation? I mean, I was just patting myself on the back for being so proactive when I sent out that memo letting everyone know the company policy on discrimination. I wrote it not thinking we had any problem at Triton. But just in case we did, I figured that memo would take care of it."

"Well, it looks like it's not enough just to have a corporate policy if the people in the ranks aren't on board. Obviously it didn't have much of an effect on Ed."

"So what am I supposed to do? Fire Ed?"

Being asked for my honest opinion by my CEO was a new experience for me and I appreciated it, but I wasn't going to touch that last question with a ten-foot pole. Instead I went on to another aspect: "And even if you get your managers behind you, your policy won't work if the people it's supposed to help don't buy it. Ruth was the first woman to complain around here. Are the others afraid to speak up? Or do they feel like Ed about a woman's place, or have husbands who do? Maybe they lack confidence even to try for better jobs, that is, if they knew about them."

"Okay," he said, "I'll admit that our system of having the VPs make recommendations, our 'old-boy network,' as Ruth called it, does seem to end up excluding women, even though the exclusion isn't intentional. And it's not obvious discrimination, like Ed's claim that Ruth is unqualified for a position because she is a woman. But wouldn't open job posting take away our right to manage as we see fit? Maybe we should concentrate instead on getting more women into the social network, make it an old boys' and old girls' club?"

"To tell you the truth, George, I don't much want to play squash with you," I replied, "but maybe we're getting off the subject. The immediate question seems to be how we're going to get more women into executive positions here, or, more specifically, do we give Ruth the director of marketing position that we just gave Dick?"

"On that score, at least, it seems to me that Ed has a strong argument," George said. "Dick is more qualified. You can't get around that."

I had wanted to challenge Ed on this point when he brought it up earlier, but I wasn't quite sure of myself then. Now that George was asking me for advice and seemed to be taking what I had to say seriously, I began to think that I might have something valuable to offer. So I charged right in. "George, maybe we're cutting too fine a line with this qualifications business. I know a lot of people think affirmative action means promoting the unqualified over the qualified to achieve balance. I think that argument is hogwash at best and a wily diversion tactic at worst. To my mind, Ruth and Dick are equally qualified, or equal enough. And wouldn't it make good business sense to get a diverse set of perspectives—women's, men's, blacks', whites'—in our executive group?"

"But isn't that reverse discrimination—not promoting Dick because he's a man? How would a judge respond to that? That's a question for a lawyer."

George leaned forward. "Let's talk about my last point, the one I think we've both been avoiding. What about this affair between Ruth and Steve? Boy, this is one reason why women in the work force are such trouble—no, just joking, Barbara, sorry about that. Look, I don't like lawsuits any more than anyone else, but I'd do anything to avoid this one. We'd be a laughing stock if it got out that Triton promoted unqualified people because they slept with the boss. I don't know how I'd explain that one to my wife."

"Look, George," I said, "in the first place, Dick's superior qualifications are debatable; in the second place, we have no proof that Ruth and Steve are involved in that way; and in the third place, what if they were once involved but no longer are? Does a past relationship condemn them for life? Isn't there a statute of limitations on that kind of thing, or are we going to make her put a scarlet letter on her briefcase? I thought these discrimination laws were supposed to protect women, but now it looks like a woman can be denied a promotion because someone thinks she's a floozy."

"Wait a second, Barbara. Don't make me look like such a prig," George said. "I realize that when men and women work together sexual issues are bound to crop up. I just don't know what I'm supposed to do about it, if anything. In some cases a woman may welcome a guy coming on to her, but what if it's her boss? And then there's that subtle stuff Ruth brought up—the calendar, dirty jokes, the male employees excluding women by going to bars to watch TV—and other women. And Ruth's treatment at that factory—how can we control our clients? I'm not sure these are things you can set policy on, but I am sure that I can't ignore them any longer."

And there we were. All the issues were on the table, and we had about 21 hours to make our decisions and act on them.

What would you do?

We asked the following business leaders—people who actually have to deal with such problems—how they would solve this dilemma. Here are their responses.

Donald J. Comeau *is corporate senior vice president of the Stop & Shop Companies, Inc., where he has served in a variety of positions since 1960.*

The facts indicate clear discriminatory practices.

It is clear that Triton's historical methods of hiring, developing, and ultimately promoting its people systematically discriminate against women. The mere issuance of a "policy statement" from the CEO without the proper training and understanding of the people who must carry out the policy is ludicrous. Triton has obviously made an attempt to bring in qualified, high-potential women but has paid no attention to integrating them into the old-boy network, and even less attention to evaluating their qualifications on a nondiscriminatory basis.

It's not unusual that these issues came to light as a result of a specific situation. As Triton brings more highly educated and trained women into the company, management must change its policies on development and promotion.

The facts as presented indicate clear discriminatory practices. Since a possible lawsuit is a real threat, Barbara and George's time should be spent deciding: how they will handle the decision to promote Dick ahead of Ruth, what steps must be taken to correct the practices that put them into this situation, and how to handle Ruth.

The decision to promote Dick must stand. To do otherwise would put Triton at risk of losing two very good people—Dick and Ruth. Reversing the decision, while it would make Ruth director of the marketing division, would also position her for failure. The organization would perceive the reversal to have occurred simply because she was a woman, not because of her qualifications and ability to do the job. Dick, on the other hand, might resign and/or file his own lawsuit.

George as CEO must institute an affirmative action plan that his office controls and follows up. It must be understood and practiced at all levels of the organization and be recognized as part of the company's business plan, on which managers are evaluated. Important elements in the plan must include but not be limited to:

Elimination of the old-boy network.

A promotion policy based on qualifications—perhaps a bid system or other nondiscriminatory method of judging abilities.

A comprehensive development program for all managers to immediately begin educating them in Triton's affirmative action plan, with ongoing follow-up sessions.

Individual counseling that addresses women in management and how to deal with the issues, for example, for people like Ed. In this case, an affair should only be a consideration when job performance is affected, and that applies equally to men and women.

Communication of the plan to all employees and clients.

Once the outline of this plan is put on paper, George and Barbara should sit with Ruth and talk with her about the following:

The decision on Dick and the reasons for going ahead with him as the new director of the marketing division.

Plans for revitalizing an affirmative action strategy.

Since Ruth obviously has some strong and constructive feelings about integrating women into Triton, offer her the opportunity to work directly with Barbara and George to develop and implement the revitalized affirmative action plan.

If after this discussion Ruth decides to file a lawsuit, then she should do so; the affirmative action plan, however, must be carried out.

Zoe Coulson, *the first woman corporate officer of Campbell Soup Company, is vice president— consumer issues. Previously, she held positions at the Good Housekeeping Institute, J. Walter Thompson, and Leo Burnett Company in Chicago, and Donnelley/ Dun & Bradstreet in New York.*

It takes more than a memo to promote qualified women.

Women—and men—climbing career ladders need to recognize that so-called old-fashioned values, ethics, and morals still have credence. Many men and women heading today's major American companies and participating on boards of directors have been molded by another era; it is not surprising that they use their own standards when evaluating the personal traits of someone being considered for advancement.

In this case, Ruth's corporate accomplishments are not reported as exceptional to the man's; in fact, Dick "had seniority and a little more experience in the industrial sector," according to Ed, a vice president. Ed's subjective evaluations, however, seemed to be influenced by traditional views some men have about women; a woman working in industry may be unsettling to a man raised in a background where women only worked at home.

Since men like Ed make management decisions, it is essential for women with high corporate goals to recognize the corporation's customs as well as management's standards on personal characteristics, and act accordingly. After the successful team project, Ruth did not mention if each male specifically was invited to celebrate afterwards; it sounds as if a spontaneous team event happened and Ruth didn't "read" it. While some men also don't correctly evaluate such customs, women, who may be new to these environments, need to be especially aware.

Different corporations have different customs, and if a company's atmosphere is tightly tra-

ditional, people of high ambition should respond accordingly. In this case, when Ruth was employed in another company, she did not consider the implications of her personal actions (her affair with Steve) if she changed companies. But the custom of informal meetings between candidates and other officers was one of Ed's methods of evaluating promotability, and Ruth's "reputation" didn't encourage the informal interview custom. In today's world of corporate mergers and executive job changing, managers overlap between companies and, indeed, areas of the country, so implications can be far-reaching.

While the people in this case are in middle management, they should be aware that traditional values and customs are important to upper management in many of today's big companies. And top executives send down signals; how they act is how they expect their peers to act. They may not promote someone with entirely different customs from theirs.

Ruth commented that at the previous company her brief affair with Steve "was discreet; it never interfered with business, and we ended it." Her previous personal behavior introduced an issue.

This case does not state the marital status of these employees. As the legal counsel of a big corporation commented recently, "When a senior manager 'bends the rules' on one corporate policy, he sends a message that his employees apply to lots of rules," which can lead to staff dishonesty. Marriage, of course, is a legal contract, as well as a personal commitment; therefore, some corporate managers use fidelity as one criteria when promoting someone.

In another corporation, the chief executive officer was removed by his board of directors a few years ago because of an extramarital affair. In another company, an officer was asked to resign because of his approach to a secretary. In yet another, the president suggested to a divorced senior executive that he marry the woman with whom he was living; the board chairman was a traditionalist. The man married the woman and probably removed a concern of the board.

Since these situations have affected men's careers, women need to be doubly cautious. Meeting with a male business friend occasionally for a drink or dinner should cause no stir in today's world if the ambiance of the place is pleasant and if the couple's demeanor portrays friendship, not sex; many corporate cultures accept this. In other environments, however, even a meeting with a nonemployee date that might reveal sexual overtones should take place in private, or at least not in a public place where a "message" might be extended.

Since Ruth seems to be one of few women in her company, she is more visible than a man, whether she likes it or not. She needs to recognize that she is being reviewed at all times.

All this is not to say there is no problem. Even though George sent a policy statement to staff on affirmative action, women in this corporation are still at risk. It takes more than a memo to promote qualified women! Senior management could consider these and perhaps other steps to send strong signals to employees:

Should men be trained in reviewing women's qualifications?

Should there be special programs for all minorities on "keys to success"?

Can top officers become informal mentors to potential executive women—and men—so that they better understand the company's customs?

Should male managers be evaluated on their progress in promoting women?

Since Ruth has stated her dissatisfaction, in my opinion she has two courses of action. She could continue to execute her job as well as possible and avoid situations that might be misinterpreted by associates. Or she could go work for another company and learn its pattern at the beginning.

With more dedicated, educated women in the work force, some discriminatory beliefs about women's roles indeed will erode in the future. Women like Ruth, however, should learn now how to put themselves in the man's chair, to better understand and respect male values. Also, women who are achievers are setting examples for women who follow them, so they have another responsibility.

Top executives can make efforts to discuss their values (and practice them), so aspiring men and women managers can learn their scoring system.

It is to be hoped that Ruth will now understand the scorecard at her company better so that next time an opening occurs she will be judged with higher points.

R. Marilyn Lee *is corporate director of human resources for The Times Mirror Company. Before joining Times Mirror, she was a deputy city attorney for the city of Los Angeles.*

All employees should feel comfortable and have an equal chance to advance.

Triton is about to have its first sex discrimination and sexual harassment complaint. This case has it all—a predominantly male work force with an old-boy environment, a secretive promotion sys-

tem, a qualified woman loses a job to a qualified man, rumors of a personal relationship, sexual stereotypes, and good old-fashioned bias.

How did a nice company like Triton with a concerned CEO like George end up in a mess like this? From the facts given, it appears that Triton hasn't done well in keeping pace with a changing workplace. Women generally make up more than 45% of the nation's employees, yet Triton has only 20%, low for even an industrial setting. There are no women in the executive group at Triton and only two in middle management. From Ruth's perspective, the women at Triton are made uncomfortable by the good-old-boy atmosphere of talking sports and going to bars. Management has an antidiscrimination policy but apparently has taken no steps to make the work environment hospitable for all employees.

The case does not look good for Triton. Ed found Dick's and Ruth's qualifications to be nearly identical. The additional criteria that Ed considered—intuition, socializing with Dick at club events, Dick's being a family man who needed the extra money—were subjective at best and irrelevant at worst. Add Ed's belief that women don't belong in certain work settings, his discriminatory treatment of Ruth, and his hasty assumptions about Ruth's relationship with Steve, and this case could be a plaintiff lawyer's dream come true.

Can the problem be resolved in the next 24 hours? Probably not, but there is time for Barbara to review the facts and discuss options with George and Ed. Triton's legal department or outside lawyers should be consulted as management proceeds.

Here is one approach the company might take. Barbara could meet with Ruth the next day and explain that the company takes seriously her claims of discrimination. Let Ruth know that George has been briefed and has asked Barbara to immediately proceed with an investigation that will include more detailed interviews with Ruth, Ed, and others.

It would also be a good idea to find out what Ruth wants at this point. When she first saw Barbara, she was very upset. Barbara needs to find out if Ruth really would like to continue working for Triton, or have recent events soured that possibility? If the situation is salvageable, Barbara should ask Ruth to give the company time to do the right thing. (That does not mean giving her the disputed promotion. Since it appears that the company's selection of Dick has been announced, it would be unwise to reverse the decision and thereby create a second personnel dispute.)

Either Ruth will agree to work with the human resources manager on the complaint, or she will tell her that it has gone too far and she would rather go to court. Perhaps the prospect of a future promotion for Ruth can be suggested and discussed with George. In either event, the company should investigate her claim, take appropriate corrective action, and move forward with new personnel programs.

The long-term goal for Triton's management should be to open up the atmosphere so that all employees are comfortable and have an equal chance to advance. Some steps are quite simple.

First, an internal job posting procedure should be established. Promotional openings should not be communicated only through the grapevine. Job posting increases accountability in hiring decisions and encourages women and minorities to apply.

Second, supervisory training on equal opportunity and a diversified work force is clearly needed. Managers and supervisors should understand that offensive language and insensitive actions can create a hostile, discriminatory environment. Ruth's case contains several examples: calling her ''honey,'' not introducing her on sales calls, not including her in social activities on business trips, and allowing locker-room calendars to be posted on office walls. Many men are genuinely surprised that some of these actions are offensive. A discussion between male and female colleagues, including suggested ways to handle travel assignments and introduce new employees, would help.

In addition, training can address sexual stereotyping. For instance, Ed assumes that a saleswoman would not relate well to a client in a factory setting because she may not talk about hunting or sports. Ruth has already shown that notion to be false because she is one of Triton's best salespeople. Ed also wrongly assumes that women leave jobs at a greater rate than men. Men tend to leave jobs just as often—for promotional opportunities, career changes, and, yes, even because their wives have been transferred to new jobs.

A good training program will also develop ways to deal with customers who seem to prefer a male account executive. Here Ed might have suggested to Dryden Industries that Ruth was one of Triton's top people and capable of doing the needs assessment, or that Ruth work with a man to do the survey more quickly.

Training can instill a better understanding of affirmative action and employment law generally. Ed, playing armchair lawyer, is confused about reverse discrimination. Selecting a qualified woman candidate over a qualified man is lawful when women are underrepresented in that job category—certainly the case at Triton.

Training classes could review Triton's employment data and identify the problem areas. Affirmative action hires and special attention to the promotion of women and minorities may be needed until the work force is more balanced. Once employees understand that concept, some of the anxiety about affirmative action is eased.

Ed will need some individual coaching since he obviously has strong opinions on this subject and may adversely influence others he supervises.

Third, Triton's management must show that its affirmative action policies have a clear direction. Issuing an antidiscrimination policy is fine but is a small piece of a larger pie. The company needs to take firm steps to increase the number of women in the general work force and in management.

A directive from the top is always the best way to start. George should meet with his vice presidents and convey his expectations: that they will increase the number of women employees in each department where women are underrepresented and establish programs to assure career development for women. George could make affirmative action goals a part of each executive's annual bonus plan and withhold payment if goals are not met. It is not surprising to find that those people who are good at meeting sales and other business goals become equally good at meeting affirmative action goals, once the company's commitment is made clear.

Last, the human resources department should become more involved with the promotion process. If Triton had well-defined affirmative action goals, Barbara could have advised Ed that all things being equal, Ruth should have been selected over Dick in order to diversify the director group. Promotional selection by a committee of vice presidents appears to be a holdover from the old days and does cloud the issue of who is actually making the promotional decision. Hence, Ruth's past affair with Steve is brought up even though Ruth, in marketing, does not have a direct reporting relationship to Steve, in production.

As Triton implements some of these long-range solutions, there will be plenty of questions and issues to address along the way. Barbara is perceptive to acknowledge that other women may also have complaints but may have been afraid to come forward. The issues are clearly under the surface, and it would be far better to take remedial action now before another ''case of the mismanaged Ms.'' appears.

Joseph Posner *is a trial and appellate lawyer in the Los Angeles area. His practice concentrates on representing plaintiffs in wrongful firing and employee harassment cases.*

Coulter has to go.

Ed Coulter is going to cost this company some real money. Any way you look at it, the company is going to have to pay some big bucks to get out of the mess in which it finds itself and, perhaps more important, to prevent the same thing from happening in the future.

Apparently, Triton already gave Dick Simon the promotion to director of the marketing division. Even without considering the issue of reverse discrimination, the company can't very well take the promotion away from him. If it tried to do this, Dick would probably have a good lawsuit against the company without regard to whether the action constituted reverse discrimination. At least under California law, I think that he could sue and win.

When Ruth came into Barbara's office, she had more suspicions than facts. But her suspicions proved to be far more true than even Ruth probably realized. It is apparent to me that this company, which seems to be a fairly good-sized operation, has engaged in a systematic pattern of making it virtually impossible for a woman to receive any significant promotion. On the one hand, you had Ruth with an outstanding record, a sensible, intelligent person, and quite stable; the fact that she was provoked by this incident is not only understandable because of its gravity but it also shows the extreme impact on her.

Taken by itself, deciding to promote Dick or to promote Ruth to the director's job could probably each be defended, as they appear evenly matched. But when I see: (1) all the top jobs controlled by a tight group in the old-boy network and the openings not made known to others; (2) the situation at the customer's factory where Ed refused to back up Ruth by telling the customer that Ruth was the person in charge and had to do the interviewing; (3) the use of a mere suspicion about a subject which is none of Ed's business in the first place, i.e., Ruth's friendship with Steve; (4) Ed's admission that a factor in promotions is off-hours socializing at the country club (leading to the conclusion that off-hours socializing at the local bar is a part of business activities); (5) Ed's candid statement that he doesn't think women are good for certain jobs because they should stick to things that are in his words "real soft, person to person"; (6) his statement that women aren't dependable because of marriage, dependence on a husband, pregnancy, or the like—these factors all add up to the reality that the company did exactly what Ruth suspected it of doing.

In that connection, the other points, such as the fact that there is a pinup calendar in the sales room, don't carry a lot of weight with me. In a trial, these, however, as well as the most important factors I already mentioned, would certainly be something for the jury to think about.

In my opinion, Ed Coulter has to go. The company simply cannot afford to keep a man in his position with his attitudes and demonstrated actions. Perhaps a transfer could be arranged for him and/or a job found for him at another company or related entity. But one thing is for sure—the longer he is there, the more he is going to cost the company, if not today, then later.

Next, even George, the president, needs to have his consciousness raised. He is not in the same league with Ed, by any means, but he needs to realize

that he has a problem, and he needs to do something about it. That would include calling together the five or six remaining vice presidents and laying the law down in no uncertain terms that the way people are selected for the top jobs is going to change, and change now. And then George has to monitor the situation to see that his subordinates do what he tells them.

This leaves us with the big question, what to do about Ruth, and this is a real dilemma. If Ruth were to sue, and if she ever could get testimony about the conversation in George's office, she would win in a walk. And since the company appears to have been selecting people for the top jobs this way for some time, I am willing to bet that there are more "Ruths" out there.

The company should think about a substantial monetary settlement with Ruth *right now*, whether she stays with Triton or not. Certainly, nothing should be said to her about leaving, and she should be promised that she would be the preferred candidate for the next slot that opens up. Moreover, Triton should look around to see if there are any such positions to which she could be promoted now. In addition, the company should think about doing some reorganization, if that is possible and makes good business sense. The one thing that Ruth will have to accept is the fact that Triton can't very well take back its promotion of Dick Simon.

T. Gary Rogers *is chairman of the board and chief executive officer of Dreyer's Grand Ice Cream, Inc. and director of several other corporations and associations.*

Put the responsibility for human resources where it belongs.

If George Drake were to ask me for advice on dealing with the issues raised by the Ruth Linsky controversy at Triton, I would offer him the following five observations:

1   Triton's policy is equal opportunity, and Ruth hasn't had it yet. Affirmative action has to be more than a toothless memo. Equal opportunity in hiring means the person with the best *relevant* qualifications (more on that below) gets the job. Triton has an obligation to let its people know when an opening occurs and to interview any applicants from within the company who may be qualified. Because minorities and women *are* often discriminated against in hiring decisions, Triton must be especially careful to ensure such candidates for promotion a fair opportunity to present their credentials and make their case. Ruth clearly deserved an interview for this job, but

she did not really get one, and this must be remedied immediately.

2   The relevant qualifications are only those related to job effectiveness. Triton's first responsibility is to its shareholders. Its managers should be selected on the basis of their ability to further the company's goals and maximize its earnings. In choosing between Ruth Linsky and Dick Simon for director of the marketing division, only factors that affect job performance in that role should pertain. Ruth's relationship with Steve Baines is irrelevant unless it somehow affects her ability to perform the job. The assertion that she will get married and move or want time off to have a family is not germaine unless those really are her plans. Similarly, Dick's being a family man, or needing a raise, or playing squash obviously should not enter into the equation.

On the other hand, it *is* appropriate to consider that a director of marketing in the industrial drill business has to deal and be effective with many types of men, including some who have deep-seated (albeit unfair) prejudices toward women in business. Triton has no obligation to change the culture of its industry and has to be realistic about the skills and attitudes its managers require to cope effectively within that culture. Therefore, it *is* appropriate to compare Ruth and Dick in terms of their maturity, experience, and demonstrated ability to function in what is largely a "man's world," even though that requirement poses a much tougher challenge for Ruth than it does for Dick.

3   Let Ed Coulter make the decision, but require him to explain his thinking. Ed is charged with responsibility for marketing at Triton and has the right and duty to select the management team for his department. If Ed wants the advice of the other vice presidents, that's fine, but the final decision should be his responsibility alone—not that of a committee. In making his decision, however, Ed must comply with the company's affirmative action program and be able to satisfy his boss that he has done so.

Given the sensitivity of this matter and the questions about Ed's understanding of the issues, George should have a long talk with Ed about equal opportunity, relevant hiring criteria, and the law. At the end of this discussion, George should ask Ed to interview Ruth with an open mind, reconsider his decision, and then come back and share his thinking with George. In his conversation with Ed, George should be careful to have Ed understand that he is not campaigning for Ruth but only ensuring that she receive fair consideration as an applicant for the job.

4   Don't let potential lawsuits affect your business decisions. The real issue for George is whether Triton's policies and practices comply with his desires (and the law) on an ongoing basis. If they do, George should assume Triton will prevail, if sued. Unfortunately, defending lawsuits, particularly in the personnel arena, has become a cost of doing business, even for the best-managed companies. If George is satisfied that Triton is acting appropriately, then he should not let Ruth's threat of legal action affect his thinking—except, perhaps, as an indication of immaturity or poor judgment on her part.

5   Consider reassigning human resources responsibilities at Triton. The first and most important responsibility of any manager is for his (or her) human resources, and good managers will demand direct control over the hiring, training, motivating, and developing of their people. Triton appears to exhibit a problem common to many companies with a high-profile human resources department—management has abrogated much of its most important responsibility. Triton's managers should understand, be thinking about, and be experienced with the subtleties of equal opportunity and other people-related issues. At Triton, it appears the human resources department "takes care of that."

For example, it would have been much more appropriate and efficient for Ruth to take her complaint directly to Ed—or to George, if necessary—rather than to the human resources department. Choosing properly between Ruth Linsky and Dick Simon requires integrating judgments about job requirements, industry culture, and individual capabilities. If Ed Coulter is qualified for his job, he should be able to make these judgments appropriately without help from a staff department. If Ed cannot be trusted to do this, he should be replaced. George should reduce the role of his corporate staff in personnel matters to only technical support and record keeping and put the responsibility for human resources where it belongs—squarely in the hands of his managers. ▽

Special Report

David N. Campbell,
R.L. Fleming, and
Richard C. Grote

Discipline without punishment— at last

Why and how you should implement a nonpunitive approach to discipline

When a foreman at Tampa Electric Company blew up at a lineman and earned a suspension from work, the company's labor relations manager knew it was time for a change in the discipline system. Tampa Electric's switch to a nonpunitive approach is only one example of a growing trend to a disciplinary method that is now winning broad acceptance. In part, a nonpunitive approach simply fits the times. Shifting attitudes toward corporate culture, new competitive requirements, a changing work force, and reforming views on the importance of discipline all add a new relevance to an issue that was first broached in HBR 20 years ago by John Huberman, who introduced a nonpunitive system of discipline at a Canadian pulp mill.

But most important is the qualitative difference of the nonpunitive approach. It simply represents a more realistic, more adult, and more positive way to encourage a disciplined work force. The nonpunitive system recognizes that workers themselves must be the real source of disci-

pline and sets up a workable program that reinforces self-discipline. To be effective, the new system must be linked in a consistent manner with the rest of a company's human resource management programs. In this way discipline becomes part of the company's philosophy, reflecting management's view of itself and its work force.

Both Messrs. Campbell, senior vice president, administration, and Fleming, director of labor relations, participated in the implementation of a nonpunitive system of discipline at Tampa Electric Company of Tampa, Florida. Mr. Grote is president of Performance Systems Corporation of Dallas, Texas, a management consulting firm that specializes in helping organizations implement nonpunitive performance management systems.

Authors' note: We thank Eric L. Harvey for his contributions to this article.

1 John Huberman,
  "Discipline Without Punishment,"
  HBR July-August 1964, p. 62.

It was a particularly nasty incident involving a foreman that triggered Tampa Electric Company's decision to switch to a nonpunitive approach to discipline. The labor relations manager recalled the 1977 confrontation between the foreman and a lineman this way: "The lineman's confrontational behavior caused the working foreman to grab the lineman by his shirt collar and shake him severely. This is unacceptable behavior for a working foreman, and he was suspended for 13 days. I had no choice under the existing policy but to support that suspension, but I never felt good about it. All I did was penalize an employee and his family; I did not change his behavior in any way. I believe he would have done the same thing again. I forced compliance, but he will still believe the company was wrong."

His prediction was accurate. Five months later another disciplinary situation arose with the same foreman. The previous suspension had proved ineffective in improving behavior.

The labor relations manager's frustration with the company's punitive approach resulted in a search for an alternative. The organization wanted a system that provided consistency, fairness, and lasting corrective measures without resorting to punishment. In September 1979, the production operations and maintenance groups replaced the old approach with a nonpunitive system for a one-year trial period. By January 1981, the new system was in effect companywide. The pilot project, which covered 1,000 employees, grew to include nearly 3,000.

After the program had been in place in production operations and maintenance for about a year, Tampa Electric surveyed the 100 managers and supervisors in the affected departments. All but 2 not only agreed that the program should be continued but also recommended its expansion. "When you get 98 out of 100 managers agreeing on anything," one senior executive commented, "you know you've got something that's very successful." Shortly thereafter, Tampa Electric expanded its nonpunitive approach to all operating, service, and administrative departments.

Since the program was adopted companywide in January 1981, Tampa Electric reports only favorable results: more effective and accepted disciplinary measures, fewer successful unemployment compensation claims after employees have been terminated, less absenteeism, and fewer arbitrations. In fact, in 1982, *no* union grievance proceeded to arbitration.

The decline in absenteeism alone resulted in sizable financial savings for the company. Sick time usage in maintenance and production operations dropped from an average of 66.7 hours in 1977 to 36.6 hours in 1983. In one operating department, the average use of sick time per employee dropped from 58.8 hours to 19.5 hours per year in five years. Based on a 1983 average wage rate of $11.78 per hour, this reduction in sick time use saved the company $439,404, or 1.38% of the 1983 payroll—the equivalent of having 18 additional people on the job.

Tampa Electric's experience with its nonpunitive system was best captured by the words of a long-term supervisor who expressed relief over the elimination of the unpaid suspension. "I've never yet seen a guy come back from an unpaid suspension," he said, "feeling better about his boss, his job, the company, or himself." (See the insert, "Similar Results in Dissimilar Organizations," for more information.)

Resistance & acceptance

Twenty years after its introduction, a growing number of companies are finally moving to implement John Huberman's "discipline without punishment" approach.[1] Five reasons explain why it has taken so long for the new system to gain acceptance:

1   **No perceived need.** Throughout the 1960s and much of the 1970s, existing approaches to discipline were perceived as adequate, if imperfect. In the industrial sector of the economy, the traditional disciplinary series of warnings and suspensions was comfortable and familiar; managers didn't expect to bring about behavioral change and commitment to the organization's goals. In the professional and technical sector, organizations tended to discount the need for a formal discipline system. Formal disciplinary action was somehow seen as inappropriate for this more sophisticated, bet-

ter educated portion of the work force; problems were as likely to be avoided as confronted.

Today, the old standard is not good enough. Pressures for quality and productivity demand a work force committed to meeting organizational goals and requirements. Companies are implementing nonpunitive discipline systems as a strategy to build commitment and productivity.

2   **Understanding "corporate culture."** Until recently, few companies recognized or cared whether they had a corporate culture that influenced the collective behavior of its members. Discipline was not perceived as a reflection of culture—represented, for example, in the idea of a well-disciplined organization. Rather, discipline was merely something "done to someone" in response to misbehavior. With the new interest in a company defining its corporate culture, however, has come a recognition of the way discipline defines the relationship between managers and workers.

3   **Lack of an effective implementation process.** Huberman's 1964 article merely suggested replacing a series of punitive steps with a series of nonpunitive steps. But simply renaming the steps has little impact on the day-to-day behavior of supervisors confronted with employee misbehavior. For an organization to change its approach to discipline, it has to review and reevaluate its entire approach to performance management. With more experience, managers have found methods to use in moving an organization from the old style to the new one.

4   **Changing work force values.** At the time Huberman introduced his approach, the "baby boomers"—the huge population born between 1946 and the mid-1960s—had not yet entered the work force. The traditional values of hard work, diligence, obedience to authority, and self-discipline still prevailed. Today, with approximately 48% of the work force consisting of people born between 1946 and 1964, managers have to deal with employees who grew up in an era that spurned discipline for permissiveness, rejected authority figures, and insisted on immediate gratification and participation in decision making. When man-

agers today complain that the "new breed" is different, they're right.

Moreover, baby boomers not only make up the great majority of young employees in an organization, but also "senior boomers," in their middle and late thirties, are now assuming positions of authority where they are required to set disciplinary standards. In their new tasks, many continue the unconventional attitudes and approaches they brought with them to the organization.

5   **Changing perceptions.** Twenty years ago, discipline was perceived as a distasteful task best left to line supervisors and the labor relations department. Discipline did not deserve senior management's attention.

Because of the tremendous increases in wrongful termination suits and challenges to disciplinary action by outside third parties, discipline has assumed a more significant place on the corporate agenda. Senior managers are recognizing that the traditional approach to discipline is out of alignment, both with other human resource systems and, more important, with most of our beliefs about the worth of the individual and the best ways to manage human resources.

These five factors have contributed to the increasing interest in and introduction of nonpunitive discipline systems in a variety of organizations. As a result, the purpose of the disciplinary transaction has changed from a punishment meted out in response to a violation to a process that requires individuals to accept responsibility for their own behavior, performance, and continued participation in the enterprise.

The discipline dilemma

Few systems in American organizations seem more accepted yet less productive than the old-line "progressive discipline." In the desire to enforce rules in the work force, organizations frequently act in ways that prevent real self-discipline. Consider:

☐   In a plant of a major food-processing company, disciplinary prob-

Similar results in dissimilar organizations

Many organizations that have adopted a nonpunitive system have found results similar to those at Tampa Electric. The Texas Department of Mental Health and Mental Retardation, with 26,000 employees spread over 30 facilities, was suffering from high turnover and absenteeism, low morale, and low quality of patient care. It was also plagued with assorted labor relations, recruitment, and regulatory problems. The implementation of its system, similar to Tampa Electric's, produced significant and sustained results. The first quarter alone produced a retention of 853 employees, a 30% reduction in turnover from the baseline evaluation period. Using a conservative replacement cost of $2,000 per employee, the change to a nonpunitive system saved the department more than $1.7 million.

Union Carbide has reduced absenteeism, turnover, and disciplinary actions at ten locations with its positive discipline program and is now expanding its use of the system. W.R. Hutchison, director of personnel programs at

Union Carbide, believes that the company is in a better position to defend itself against wrongful termination suits because the system obliges a poor performer to make the decision about his or her job. "In 90% of the cases where an employee has been placed on a decision-making leave and confronted with the need either to quit or to formulate a list of actions he will take to keep the job," explains Hutchison, "employees choose the latter alternative, improve their performance, and save their jobs. Once employees set their own standards and agree to them, it's a lot more difficult for them to say they didn't understand the rules."

According to Susan N. Cook, vice president of personnel at Liberty National Bank, the Oklahoma bank's implementation of a discipline-without-punishment approach produced significant reductions in absenteeism, turnover, and disciplinary problems. "The intangible benefits have also been great," she explained. "We have found a noticeable improvement in morale and greater supervisory self-confidence in confronting employee problems as well as reduced exposure to equal opportunity complaints or lawsuits resulting from unfair or inconsistent disciplinary action."

The Somersworth meter business department of General Electric, recently featured in an article on rehabilitated plants, adopted the approach in April 1981.* According to Alan W. Bryant, employee and community relations manager, while disciplinary problems had never been significant in this nonunion facility, it made operational the company philosophy of positive, mature employee relations: "Implementing a positive discipline program produced the results we expected—fewer disciplinary problems and transactions, improved employee morale, greater supervisory self-confidence, more consistency in administration. Our experience in installing positive discipline, moreover, provided two other subtle but important benefits. First, it fostered the development of a more collaborative climate between operating managers and the employee relations function. Second, and most important for us, it promoted a shift in supervisory attention toward the 'forgotten workers'—that greater majority of employees who do their jobs well and never encounter any disciplinary problems."

In installing its system, General Electric tracked not only the number of disciplinary discussions but also "positive contacts"—formal discussions between a supervisor and a subordinate about a job well done. In a two-year period, the company recorded over 6,200 positive contacts.

The solid data collected from a variety of organizations (see Exhibit II), reinforced by the personal reactions of the managers themselves, supports the case for a positive approach to the application of discipline. By confronting the issue from this different, more adult perspective, managers perceive the entire issue of discipline from a different angle. No longer caught up in trying to determine the punishment that fits the crime, managers now explore positive ways to build commitment, generate self-discipline, and ensure individual responsibility.

*See Jonathan King and Robert E. Johnson, "Silk Purses from Old Plants," HBR March-April 1983, p. 147.

---

lems became so severe that in a space of nine months, managers fired 58 of the 210 employees. Supervisors eagerly wrote up infractions with the intent of running off "troublemakers." The atmosphere turned poisonous; obscene messages began appearing in the plant's products.

☐   A Midwestern office-furniture manufacturer, responding to demands from supervisors for a consistent discipline system, concocted a point scheme that rated the seriousness of every conceivable disciplinary offense. An employee accumulating 200 points earned a written warning; an employee accumulating 350 points in a 12-month period earned automatic termination. Supervisors passing workers loitering by the time clock called out, "That'll cost you 25!" Every disci-

plinary action was grieved; "point shaving" was commonplace.

☐   A glass factory's system made final action an unpaid suspension, the length to be determined by the facts of the case and the employee's record. An employee who had previously been suspended for one day would be suspended for three days for repeating the offense; a five-day suspension might be ten the next time. A frustrated personnel manager complained of one individual who was now on his fifth suspension—this time for one month—and admitted that when he returned he would be no better than when he left. "What should we do next?" he asked. "Suspend him for a year?" In the meantime, production was disrupted as less-skilled employ-

ees had to fill in. Overtime increased, and other employees kidded the supervisor about how they too would like a month's "vacation."

☐   A middle manager in a fast-growing high-tech company was disturbed by a senior engineer's performance. A long-term employee, the engineer demonstrated his apparent resentment of younger colleagues by leaving work early, disregarding deadlines, and producing second-rate work. The manager, asked if he had talked to the engineer about the situation, replied, "No. I know I should, but I hate that kind of confrontation. I'd really like to give him a written warning, but that's only for factory types."

These examples illustrate the dilemma of discipline. Attempts to establish a disciplined environment by using a traditional approach cannot produce employees who are committed to the goals of the company and the policies and rules by which it operates.

Other problems abound. Supervisors resist and resent a discipline system in which they suffer more pain than do the employees on the receiving end. Simply from doing their job, supervisors may face apathy, hostility, reduced output, and an uncomfortable personal relationship with a subordinate.

Old-line approaches require the supervisor to play the heavy and wear a black hat. By definition, the job demands that he or she write up, suspend, place on probation, or deliver a "final warning" to members of the work group. Because they consider it an obstacle to developing a professional image, most supervisors today avoid this role.

Not only do they catch flak from below but supervisors also discover that maintaining discipline may produce reversed decisions "upstairs," pressure from peers and bosses who are more tolerant of rule violations, or subtle messages not to "rock the boat." Even more insidious is the perception that a supervisor who takes many disciplinary actions demonstrates a lack of administrative competence.

Furthermore, some supervisors believe that the goal of a disciplinary action is to build a case justifying an individual's termination. Reluctant to enter a one-way street, supervisors often spend too much time in unproductive counseling sessions to avoid taking any formal measures before they have made up their minds that discharge is the answer. They then begin the discipline process with the objective of termination rather than rehabilitation. But this approach has its own perverse twist: should the employee improve following a disciplinary step, the supervisor may feel frustrated about losing the grounds to justify recommending dismissal.

Finally, the most significant problem with a traditional punitive approach is that it leaves the worker freed of responsibility for future good performance. To the employee, the slate is now clean: "I did the deed, I paid the price, now everything's back to normal." But management has neither requested nor received commitment to future good performance or acceptance of reasonable standards. The worker has been absolved of wrongdoing by accepting the punishment.

The traditional industrial system assumes that crime must be followed by punishment lest chaos reign. It requires managers to sit in judgment of the individual to determine the penalty that fits the crime. It seems irrelevant that this approach produces few beneficial results.

While layoffs, probations, final warnings, and so on may produce initial compliance, over time this approach generates more problems than it solves. A worker punished with a written warning or unpaid suspension responds with resentment or apathy; absenteeism and grievances increase; communication and trust decline; "get by" or "get even" performance results. In fact, it is the prevalence of these very problems that has led organizations to change to a nonpunitive approach.

Basics of a nonpunitive system

Like Tampa Electric, many organizations are now adopting an approach modeled on Huberman's system. The differences in method show up not only in the formal steps but also in the organization's administrative policies and in management's attitudes, beliefs, and behavior.

The first step of formal nonpunitive discipline is to issue an "oral reminder." The manager meets privately with the employee to discuss the problem. The manager's primary goal is to gain the employee's agreement to solve the problem. Instead of warning the employee of more serious disciplinary action to come, the manager reminds the individual that he or she has a personal responsibility to meet reasonable standards of performance and behavior. In most organizations the manager documents the discussion but retains the documentation in a working file. In this way the manager extends a strong incentive for improvement by advising the individual that although this is the first formal step of discipline, no record of the transaction will appear in the employee's permanent record unless the problem arises again.

Should the problem continue, the manager moves to the second step, the "written reminder." The manager talks to the employee again in a serious manner but without threats. The manager reviews the good business reasons why the rule or standard must be observed, discusses the employee's failure to abide by the original agreement, and, through counseling, again gains the employee's agreement to solve the problem. Together they create an action plan to eliminate the gap between actual and desired performance. Then the manager writes a memo to the individual summarizing the conversation, and places a copy in the employee's personnel file.

In both steps, the main objective of the conversation is to gain the employee's agreement to change. This agreement is important for several reasons. First, the employee is more likely to improve if he or she makes an agreement to change than if the company mandates compliance. Second, and more important, if the problem continues and another disciplinary discussion is necessary, the subsequent discussion will focus not only on the continuing problem but also on the employee's failure to abide by the original agreement—a much more serious concern. Finally, should the employee refuse to agree to meet reasonable employer expectations, the documentation of that refusal in the second step strengthens the company's position if a record is needed to justify the employee's termination.

Issuing reminders instead of warnings involves more than a mere semantic sleight of hand. *Warnings* threaten future disciplinary action should the employee be caught misbehaving again; *reminders* restate the essentialness of the rule and the individual's responsibility to uphold it (see *Exhibit I*). The point is not to reprimand for past misbehavior but rather to create an action plan for the future.

The decision-making leave

When disciplinary discussions have failed to produce the desired changes, management places the individual on a paid, one-day, "decision-

Exhibit I Warnings vs. reminders

	Warnings	Reminders
Timing	Before the conversation	After the conversation
Focus	Next step	Individual responsibility
Purpose	Threaten further negative consequences	Remind employee of performance standard
Time perspective	Past	Future
Responsibility for action	Supervisor	Employee
Supervisor's role	Judge	Coach

making leave." The company pays the employee for the day to demonstrate the organization's desire to see him or her remain a member of the organization and to eliminate the resentment and hostility that punitive actions usually produce. But tenure with the organization is conditional on the individual's decision to solve the immediate problem and make a "total performance commitment" to good performance on the job. The employee is instructed to return on the day following the leave with a decision either to change and stay or to quit and find more satisfying work elsewhere.

On returning to the job, the employee does not immediately begin work. He or she first meets with the supervisor to announce the decision. If the decision is to change and stay, the employee and supervisor set specific goals and develop an action plan. The supervisor expresses confidence in the individual's ability to live up to the requirements of the action plan but also tells the employee that failure to live up to the organization's performance expectations will lead to termination. This statement is repeated in a formal memo documenting the step; the original is given to the employee and a copy is placed in the personnel file.

The rationale for a nonpunitive system

While most managers can accept the philosophy of dealing with poor performance or misconduct in a nonpunitive way in the early steps, the concept of a paid disciplinary suspension still disturbs many managers. Two issues are involved here. First, why suspend someone as a final disciplinary step? Second, why pay the person during that suspension?

The benefits of suspension as a final step are many: suspension clearly demonstrates to the errant employee the seriousness of the situation; it provides an opportunity for cool reflection and decision making for both the employee and management; it proves that the company means business; and, perhaps most important, it has been universally accepted by arbitrators as sufficient notice to the individual that the job is at risk.

Given that suspension can offer some benefits uncharacteristic of other "final step" strategies, what does the company gain from paying the employee during the leave?

☐ Paying the employee reduces the need for the individual to "save face." In contrast, when an individual returns from an unpaid suspension, the anger, resentment, or apathy provoked by the layoff often results in martyrdom, reduced output, subtle sabotage, and other forms of costly antiorganization behavior.

☐ Concerns about employee abuse of the system, such as intentional misbehavior to gain a "free day off," have proved unfounded. Organizations using the system have found that employees treat the leave seriously.

They do make a decision about changing their behavior and maintaining employment. Unlike the traditional unpaid suspension in which the individual must do no more than "serve time," now the employee must take responsibility for future performance and behavior. Employees discover that, in spite of the pay, they are confronted with a far tougher company response to their failure to meet standards. A Tampa Electric Company employee who returned from a decision-making leave commented, "Believe me, brother, that was no vacation!"

☐ Good workers do not resent the paid suspension. Virtually all employees view the leave as a grave step. Interestingly, what good workers do resent, we have found, is management's failure to confront a poor performer, since they usually must shoulder the work not done by their colleague.

☐ While the cost of paying the employee for the day he or she is absent is a visible one, it usually is the only cost associated with using the nonpunitive system. Unpaid suspensions often generate much higher hidden costs in overtime, inefficiency, disruption of others' work, and reduced output.

☐ In unionized organizations, grievances and arbitrations take on a totally new perspective. The system makes moot the question, "Does the penalty fit the crime?" Consequently, it eliminates attempts at penalty reductions, claims of punitive inconsistencies, and deal making. In addition, a nonpunitive system reduces the number of discipline-related grievances and arbitrations.

☐ Finally, the paid suspension is evidence of the company's sincere, good-faith effort to convince the individual to change and accept responsibility for appropriate behavior. Should the company ultimately fire an employee, this step reduces the chances of a third party's reversal of the decision or a wrongful discharge suit.

Most important, a nonpunitive approach to discipline represents the company's refusal to make an employee's career decision. Traditional methods of discipline force management to make all the decisions. Is the offense serious enough to warrant a disciplinary transaction? Given the seriousness, what is the appropriate level of punishment? Is the punishment for employee A similar to what we did to B and C in like situations? Then management caucuses, analyzes the available data, and decides what action is most appropriate. The decision is then announced to the employee, who from the outset, has been outside the process.

Organizations in the white-collar professional and technical sectors have found this approach more palatable. Problems that arise on the factory floor are frequently the same as those that arise in the office. A final warning or unpaid suspension for an engineer, a programmer, or a manager seems somehow inappropriate, but most managers can accept a strategy of reminding a professional to meet the organization's standards. The use of a decision-making leave can be as powerful in the executive suite as on the factory floor.

Making the move

Accepting a new disciplinary approach leads organizations to develop a complete human resource system that integrates the nonpunitive disciplinary method with all its other human resource programs.

Employees recognize that through its approach to discipline, the company displays its true attitude about people, professionalism, and productivity. Consequently, the company's disciplinary program can create either trust or distrust and produce either positive or negative results in the rest of the human-resource-management system. Discipline touches on the largest organizational questions: How will good performance be recognized? How will problems be dealt with? Who has the responsibility for ensuring acceptable behavior? Who will be expelled from membership in the organization family? How and by whom will that decision be made?

Since the implementation of a nonpunitive system affects the entire organization, its philosophy, and values, a major organizational effort is required. Formal policies and informal day-to-day practices must be reviewed and reconsidered. Supervisors need to be trained in the new approach, the belief system behind it, and the methods

for holding nonpunitive disciplinary discussions. They must learn how to develop action plans that lead to an employee's agreement to change and to recommit to the company's objectives. Management must communicate to everyone concerned both the general purpose of the system and the specific administrative practices.

Finally, management must link the system with all other existing human resource programs and policies such as performance appraisal, attendance management, grievance and appeal procedures, and employee assistance programs. After installing the new system, managers must measure, monitor, and maintain it. The process typically involves several months of alternatives analysis, decision making, and training, and requires the efforts and involvement of a large number of supervisors and managers.

To develop the system, most organizations appoint a team of supervisors and managers from different levels and functions. The team's task is to manage the transition to the new system by answering questions like:

What are the appropriate roles of personnel and line management? To which categories of employees will the system apply? How will the severity of different problems and offenses be determined? How will unrelated problems with the same individual be handled? What authority and responsibility will first-line supervisors have for each step of the system? How will they be trained?

While initial answers to these questions can come from the experience of other organizations that have adopted similar systems, ultimately no answers can be adopted off the shelf. For the policies to be workable and appropriate, they must take into account the organization's culture and history.

Once all managers have been trained and top management has formally approved the policies, the company communicates the change to all employees. It holds meetings with all company members to review the key elements and operation of the system, the reasons for the change, and the philosophy behind the program. Managers also hold meetings with employees already on a discipline step to advise them where they will stand when the new system begins.

Managers maintain the program by measuring the results, feeding information back to higher level managers and senior executives at regular intervals, and reinforcing supervisory counseling skills.

Ensuring a successful implementation

The secret of nonpunitive discipline is that there are no secrets. To produce a committed work force of professionals, this program, like any other change process, must be installed in an open, collaborative, and honest fashion. Inevitably, problems and pitfalls present themselves. For example:

☐ Some senior managers oversimplify the cultural and operational differences between nonpunitive performance management and traditional approaches. Many executives overestimate the ability of supervisors, managers, and employees to translate their intellectual appreciation of this type of system into a practical approach. Conversely, senior executives may also fail to appreciate the ease with which some supervisors, especially those most experienced with the dismal results of a a punitive strategy, will accept the new approach.

☐ Senior managers may recognize the benefits of a new approach; those benefits, however, must also be perceived by everyone affected, including the great majority of employees who are never affected by formal disciplinary procedures. Every employee and every manager will evaluate the program from the perspective of "What's in it for me?" The answers must be built into the development, communication, installation, evaluation, and management processes.

☐ Some managers believe that once a sensible program is installed, it will somehow run on automatic pilot. But experience suggests that unless the program is tightly managed and maintained, it is very easy for old procedures and practices to creep in. Then, like so many other well-intended programs, it will become an event that occurred some time in the past rather than a part of the practices ingrained in the company's culture.

Exhibit
II
Advantages of nonpunitive systems

Reduction in turnover
Texas Department of Mental Health

Percentage
of
turnover

50	48.5%	
45		
40		
35	31.3%	
30		
25		
20		18.5%
15		

| Year before nonpunitive system | Year 1 after nonpunitive system | Year 2 after nonpunitive system |

Reduction in disciplinary incidents
General Electric

Reduction
in disciplinary
incidents

40	39	
35		
30	Written warning	
25		23
20		
15		
	10 11	12
10	Suspension 6	7
5	Discharge 3	0

| Year before nonpunitive system | Year 1 after nonpunitive system | Year 2 after nonpunitive system |

Reduction in grievances
General Telephone

Reduction
in
grievances

90		
80	All grievances	
70	71	
60		63 % decrease
50		
40		
30	Disciplinary grievances	26
20	22	86 % decrease
10		3

| First quarter-year before nonpunitive system | First quarter-year after nonpunitive system |

Reduction in sick leave usage
Tampa Electric

Hours
per
employee

70	66.7
65	59.9
60	56.2
55	50.1
50	
45	43.4
40	38.7
35	
30	

| Year before non-punitive system | Year 1 | Year 2 | Year 3 | Year 4 | Year 5 |

☐ Finally, excessive dominance by the personnel function in the development and implementation process can undermine a new approach. While expertise in human resource management is critical to successful implementation, it is only one critical aspect. Significant issues dividing personnel and the line organization responsible for managing the discipline system often go unresolved if personnel is perceived as bearing full responsibility for the program's success.

Building momentum toward change

The results speak for themselves: organizations that have adopted a nonpunitive strategy for handling performance problems have found measurable reductions in absenteeism, dismissals, disciplinary actions, grievances, and arbitrations. Less measurable but equally significant results include improved morale and increased respect for management, a reduction in wrongful termination suits, and a sharper focus on the great majority of employees who are performing well. The responsibility for action shifts from the supervisor to the employee; the time frame changes from past to future; and the objective becomes commitment and not mere compliance (see *Exhibit II*).

But in the 20 years since Huberman proposed the concept, many organizations still seem reluctant to move away from traditional strategies. What is the source of this hesitation?

The most common criticisms managers make—a nonpunitive system won't be taken seriously by employees, employees will take advantage of it to get a "free day off," it won't be upheld in arbitration—have all been proven groundless by the many organizations that have adopted the approach. A deeper and more subtle concern is the hesitation to abandon the traditional parental role of total control. But the decision to perform well or perform poorly, to follow the rules or to disregard them, is the employee's. Only when managers recognize this can they create a system that not only encourages individual responsibility but also requires it.

Perhaps the greatest difficulty in changing an organization's approach to discipline is in readjusting managers' ingrained attitude that punishment is the appropriate response to employee failures in behavior and performance. Like most people in our culture, many managers have grown up believing that misconduct must be followed by punishment. At home, misbehavior earned a spanking; at school, it earned a visit to the principal's office. More serious violations were met with more severe punishments, all in the sacred name of "justice." But is justice the ultimate and appropriate objective of an organization's discipline system?

Organizations have legitimate and reasonable rights: the right to expect employees to be on time; to attend regularly; to put in a full day's work; to be mentally and physically prepared for the tasks at hand; to respond positively to direction; to learn the job at hand and the jobs to come; to adapt to change; to get along well with customers, supervisors, and fellow employees; to know and to follow the rules and procedures; and to meet the technological and ethical standards of the enterprise. In other words, the employee must fit into the culture of the organization—which is not too much to ask of anyone who draws a paycheck. Most people do fit in. But when they do not, the need arises to confront the difference between what is expected and what is delivered.

Organizations that have adopted a nonpunitive approach to discipline reject the use of punishment, not only because it seems to create more problems than it solves but also because few counterbalancing positive effects can be identified. It seems impossible that people will become better workers if management treats them progressively worse.

The ultimate problem with traditional approaches to discipline is that they take problem employees, punish them, and leave them punished problem employees. A nonpunitive approach to discipline requires problem employees to make a choice: to become either committed employees or former employees. ▽

Ideas for Action

Edited by
Timothy B. Blodgett

How to deal with bizarre employee behavior

*Terry L. Leap and
Michael D. Crino*

☐ While engaging in horseplay, an employee of an equipment company threw a pie at a management consultant. The company fired him.

☐ A man lost his job for pounding on a broken vending machine, then shouting abuse at the vending company representative.

☐ An airline ground employee was terminated when, after completing his night shift, he "streaked" along a traffic island fronting the airport to win a $20 dare from his coworkers.

☐ A driver for a bottling company was discharged after urinating on the floor of his delivery truck even though there were rest room facilities nearby.

In each of these true cases, on appealing to a labor arbitrator, the employee either won reinstatement or had the disciplinary penalty reduced.[1] Eccentric employee behavior occurs often enough to pose problems for personnel administrators and supervisors who must decide on proper disciplinary measures. Understandably, they tend to react to the peculiarity of an incident, not to its seriousness.

Often these incidents are not amenable to quick solutions. In imposing discipline after such incidents, management sends its employees (and

in some cases the public) a message reflecting the sense of fairness, sensitivity to personal and organizational concerns, and even political acumen of the decision makers.

The rules and procedures organizations have for handling disciplinary incidents generally contain a list of offenses or categories of offenses along with penalties ranging from oral reprimands to discharge, depending on the seriousness of the offense, previous violations by the employee, and extenuating circumstances. These "progressive discipline" systems are adequate for common problems of employee theft, absenteeism, incompetence, and insubordination, but are often inadequate when applied to unusual incidents. Here are some criteria to keep in mind when confronted by a matter whose resolution is baffling.

Eight questions

Did the employee's action damage equipment or products? A machine shop worker was discharged for writing obscenities on rest room walls. A truck rental firm employee was fired for throwing an aerosol can of paint in

anger—it ruptured on impact. In both cases arbitrators reinstated and imposed a less severe penalty on the employees.[2]

You can quantify the seriousness of any damage simply by placing a dollar value on minor, moderate, or serious violations. It may also be a good idea to distinguish unintentional from willful damage. Unintentional damage may stem from incompetence, ignorance of proper procedures, or sheer carelessness.

Cases of willful damage, however, are sometimes difficult to assess. There is willful damage that is accidental, where the behavior was deliberate but the resulting damage was unintended, and willful damage that is intentional (the results were intended too). While the damage caused by the ruptured aerosol can involved an intentional action (the employee threw the object), the damage caused by the ensuing explosion was accidental. Writing obscenities on a wall, however, involves both intended actions and results, thereby increasing the potential seriousness of the incident for disciplinary purposes.

Did the employee's actions disrupt the work flow? A labor arbitrator supported a company's decision to fire a day-shift employee who complained to those working the night shift that their high production rates were creating problems for the day shift. A company rule prohibited the hindering or limiting of production by employees. In another case, two chemical company employees lost their jobs when a supervisor learned they were making loans and collecting payments from coworkers during working hours.[3]

The main issues in cases like these are whether the work routine was disrupted enough to warrant severe punishment and the extent to which the employee's behavior was intentional, accidental, or preventable. The expense incurred by the company and subsequent production or service

The authors are full professors in the department of management, Clemson University. Both teach personnel management. Terry Leap has published before in HBR; with Larry R. Smeltzer, he wrote "Racial Remarks in the Workplace: Humor or Harassment?" (November-December 1984).

delays are also consequences bearing on the seriousness of the offense.

Did the employee's action create a safety hazard? Although the pie-throwing and aerosol-can-throwing incidents may have created safety hazards, neither could be regarded as seriously threatening injury. This was not the case for a prankster whose discharge was sustained after he put lighted cigarettes in the back pockets of two fellow employees. Although neither victim was injured, one of them worked in a spray-paint booth containing highly combustible paints, lacquers, and solvents. Thus a potentially unsafe act or condition is probably a sufficient ground for disciplinary action, especially when it shows disregard for the safety of others.[4]

"Understandably, supervisors tend to react to the peculiarity of an incident, not to its seriousness."

A public utility employee was discharged when it was learned that he planned to throw a "fit" during which he would kill a district superintendent. His threat, coupled with his erratic and undependable work record and history of disruptive behavior, convinced management that this individual posed a potentially life-threatening hazard.[5]

Should the employee have known better? More tact and refinement in judgment are usually expected of supervisory, skilled, and professional employees; an act that might be tolerated from an unskilled employee may be unacceptable if committed by a professional.

A supervisor was demoted for failing to take decisive action to bring under control a fight between two employees, one of whom was armed with a knife and the other with a piece of steel pipe. A police officer incurred suspension for behaving in an unprofessional manner by handcuffing and berating a man who, while walking in the alley behind the officer's home, had thrown a rock at his barking dogs.[6] In both cases the arbitrators supported the disciplinary action on the ground that the men had exercised poor judgment.

Even so, these cases do not offer much help in fixing the appropriate range of acceptable behavior for professional and supervisory people. Factors such as their education and training, policies and rules that outline the organization's standards of professional conduct, and the speed and stress level under which decisions must be made should be prime considerations in judging whether a particular action is imprudent.

Compare a case involving a nonprofessional worker, a machine shop employee whom an arbitrator reinstated following his dismissal for immoral conduct after he had made a sexually explicit gesture at a female employee. Rumors had spread through the shop and exaggerated the incident. The arbitrator determined that the offender had not been warned that such conduct was inappropriate, nor did the company have a "specific code of conduct governing [the] industrial relationship between the sexes."[7] It is unlikely that the lack of a code of conduct would protect professionals or supervisors guilty of such behavior.

Is the behavior correctable? A pivotal consideration, especially in discharge cases, is the likelihood of repeated violations. Many of the aberrant incidents discussed here involved employees with no record of discipline problems. Counseling could probably resolve such matters. Behavior correctable only through extensive training or psychiatric counseling—if then—presents a more serious prospect.

If the offense stems from an alcohol or drug problem, personnel managers and labor arbitrators often condition reinstatement of a discharged employee on adherence to a prescribed treatment program. This approach gives the offender the benefit of the doubt and a second chance, while also making the person responsible for rehabilitation and job retention. Of course, the employee must be given a reasonable amount of time to comply.

Did the behavior violate the law? Illegal activities on the job clearly require disciplinary actions. Theft and drug-related violations are the most common offenses. A dilemma arises when deciding whether to also press criminal charges, and extenuating circumstances, such as a history of alcohol or drug abuse, mental problems, or ignorance of the law, often complicate this decision.

Illegal conduct off duty presents a thorny dilemma: To what extent, if any, should scrapes with the law away from the job subject the employee to disciplinary measures at work? A Social Security Administration employee accused of illegal sexual activity with a minor was let go but then won his job back because his employer, the arbitrator decided, "could not show a nexus between an employee's off-duty sex and efficiency of service." An airline flight attendant was reinstated after dismissal for making a homosexual advance toward a 15-year-old motel employee who had been summoned to the man's room to investigate a plumbing problem.[8] (Of course, the fate of these offenders presumably would have been different if their jobs had involved contact with children.)

An arbitrator ruled that an employee had been improperly discharged when he was arrested and incarcerated on a felony charge that did not result in a conviction. A discharged employee jailed for armed robbery was not reinstated, however, when he confessed to the crime. Similarly, a man convicted of a felony and sentenced to life imprisonment permanently lost his job rights even though he later won a new trial and eventual acquittal.[9] Offenders who either confess to or are convicted of felonies presumably face long prison terms and so may forfeit their employment rights.

Did the behavior damage the organization's image, customer relations, or competitive position? For the sake of projecting an image, companies generally have a right to set grooming, dress, and appearance standards for employees. Take the case of an overweight Disneyland employee who was fired for failing to lose a large amount of weight in 30 days. While its deadline may have been unreasonable, and, in fact, was extended by an arbitrator, Disneyland had a legitimate reason for imposing the weight-loss regimen because the employee had to fit the range of costume sizes for her job as a ticket seller at the main gate.[10]

In another case, an arbitrator determined that an obese municipal worker was properly discharged because his bad eating habits, weight, and health problems apparently caused him to sleep on the job. "The presence of an employee who is asleep at work," the arbitrator noted, "is not conducive to [the] public image of [an] efficiently operated employer."[11]

Employees whose bizarre behavior alienates customers are fair game for punishment. A uniform rental service sacked a driver-salesman who persisted in preaching his religious beliefs to customers along his route despite the employer's warnings, customers' complaints, and loss of business.[12] A retail food employee, on being told to "have a nice day" by a customer, replied that he would if the customer did not come back to the store. He also referred to another customer's children as "brats." Those two remarks culminated in his dismissal.[13] Two sales clerks in a clothing store met a similar fate when, in the presence of customers, they engaged in a loud, profane shouting and shoving match over a sales commission. The latter case also illustrates poor judgment that by any standard falls outside the bounds of prudent behavior.

A nursing home attendant refused to wear the uniform customarily worn by male employees because of his contemplated transsexual surgery and desire to wear the female uniform. After wearing the female uniform for three years without undergoing surgery, he was discharged. The arbitrator supported this action and commented that nursing home patients have the right to know the sexual identity of employees who treat them.[14]

Sometimes an organization's supersensitivity to image or competitive position causes management to overreach. A clerk in a retail bakery offered to make a birthday cake for a friend, whereupon the friend canceled her cake order at the store. The bakery fired the clerk for causing a mere $10.95 sales loss. The U.S. Immigration and Naturalization Service suspended a criminal investigator for ten days because he served as a "padrino," or sponsor, in a wedding between a coworker and an "undocumented" alien.[15] Any potential conflict of interest in this

case is at worst quite minor, especially considering the size, scope, and mission of this agency.

Recently a trivial incident created embarrassing publicity across the country for the employer. A supervisor at the Coca-Cola bottling plant in Anniston, Alabama, suspended a worker for three days without pay after someone saw him drinking Pepsi-Cola on company premises. The employee claimed he was unaware of the brand of cola because his wife had brought it to him in a food chain's paper cup. The newspapers picked up the story and spread it wide, whereupon the company rescinded the punishment.

Has the employee's action damaged morale? Probably the most significant question surrounding unusual employee transgressions is the impact they have on others in the organization. Numerous cases of sexual harassment and racial slurs have been filed under fair employment laws because of the uncomfortable and hostile working atmosphere that such behavior often creates. Pranks, obscene language, and vendettas as well cause morale problems and tensions among employees.

An arbitrator held that a man was properly discharged because he habitually used lewd and vulgar language in the presence of objecting female coworkers. Several employees of a grocery chain were dismissed, either directly or indirectly via forced resignations, after attending a "lesbian show" staged at the home of an assistant check-stand manager. Hostility between homosexual and heterosexual employees and knowledge of an extramarital affair between a male manager and a female employee had made the atmosphere tense before the dismissal. Nevertheless, an arbitrator ordered reinstatement for each employee since the problems involved off-duty conduct that did not harm the grocery chain's business, no customers had complained, and employee fears about working with gays appeared unfounded.[16]

Recurring incidents, like the use of foul language that eventually amounts to sexual harassment of female employees, are the most likely to damage morale. When a competent and hitherto accepted worker commits some offensive act that threatens to hurt morale, the company sometimes

can transfer the person to a different location and eliminate the threat of further friction.

If executives overreact

Some behavior, like sexual misconduct, racist acts, and cruelty, is not only bizarre but also repugnant. Some years ago, two Portland, Oregon, policemen on night patrol encountered and killed five possums. After rendezvousing with eight other officers, the two men (who were white) threw the dead animals on the sidewalk in front of a black-owned and -operated restaurant. The incident got great play in the news media, and the police chief dismissed the two ringleaders from the force. An arbitrator later reduced the penalty to 30-day suspensions without pay.

Did management overreact? Perhaps not, when you consider the racial overtones of the possum caper and the need the Portland authorities felt to make a statement. In imposing its penalty, the city contended that the police officers' behavior betrayed the public trust, violated the police department's code of professional conduct, and generated bad publicity that would have impaired their effectiveness on the force.[17]

An employer may believe that in an extreme case a departure from the established disciplinary system is warranted. To what extent, however, can you justify a trade-off between the integrity of that system and a gesture designed to soothe outrage or convey a moral message? If the disciplinary action is later canceled, will the offending employees be regarded as victors? Moreover, management may appear to be satisfying political pressures by using due process as a sacrificial lamb. Therefore, inflicting punishment more severe than the system calls for is often unwise.

Instead, management might take a public stand against the behavior while at the same time penalizing the employee to the justifiable limit of the disciplinary system. For example, a statement to employees (and even to the public if the press has become interested in the case) outlining management's opposition toward a particular employee's action may be more effective than termination.

Because many employees have neither a contractual right to employment nor other legal recourse, most overreaction by management will go unchallenged. A question of fairness then arises. Should a person with no chance for appeal be sacrificed as an example to other employees? This approach to discipline may backfire and cultivate a climate of distrust, suspicion, and insecurity.

Keep the right focus

We suggest that, before taking disciplinary action, management examine the ramifications, rather than the peculiarities, of unusual behavior. It is important for supervisors to deal with this behavior in as systematic a manner as they do routine discipline problems. Their aims should be to:

☐ Avoid inappropriate reaction in matching offenses and sanctions.
☐ Ensure due process and equal protection as a means of creating an organizational culture that supports employee dignity and rights.
☐ Minimize the need for employees to pursue their rights through external channels such as arbitration, federal and state EEO agencies, and the courts.

References

1 In order, these legal citations are
Clay Equipment, 73 LA 817 (undated),
W-L Molding Co., 72 LA 1065 (1979),
Air California, 63 LA 350 (1974), and
Pepsi-Cola Bottling Co., 76 LA 54 (1980).

2 Prototype Development, Inc., 78 LA 652 (1982), and
Ryder Truck Rental, Inc., 78 LA 542 (1982).

3 Dover Corp., 74 LA 675 (1980), and
Mobil Chemical Co., 76 LA 585 (1981).

4 Decar Plastics Corp., 44 LA 921 (1965).

5 Georgia Power Co., 76 LA 761 (1981).

6 Fry's Food Stores of Arizona, Inc., 76 LA 744 (1981), and
City of El Paso, Texas, 76 LA 595 (1981).

7 Powermatic-Houdaille, Inc., 71 LA 54 (1978).

8 Social Security Administration, 80 LA 725 (1983), and
Hughes Air Corp., 73 LA 148 (1979).

9 Owens-Illinois, Inc., 71 LA 1095 (1978),
Dorsey Trailers, Inc., 73 LA 196 (1979), and
3M Company, 72 LA 949 (1979).

10 Walt Disney Productions, 78 LA 1044 (1982).

11 City of Iowa City, 72 LA 1006 (1979).

12 Charles Todd Uniform Rental Service Co., 77 LA 144 (1981).

13 Great Atlantic and Pacific Tea Co., Inc., 71 LA 805 (1978).

14 Greater Harlem Nursing Home, 76 LA 680 (1981).

15 Patton Sparkle Market, 75 LA 1092 (1980), and
U.S. Immigration and Naturalization Service, 72 LA 1095 (1979).

16 Fairchild Industries, 75 LA 288 (1980), and
Ralph's Grocery, 77 LA 867 (1981).

17 City of Portland, Bureau of Police, 77 LA 820 (1981).

Beyond Testing: Coping with Drugs at Work

by JAMES T. WRICH

It is hard to overestimate the impact of substance abuse on the workplace. Even the most conservative estimates are staggering. The National Institute on Drug Abuse (NIDA) and the National Institute on Alcohol Abuse and Alcoholism (NIAAA) estimate that at least 10% of the work force is afflicted with alcoholism or drug addiction. Another 10% to 15% is affected by the substance abuse of an immediate family member. Still more bear the scars of having grown up with an addicted or alcoholic parent.

All in all, even after eliminating duplicates, at least 25% of any given work force suffers from substance abuse—their own or someone else's. As a chronic alcoholic from the ages of 15 to 27, I have personal experience of the problem and know the devastation it can cause. Managers are right to be apprehensive about drugs in the workplace, but a punitive response is inappropriate. Drug testing may be necessary where compelling issues of safety or na-

tional security are involved, but drug testing alone will not make the problem go away. Inexplicably, our efforts to deal with drug abuse ignore nearly 50 years of experience in the workplace treatment of alcoholism. We have had Broadbrush employee assistance programs for more than 15 years, and they continue to be used with great effectiveness to reduce absenteeism, promote recovery, minimize relapse, cut treatment costs, and improve productivity among drug abusers as well as alcoholics.

Assessing the problem

For practical purposes, alcoholics and addicts are not two groups of people but one. Alcoholics cannot safely use drugs, and drug addicts cannot safely use alcohol. Moreover, treatment centers have reported for at least ten years that a majority of patients under the age of 40 are dually addicted to alcohol and at least one other drug. Because it is legal, we seem to find alcohol less frightening, but the

effects of alcoholism are at least as devastating.

A recent estimate by the Alcohol, Drug Abuse and Mental Health Administration indicates that alcohol and drug abusers together cost the country more than $140 billion annually, including $100 billion in lost productivity. And these are only the direct costs. If we include family members in our calculation, the total will rise still higher.

An NIDA survey indicates that 19% of Americans over the age of 12 have used illicit drugs during the past year. Among 18- to 25-year-olds—the population now entering the work force—65% have used illicit drugs, 44% in the past year.

Given these figures, it is hardly surprising that many companies have opted for hardball methods, heeding the law and conventional notions of human rights only when faced with unequivocal prohibitions. In general, managers are not only extremely concerned about drugs, they are also convinced that fast action can solve the problem quickly and that they have the muscle and the means to do it. They have been encouraged by the attorney general's drug-testing initiative and by testimony from the commissioner of baseball claiming that the drug problem in the major leagues has been resolved. The first lady's "Just Say No!" slogan gave the ef-

James T. Wrich is president of Employee Assistance Services for Parkside Medical Services Corporation in Chicago. He has played a leading role in developing techniques for early identification of chemical dependency. In the mid-1970s, he was executive director of the Minnesota alcohol and drug authority. From 1978 to 1984 he was director of the United Airlines employee assistance program. He is author of The Employee Assistance Program, Updated for the 1980s *(Minneapolis: Hazelden, 1980).*

fort an appealing simplicity that encouraged everyone to overlook the complexities involved. In essence, many *managers* just said "No!" They resolved to get drug abusers out of the workplace one way or another, and drug-testing initiatives (DTIs) became their weapon of choice.

Drug-testing initiatives usually employ the following sequence of elements. The company:

Prepares a written policy and procedure statement.

Trains supervisors to recognize the signs and symptoms that would justify reasonable suspicion of drug use.

Instructs supervisors to refer employees for testing if these criteria are met.

Obtains and tests a sample of the employee's urine.

Confirms all positive test results with a second, more accurate test.

Gives those with confirmed positives a choice between treatment and disciplinary action up to and including termination.

Requires retesting without notice for those who complete treatment.

Establishes serious disciplinary measures, often termination, for those who test positive after undergoing treatment.

More than 35% of the country's largest companies have DTIs, and the number is growing fast. This overwhelming response may be seen as a clear indication that business is ready to tackle the problem. Nevertheless, I believe these programs are based on a number of questionable assumptions, many of which were proven false by programs instituted as long ago as the 1940s to deal with alcoholism. Drug-testing initiatives assume:

That we can adequately train supervisors to recognize the telltail signs and symptoms of substance abuse.

That supervisors will find reasonable suspicion an adequate basis for referral.

That supervisors can be motivated to make such referrals.

That testing will be accurate.

That the positive tests will be accurately interpreted.

That the imposition of treatment or disciplinary action will be appropriate and that employees will respond appropriately to whichever course is pursued.

Our experience with alcoholism

Substance abuse is nothing new. Heroin was once considered a wonder drug to cure morphine addiction in soldiers returning from Civil War hospitals. Cocaine was first used in the United States in the 1880s—not the 1980s—and was outlawed in 1914, whereupon amphetamines more or less took its place until recently.

Alcohol, our national legal drug of choice, has been with us practically forever, and, with 11 million alcoholics and another 7 million alcohol abusers, it is by far our most serious chemical dependency. Employers who recognized the problems that alcohol creates in the workplace have tried a number of remedies over the past 45 years. Employee assistance programs have been the most effective.

Until the 1970s, the great majority of companies addressed employee alcoholism with an informal policy of concealment and denial. When the alcoholic employee's condition became so severe as to be obvious to everyone, he or she was fired, or retired, or died. Some companies have tried to weed out alcoholics before they reached that stage, but managerial naivete and a lack of supervisory cooperation have usually thwarted such efforts.

The problem has always been twofold: how to identify afflicted employees and what to do with them. The success of identification programs depended greatly on what the work force perceived to be the consequences to the employee. Progressive companies like Eastman Kodak and the Northern Pacific Railroad (now part of the Burlington Northern) launched formal efforts decades ago to help alcoholics. Program staff usually consisted of a recovering alcoholic and sometimes a sympathetic company doctor or nurse who encouraged the employee to attend meetings of Alcoholics Anonymous.

These early efforts greatly helped those few alcoholics who were referred, but the vast majority went unidentified and untreated. Naturally, employees were concerned about confidentiality, job security, the possible stigma, and the quality of case handling.

Experience brought other problems to light through the 1940s and 1950s. Training was difficult to deliver, and its impact was

> Drug abuse touches one worker in four — but there is an effective remedy.

short-lived. In the course of their regular work, supervisors had scant opportunity to practice what little they had learned. The training taught them to look for bloodshot eyes, slurred speech, and the smell of alcohol on the breath, but supervisors were neither comfortable nor proficient as amateur sleuths and pseudo-diagnosticians. Much of the current DTI training to help supervisors establish "reasonable suspicion" resembles those early efforts to cope with alcoholism.

When DTIs Are Called For

The value of drug testing is so questionable and the drawbacks so great that no organization should even consider a DTI without compelling safety or national security reasons. An airline, for example, might decide to saddle itself with a DTI to increase the safety of its passengers, and a defense contractor might consider weapons secrets worth the small extra protection that an expensive and troublesome DTI could provide. Even in such cases, however, careful planning and administration are essential if the DTI is to solve more problems than it creates.

In order to set up a workable drug-testing program, an organization should:

1. Have an effective employee assistance program already in place.

2. Familiarize itself with the technical and legal limitations of a DTI and consider the possible negative effect on employee relations.

3. Place control and direction of the DTI in the hands of its human resource department, with input from its legal department—not the other way around.

4. Convince supervisors and employees of the need for drug testing and give them reason to trust and support the program.

5. Require drug testing of everyone in the organization from the CEO on down.

6. Establish criteria in advance for maintaining confidentiality and evaluating effectiveness.

In those early programs, the training was seldom offered to managers above the supervisory level, and instructional anecdotes focused almost exclusively on nonmanagement employees, which implied that no one above that level had a problem. Addicted supervisors rarely saw the problem anywhere. Supervisors with a strong bias against alcohol tended to see it everywhere.

All the while, the alcoholic senior manager remained completely hidden. These inconsistencies did not go unnoticed by employees and unions. They are also analogous to situations found in many of today's DTIs. It is rare for company officers to be tested, even though the problem is certainly present at that level.

Finally, there was the dimension of the disease that still amazes experts—the alcoholic's profound capacity for denial and deception. By the time addicted people were confronted, they had often spent years developing their alibi systems and their unique capacity to manipulate. Matching an alcoholic against a supervisor with one or two hours of training in late-stage symptoms was usually no contest. Moreover, when alcoholic employees learned what supervisors were looking for, they stopped displaying those symptoms, at least until the very latest stages when they completely lost control. When today's addicted employees learn their company's criteria for "reasonable suspicion," they too will work hard to avoid such behavior. Today's addicts are at least as cunning as yesterday's.

In the 1960s, programs shifted their focus from symptoms to job performance. Because supervisors were so often outmaneuvered, the experts decided to take the game out of the alcoholic's ballpark and put it into the supervisor's. Job performance became the principal criterion for referral. Supervisors were told to stop diagnosing and, moreover, not even to discuss alcohol. Of course if they thought an employee had a drinking problem, they were to refer him to the company program.

This ambiguous message confused everyone. Obviously, if supervisors did not make some kind of diagnosis, however amateurish, they certainly were not going to refer the employee to an alcoholism program.

On the positive side, these programs were sincere efforts at rehabilitation, recovery rates were encouraging, and the testimonials of participants were glowing. Even so, feelings of suspicion ran high among employees. Confidentiality was so often compromised that laws were later written to safeguard it. Supervisors disliked the confrontational role, and they feared sending someone to the program who wasn't really an alcoholic, thus hurting the employee and damaging their own credibility. A 1976 review showed that only one-third of 1% of all employees made use of such programs each year. In addition, those who used the programs tended to be in late stages of the disease and had already experienced great personal suffering and productivity loss. Because of the denial inherent in the disease, and because coercion as a method of referral so closely resembled punitive action, there seemed little hope of seeing significant numbers of self-referrals without a change in approach.

Ironically, had there then been a test to prove conclusively that an employee had been drinking on the job, it is doubtful that it would have improved overall program effectiveness. Then, as now, you can't test what you can't refer; you can't refer what you can't find; you can't find what you're

Developing an Effective EAP

Building an effective EAP requires time, insight, and a lot of work. We cannot simply slap together a few outmoded ideas, dress them up with word processors, add a testing gimmick, and peddle them as a package.

For the most part, an EAP should be custom designed for its specific workplace. To be effective, it should see and refer for drug-abuse treatment at least 1% of the work force each year. To do this, the program must be properly staffed. Generally this means one full-time equivalent assessment and referral (A&R) resource professional for every 3,500 to 4,200 employees, plus adequate clerical support.

The A&R staff must have considerable training and experience working with chemically dependent people. Whatever their academic degrees, professionals without vast experience working with alcoholics and drug addicts can do as much harm as good. Resourceful addicts and alcoholics often can deceive them, which leads to inappropriate care and drives up employee health-care costs without solving the problem.

A sufficient budget, an effective training and communications program, a good management information system, a valid outcome evaluation program, a credible benefit-to-cost analysis, an appropriately designed benefits package, ongoing education for EAP staff, and lots of attention and support from senior management are among the other key ingredients for a successful EAP.

not trained to find; and training alone will not inspire those with a vested interest in the status quo. Experience indicates that a disproportionate number of chemically dependent employees end up working for others who are addicts, substance abusers, or the untreated adult children of alcoholics. Such individuals—perhaps as many as a third of all supervisors—are unlikely to do well as police officers.

Broadbrush employee assistance programs

In 1972, NIAAA launched a new workplace alcoholism program called the Broadbrush approach and sent 100 program consultants, of whom I was one, into the field to sell the idea to management and labor.

The Broadbrush approach—what we now call employee assistance programs or EAPs—took into account the limitations of earlier efforts as well as the nature of addiction. Knowing that alcoholic denial and manipulation were more than the typical supervisor could learn to cope with, it likewise stressed that supervisors were not to diagnose.

But for the first time, it also provided a structure for implementation. Rather than focus only on alcoholism, the program was broadened to cover a wide range of personal problems including emotional, marital, family, and financial difficulties, and of course, drug abuse. The alcoholic label was no longer attached automatically to anyone using the program. The new approach not only reduced the stigma but also encouraged supervisors to refer a troubled employee without first trying to figure out the nature of the problem. Previously, when alcoholic employees argued that the problem wasn't really drinking but a bad marriage, say, or indebtedness, they generally got off the hook. Now there was a program that dealt with these other, "respectable" issues as well. EAP staff assessed the nature and severity of problems, referred employees to appropriate care in the community, and followed up.

By the late 1970s, employees could get help even without a documented job performance problem, and EAP professionals had developed new outreach and intervention techniques to generate referrals by peers and to identify substance abusers at an earlier stage of their dependency. For the first time, self-referrals began to outnumber referrals from supervisors.

The results were gratifying. Employees were getting experienced, professional help, and getting it sooner, which reduced both personal suffering and productivity losses. Earlier treatment also meant lower costs, since someone in the later stages of any problem is less likely to respond to outpatient care. Both diagnosis and treatment were confidential. Managers liked the idea of attacking a wider range of problems, since their goal was to reduce losses in productivity regardless of their cause. Many managers had wanted to address alcoholism more aggressively for years but had hesitated because previous approaches so often looked like witch-hunts.

Most important, the programs were reaching nearly three times as many alcoholics as before. Burlington Northern changed from a straight alcoholism program to the Broadbrush approach and achieved utilization rates of more than 1% for alcohol and 2% to 3% for other problems. This meant that the time required to reach a number of alcoholics equivalent to the population at

The Medical Case Against Drug Testing

A drug's detectability depends on many variables: dosage, absorption rate, location of entry, drug purity, individual metabolism, frequency of use, and whether drugs are consumed singly or in combination. A urine test does not test for the presence or absence of the drug, but for a critical quantity of it. If the concentration drops below a certain level, the test will not usually detect it. Knowing how long it takes for abstinence to reduce concentrations below these critical thresholds—e.g., 2 to 4 days for cocaine, heroin, and amphetamines; 3 to 10 days for occasional use of marijuana; 5 to 13 hours for alcohol—allows chronic users to feign illness and postpone their tests long enough to free their bodies of the drug and its metabolites.

Abstinence is not the only way to beat the tests. Employees have been known to smuggle in clean urine (and to keep it at body temperature to fool the medical attendant), to drink large quantities of water to dilute their samples, even to obtain prescriptions for legal drugs known to test positive in order to provide themselves with a "legitimate" explanation of their own more genuine positives. Marijuana users can add salt, sweat, or Drano to increase the pH of their urine samples. Besides, there is a 5% to 10% chance that drug abusers will falsely test negative despite the drugs in their bodies.

There is also a chance that positive tests will be false. Even if the test is accurate, the mere indication of the drug does not tell us whether the employee has used the drug once or a hundred times—or at all.

Most laboratories screen for illegal drugs with the so-called EMIT method, which is hardly foolproof. A number of harmless—or in any case legal—substances have molecular and electrochemical patterns similar to the hard drugs EMIT was designed to identify. Over-the-counter cough and cold preparations may test positive for amphetamines. The opiate-like drugs and alcohol found in other legal medications may also confound test findings. Poppy seeds eaten in quantity may produce a trace opiate indication. Some herbal teas have been associated with positive tests for various illegal drugs.

Ibuprofen, a painkiller found in Advil, Datril, Rufen, and other over-the-counter medications, can cause a false positive for marijuana. Ephedrine, an ingredient of Nyquil, can test positive for amphetamines. Dextromathorphon, found in many cough suppressants, has tested positive for opiates. False positives may also result from laboratory errors such as mislabeling urine or transposing results, or from improperly cleaned equipment, incompetence, or out-and-out fraud.

Several years ago, the navy found that more than 30% of positives were erroneous. In one methadone maintenance program, accuracy was no better than 50%. In a litigious society, employers are well-advised to do two confirmatory tests. Even so, they run the risk of lawsuits. In May 1987, San Diego Gas and Electric lost a court case to a "false positive." The cost of defending the suit, settlement, and other fees was publicly stated as $80,000.

Even without litigation, testing is expensive. Most tests range from $7.50 to $70 each and companies must add the costs of administration, supervision, and lost work time. Last but hardly least, the cost to employee morale cannot be measured.   —DAVID BEARMAN, M.D.

David Bearman is medical director of the Santa Barbara Health Initiative, a Medicaid demonstration project. He is former director of the student health center at San Diego State University and has spent 20 years in drug abuse treatment and prevention.

risk had been reduced to as little as seven years in some programs. We thought we had discovered pure gold.

The new approach had its detractors, of course. Some alcoholism professionals feared that alcoholism would get lost in the shuffle if it weren't the sole focus of the program. Some managers disdained rehabilitation as an organized form of coddling undesirables. Some unions thought that EAPs infringed on their turf. But EAPs worked, and by 1979, more than half of the country's largest companies had EAPs in one form or another, and about 80% of new programs were some variation of the Broadbrush approach.

My own experience is representative. From 1978 to 1984, I was director of the EAP at United Airlines. Of the first 5,100 employees using the program, 65% came in on their own or on the encouragement of their family, friends, or unions. About 2,000 of these were in trouble with alcohol or drugs, often both. Of the 35% referred by management, less than half had developed job performance problems. Our evaluation showed the following:

Absenteeism among program participants, measured from one year before entering the program to one year after, went down 74% in Chicago and 80% in San Francisco, to cite two cities.

Recovery rates the first time through the program were 74% for ground employees, 82% for flight attendants, and 92% for pilots and copilots.

Recovery rates for those who relapsed and reentered the program were about 40%.

The benefit-to-cost ratio, based on reduction in sick leave and including cost of program operations, treatment, and time off work while receiving treatment, was 7 to 1 projected over five years and nearly 17 to 1 when projected over the expected career of participants.

Job performance improvement, rated by supervisors on an 11-point scale ranging from −5 to +5, was 3.5 points on average.

Other companies have reported equally encouraging results.

Kimberly-Clark documented a 43% reduction in absenteeism and a 70% reduction in accidents among a sample of employees who had participated in its employee assistance program.

Chairman Roger Smith of General Motors announced in 1983 that, of some 60,000 employees who had taken part in its EAP, between 60% and 70% were still abstaining from alcohol or drugs one year later.

Phillips Petroleum reported that its EAP had netted more than $8 million a year in reduced accidents and sick leave, and in higher productivity.

The Kelsey-Hayes EAP tracked 58 plant workers involved in its program and documented the recovery of 18,325 hours in one year, an average of 316 hours per employee.

An AT&T study in 1982 showed declines of 78% in overall absenteeism, 87% in absence due to disability, 81% in on-the-job accidents, and 58% in off-the-job accidents.

The solution that acts like a problem

In our eagerness to attack the current crop of devastating drugs—particularly cocaine—we have ignored not only the pitfalls of the past but also the effectiveness of our present employee assistance programs. We have somehow convinced ourselves that the solution should be easy—an inference easily drawn from the Reagan administration's simplistic approach and the blandishments of those consultants who market DTIs.

But solving tough problems is seldom easy. Even a superficial study of past efforts suggests a number of hard questions: If it was difficult to train supervisors to identify late-stage alcoholics whose drug was familiar and whose problems developed slowly, how difficult will it be to train supervisors in the various effects of a wide spectrum of unfamiliar drugs that can cause extreme problems in the course of a few months? If it was difficult for supervisors to overcome their fear of stigmatizing subordinates with an alcoholic label, how hard will they find it to refer employees for possible termination? If the alcoholic supervisors of the past failed to refer alcoholic subordinates for fear of exposing themselves, what are the chances today that a supervisor who abuses illegal drugs will refer an employee for testing?

The basic approach and underlying philosophy of many DTIs pose serious obstacles to their effectiveness. While EAPs generally assure employees that only substandard performance or rule violations—not EAP participation—will jeopardize their jobs, drug testing can mean job loss even where performance problems and rules violations are not evident. DTIs are essentially punitive in nature and therefore legalistic in tone and approach. They are often based on a number of misjudgments.

For example, we take it for granted that supervisors will support tough tactics because the problem is so serious, but experience shows that supervisors often identify more closely with the subordinates they work with every day than they do with top management.

We figure that if we can make examples of the worst offenders, others will change their behavior. This may work with some people,

but not with alcoholics and other addicts. Addicts believe they can get away with it because they nearly always do. Until the late stages of the illness, their deception skills will be much more effective than the detection skills of the company.

We assume that a positive or negative test result will help us to identify problems and limit their effects. But the tests in use today

> **Addicts believe they can get away with it because they nearly always do.**

are not entirely reliable, and many practiced drug abusers know how to beat them. Even a true positive can mean many things. The employee could be an addict, an abuser, an occasional user, or merely someone who likes his sandwich on a poppy-seed roll. Moreover, a non-addicted employee who smoked marijuana ten days ago could test positive, while a chronic alcoholic who was drunk ten hours ago might very well test negative. Even error-free test results would need professional assessment.

We argue that cocaine and other drugs require special attention and effort because they are against the law, but alcohol is legal and does no less damage in the workplace. The problem for businesses and their employees is chemical dependency, and that, fortunately, is a problem we know how to address with EAPs.

We tell ourselves that drug testing can't hurt so we may as well try it. But if drug testing ignores the human element and damages employee relations, it can hurt greatly. Worst of all may be the mistaken belief that something of value has been done.

Finally, we tend to assume that as long as drug testing is legal, it is all right. But the tone, approach, and perceived objectives of DTIs are adversarial, and the courts and legislatures have not yet spoken their final words on the subject. Drug-test procedures are essentially legal treatises designed to defend the company in a grievance hearing or courtroom, but that is the last place anyone but a lawyer wants to be.

The fact that DTIs emphasize "reasonable suspicion" as a basis for referral reveals the essentially combative nature of such programs and explains why they are so ineffective. Establishing reasonable suspicion requires a focus on the more obvious, late-stage symptoms—the more conclusive the evidence, the safer the process legally. But winning in court is not the same as winning in the workplace. Later and fewer referrals mean a return to the intake levels of the 1940s.

Moreover, skewing tests to avoid the legal fallout of false positives will only produce more false negatives. And these particular false negatives are likely to render the DTI ineffective, since the people we most want to catch in a drug-testing net are the very people who are most skilled at achieving negative or ambiguous results by devious means.

Drug testing, even when necessary, should be seen not as a program in itself but rather as one element in a larger effort, an effort that begins with a properly designed and staffed EAP.

Our leaders suggest that we may be able to eliminate this problem in two or three years if we really get tough. But until we find a way to prevent 10% of the population from becoming addicted, the problem will continue. If all employers were able to pre-screen with 100% accuracy, the resulting rise in unemployment would be staggering, and we would also find an increase in the suffering and disruption of other family members still in the work force. By the same token, if all employed alcoholics and addicts could be identified in the next three years, our current treatment

Is a drug-free workplace a realistic goal in a drug-filled society?

capacity could not possibly handle the load.

Creation of a drug-free workplace in a drug-filled society is an illusion. It emphasizes supply rather than demand. It suggests that eradication of cocaine and other hard drugs will solve the problem generally. It insists that drug addicts and alcoholics are separable groups, the former far more intractable than the latter.

Our goal should be an *addiction*-free workplace. And that means focusing on all addictive substances, not just those portrayed in the scariest colors. It means treatment of the whole problem, not just punitive measures for the small portion currently in the spotlight. It means concern for all employees at all levels, not just those in the lower echelons. We could have a drug-free workplace today if that were the only freedom we valued. We certainly would not be free of addiction. Untreated, addiction will always resurface in some new and equally destructive form.

Reprint 88114

IDEAS FOR ACTION

New data conversion devices have opened job opportunities for this willing but underused group.

How Technology Brings Blind People into the Workplace

by Julia Anderson

In these days of low unemployment, many corporate and other organizations find it necessary to track the whereabouts and profiles of underused sectors of the labor pool. One sector seldom tapped by business has an unemployment rate as high as 70% – even though the advent of new data-processing technology has opened a window of opportunity for the group. What's more, people in this sector who do find employment historically have had a lower than average turnover rate.

They are the thousands of sightless or visually impaired people who possess desirable skills but who have difficulty finding work, or at least work commensurate with their skills. Many of them have received training as computer programmers, but there are quite a few other functions where blind persons have worked effectively, including customer service and repair service representatives, staff writers, quality control inspectors, receptionists, and curriculum specialists.

The advent of the microchip has been a boon for people with vision loss. Information encoded as a magnetic signal in a computer can be variously decoded into speech (through a speech synthesizer), braille (through a hard-copy printer or a refreshable cassette tape), or enlarged print visible on the computer monitor. Other recently developed aids include a computerized tape recorder that enables the user to speed-read by ear and a talking calculator.

The result has been a virtual explosion of opportunity for independent reading and writing by people who cannot use print. No longer do they have to depend on someone else's eyes to translate printed information. This technology revolution has forced corporations to rethink notions of the physical limitations on job performance in information processing.

Let's look in on a job interview held by several skeptical telephone company division managers. The applicant, Russell, blind since the age of two, had had five years of experience as a customer service representative with a government agency before attending a computer programming school. Russell demonstrated a device attached to a computer that allows the information on the screen to be read in braille on a tactual display. While he talked about his research in adaptive devices, he wrote a program to perform a simple data sort and then inputted the names of his interviewers. As the screen displayed the sorted material, Russell read it aloud by means of the attached display.

Intrigued, the managers showered him with questions about debugging programs and the comparative versatility of braille and speech in accessing visually presented information. He answered them readily while he broke down the equipment and packed it up. As he left, Russell offered to show them "a piece of the most impressive technology ever developed," and in one motion he snapped his folded cane into extension.

Earlier, several of the managers had expressed reservations about bringing a blind person into the department. "What if there were a fire?" one asked. "How would he find his way to the restroom?" another wanted to know. But their interview with Russell convinced them that he would be an asset, so they offered him the job.

Gambling with the unknown

One employment roadblock for the visually impaired job seeker is the view most sighted people hold about a blind person's dependence and passivity in the world. From this

Now a doctoral student in clinical psychology at Boston University, Julia Anderson has been connected professionally with the Perkins School for the Blind in Watertown, Massachusetts for more than a decade. For three years she coordinated the Perkins Project with Industry.

stereotype, it's a short step to the assumption that a fast-paced corporation is no place for a person without sight. It takes exposure to a person like Russell to explode these misconceptions; on the strength of his personality and his talent, he was able to put his listeners at ease.

To many managers, hiring a sight-impaired person is taking a big chance. An executive once said to me: "The main risk on my mind was that I might have to let her go. I figured this person had suffered enough in her lifetime, and now, what if she really can't perform? I don't think we would have fired her, but we would have found her a different job."

For three years in the mid-1980s, I coordinated the Perkins Project with Industry, a federally financed project to expand job opportunities in New England for people with visual disabilities. Together with our colleagues at the Massachusetts Commission for the Blind, we encouraged our corporate clients to expect the same quantity and quality of work from visually impaired employees as they would from sighted employees, and to supervise them accordingly.

The results of our placement efforts were various: some blind employees learned their jobs and stayed on; some moved up; others quit to return to school; some got laid off or never mastered their jobs and were terminated. The same happened to their sighted peers. But certainly, most of the people we helped are either still holding their initial jobs or have advanced to better positions in the same or different organizations.

It was crucial for the employers with whom we dealt to find out the reality of a blind person's independence, which belies the misperception of dependence. When someone who is sighted observes how a person with vision loss manages in the world, and manages differently from a sighted person when necessary, the demystification of the disability begins. At that point, the sighted person starts looking past the disability to see the person behind it.

The feeling that blind people are somehow different—as though in experiencing the world differently, they are living in a different world—

is often responsible for the rejection of a candidate early in the job application process. The manager's question, "Will I be comfortable working with this person?" is a legitimate question, often answered negatively because of a lack of information and familiarity.

> ## When managers ask, "Will I be comfortable with this person?" too often the answer is, "No."

Few of us can view calmly the prospect of spending time with someone we perceive as being very different from ourselves, for we fear not knowing what to do. In not knowing what to do, we risk appearing foolish. The Project with Industry aimed to give employers the information they needed to become more comfortable, especially information about the disability and about the types of job adaptations in place around the country.

Time after time, we observed that once a manager had decided to make the move and incorporate a blind person into his or her work group, the climate there became a very positive one for the new employee. The failures were always due to factors other than vision limitations, factors that can disrupt any employer-worker relationship. Yet even in those cases, the work group often felt a strong desire to recruit another visually impaired or blind person. They had an investment in the cause.

Even so, the problem of social isolation in the work setting has to be dealt with. A month after hiring a blind individual, an executive described the social situation this way: "It's easy for a sighted person to go visit somebody in the next department. But Sharon can't do that. A sighted person can see that someone's busy and decide not to interrupt. So Sharon, as a result, just stays in her office. It's up to everyone else to come by and say, 'How are you do-

ing?' And most of them won't because they feel embarrassed. Nobody asks her to go to lunch because that takes a little bit of effort: you've got to be able to guide her. It's very uncomfortable for somebody who isn't prepared for it, unless you're a strong personality."

This executive arranged for his group to participate in a workshop that featured role playing and discussion of the facts and misconceptions about blindness. Back in the workplace, the manager noticed that employees seemed to feel more at ease with Sharon, and she was less shy with them.

He also devoted some thought to how he could communicate with his subordinates in a way that would not exclude the worker with limited sight. He learned to use the office's electronic mail system instead of relying on handwritten or typed memos, and he encouraged everyone in the office to do the same. The result was clearer communication for the entire department. His supervision of the staff improved, he was convinced.

Corporate initiative

In this age of 6% unemployment, organizations looking for talent may have to do some creative recruiting. Individuals with little or no eyesight can be prime candidates for those recruiting efforts.

The first step should be an analysis of the problem from a logistical standpoint. What are the visual requirements of the jobs available? Can any reading demanded in the job be done with a computer screen? Other factors include the layout of the building, the frequency of disruptive environmental changes, and the expectation of field travel or out-of-the-office meetings. None of these factors precludes consideration of a blind person, but it's important to discuss all these job components with the candidate.

Every job deserves to be considered with a particular person in mind, partly because it's essential to understand the applicant's visual capacities. Most legally blind individuals have enough functional vision to use large or regular print. The applicant will probably have a reading preference among the options of regular or large print, braille, or a personal reader. It is also important to determine whether the applicant gets eyestrain when reading from a computer screen.

The rehabilitation agency for the blind in any state, often called the Vocational Rehabilitation Commission, has specialists who help organizations in recruiting and in adapting jobs to the needs of candidates. Such agencies in many states lend adaptive devices to blind people to use on the job.

Public agencies provide guidance and a clearinghouse for employers.

Rehabilitation specialists can help an employer investigate appropriate devices and can advise him or her on applications for tax advantages connected with purchases of this equipment. Another resource is the local Project with Industry, from which businesses can get help through networking activity.

In some states, rehabilitation agencies have built excellent communication networks with private-sector employers, and both benefit. In other states, rapport has not been established, and differences in vocabularies and technological expertise present obstacles. There are enough successful collaborations, however, to serve as models for any corporation interested in pursuing this idea.

When initiative from employers is backed with expertise from the public organizations specializing in help for visually impaired job seekers, this resource can be better exploited for the benefit of both employer and worker.

Reprint 89201